Publishing Romance

Publishing Romance
The History of an Industry, 1940s to the Present

John Markert

McFarland & Company, Inc., Publishers
Jefferson, North Carolina

LIBRARY OF CONGRESS CATALOGUING-IN-PUBLICATION DATA

Names: Markert, John, 1945– author.
Title: Publishing romance : the history of an industry, 1940s to the present / John Markert.
Description: Jefferson, North Carolina : McFarland & Company, Inc., Publishers, 2016| Includes bibliographical references and index.
Identifiers: LCCN 2016002870 | ISBN 9780786494903 (softcover : acid free paper) ∞
Subjects: LCSH: Romance fiction—Publishing—United States—History. | Harlequin Enterprises—History. | Silhouette Books—History.
Classification: LCC Z473.R66 M37 2016 | DDC 070.509—dc23
LC record available at https://lccn.loc.gov/2016002870

BRITISH LIBRARY CATALOGUING DATA ARE AVAILABLE

ISBN (print) 978-0-7864-9490-3
ISBN (ebook) 978-1-4766-2124-1

© 2016 John Markert. All rights reserved

No part of this book may be reproduced or transmitted in any form or by any means, electronic or mechanical, including photocopying or recording, or by any information storage and retrieval system, without permission in writing from the publisher.

Front cover images © Digital Vision, Hemera, iStock/Thinkstock

Printed in the United States of America

*McFarland & Company, Inc., Publishers
Box 611, Jefferson, North Carolina 28640
www.mcfarlandpub.com*

To Gail
My Heroine

Acknowledgments

There are many people to thank for their participation in this study. There are all those who warmly gave input about what they or their company was doing. The time they generously allocated me from their extraordinarily busy schedules is greatly appreciated. I wish also to express my appreciation to Cumberland University for its moral and financial support. I am particularly grateful to Laura Vivanco and Kristin Ramsdell for their comments on an early draft of this book.

Table of Contents

Acknowledgments	vi
Introduction	1
1. Paperbacks in Society	15
2. The World of Harlequin: 1949–1979	26
3. The Four Phases of Love: American Romance Publishing in the Seventies	44
4. Silhouette Books: Challenging Harlequin's Supremacy	66
5. The New Dawn: Romance Publishing Comes of Age	85
6. Risky Business: Rushing to Cash In on the Romance Craze	105
7. The Editorial Ear: Selective Listening	126
8. Alive and Kicking: Harlequin Regains Market Supremacy	140
9. Line Diversification: The Byword of the New Millennium	198
10. Romance Publishing at the Outset of the New Millennium: Market Share, Competition and Content Innovation	265
Conclusion	284
Chapter Notes	301
Selected Bibliography	326
Index	331

Introduction

Mass-market paperback books were introduced in the United States on June 19, 1939. The first series of ten paperbacks published were test-marketed in New York City. A full-page ad in the *New York Times* proclaimed their debut: "OUT TODAY—THE NEW POCKET BOOKS THAT MAY REVOLUTIONIZE NEW YORK'S READING HABITS."[1]

Robert Fair de Graff, the originator of American paperbacks and president of Simon & Schuster's newly formed Pocket Books division, received numerous calls that Monday morning from industry skeptics who had seen the ad and telephoned to urge him to retreat before it was too late.[2] He didn't, and he went on to make publishing history.

Today, mass-market paperback publishing is big business. There are even those who contend that paperbacks have saved the publishing industry by pumping hundreds of millions of dollars of reprint royalties back into trade publishing.[3] The claim may be hyperbolic, but it is not unwarranted, since paperbacks surpassed adult trade hardcover sales as early as 1959.[4]

The half-century since their appearance notwithstanding, paperbacks have only recently gained legitimacy within the industry. Trade publishers have for decades looked down their long, bookish noses at these cheap, mass-produced reprints of hardcover books. It was not until the early 1970s that paperback houses directly challenged their older siblings by publishing original novels.[5] The furor that might have arisen over this territorial infringement was forestalled by an intense period of merger activity. Paperback houses merged with hardcover firms, which were, in turn, being bought by conglomerates, such as RCA and Gulf + Western, who were more interested in the bottom-line profit margin than upholding some nebulous standard of literary excellence. The new parent corporations provided mass-market paperback firms with a competitive edge over their hardcover siblings by pumping large amounts of needed financing into their heretofore undercapitalized offspring.[6]

The quest for profitability helped make mass-market paperback publishing competitive, and the newly formed alliances between hardcover and paperback houses has muddied their previous rivalry.[7] The largely genre-driven nature of paperback publishing[8] has also gained legitimacy over the last few decades as the once-defamed "popular" genres of science fiction, detective mysteries, and Westerns began to be regarded by critics as literary contributions in their own right and not as shallow imitations of Ernest Hemingway.[9]

The increased acceptance of paperbacks and genre fiction has not been unreserved. Romance novels, traditionally relegated to the bottom of the paperback hierarchy by mass-market publishers, continue to be consigned to the trash heap of literature, despite the fact that romances over the last decade (2000–2010) have consistently accounted for 14.3 percent of all consumer books bought and sold in the United States and added $1.355 billion to the industry's $10.11 billion in net revenue in 2010.[10]

Romances account for one out of every four books sold[11] and one out of every two mass-market books sold.[12] They dominate other genres with a 39.3 percent share of the market. Their closest genre rival are mystery/thrillers with a 29.6 percent market share.[13] The widespread consumption of these slim paperback stories of love and marriage, however, has not helped them gain respectability, despite their heavy presence on best-seller lists.[14] In an otherwise excellent analysis of the publishing industry, the co-authors of *Books: The Culture and Commerce of Publishing* could not refrain from commenting that romances are "created by hack writers" reminiscent of the Grub Street authors of the eighteenth century, with one difference: "The art of manipulating [romance] readers has been refined and the degradation of public taste, it would seem, is now pursued without the least shred of bad conscience."[15] Few in the industry would disagree; in fact, many would vigorously concur with one publishing veteran who summarized his colleagues' views of the romance reader as "women deprived of intellectual stimulation: run-of-the-mill tired people who are looking for a way of spending their time and losing themselves in a dream."[16]

Popular Literature and the Romance Formula

Romance literature can be traced back to the early Middle Ages lyrics of the troubadours and trouveres; its more modern guise took shape early in the eighteenth century with the birth of the novel. The triumvirate responsible for developing the most popular form of literary expression of future generations consisted of Daniel Defoe, Samuel Richardson, and Henry Fielding.[17] These early novelists abandoned literary tradition by giving their characters common names, locating narrative events in a detailed here-and-now time scheme, and relying on everyday human experience to supply them with plot devices, rather than building on esoteric literary conventions.[18] Decried by critics in their own day for portraying the world too realistically, the novels of Defoe and Fielding have taken their place among the classics, while Richardson's romances have all but passed into obscurity.

Richardson's omission from the literary pantheon seems undeserved, judging from the critical appraisals of his work during his lifetime. No less a personage than Dr. Samuel Johnson considered Richardson to be the most insightful of the new novelists, calling him "the greatest genius that had shed its luster on this path of literature"; Rousseau added that "no one, in any language, has ever written a novel that equals or even approaches [Richardson's novel] *Clarissa*."[19] The relative obscurity of Richardson today may have less to do with the specific merits of his work than with the fact that women, not men, took up the romance pen.

Women have traditionally been considered inferior to men. Their role, especially in the eighteenth century, was relegated to the domestic arena. Rousseau summed up the prevailing view toward women in his day when he had one of his characters in *Emily* say, "Little girls always dislike reading and writing, but they are always ready to learn how to sew."[20] The attitude toward women would not change markedly during the nineteenth century. Comte, for example, saw femininity as a kind of prolonged infancy; Balzac felt that women were incapable of reason or absorbing useful knowledge from books; Hegel considered them capable of education only in the lower arts, but not in the advanced sciences or in philosophy; and Schopenhauer viewed the sex as advanced along the phylogenetic scale, definitely of the order *Homo sapiens*, but stuck somewhere between a child and a full-grown person: "The only business that really claims her earnest attention," he wrote, "is love, making conquests, and everything connected with this—dress, dancing, and so on."[21] These views remained firmly entrenched during a large swath of the twentieth century, despite women winning the right to vote in 1919. They would not be seriously challenged until Betty Friedan's best-selling 1963 critique of the housewife's position in society, *The Feminine Mystique*, launched the popular discourse about women's place in society and added fuel to the nascent (second-wave) feminist movement.[22]

The ease with which romances have been dismissed from critical examination is due in part to their female base—women writing for other women—and in part to their formulaic nature. Romances constitute the oldest of the novel's genres. Detective stories, mystery novels, science-fiction fantasies, and Western novels all developed a century or more after the romance. These genres also received little initial critical acclaim because of their formulaic plotlines. It was only after a protracted debate on popular art forms that followed the dissemination of entertainment for the masses after World War II that popular, mass-produced literature began to be considered worthy of study.

John Cawelti's seminal work on popular genres did much to bring the study of formulaic fiction under examination by literary critics.[23] Cawelti pointed out how formula fiction, despite its largely escapist nature, still conveys and teaches new attitudes and values to readers, a function of fiction heretofore considered the exclusive domain of the classics. The debate over the place of formula fiction did not succeed in establishing the supremacy of mass literature. It did, however, succeed in establishing that popular books transmitted values and thus were as worthy of study as "real" literature, even if he devoted little space to contemporary romance novels.[24] There are many, in fact, who contend that formula fiction deserves more attention than the classics because it is so widely produced and consumed. Romances, however, continue to be burdened by a humanistic evaluation, which is to say, they are often dismissed as not being worthy of study. This is because romances are perceived by literary critics as unchanged and unchanging, a point made emphatically by one critic of the genre, writing about consumer behavior in *Advances in Consumer Research*, who castigates the romance novel, its writers, and its readers as "atrociously written [books] mindlessly consumed, and concocted according to the same tired and tiresome recipe."[25]

Gothics, for example, have received considerable critical attention, primarily because they are the oldest of the romance subgenres. One humanistic, feminist scholar critiquing the subgenre argues that their continued popularity "perpetuate[s] the cycle of victimization which occurs between fathers and mothers, mothers and daughters."[26] Contemporary critics of the gothic novel seem to be unaware that, as Janice Radway points out and briefly puzzles over, this subgenre peaked in popularity between 1969 and 1972, after which it fell out of favor with consumers because of its "dated" storyline.[27]

Other romance subgenres have received similar treatment. Harlequin books are widely decried for their formulaic plots, but seldom is the distinction made between Harlequin Romance and Harlequin Presents.[28] Consumers, however, were quick to recognize the difference between the two lines, and sales of the Presents line would surpass those of Harlequin Romances not long after it debuted in 1973. Likewise, the sensual "bodice-ripper" romances of the 1970s received considerable attention in the popular press and among feminist scholars, yet these novels were never as widely consumed as critics lamented, nor did Harlequin, the most popular romance publisher of the 1970s, incorporate the bodice-ripper dimension into either of its romance lines. The more liberated sensual romances that debuted in the 1980s are often confused with the bodice-rippers, even today, though they are distinctly different in their depiction of sexuality.

The romance novel has undergone substantial changes since Harlequin first turned its attention to producing primarily romance novels in 1964. This analysis sidesteps judging the content of romance novels by looking not at the novels themselves but at the structure of the romance publishing industry and, in particular, the key role of decision makers within the industry who decide what novels to select or reject. Content is, of course, addressed, but it is appraised through the publishing lens. In other words, the focus on content, which cannot be escaped, is predicated on the decisions made by those in publishing as to what themes might sell and thus be entered into the production cycle, or why other romantic themes would be dismissed as irrelevant to contemporary tastes and rejected. The success or failure of these decisions is evaluated by assessing sales figures.

Decision Making Within the Publishing Matrix

Scratch marks on paper are transformed into a book only after those scratches are deemed acceptable to a publishing house. This observation is not as banal as it may at first appear when one considers that for every manuscript selected by an editor for the mystical transformation process, scores of others are returned with standardized postcard-size rejection slips (or curt emails) to crush the hopes of budding authors.

The history of publishing is studded with stories of editors who turned down a manuscript that was later published by another house and went on to sell millions or achieve literary fame. For example, as an editor for McGraw-Hill, William Styron rejected Thor Heyerdahl's *Kon-Tiki* (1948), which later as a Rand McNally book sat atop the *New York Times* best-seller list for two years. "This is a long, solemn, tedious, Pacific voyage," Styron wrote, "best suited, I would think, to some kind of dramatic abridgement in a journal like *National Geographic*"; another publisher more straightforwardly inquired, "Who the hell wants to read about a bunch of crazy Scandinavians floating around the ocean on a raft?"[29] A similar assessment plagued Christina Baker Kline's recent bestseller, *Orphan Train* (HarperCollins, 2013). The author remembers the marketing meeting where she was told that that her characters, "a grumpy old woman and a disaffected Goth teenager," didn't make for "great [sales] demographics." The publisher optimistically ran 55,000 copies of the novel; it sold 1.1 million copies in the first six months of 2014.[30]

A more trenchant example of editorial rejection is John Kennedy Toole's posthumously published *A Confederacy of Dunces*. Written in the 1960s, *Dunces* was rejected by every major publisher and most minor ones in North America. The author, in a state of severe depression over the accumulated pink slips, committed suicide in 1969 at the age of thirty-two. The remains of his manuscript—a badly smeared, scarcely readable carbon—would have ended in the trash bin had it not been for the persistence of Toole's mother, who badgered the distinguished novelist Walker Percy, at the time teaching at nearby Loyola University in New Orleans, to read her son's novel. Percy, impressed by the author's tale, used his considerable influence to get Louisiana State University Press to publish the book.[31] It won the Pulitzer Prize in 1981.

"A writer does not write just for his files," says a character in the Isaac Bashevis Singer short story "The Colony." He might add that, contrary to popular belief, a writer does not write just for the public, either. The first and often last court of appeals for a writer is the editor. This is why the editorial role is the most esteemed job within the publishing industry. It is the editor who stands between the writer and the consumer. By examining the structure of the industry, rather than the novel itself, we will see why certain themes were resisted while others were found to be appealing and what happened to open the floodgates to the "romance revolution" of the 1980s that changed the nature of romance publishing and paved the way for the wide range of successful romance subgenres that flooded the market at the outset of the twenty-first century.

Editors are important in transmitting ideas originated by writers because they act as gatekeepers. Gatekeepers are those key individuals who, by virtue of their formal position within organizations, screen and selectively choose what new products or ideas to offer the public. The importance of these key individuals in determining what to allow through the sluice gates has been the subject of considerable attention since Kurt Lewin first identified the crucial role these decision makers play in shaping what ultimately reaches the public.[32] The pivotal role played by those who inhabit formal decision-making positions has been well documented in a wide range of disparate organizations and markets.[33] Gatekeepers have garnered particular attention in media organizations,[34] with editors as the focus of attention within the publishing industry because of their strategic position in sifting through manuscripts.[35] They are the ones who decide the fate of the manuscripts that cross their desks every day.

Management's role in the gatekeeping tradition has been largely ignored. This is because managers are viewed as setting general parameters on what types of books the house will publish and how many manuscripts they would like transformed into books, but they seldom interfere with the day-to-day selection of manuscripts. This is not the case with romance publishing, where management has sometimes played a critical gatekeeping role in shaping the content of the novels that some houses publish. The direct intervention of management in romance publishing in shaping content suggests its role in promoting certain themes has not been fully appreciated in studies of the editorial decision-making process within publishing and perhaps other organizations as well.

The failure of management in publishing houses in the United States to bother much with romance novels in the 1950s and 1960s ensured that Harlequin would dominate the romance field. This dominance by Harlequin was established less by editorial savvy than by an astute marketing campaign orchestrated by management. Harlequin management not only decided to focus exclusively on romance novels, but it was also instrumental in the 1970s in forcing reluctant editors to introduce new content in their existing lines of increasingly "dated" books that immediately proved successful with consumers.

Harlequin's domination of the North American market would last through much of the 1970s, despite dramatic changes in the content of romance novels produced in the United States that were introduced by Nancy Coffey, the editor at Avon in 1972, who, in the best gatekeeping tradition, published Kathleen Woodiwiss's now classic *The Flame and the Flower* because it was a "good read." Despite the outpouring of the so-called "bodice-ripper" themes by other houses in the United States during the 1970s, publishing houses in the United States still deferred to Harlequin's dominance of the market. The failure of many of the new romances to capture more than a slice of the romance market at the time is laid on management's rush to cash in on the new romance "craze"—and never fully understanding what it was that made the content so appealing to consumers—and the general inexperience of many recently promoted female administrative assistants to the editorial ranks to oversee romance production. The promotion of these young women to key editorial roles would mean that, for the first time, there were editors in place who were monitoring events in the 1980s, so that when Vivian Stephens, the editor at Dell in 1980, filtered a new, more sensually liberated heroine into the novel and debuted the Ecstasy line, other houses were quick to capitalize on the new theme.

The 1980s witnessed challenges to Harlequin's domination of the romance market for the first time. This was not only because Harlequin was trying to keep up with the potpourri of American houses rushing to capitalize on the new themes that were garnering readers' attention, but they were also trying to stay competitive with the formation of Silhouette Books by Simon & Schuster. Silhouette was formed to directly challenge and wrest away from Harlequin its market share after Harlequin terminated its decade-long distribution contract with Simon & Schuster's Pocket Books. As the distributor for Harlequin in the United States market, Simon & Schuster was one of the few publishers to recognize just how lucrative the romance market was. By the middle of the 1980s, it became obvious to many within the industry how popular romances were, and everybody in the industry was clawing to get a piece of the market. Some succeeded; many more failed. In fact, the 1980s have been referred to as the romance revolution because so many publishers were rushing to capture a slice of the romance market. It was a particularly confusing time because the market had become so turbulent.

Studies of the decision-making process by gatekeepers tend to situate them in placid, stable competitive environments. This stability allows the gatekeeper to sift proposed products and ideas with minimal difficulty. Gatekeepers, whether managerial or editorial staff, generally make their decisions as to what to pass through the gates on one of two criteria. The first is based on personal taste. Gatekeepers tend to assume that if they like it, others will too.[36] Gatekeepers in stable environments have a great deal of faith in their judgment because the consumer has been accepting the proffered items, often for some time, so they feel they know what the public likes. The second is based on an assessment of market conditions. In this instance, gatekeepers seek to find a niche for their product by surveying the competition; they attempt to find something similar to, but slightly different from, the competition to offer the public.[37] Gatekeepers in stable environments can easily survey the competition to find their special place. Since many markets, like publishing, have only a dozen or so major firms, it is easy to monitor their competitors' products.[38] Products selected in stable environments tend to be somewhat homogeneous.

Change in product uniformity does occur, however. Sometimes gatekeepers allow something new into the system because they like the new product or idea. Gatekeepers, however, tend to be conservative, fearful that something too different might be rejected by consumers. The new item is often only marginally different from that which presently exists; however, it is possible that someone is occasionally "ahead of the times" and introduces something so new that it disrupts the environment.[39] Greater product change may follow as other gatekeepers seek to provide an alternative to that which has been recently introduced by moving beyond simply providing an imitative product. In this case, they may be moving ahead of the classic concept of gatekeeper since they are actively seeking something different and not simply filtering products into the marketplace. They remain steadfastly locked to the gatekeeper tradition, however, because they do not set out to create the product but simply sift through available products—romance manuscripts that cross their desk—looking for something different. Once again, there is an inherent conservativism. The gatekeeper seeks only to differentiate his or her product from others in the same market, but not so much so that it is too different, since the consumers may reject radical differences. Sometimes, however, the product is dramatically different, more different than even the gatekeeper had intended, which means that even he or she is unsure of what it is about the product that the consumer likes. Such confusion can destabilize the competitive environment. Turbulent environments are problematic for gatekeepers because they no longer know exactly what the public wants. It is under these conditions that they may move from gatekeepers to gatemakers, where the product or idea is initiated and shaped by them; in a sense, they are now *making* the product, not just keeping an eye open for something a little different.

The classic concept of gatekeeping is rather passive. Nevertheless, it has been recognized for some time that gatekeepers are more active in the selection of products and ideas. They sometimes do more than select from a host of ideas; they shape the idea. Ryan and Peterson, for example, show that while the gatekeeping influence is strong in the initial selection of songs by music publishers, the songs are rewritten or reinterpreted at several points along the production line, sometimes so much so that the finished product may bear little resemblance to the original intention of the songwriter.[40] Similar shaping mechanisms have been found in other industries.[41]

These producers do not set out to shape the product; they simply modify it. They are still considered gatekeepers because they do not consciously set out to create something unique. These modifications, like the original selection of the new product, are based on personal taste or assessments of market conditions, e.g., "We think this song would be a little better if trumpets were played in the background, since so-and-so's successful new song had trumpets in the background." The changes, then, are not dramatically different from the products available in the marketplace. The economist Joseph Schumpeter felt that the more unique the "recombination of existing factors of production," the greater the amount of disruption that will occur in the competitive environment.[42] Faced with a new competitive product, producers scurry to imitate the latest innovation. One response to a turbulent environment is the emergence of gatemakers. Gatemakers attempt to deal with chaos by imposing rigid restrictions on the new product based on their assessment of what the consumer wants. The gatemaker role appears to be a temporary adaptive condition that allows entrepreneurs to deal with a rapidly changing, highly competitive environment.

Romance publishing provides a strategic opportunity for examining the infusion of innovation into the system. The content changes that took place in the early 1970s did not cause anywhere near the confusion as did the content changes that took place in the early 1980s. This is because there were so many "new" aspects to the romance novel in the Ecstasy books that other publishers were not sure exactly what it was about them that the public liked. The result was that editors proactively latched on to one of the multiple dimensions of the Ecstasy novels to differentiate their books from all the others. The editors had no time to filter manuscripts because management wanted them to do something while romances were "hot," so editors had to tell writers how to write the books they wanted. By the end of the 1980s, the romance market had stabilized and editors returned to the more traditional role of gatekeeping.

While the market settled down in the 1990s, the aftermath of the romance revolution of the 1980s is still felt. Harlequin purchased its major rival, Silhouette Books, in 1984 and by 1990 had regained its supremacy over the romance market. Its share has fallen, however, and it is now more diligent in actively surveying the market to find new product niches. Many of the American houses that entered the fray during the 1980s, once the dust settled, have finetuned their offerings to stay competitive, while a potpourri of smaller romance houses have emerged, and an old one, Harlequin, has been subsumed by HarperCollins. The result is that not only are more publishers competing in the romance market than ever before, but there is now a wider range of thematic choice in the novels. Indeed, the market is more vibrant than ever. How it got there, and what it is doing to stay there, is the subject of this book.

This analysis of the romance industry begins with the introduction of paperback books to the United States in 1939. Chapter 1 sketches the origin of mass-market paperbacks. The rapid growth of mass-market paperbacks in the aftermath of World War II stalled in the 1950s. Paperback houses continued to thrive, but the public's anti–Communist fervor would affect the content of mainstream fiction through much of the 1950s. That would spill over and affect the format of many romance novels of the day.

Chapter 2 looks at how Harlequin, like rival mass-market paperback houses, started in the 1950s as a publisher of general fiction and nonfiction. The chapter progresses by looking at the dynamics that moved Harlequin to become an exclusive publisher of romance fiction and then at how it gained dominance over this field. The switch to romances was not dramatic (or particularly lucrative) until the 1970s, when Harlequin moved beyond its geographic boundaries in Canada and formed an alliance with Pocket Books to distribute its romance novels in the United States. The new president of Harlequin, W. Lawrence Heisey, then embarked on an intense marketing campaign that would make the Harlequin name synonymous with romance novels. But it was not just marketing that made Harlequin *the* romance publisher of North America. Two innovative types of content were introduced that helped sell its books. The first change was to modify the existing line of Harlequin Romance and introduce Harlequin Presents, a more socially relevant line of romances. The second was to introduce Janet Dailey, their first American author, who focused on romances set in the United States; Dailey would go on to become one of Harlequin's most successful authors. Harlequin capitalized on the first change but did not take advantage of the second, a mistake that would cost them dearly in the 1980s.

Chapter 3 explores American romance publishing during the 1970s. American publishers at the beginning of the decade published two types of romances: contemporaries (or romances set in the here-and-now) and historicals (romances set in some bygone era). By mid-decade, most had switched to historical romances in an attempt to mimic the success that Avon Books had when it introduced a new romance subgenre in 1972. I prefer to label this subgenre "sensual historicals" to avoid the negative connotation associated with the term "bodice-rippers" that was hung on these novels because the heroine often had her bodice ripped off in the course of the story, often numerous times. The new subgenre gained wide popularity among American romance publishers. The books were only modestly successful among consumers, however. Nevertheless, the sexual content of the novels would pave the way for the more liberated treatment of sexual relations by romance novelists in the 1980s.

Chapter 4 looks at the development of Silhouette Books, the first real challenger to Harlequin's domination of the romance market. Silhouette launched within a year of Harlequin serving notice that it would no longer use Pocket Books to distribute Harlequin books in the United States. This chapter examines how Silhouette was able to launch a completely new book division and have books on the shelves within a year and in doing so carve away a hefty slice of Harlequin's business. The chapter goes on to examine how Harlequin competed with Silhouette and how the buy-out of Silhouette by Harlequin in 1984 unfolded to the satisfaction of both publishers.

Simon & Schuster's decision to launch Silhouette was a sound business decision that might have remained lucrative had the romance market not suddenly undergone dramatic change and sliced into both Silhouette's and Harlequin's sales. Chapter 5 looks at how an editor at Dell, Vivian Stephens, acting in the best gatekeeper tradition, tentatively debuted a radically different thematic content, and when, as she says, "nobody screamed," she launched Dell's highly successful Ecstasy line. The chapter examines just what it was that appealed to Stephens and how the new content resonated with readers. The chapter concludes by looking at the first two lines that successfully tapped into nuances in the Ecstasy series and the decision by editors at one house to launch Second Chance at Love and at another house to transform the lackluster Circle of Love series into the highly successful Loveswept line.

Chapter 6 looks at the problematic entry of all those lines that followed and explores why so many were a failure, while a few succeeded. Once an understanding of what took place during the volatile 1980s has emerged, attention can be turned in Chapter 7 to assessing the selectivity of the editorial ear in listening to readers. It also looks at the problem many editors had when they moved from their comfortable role of gatekeeper to the more problematic one of being a gatemaker.

The market settled down by the end of the 1980s, and editors returned to their more traditional gatekeeping roles. Chapter 8 examines Harlequin's purchase of Silhouette and why the Canadian-based publisher did not simply "kill" its New York–based rival, as many in the publishing field thought they might, but instead co-opted the Silhouette line into the Harlequin family, and why, twenty-five years later, it finally disbanded the Silhouette imprint. The chapter goes on to examine the multitude of Harlequin lines today and how Harlequin attempts to stay competitive, both in North America and in the international arena. Torstar, Harlequin's parent company, relied on its little stepdaughter to provide solid profits for decades, and Harlequin's contribution was a major factor in keeping Torstar afloat during the costly newspaper wars in Canada. The chapter concludes by examining what prompted Torstar to sell its feisty stepchild to HarperCollins in 2014.

Chapter 9 examines the vitality of the market over the last twenty-five years (1990–2014) and the assortment of small romance lines available in the United States. It assesses how mainstream publishers are rather lackadaisically monitoring market conditions and allowing numerous small romance presses to carve out a slice of the market for themselves. The chapter examines the multiplicity of niche lines today that attempt to capitalize on market conditions, such as BDSM romances, GLBT romances, minority romances, and other romance lines that mainstream publishers like Harlequin may or may not be attempting to replicate.

Chapter 10 attempts to make sense of the market today. It examines how the small presses have achieved a slice of the romance pie and what mainstream publishers are doing to stay competitive. The impact of the new digital age is appraised, as well as how the market may be affected now that HarperCollins has become, almost overnight, *the* romance publisher of the twenty-first century with the purchase of Harlequin. The conclusion wraps up this assessment of the romance industry and ends with some suggestions for further research that have arisen in the process of assessing contemporary market conditions.

Methodological Note

The primary research for this study consisted of interviews with key informants and observations of significant individuals within the publishing industry. One round of interviews took place in 1983 and 1984 (supplemented by follow-up interviews in 1988). The first series of interviews addressed decisions taking place during the 1970s and 1980s. A second round of interviews took place between 2013 and 2014 and addressed decisions that took place between 1990 and 2014. Senior management at some of the major publishing firms, such as Harlequin, Silhouette, Simon & Schuster, and Kensington, among others, were interviewed at both points in time, as were key editorial personnel at these and other publishing houses. Other individuals were also interviewed, including functionaries in other departments (e.g., art, advertising, and public relations), editorial assistants, and personnel in support industries (romance newsletters and trade publications).

The primary means of eliciting information was by telephone interview. Editors overwhelmingly preferred this method because they saw it as less time-consuming than completing a detailed questionnaire. The author also favored this method, since personal interviews allow information about the publishing goals to be explored in greater depth, especially the knowledge, attitudes, and behavior of managers and editors that led them to make decision pertaining to the growth and content of romance lines.

In general, there are two types of personal interviewing techniques: informal (or open-ended) and formal (or closed). The informal approach allows the respondent to talk freely about his or her experiences and offers the advantage of allowing the interviewer to catch glimpses of decision-making that might not otherwise emerge in a question-and-answer approach. The disadvantage is that the interviewer might get diverted by the unstructured discussion and forget to ask key questions. A more formal, or structured, approach has the opposite advantages and disadvantages. My own approach was to combine both techniques. Discussions were informal and allowed the respondents to go in whatever direction their comments took them. At the same time, a list of specific questions was drawn up to ensure that key points were not overlooked. During our discussion, I checked off questions as they were answered. Points not raised during the interview were then covered before the discussion terminated; clarifying, follow-up calls often occurred. For those who preferred to respond in writing, more frequent in the latter period (25 percent) than the former, questions were posed in an open-ended manner. Some of the answers needed clarification, and these were typically addressed in follow-up email exchanges.

Four broad categories of questions were identified: (1) editor demographics; (2) the decision-making process involved in conceiving and formulating new lines of romance novels and/or the decision to modify or discontinue an existing line, including the relationship and attitude between management and the editorial staff; (3) the editor's perception of the romance audience and other romance publishers; and (4) trends that editors/managers saw in romance publishing and their responses to them. There are some disadvantages to the interview process when asking about past decisions. Input may be inhibited by fading memory, intentionally distorted to make the interviewee look better than she might otherwise appear, or hampered by the respondent's ability to recall the multiple factors that promoted the initial decision and/or reaction to events. Every endeavor was made to verify statements made by interviewees. Trade sources were checked so that at the time of the interview, I was generally aware of events that had occurred within the house and could raise specific questions. In those instances where input from people at the house conflicted with other input, respondents were called back to clarify contradictory statements. Verifying respondents' comments was facilitated by the mobility that naturally occurs within publishing. Many editors either previously worked at other houses or were aware of ongoing developments at other houses. The situation allowed me to cross-check input. I talked with Vivian Stephens about events that took place at Dell in 1980 when she was the editor for Dell's moribund Candlelight line. At the time of our discussion, Stephens was the editor of Harlequin American Romances and could also confirm comments I had received from other sources at Harlequin. Stephens's comments regarding managerial and editorial decisions at Dell could, in turn, be cross-checked with Kate Duffy, who was senior editor at Pocket Books and Stephens's boss, and who I interviewed after she took the helm as editor-in-chief of Silhouette. The same scenario held for a number of managerial personnel who were interviewed in 2013–2014, many of whom had worked in an editorial capacity at another house between 1990 and 2014. Glenda Howard, for example, was an editor with Arabesque at BET after BET purchased the African American romance line from Kensington; she would move to Harlequin when Harlequin bought Arabesque from Kensington, and in 2014, when we talked, she was senior executive editor at Kimani and shed light on activities at both BET Arabesque and at Harlequin Kimani.

The telephone interviews at both time periods typically lasted between one and two hours. The interviews were taped and then transcribed to ensure the accuracy of quoted material; interviewees were informed that the conversation was being taped and that they could be quoted in subsequent printed material. Off-the-record comments are not attributed. The first round of interviews was augmented by visits to publishing firms in New York City and Toronto in 1984, during which time editors, their assistants, and other, non-editorial personnel, including senior management, were interviewed. Subsequent interviews relating to events that took place during the 1970s and 1980s were conducted between 1986 and 1988. The second series of interviews focused on events taking place between 1990 and 2014 and took place between 2013 and 2014. The telephone interviews that took place during the second period were augmented by a visit to some publishing houses in New York in 2014.

Chapter 1

Paperbacks in Society

The debut of Pocket Books in 1939 shaped the course of publishing history. But Pocket Books had its precedent. There were two unsuccessful paperback revolutions that set the stage for this, the third paperback revolution.

The first two paperback revolutions occurred during the nineteenth century. The first took place between 1830 and 1845; it was sparked by advances in printing technology and fueled by an increasingly literate society. The second began a decade after the first ended and reached its peak between 1875 and 1895; its momentum was stoked, much like Pocket Books would be a half-century later, by publishers taking advantage of new market conditions.

The first and second paperback revolutions each came to an abrupt end. Legal decisions affected the ability of paperback firms to compete economically with hardcover publishers. The lapse of nearly half a century between the end of the second paperback revolution and the beginning of the third was the result of the introduction in 1895 of buckram binding, which allowed hardcover publishers to produce inexpensive hardcover editions.

For nearly fifty years, hardcover publishers dominated the book market. Without the keen edge of competition to sharpen their practices, however, they became lackadaisical in their business habits, leaving the door ajar for paperback publishers to reenter the field. A 1931 survey undertaken by Orin Cheney for the National Association of Book Publishers and dubbed the Cheney Report scathingly denounced the publishing practices of the day, to the surprise of many on Publishers' Row.[1] Editorial, distribution, and promotion procedures were criticized as unorganized and inadequate, and waste excessive. Book sales were compared to the sales of such luxury items as jewelry and automobiles: they were costly and not getting to the people. De Graff, the founder of Pocket Books, must have nodded his head sagely when he read the Cheney Report. Ever since entering publishing as a salesman for his cousin Nelson Doubleday in 1922, de Graff had been toying with various methods of selling cheap books.[2]

There was nothing innovative in de Graff's venture with Pocket Books' paperbacks. Indeed, he merely imitated the highly successful Penguin Books, launched in England by Sir Allen Lane four years earlier, adapting Penguin's merchandising and distribution techniques to the American marketplace. The sales of the new paperbacks soon became obvious, but other publishers were unable to take advantage of the new market conditions because of the paper shortage during World War II. The boom in mass-market publishing firms would not take place until the second half of the 1940s. It was during this period that many of the large paperback houses of today, including Harlequin, had their origin.

The growth in mass-market publishing during the late 1940s and early 1950s led to a period of intense industry-wide competition. Paperback firms vied with one another for the consumer's dollars by packaging their books with sexually suggestive illustrations. The provocative covers caused a public furor that led to a toning down of book jackets. The moral outrage of the 1950s also would affect the content of fiction over the rest of the 1950s and have consequences for the "hardcore decency" content of the romance genre throughout the 1960s.

The Introduction of Paperback Books

The rise of modern publishing in the United States had its beginning in the early nineteenth century. Until then, the field had been a relatively restricted occupation, catering to a semi-scholarly audience; readers of secular books represented a small aristocracy of written culture.[3] By 1830, the beginning of the first paperback revolution, publishing was fast becoming "a hardcore, competitive scramble in which it was difficult and sometimes impossible to maintain the façade of gentility that nevertheless continued to characterize publishing."[4]

The paperback "scramble" was facilitated by technological and social changes. The first major technological changes in printing since the fifteen century—the metal press, the foot-operated cylinder press, the mechanical steam press, stereotyped plates, and cheaper methods of making paper and binding—all opened the way to producing low-price books.[5] The period of large printings began. The public was ready.

The most important social factor influencing the proliferation of book publishing was the spread of literacy. The increased literacy of the American population was fostered by the growth of the public school system. Education was no longer ornamental or restricted to an elite ruling class, but was becoming functional and general.[6] The spread of literacy was augmented in the United

States by various education societies, such as the Boston Society for the Diffusion of Knowledge, which published a series of secular nonfiction books for popular consumption. The Boston Society, like many other similar groups, proposed to "issue in cheap form a series of works, partly original and partly selected, in all the most important branches of knowledge."[7] The success of the Society's project was limited; the mass audience it sought to attract was more interested in fiction than nonfiction. Nevertheless, the books published by the Society's American Library of Useful Knowledge made up a seminal event in publishing because they reflected the increased literacy of the American population.

To reach the growing literate populace in America and to tap the widespread interest in fictional books, Carey and Lea Publishing initiated an imprint called Carey's Library of Choice Literature. These were fictional books issued in weekly parts for about ten cents and delivered through the mail. A rise in postal rates forced Carey and Lea to abandon the experiment in 1837.[8]

In an attempt to circumvent postage costs for books, a number of publishers began issuing "books" in newspaper format. These were newspaper-sized publications, printed in large-page format. Instead of news, however, these "paper" books contained pirated serials of British novels.[9] They were sold by newsboys on the street as well as by mail. For street sale, the front page was in lurid color. For mail subscriptions, the publisher simply removed the cover, thus maintaining the pretext that the publications were really newspapers, and thereby avoiding the higher cost of postage for books.[10]

Newspapers soon joined the competition by adding fiction supplements themselves. The price of a paper was twelve and a half cents. Legitimate book publishers began to drop their price to a quarter in 1843, but this was still too high.

Unable to compete with the paper book bonanza, the larger publishing houses used their political and financial resources to press the government to more stringently enforce postal rates. In 1843, the United States Postal Service ruled that paper book supplements were no longer eligible for newspaper rates but must be mailed as books.[11] Brother Jonathan, the most popular publisher of these paper books, went out of business seven months later, in January 1844. The New World, the last of the paper book publishers, suspended publication in May 1845. The first paper book revolution had come to an end.

Revitalizing Paperback Books

The first paperback book revolution proved that inexpensive literature could be brought to a large number of people who could not otherwise afford clothbound editions and also that there was a demand for these cheaper books.

In less than a decade after the first revolution ended, the publishing industry was beginning to issue paperback books again. By the 1880s, the market was flooded with paperbacks. In 1893, the year the paperback industry collapsed, there were fifty paperback publishers printing ninety-four series. A decade later, only three publishers continued to print paperback books.[12]

The precursor of the second paperback revolution was a book by Mrs. E. D. E. N. Southworth, published by T. B. Peterson & Brothers.[13] Southworth's romance manuscript, *The Lost Heiress*, had been turned down by several of the larger publishing firms before Peterson agreed to publish it and signed her to a long-term contract in 1854. Peterson accepted Southworth's novel in the gatekeeper tradition and with an astute eye on the marketplace, which he saw as especially favorable "for books at low prices, especially cheap, sensational fiction."[14] He invested $6,000 in advertising before the book came out, an unheard-of sum for a paperback novel. He received a good return on his investment. *The Lost Heiress* was an immediate success, and Peterson soon signed up a number of other women to write romances, many of whom continued to sell well during the second paperback boom of the 1880s.

Not unlike Harlequin Books of the 1960s and 1970s, Peterson & Brothers built its business on these romance novels, published for a predominately female readership.[15] Many, like Mrs. Henry Wood's successful *East Lynne* (1861), were filled with sentiment and romance. Like the male-oriented blood-and-thunder novels introduced by Beadle & Company during this period—which sold for a dime, were packaged in yellow or orange wrappers, bore a dramatic woodcut illustrating the content, and averaged one hundred pages in six and five-eighths by four and one-half sizes—these paperbacks were referred to as "cheap" because of their content as well as their price.[16]

The Civil War intervened, and while Beadle's sensational blood-and-thunder books were shipped in bales to the troops, the price of paper rose, which discouraged printing. Prices fell after the war, accelerated by the development in 1867 of a new process of manufacturing paper from ground wood pulp. Despite the decline in paper costs, however, manufacturing costs more than doubled after 1875. It was this cost increase that precipitated the increased printing of cheap, paperbound, pirated quarto novels.

Cheap paper books had, of course, been introduced before the Civil War. But for the first time publishers made them uniform in size: quartos (the page size obtained by folding a whole sheet into four leaves) contained two or three columns of closely printed type to a page. This standardization helped make the price for paperbacks extremely low, and the cost was further reduced as reprinters issued books for which regular hardcover publishers had already created a demand. Paperback book publishers proliferated.

Donnelley Loyd and Company of Chicago was one of the first publishing houses to introduce a line of uncopyrighted "pirated" novels in 1875 under the imprint Lakeside Library.[17] By 1877, fourteen similar "libraries" were available. Scores more were introduced over the next decade by other major hardcover houses, including Harper, Holt, Houghton-Mifflin, Appleton, and Scribner. In 1886 alone, nearly 1,500 titles were *added* to these series and were mostly fictional works. By the end of the 1880s the market was glutted.[18]

The proliferation of paperback books was one factor that contributed to the end of the second paperback revolution; by the late 1880s, anything and everything worth publishing had been reprinted. Also, the public's taste was changing. More literate and more discerning, the public demanded quality books at affordable prices, not just affordable books. The major hardcover publishers responded to this demand by not only improving the type of literature available but by enhancing the aesthetic appeal of their packaging. According to *Publishers Weekly* (1887), the new books were "handy in shape, set in readable type, carefully printed on substantial white paper, with black not muddy ink—and above all, daintily bound in cloth with paper sides—these are books that are not only an intellectual feast, but decidedly pleasing to the eye."[19]

Another major factor contributing to the demise of "cheap" paperback publishing was the International Copyright Act of 1891, which protected foreign authors from being pirated. Publishers were now required to pay royalties to foreign authors whose work they reprinted.[20] The period between 1884 and 1893 was also marked by acute financial fluctuations in the American economy,[21] and paperback publishers, suddenly forced to compete for new books with hardcover firms during an economically depressed period, found it impossible to continue production at their former low prices. The New York financial panic of 1893 forced the last major paperback publisher, Lowell's United States Book Company, into bankruptcy. The second paperback revolution had come to an end.

The Origin of Mass-Market Paperback Publishing

The end of the second paperback revolution at the close of the nineteenth century did not mark the end of cheap books, but merely the end of cheap paperback books. Publishers of clothbound books filled the consumer demand for inexpensive editions by offering reprints of hardbound volumes. They were able to do this because of the introduction of the less costly buckram binding process in 1895. This practice of reprinting original works in inexpensive cloth editions would continue in the United States until Simon & Schuster founded Pocket Books in 1939 and set a worldwide pattern for mass-market paperback book publishing that remains basically unchanged today.[22]

The Early Years: Pre–World War II

Pocket Books copied and improved upon the success of Penguin Books in England, which had been founded by Sir Allen Lane four years earlier. The first Penguins were six-penny paperbacks in red-and-white jackets. The initial set sold poorly until Lane arranged for distribution with Clifford Prescott, the buyer for Woolworth's five-and-ten-cent stores.[23] From then on, Penguin sets did extremely well. When the line launched in England, it was estimated that two million volumes a year would ensure success. By 1938, sales totaled twenty-five million.[24]

The solid success of Penguin led Robert Fair de Graff to develop a twenty-five-cent American version of the paperback. At the time, de Graff was president of Blue Ribbon Books, a subsidiary of Doubleday. He suggested the idea of an American version of Penguin to Nelson Doubleday. Doubleday, strongly committed to hardcover reprints that would be competitive with those of other publishers, turned the idea down.[25] De Graff resigned from Blue Ribbon in February 1938 and took the idea to Simon & Schuster.

Initial printings were modestly planned at 10,000 copies per title. To make sure the readers would not feel that they were somehow being cheated by the small editions, the jacket cover guaranteed that the book was "complete and unabridged."[26] To further ensure the success of the new firm, the first series of ten books was carefully chosen to appeal to the broadest range of reader habits; it included proven best-sellers such as *Lost Horizon*; *Wake Up and Live*; *Topper*; *The Murder of Roger Ackroyd*; *Enough Rope*; *The Way of All Flesh*; *The Bridge of San Luis Rey*; *Bambi*; the first movie tie-in, *Wuthering Heights*; and *Five Great Tragedies* by William Shakespeare. The new Pocket Books took New York by storm, and the rest is publishing history.

Two factors contributed to the success of the pocket-sized paperbacks: the format and method of distribution. Format includes the design, size, and price. The design was, as de Graff himself proclaimed, "pleasing to the eye and agreeable to the touch." They were four and one-half by six and one-half inches, with attractive multicolor cover designs, and they were easily carried in a workingman's hip pocket. The covers were made of sturdy cardboard, with a thin and transparent waterproof coating, which gave the books a shining freshness. The price was twenty-five cents, well below the thirty-nine cents to $1.98 range of their lower-priced cloth reprint competitors. Their readers were working people—locomotive engineers, mechanics, salesmen, clerks, waitresses, ranchers, and farmers, among others—and the books reached this heretofore mostly untapped audience through a unique distribution system.

It was the method of distribution, perhaps more than any other single factor, that influenced the success of the third paperback revolution. As early as 1935, department stores and chain variety stores were playing an increasingly important role in the distribution of books. Pocket Books utilized these outlets, pioneered by Penguin Books, and tapped another—magazine wholesalers.

When Pocket Books first appeared, regional magazine distributors had room for additional items and wanted something other than magazines. At the same time, Pocket Books was seeking an alternative source of distribution, since traditional book retailers were cool to the new pocket-sized paperbacks, thinking they wouldn't sell, and took only limited quantities.[27] Because magazine wholesalers distributed to nontraditional book outlets—newsstands, drug and cigar stores, railroad terminals—Pocket Books greatly expanded its potential book market. In Columbus, Ohio, for example, readers of traditional books in 1939 had a choice of six bookstores, but those who wanted a pocket paperback could find them at 210 other outlets around the city.[28] The limited distribution channels for hardcover publishers had been cited in the Cheney Report nine years earlier, but until Pocket Books, no one had taken steps to expand the traditional outlets or examine new methods of getting books to the consumer.

These new wholesalers changed distribution in a powerful way. Besides reaching a previously untapped audience with books the working person could afford, the wholesaler greatly reduced sales and distribution costs to the publisher. A publisher could now ship to one location and be assured the books would reach a multitude of outlets. Buying decisions were eliminated by this new method because the distribution decisions were essentially made by the publishers themselves, who allocated copies among the magazine distributors based on the amount of space they were allocated by the outlets in their region. The cost of covering an account was dramatically lowered as the salesperson no longer had to stop at each outlet and pitch the books—a costly, time-consuming process, which hardcover houses would continue to use until the bookstores themselves started to disappear toward the end of the twentieth century.

Boom Years: Post–World War II

The Second World War, much like the Civil War three-quarters of a century earlier, both helped and hindered the spread of paperbacks. Paper shortages during the war years forced many publishing firms to curtail their offerings.[29] Nevertheless, in May 1943, the Council of Books in Wartime announced a plan to send approximately thirty-five million copes of fiction and nonfiction over the next year to men and women serving in the armed forces abroad. These books, popularly known as Armed Forces Editions, were designed with paper covers, bound by staples, with two columns of print on a page; they were designed cheaply to minimize production cost, but also to provide easy reading in a size that could be slipped into the pocket of any uniform.[30] Books were thus disseminated to countless individuals, many of whom might otherwise never have acquired the habit of reading for entertainment. The Armed Forces Editions also helped pave the way for the incipient paperback revolution because they were pocket-size and paperbound.[31]

The boom in mass-market publishing began two years after the end of the war, in 1947. As in the period following the Civil War, paper was more readily available, but manufacturing costs began to rise rapidly. Paperback reprints thus "offered the best chance to keep a wide range of books available to the public at prices that large numbers of people could afford to pay."[32]

The boom in mass-market publishing can be gauged by the number of new paperback firms that started between 1948 and 1955, all following the distribution pattern established by Pocket Books. Among the new paperback house were New American Library (1948), Harlequin (1949), Pyramid (1949–1977), Fawcett (1950), Ace (1952), Ballantine (1952), and Berkley (1955). Many of these houses continue to be dominant mass-market publishers today, though some, like Penguin, have shifted their emphasis to "quality" paperbacks, and others, such as Berkley, Jove, Fawcett, and, more recently, Harlequin, have merged with other firms but continue to publish paperback book under their original names.

In the midst of this explosive growth of mass-market paperback publishers, "quality" paperbacks evolved. The distinction between "quality" trade paperbacks and mass-market paperbacks was introduced in the early 1950s. Quality paperbacks, which included serious nonfiction titles and reprints of literary classics, were introduced to meet the growth in the educational market.[33] Established hardcover publishers—such as Doubleday, Macmillan, Harper & Row, and Random House—expanded their book lines in the direction of "quality" paperbacks, while the newer houses, cited earlier, entered the mass-market paperback field. This emphasis on "quality" paperbacks suggested, at least obliquely, that the content of mass-market paperback books was "cheap" and served as justification by hardcover publishers for not entering this field, since hardcover publishers have traditionally viewed themselves as guardians of the public's taste.[34] The quality/cheap distinction was further underscored by the dispersion of the former paperbacks in colleges, while the latter were distributed in such "common" places as railroad terminals and cigar stores. The line dividing the two types of paperback books is less sharp today but still lingers over romance publishing.

The Social Climate of the Fifties

Growth in the paperback industry between 1948 and 1955 resulted in a period of intense publishing competition. Genre fiction, always a mainstay of the paperback industry, was widely circulated by paperback houses, and because the books were largely reprints of hardcover releases, the paperback firms of the day attempted to differentiate their products from one another by designing the book covers to appeal to a mass audience. This led to a trend that Kenneth Davis called the lowest-common-denominator appeal.[35] Titles such as *The War of the Sexes* and *Three Gorgeous Hussies* were carefully chosen for their sexual connotations; illustrations were designed with suggestive images and usually featured a woman in some state of undress; in addition, otherwise innocuous

Risqué covers work to entice the reader. Left: *The Men She Knew* (Venus Books, 1951); right: *Gutter Girl* (Beacon Books, 1960).

passages in the book would appear suggestively misrepresented on the cover. Over the next decade, the public furor over the content of some of these books and the images on most would result in a toning down of both.

The censorious climate in America during the McCarthy era (1946–1957) affected the content of all entertainment media during the period. Immorality became a pseudonym for Communism, morality for patriotism. Complaints, censorship suits, and legislative investigations, such as the U.S. House of Representatives' Gathings Committee, began to affect what was published. By 1952, paperback bannings were no longer isolated instances of prudish Puritan "Banned in Boston" regionalism, but were sweeping across the country. The 1957 Roth decision, in which the Supreme Court held that publishers were liable for offensive material, formalized the ban against "pornographic" books that had been in effect in America since the early to mid–1950s.

Censorship during this period was aimed at any "immoral" form of entertainment. In publishing, the mass-market paperback industry came under attack for its lewd books. It was not the content, however, that was "lewd" so much as the packaging, especially on such spicy titles as *Impatient Virgin*, *Hard-Boiled Virgin*, and *Kept Woman*. The concern was that the widespread availability of these books—they *seemed* to be everywhere—would corrupt the masses through their putatively "dirty" content. Romances in particular came under attack, probably, as Ian Watt suggests, because, like Richardson's *Pamela*, the genre concentrates much more exclusively on the sexual relationship itself and on arousing sexual interests.[36]

The effect of the McCarthy era on romances can be gleaned by the changes in Avon's publishing decisions over the next decade. Like many early paperback publishers, Avon had been eclectic in its choice of books and reprinted a wide range of fiction titles and authors, from classical translations to fantasies and from Erskine Caldwell to Agatha Christie. Avon's major success, at least initially, was in mystery and romance novels. Then, in 1948, mysteries took precedent over romances. By 1953, Avon published only five or six romances in a list which now accentuated detective novels, thrillers, and westerns. There was a slight increase in romances in 1955 (up to nine); this level continued until 1947–1958, when, in the wake of the Roth decision, Avon cut its romance list by half. In 1959, only two sexually explicit books appeared, and neither were romances: *More About Girls* by the respected Italian author Alberto Moravia and R. Rogers's *Born Reckless*. Much of Avon's list in the late 1950s and early 1960s, like those of most other paperback publishers, consisted of "safe" (sexless) mysteries and westerns.[37]

The legal climate began to change in the late 1950s and early 1960s. The change was slow, however, and would not affect genre fiction for another decade.

In a number of separate legal decisions, numerous books were found not to be obscene, including D. H. Lawrence's *Lady Chatterley's Lover*; Henry Miller's *Tropic of Cancer*; and John Cleland's *The Memoirs of a Woman of Pleasure*, more popularly referred to as *Fanny Hill*. All of these rulings were based on the literary merit of the books in question.[38] This helps explain the "sexually explicit" books that Avon and other paperback houses began allowing to pass through their editorial gates in the late 1950s through the early 1960s. There was less fear of prosecution for books that met the "literary merit" standard. No publisher attempted to argue that genre fiction met this stringent criterion, least of all the highly dubious romance genre. The few romance novels that were published by American paperback houses were sweet and sexless, released to meet what was viewed in-house as a limited demand for these novels.

Conclusion

Paperbacks were a long time coming. They were constantly resisted by hardback publishers who feared that paper books would cut into their profits. Certainly a major appeal for many consumers was their low cost. But this is not the primary reason the books were called cheap. The label was aimed less at the cost than to designate the often-sensationalized content of these paper books. The denigrating label was also applied to the "common" man who was viewed as less educated—the books were, after all, designed for "the masses." This suggested that the reader of paperback novels could not appreciate the "literary" books produced by hardback publishers, a distinction more finely made with the introduction in the 1950s of mass-market "quality" paperbacks that were aimed at the college market. It didn't help that many of the novels during each of the three paperback phases, inclusive of the present one, were romances aimed at women who were relegated to a rung substantially beneath the common man. The contemporary outpouring of romances in paperback form would continue to hamper their "acceptance" among scholars and by others in publishing, including other mass-market houses. Even devotees of the genre often feel a certain "guilt" over their fondness for romance novels.[39] These thin—and sometimes not so thin—mass-market romance paperbacks, as we step into the twenty-first century, are beginning to gain a certain degree of respectability, but the cloud of "cheap literature" still hangs over the genre.

Chapter 2

The World of Harlequin
1949–1979

One of the early publishing houses to emerge during the post–World War II boom in mass-market paperback publishing was Harlequin, established in 1949. Like many of the other publishing firms that began during this period, Harlequin was at first a reprint publisher of mass-market general fiction and nonfiction. It was not until 1957 that Harlequin began publishing romance novels. Three years later, romance titles began to dominate Harlequin's list, and in 1961, the books took the imprint "Harlequin Romance." In 1964, Harlequin devoted its entire list to reprinting Mills & Boon romances in paperback.

Harlequin's success throughout the 1960s was limited primarily to Canada. Sales did not climb until 1970 when the Toronto-based publisher made arrangements with Pocket Books for widespread distribution of its romance line in the United States. In 1969, Harlequin sold 19 million books and netted $110,000 on sales of $7.7 million. By the mid–1970s, Harlequin was selling 100 million copies of its romances in North America and another 50 million overseas. Profits in 1977 were estimated at $11 million on sales of $75 million, with an after-tax profit margin of 15 percent, almost three times the industry average. By the end of the 1970s the number of books sold by Harlequin would almost double, falling just short of 200 million copies; sales climbed to an all-time high of $275 million, and earnings topped $25 million.[1]

In the Beginning

Harlequin Enterprises Limited was founded in 1949 by the former mayor of Winnipeg, Richard Gardyn Bonnycastle. Prior to launching Harlequin Enterprises—a name chosen to convey light entertainment—Bonnycastle owned a company that produced American paperbacks for distribution in Canada. This company provided the base for Bonnycastle's publishing venture.

In its first year, Harlequin published twenty-five novels. The next ten years were erratic. Between 1950 and 1959, Harlequin published an average of 50 books a year; some years it offered as few as 25 (1955) to 28 (1956) titles and some years as many as 61 (1953) to 65 (1950). Most of these titles were reprints of westerns, mysteries, and thrillers and included books by such authors as W. Somerset Maugham, Arthur Conan Doyle, Agatha Christie, and Edgar Wallace. The list was lightly peppered with romances. The first decade was unmarked by any notable success.[2]

The romance stage of Harlequin's enterprise began in late 1957, when it published its first British romance, a Mills & Boon reprint entitled *Hospital in Buwamba*. This transcontinental arrangement, and the consequent domination of Mills & Boon romances among Harlequin's titles, was prompted by Mary Bonnycastle, then editor of the house and the publisher's wife, who considered the Mills & Boon romances to be "fiction of good taste."[3] That Mary Bonnycastle would decide to focus increasingly on romance because she enjoyed the books should not be considered unusual; as we shall see throughout this book, editors tend to select novels they personally enjoy, assuming that their enjoyment will be reflected in the consumer's taste.

Mary Bonnycastle's personal preference for the genre may have been one reason for Harlequin's decision to increase its romance line, but it is not the only one. The arrangement with Mills & Boon was also financially sound for both publishers.

Mills & Boon, Limited, is an established London-based publisher, founded in 1908. The firm was well known for its hardcover romances. Most of its romance novels were distributed through libraries, but in the 1950s libraries began to close and the major source of sales for Mills & Boon titles was being choked off. Looking for a new outlet, Mills & Boon contacted the fledging paperback publisher Harlequin. A contract was arranged that provided for Mills & Boon to release the hardcover editions in the United Kingdom, with Harlequin having the paperback reprint rights in both the UK and North America.

There is no evidence to indicate that Mills & Boon contacted any of the American houses that were emerging during the 1950s. One reason why Harlequin likely was chosen over other paperback houses in the United States was that it was based in Canada. Since Mills & Boon authors were predominantly British, and since their romance titles had met with a degree of success among British women, it seems logical that the London-based firm would perceive a market in Canada, which continues to have strong political and cultural ties with Britain.[4] As a struggling paperback publisher in the 1950s, Bonnycastle no doubt found the reprint offer attractive since it would provide Harlequin with a steady stream of fiction titles that would already have established themselves as proven sellers in Britain. The decision must have proved satisfactory, because between 1957 and 1963, Harlequin's list of Mills & Boon romance titles increased steadily from 33 to 78. Yearly romance production rose to 96 titles in 1964, the year Harlequin began publishing Mills & Boon romances exclusively; it remained at this level until 1973, when Harlequin debuted Presents and added another 48 titles to its list.

Both the Harlequin Romance and Presents series are typically referred to as contemporary romances because the romantic relationship is set in the here-and-now, in contrast to historical romances, which are set in some bygone era. The contemporary setting has changed, however; in the late 1950s and early 1960s, most of the romances that Harlequin published were "nurse novels." The name derives from the potpourri of titles that featured romantic relationships between nurses and doctors, such as *Emergency Nurse*, *Career Nurse*, *Calling Nurse Grant*, and *Desert Nurse*. The extent to which nurse novels dominated Harlequin's list in the early 1960s can be gleaned from the number of titles featuring a nurse, doctor, or hospital. Of the 378 titles published during the first half of the 1960s, 57 percent were nurse novels. This began to track upward in 1965 at the peak of television's preoccupation with young heartthrob doctor shows, such as *Ben Casey* (1961–1966) and *Dr. Kildare* (1961–1966).[5] Though nurse romances continued to dot Harlequin's list well into the 1970s, heroines in the second half of the 1960s and after were more likely to be teachers, secretaries, and governesses, no doubt exploring the premarital side of the squeaky-

Nurse novels were an industry standard for several years. From left: *Wilderness Nurse* (Pocket Books, 1949), *Night Call* (Dell, 1961), *Nurse Sally's Last Chance* (Harlequin, 1969).

clean marital family so popular on television during the 1960s.[6] A visual depiction for the period 1970–1979 would show a marked decrease in nurse novels offset by a concomitant increase in other types of contemporary romances.

Whatever the occupation, the setting was often exotic. Nurse heroines often took jobs in the jungles of Africa or on Polynesian islands: *Jungle Hospital, Outpost Hospital, Rendezvous in Lisbon*, and *Hotel on the Loch*. Like the movies of the 1960s, these novels offered women readers a taste not only of romance but of travel, an opportunity that they were not exposed to on studio-set television shows during this period.

Besides the travelogue aspect of the Harlequin novel, contemporary romances of the period shared at least one other distinguishing feature—sexual encounters were notoriously chaste. A lot of kissing and some heavy breathing occurred in these books, but sex was banished; it was merely implied in the happy-ever-after marital endings. No sex occurred outside marriage, nor was there any description of sexual activity. These books, as their publisher once described them, stood for "hardcore decency," and Harlequin remained proud of being able to provide romantic fiction in good taste throughout the 1970s.[7] Harlequin's sexually chaste novels have come to be known as "sweet romances."

The Harlequin heroine of the 1960s and 1970s is always virginal. Typically, she is in her late teens or early twenties and has seldom experienced more than

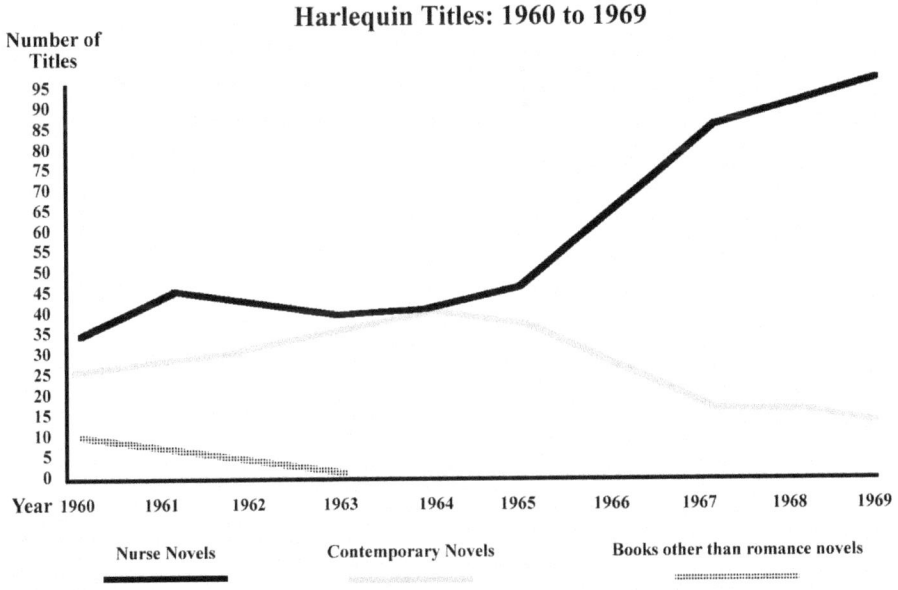

Harlequin Titles, 1960–1969.

a few kisses from the opposite sex. Heroines vary in appearance from attractive to beautiful; they are never described as ugly, homely, or plain but tend to be physically "flawed": their noses may be a little too small or their mouths a little too generous for ideal beauty.[8] The hero, on the other hand, is always her social superior (women then and now tend to marry socially upward); he is usually in his mid- to late thirties, handsome, and is well dressed; he is usually well-to-do, if not wealthy, a successful entrepreneur, and more often than not, the heroine's boss. The heroine's sexual desires have remained latent and are awakened by the hero. Despite the stirrings of passion he elicits, sexual intimacy is rarely contemplated outside the marital state.[9]

The plot of the Harlequin Romance series has received more than its share of critical attention. The firm's high visibility and product specialization led critics of the genre to vent their disdain of romances upon Harlequin's list. The most vituperative analyses came from the growing ranks of feminist literary schools in the 1960s and 1970s who, like Marxist critics, began their assessment of the novel with a series of a priori assumptions as to what constitutes "good" literature.

The feminist school grew out of the women's liberation movement of the late 1960s and gained momentum, or at least a sharpened direction, from Kate Millett's *Sexual Politics* in 1970, the first major book of feminist criticism published in the United States.[10] Feminists began to reread a host of male-authored novels, ripping the stories from their social context and finding everything steeped in sexist language and politics, from "Rip Van Winkle," in which Rip's prolonged absence from the home allows him "access to life in an all-male world, a world without women, the ideal American territory," to *The Great Gatsby*, another American "love story centered in hostility to women."[11]

The only good novels, the feminists began to argue in the mid- to late 1970s, are those written by women and that focus on sexual repression and inferiority. Attention turned to the novels of George Eliot, Simone de Beauvoir, Doris Lessing, and Fay Weldon. Novels by these women were viewed as "feminist novels" because they grappled with the experience of women's oppression. Novels by women that did not focus on the oppressive theme tended to be dismissed or condemned. This philosophical bent made Harlequin an easy target. Here were women writing for women who, by focusing on love and marriage, were hindering the development of women's true consciousness.[12]

The feminist critical interpretation of a text is distorted by a failure to examine and come to terms with the historical time period. The women who wrote and read Harlequin romances in the 1960s and 1970s were not in the vanguard of the women's liberation movement. One of the few public domain studies of Harlequin readers was conducted by Peter Mann in 1968.[13] Mann sampled 9,300 readers on the Mills & Boon/Harlequin mailing lists: nearly

3,000 returned the questionnaire. Because of the limited distribution of Harlequin in the United States in 1968, few American respondents were included in the sample; the majority were British residents, along with a smattering of Canadians. Mann's study is not representative of North American romance readers, but it does give us some idea of the social demographics of Harlequin readers.[14] The majority (58 percent) were between the ages of twenty-five and fifty-four; a quarter (24 percent) were over fifty-five. Fifty-five percent were married and listed their occupation as housewife. Only six percent had the equivalent of a bachelor's degree or above, though this is more reflective of the 1960s than the romance readers, since only eight percent of women in 1970 had a college education.[15] The Harlequin reader was thus disproportionately likely to be a married housewife with a high school degree who purchased an average of twenty to thirty paperback romances a year. It was this group that Harlequin attempted to attract, and it reached this audience initially through an astute marketing campaign and later by incorporating plot changes into the newly launched Presents series that were more in keeping with values emerging among women during the 1970s.

Distribution and Marketing Innovations: Insights Plus Hype and Ballyhoo

The content of romances being released by American publishers when Harlequin entered the American market in the early 1970s, as we'll see in the next chapter, was basically the same. The only important notable exception was the setting: Harlequin's were all contemporary; American romances were predominantly historical. They were otherwise very much alike: sweet with no overt sexual nuances, with stereotyped "fifties" heroes and heroines.[16] To compete in the American marketplace, and to set its product apart from American-based romance publishers, Harlequin had to do something unique. It did!

The first major decision Harlequin made was to appoint W. Lawrence Heisey president in 1971. Heisey was a Harvard Business School graduate. He had spent thirteen years as a marketing and advertising executive at Procter and Gamble, as well as a number of years in broadcasting in a similar position. The new president had no publishing background, but he was astute at marketing strategies and sometimes referred to himself as "an old soap salesman."[17]

One of the first tasks Heisey faced was to acquaint the American public with Harlequin's romances.[18] Two problems confronted him. First, bookstores were reluctant to accept his product, since they generally shied away form mass-market softcover titles at the time.[19] Second, Harlequin was still a small company and had little money to spend on formal advertising. Heisey solved both problems by recognizing who the audience was. It was basically the same audience he had faced in his sales and marketing position at P&G: the housewife.

Under Heisey, Harlequin bypassed traditional bookstores, or made only a minimal effort to place its romances there. Instead, distribution was concentrated on selected retail establishments. Refining the strategy pioneered by Pocket Books two decades earlier, Harlequin concentrated on supermarkets and chain variety stores, such as Woolworth's. In short, Heisey distributed his product at those retail outlets most likely to be frequented by women.

Having placed the books within reach of the potential audience, Harlequin still had to acquaint the public with its books. Media advertising, the traditional method of informing the public of a new product, was cost-prohibitive to the small company in the early 1970s. Offering a discount with a coupon is another, less expensive, means of tempting the potential consumer to sample a new product. But as Heisey recognized, couponing—though a time-honored, solid consumer technique and one that was widely used by P&G—was unfamiliar to the book industry and would require a lengthy and costly educational process to introduce. The idea was therefore abandoned, if for no other reason, recalled Heisey, than that "I was never able to find a way to do it."

Unable to utilize one traditional marketing technique, Heisey turned to another—sampling. In retailing, producers sample what they refer to as the "point of purchase." The point of purchase is one way a producer ascertains how many customers might be interested in trying a specific product; it is generally used to gauge a new product's desirability. Items are given away at various stores and/or locations, the "point" where the item is most likely to be "purchased." The success of the giveaway program is interpreted as a rough approximation of how well the item might sell. This type of product sampling poses certain problems. For example, if one is attempting to ascertain the point of purchase for a dishwashing detergent, customers often take multiple units because they can use them. However, people don't tend to reread a book, or need more than one copy. Thus, Heisey perceived the point of purchase sampling technique as a valid method of determining audience interest.

It was a short step from this insight—one person, one book—to Heisey's major marketing innovation: promotion by product line rather than single title release.

Unlike most book publishers at the time, Harlequin did not have a range of fiction and nonfiction books. The company published romance novels exclusively. The content of these novels also tended to be standardized, and because they had been "pretested" in Britain under the Mills & Boon imprint, they had proven consumer interest. Heisey reasoned that if a publisher could arouse interest in one book, they could arouse interest in a series, a point, Heisey says, that "seems terribly obvious today, but it wasn't then." It was this insight that led Harlequin to emphasize its romance line, while most publishers were attempting to arouse interest in particular authors or titles.[20]

To capitalize on its product line, Harlequin chose three to five titles over the next few years to be produced and given away in record quantities. Harlequin could afford this strategy, said Heisey, because book production costs in the early 1970s were not nearly as prohibitive as they would become a decade later.

To "hook" the consumer on its romance line, Harlequin employed numerous giveaways, which Heisey readily acknowledges as gimmicks. One of these was to distribute two million copies of the book *Dark Star*, originally published in 1969, to dealers at no cost in 1973. This book was sold to consumers for fifteen cents. By giving them to dealers, and allowing the dealers to sell the book for fifteen cents, dealers were assured a quick, straight profit on every paperback. At the same time, the consumer got a bargain. Between 1970 and 1975, mass-market paperbacks sold from $.95 to $2.46.[21] Even at the lower price range, customers saved over 80 percent on the cost of *Dark Star*. It was an incentive for the dealer to stock the book and for women to buy it.

In other introductory offers for readers who might be reluctant to spend even fifteen cents, Harlequin gave away millions of other books outright, among them five million copies of Violet Winspear's *Honey Is Bitter* in 1973. These books were not given away at random; they went to the specific audience Harlequin wished to attract, the housewife, and they were delivered in a unique way. In an arrangement with Procter and Gamble, Heisey gave away record numbers of selected Harlequin titles with the purchase of various P&G household products. One such product was Bio-Ad laundry detergent. Packed inside each box of Bio-Ad was a Harlequin romance.[22]

The success of these giveaways can be judged by the firm footing Harlequin Books established by 1976, when Heisey abandoned the gimmicks for the more traditional promotion of advertising. "We finally built a big enough business base," Heisey said, "to generate enough capital that we were able to expand and to return to formal advertising."

The basic philosophy that guided Harlequin's introductory giveaways was transferred to advertising in the mid–1970s. No single author or title was promoted. Rather, focus was on the Harlequin Romance line: the romantic theme of Harlequin books.

Writing about the book industry at the time Harlequin was moving into advertising, Benjamin Compaine underscores the advantages and drawbacks in advertising for a single-title book at the time.[23] He discusses the use in St. Louis of an inexpensive thirty-second spot commercial for the $1.95 paperback of

Jose Torres's book on Muhammad Ali, *Sting Like a Bee*. Without television spots, a sale of 450 copies was predicted. The ensuing campaign consisted of only six airings of a commercial in a one-week period and cost $1,500. Over 3,800 copies of the book were sold within thirty days. In this case, Compaine concludes that the dramatic increase in sales barely covered the cost of the television spots, though it did clearly demonstrate television's impact as a stimulus on sales. This illustration aptly depicts the problems that publishers of general trade and mass-market books encounter when advertising is geared toward a specific author or title. Indirectly, it also underscores the benefits of advertising books if the ads can focus on the overall product line.

Harlequin plunged into advertising in a big way. It spent nearly $1.3 million in advertising in 1977, substantially more than some of the larger trade publishers, such as Dell, Simon & Schuster, Avon, and Macmillan. Nevertheless, Harlequin's advertising as a percent of trade sales was close to what many other publishers spent, between two and three percent. But while most other publishers diffused their advertising among the various media, Harlequin focused on radio and television ads, spending over $1.1 million, an unprecedented media expense for a book publisher. Most of this expenditure, about 80 percent, was in daytime (Monday through Friday) television.[24] Clearly, Harlequin was gearing its ads to a specific audience, the high-female soap-opera viewership.[25]

A substantial portion of the house's success in the 1970s was based on a standardized product and a recognition of its target audience: Harlequin sold romances and sold them to women. Their books were billed as "romantic fiction in good taste," and the consumer knew exactly what she was getting every time she bought a book, regardless of title or author: a romance with a happy ending (marriage), without explicit sex or offensive language. This standardization of content and the "fine-tuning" of distribution to select retail establishments were major factors in Harlequin's success. It allowed (1) print runs to be clearly pinpointed, thus avoiding the high return rates that plagued most other trade publishers; (2) a clearer perception of the prospective consumer, since consumers at retail outlets other than book stores at the time were more likely to be female, over thirty, predominantly married, and "pleasure readers"[26]; and (3) introductory offers and advertising to focus more narrowly on the specific consumer most likely to enjoy its product.

Tweaking Harlequin Romance

The overall sweet content of Harlequin novels did not change dramatically during the 1970s. But change in content did occur. These changes are often overlooked. There is a tendency, particularly pronounced during the 1960s and 1970s, to lump Harlequin's product conveniently under the label "sweet." This label, while accurate at the time, does not take into account some subtle content changes that Harlequin introduced. These changes were lauded by readers and helped Harlequin continue to build its consumer base throughout the decade.

Harlequin Presents: Introducing a New Line of Books

The first major content change that Harlequin introduced was in May 1973 when it launched a new line of books, Harlequin Presents. Harlequin Romance were paperback reprints of successful Mills & Boon hardcover romances. The Mills & Boon hardcovers were not circulated in North America; thus, Harlequin did not have to compete with hardcover editions. Moreover, in 1971, shortly after Heisey assumed the presidency of Harlequin Books, Harlequin purchased Mills & Boon. The purchase did not affect the basic organization structure of either publishing firm; however, it did guarantee Harlequin an undisturbed flow of Mills & Boon romances.

At the time of the purchase, Mills & Boon was publishing novels in England more sensual than Harlequin was selecting for reprint in North America.[27] The main difference between these novels, later to be debuted as Presents, and the Romance line, was that the former were slightly spicier: there was more description of the actual seduction scene, and it was intimated that the hero and heroine engaged in sexual activity prior to marriage, though only if there was a firm commitment to marriage.[28]

There was some discussion among Harlequin's editorial staff as to whether the American population was ready for the steamier side of Mills & Boon's romances. The editorial staff felt these books inappropriate. This editorial advice, Heisey says, was itself "inappropriate."

Heisey's belief that the more sensual Mills & Boon romances would do well in North America was based on their success in Britain. After all, this had been the basis of Harlequin's selection for the Romance line. For some reason, the editorial staff felt this "pretest" pattern was not applicable to the more sensual Mills & Boon novels.

To determine whether the editorial staff was correct, or the success in Britain of the more sensual romances was indicative of changing consumer taste, Heisey introduced the book industry to another traditional marketing technique that was well known in the retailing world: blind sampling. In blind sampling, the consumer chooses between two or more unidentified products;

for example, one marked "x" and one marked "y." The technique had not been previously employed in the book industry because it requires an identified product line, not just a title.

To evaluate the accuracy of his editorial staff's judgment, Heisey blind tested the Mills & Boon novels with Harlequin's regular Romance product. Matched pairs of books were sent to Harlequin consumers in plain wrappers, with all identification removed, including the name of the author. The consumers were asked which book they preferred. The response, Heisey states, indicated that "it was clear they [the more sensual novels] should be published." Moreover, Heisey said that "some very good books had been held back from the basic series. They should have been published earlier."

It is difficult to determine exactly why Harlequin editors were reluctant to introduce the more sensual Mills & Boon romances to the North American audience. Some conjecture is certainly in order, however. First, Harlequin was doing well with Romance without deviating from the chasteness that had been a theme since the line's introduction in 1957. Second, the editors, according to Heisey, inaccurately perceived their readers as naïve housewives who were not receptive to the idea of sex before marriage and who preferred less sensuous, sweeter novels. The fact that in 1970 through 1972, American historical romances were also sweet no doubt reinforced the editors' view that sweet romances were what the consumer wanted.

The editors were probably right to assume that Romance readers, used to a certain style, would be put off by the sudden appearance of sensuality in the series. Heisey shared this view, which is why the new books were not incorporated into the existing Romance line. The launching of a new line was a management decision, not an editorial one. The new line was supposedly differentiated to avoid reader confusion and to indicate the more sensual aspect of Presents' books, but the reader would be challenged to tell this from the covers (see cover illustrations next page).

Janet Dailey: The New Queen of Romances at Harlequin

Heisey's decision to introduce Presents would prove to be the right one. Within two years, Presents was outselling Romance.[29] The success of Presents was followed by the 1976 discovery of Janet Dailey, who soon became the new "queen" of romance novelists. Dailey, in four short years, assumed the romance throne from historical novelist Barbara Cartland, who had worked diligently for four decades to achieve her crown. By 1982, Dailey had written 76 novels

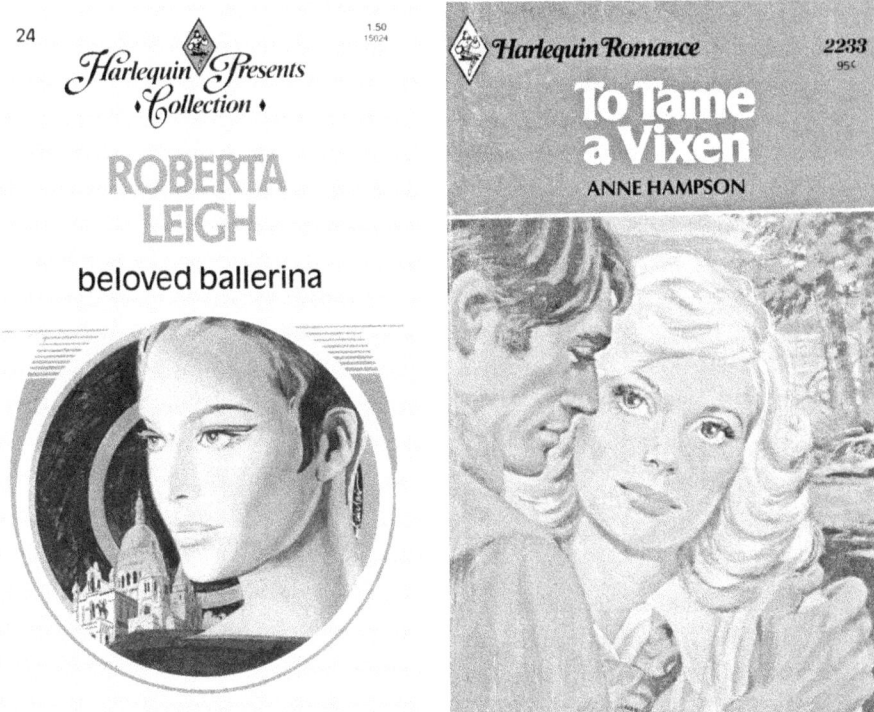

Harlequin covers from the 1970s. Left: *Beloved Ballerina* (Harlequin Presents, 1974); right: *To Tame a Vixen* (Harlequin Romance, 1979).

and had more than 90 million copies in print in 17 languages, making her the fifth most successful living author in the world; she wrote 54 of her novels for Harlequin before signing with Silhouette Books in 1980.[30]

Dailey was a significant find for Harlequin. She was the firm's first American author and its first to focus exclusively on American settings.

Though Harlequin had purchased Mills & Boon in 1971, the London publisher continued to exercise editorial control over the selection of manuscripts. The books would be printed in hardcover for release in Great Britain, with Harlequin reprinting the novels in paperback. There was little editorial selection involved for Harlequin. At most, Harlequin editors were required only to differentiate between the two content forms, assigning the sweeter books to the Romance line and the slightly more sensuous novels to the Presents line. The novels were otherwise similar to the handful of contemporary sweet romances being produced in America, though the British-authored books often were set in England or on the Continent. Dailey's first romance novel was distinguished only by the fact that the action took place in the United States.

Dailey had not previously written a romance novel prior to submitting a manuscript to Harlequin. She first became a reader of Harlequin books in 1968, when she was in her early twenties: "I felt a complete identification with the books ... [and] kept coming up with ideas for plots."[31] Dailey was not aware that the Harlequin books were written primarily by British authors for Mills & Boon.[32] Her book was published by Harlequin because it was well written and generally fit the thematic criteria for Harlequin Presents.

Thousands of American women had submitted manuscripts to Harlequin over the years without realizing that their chances of being published were remote, if only because of the Harlequin–Mills & Boon connection. These over-the-transom manuscripts were scanned by editors, and those deemed worthy of publication were forwarded to Mills & Boon. The London publisher never printed any of the manuscripts forwarded to it. Its refusal seems to have been a matter of pride—an attempt to assert its independence from the parent company by exerting editorial control. Still, Mills & Boon was under increased pressure from Harlequin management to give serious consideration to manuscripts sent to them.

The arrival of Dailey's manuscript was fortuitously timed. Author's luck, as we shall see in the following chapters, plays a major role in the editorial selection process. Her novel was accepted by Mills & Boon as a sop to Harlequin. Had Dailey decided to take up her romantic pen a year or two earlier or later, she might never have been published. Earlier, Mills & Boon editors would have probably rejected the manuscript out of hand, as they did with a host of other novels sent them from Toronto; later, Harlequin executives, appeased by Mills & Boon publishing one of the authors they sent them, turned from thematic issues and directed their attention toward expanding their empire in other directions.

We will never know exactly why Mills & Boon editors selected Dailey's manuscript from among the thousands of other unsolicited submissions. Luck and timing certainly had something to do with it, since many equally well-written, American-themed romance novels crossed the border into Canada by post and were forwarded on to London. Many of these rejected American authors later would be published by Harlequin's American-based competitor, Silhouette, when it opened its doors in 1980 to compete head-on with Harlequin.

The success of Dailey's novel had to be attributed to her American theme. It would seem a natural progression, then, for Harlequin to capitalize on this success either by introducing a new line of books, as was done with Presents, focusing on the "American" angle, or by allowing more romances set in America to filter into the existing line. Harlequin did neither.[33]

2. The World of Harlequin

Most publishers of trade and mass-market fiction sift manuscripts. They look for something that fits the type of publishing the house does but do not furnish specific guidelines for authors. Even publishers of formula fiction have no guidelines for content beyond those imposed by the dramatic conventions of the genre. In romance publishing these conventions include (1) the quest for love is a predominant theme; (2) a female protagonist; (3) a story told from the female point of view; and (4) the resolution of the primary theme in the conclusion by the attainment of reciprocal love and, typically, by marriage.[34] Editors sometimes use guidelines or tip-sheets, as they are often called, to detail nuances of these four themes so the writer knows exactly what the editors want.

Romance guidelines received a lot of caustic attention in the 1980s because of their page upon page of instructions to budding writers about who should do what to whom, when, how, and why—in some cases, even down to the page (or at least the chapter) where the first kiss should appear and what the heroine's response should be. Romance guidelines were first imposed by Harlequin in the late 1970s; they were nowhere near as stringent as later guidelines. Indeed, Harlequin's early guidelines were little more than an admonishment to the writer to read their books for a thorough understanding of Harlequin's themes:

> What distinguishes a Harlequin? How can you learn what the Harlequin editors want? The best way—the only way—to learn what constitutes a successful Harlequin romance is to obtain a number of our titles and *study* them thoroughly.
>
> Harlequins are well-plotted, strong romances with a happy ending. They are told from the heroine's point of view and in the third person. There may be elements of mystery or adventure, but *these must be subordinate to the romance*. The books are *contemporary* and settings can be anywhere in the world as long as they are authentic.

The remainder of the one-page, single-spaced guideline basically addresses often-heard editorial questions: word count; postage return inclusion to get the manuscript back; suggestions to keep a copy of the submitted manuscript; and, of course, royalty arrangements. These guidelines are like those sent out by all publishers, especially the concluding comments, the bane of publishing houses everywhere:

> We do not publish non-fiction, war novels, family chronicles or the like. Remember, a large part of being a successful writer is sending the *right* manuscript to the *right* publisher. So, *study* Harlequin and be sure you have written a Harlequin before trying to sell it to Harlequin.

In 1977, a year after Dailey's first novel was published, Harlequin established these rudimentary guidelines for their two romance lines. One reason for the development of guidelines at this point is related to the increased submission of unsolicited manuscripts Harlequin began receiving after Dailey's novel, *No Quarter Asked*, was published in January 1976. Another reason for imposing guidelines at this late stage is suggested by Harlequin's expansion program, which the organization embarked upon after 1975.

Between 1976 and 1980, Harlequin Enterprises expanded its romance series into ninety-eight countries, publishing Romance and Presents in eighteen languages. During this period, Harlequin also acquired a number of diversified companies, including the Ideals Publishing Corporation of Milwaukee, Wisconsin, a publisher of inspirational magazines and books, cookbooks, and greeting cards; Marshall Editions of London, an international book packager; and the Miles Kimball Company of Oshkosh, Wisconsin, a mail-order business for gifts, household goods, books, and assorted products. The firm also gained controlling interest in the Lauffer Company, a North American publishing group that put out entertainment and teen magazines. In addition, Harlequin established offices in New York City and acquired substantial holdings in numerous specialist magazines, including *ARTnews*, *Antique World*, *Weight Watchers Magazine*, *Photo Live*, and *Snow Goer*.[35] These expansions may have been directly related to the late establishment of guidelines for the primary Harlequin product. The guidelines that would be developed helped to ensure the consumer core for Harlequin's romance series was not eroded, as entrepreneurial managers attempted to redefine organizational goals. Formally fixing the content of their romances series helped to ensure continuity in product line, while attention was focused elsewhere. It may also have prevented the editors from looking at inventive manuscripts that didn't fit the guidelines.

The broad-based diversification effort Harlequin undertook in the late 1970s was recognized as a mistake by the 1980s. Harlequin's then-president, Dave Galloway, says the house "lost touch with its readers"—which helped diminish Harlequin's dominant position in the romance field during the 1980s.[36] Galloway insisted in an interview with this author that this will not happen again, and it didn't under his watch, though in the 1990s, as we'll see in Chapter 8, Harlequin did, once again, wander from its primary product with similar consequences. To sharpen their back-to-basics focus in the 1980s, Galloway distributed a case of the best-selling business book *In Search of Excellence* to his staff, reminding them, as Thomas Peters and Robert Waterman put in their book[37]:

> Acquisitions, even little ones, suck up an ordinate amount of top management's time, time taken away from the main-line business.... The typical diversification strategy dilutes the guiding qualitative theme.... Organizations that branch out but stick very close to their knitting outperform the others.... The least successful, as a general rule, are those companies that diversify into a wide variety of fields. Acquisitions, especially among this group, tend to wither on the vine.... [A]ny "back to basics" move is, according to the studies we have reviewed and the excellent companies' message, good news indeed.

Conclusion

Harlequin began like most mass-market publishers of the late 1940s to early 1950s and published an eclectic mix of previously published hardback books. Its shift toward romances was facilitated by two things. First, Mary Bonnycastle liked them. She was the editor at Harlequin and, unlike many editors, had a special "pull" since she was married to the publisher. The result was that more romances started filtering into the books published by Harlequin. The solid (though not necessarily spectacular) sales of these novels facilitated the second event. This was the arrangement with Mills & Boon in London to republish their hardback romances in paperback editions in both the UK and Canada. This was a satisfactory arrangement for both houses. Mills & Boon's primary library market was drying up, and the London-based publisher was looking for a means to maintain the sales of their books; Harlequin would have proven best-sellers to republish with little editorial effort. Romances steadily increased at Harlequin until 1964, when Harlequin began publishing exclusively Mills & Boon romance novels.

Harlequin romances were marked by modest sales until it arranged through Pocket Books for its novels to be distributed in the United States. The books appear to have resonated with American readers. Once Harlequin entered the American marketplace, the few houses in the United States that did release contemporary romances cut or curtailed their production, conceding organizational domain to Harlequin, choosing instead to release an alternative product, notably historical romances. Harlequin's dominance of the romance market, however, was due less to its content than to an astute marketing campaign.

The hiring of W. Lawrence Heisey as the publisher's president in 1970 was a brilliant move for the small publishing company. It probably didn't seem it at the time to others in the industry, since Heisey had limited experience in publishing. But after thirteen years with Procter and Gamble, he knew how to market a product to women. He quickly realized that he didn't have to market each book. This was a significant insight because it allowed him to market the Harlequin brand to readers of romances, the premise being that if the consumer liked the romance she was reading, she would like other romances they released.

Heisey was initially constrained in his marketing endeavors because Harlequin was a small company during the first half of the 1970s, so costly advertising, the traditional means of making consumers aware of a product, was not an option. Heisey solved this problem by forming an alliance with his old company and gave away millions of books with Procter and Gamble products. His success can be gauged by Harlequin's move to advertising in the second half of the 1970s, which was facilitated by their strong sales in the first half of the decade. Harlequin spent nearly three times more on advertising than other publishers, but Heisey could do this because he was promoting a line of books, not an individual book. He maintained his focus on Harlequin's primary consumer by advertising on the widely popular daytime soap operas that were largely viewed by housewives during the 1970s.

Marketing was not Heisey's only contribution to Harlequin. It was he, rather than the editors, who was responsible for introducing more socially relevant content in the books and launching Harlequin Presents. The decision to launch a new line and not incorporate the more sensual aspects of these novels into the existing Romance line was to ensure that devotees of the more chaste novels would not be alienated. It was a sound business decision, predicated on the success of the more sensual books in the UK: within two years, Presents was outselling Romance.

Since Harlequin books were exclusively reprints of Mills & Boon romances, the real editorial work was done in London. This meant the editors at Harlequin were not really functioning in a true editorial capacity since they had little say over content. They simply sifted from the array of books published by Mills & Boon. Since the sweet line had been doing so well for so long, they no doubt felt that there was no reason to change and did not sift the more sensual contemporaries published by Mills & Boon into the Romance line, feeling, no doubt, that while some British women might find these novels appropriate, American consumers wouldn't. Heisey demonstrated that they were wrong. The new novels, while certainly not "liberated" to the degree feminist critics of the 1970s might have liked, were more in keeping with changing social mores, if only in the acknowledgment that men and women in a committed relationship might engage in sexual activity before they got married.

The editors at Harlequin still did not have much sway, even after Presents was launched. They continued to filter "appropriate" (e.g., thematically correct and well written) romances to Mills & Boon for consideration. Mills & Boon was under increased pressure from their parent, Harlequin, to pay more attention to the manuscripts sent to them from North America. They appear to have resisted this pressure in an attempt to assert their editorial integrity. Nevertheless, in a sop to Harlequin, they filtered in *one* American author, Janet Dailey, whose unsolicited manuscript had been forwarded to them by editors in Canada. She quickly became a bestseller. The fact that the only distinguishing feature of her romances was that they were set in the United States appears to have been their main appeal to women readers in the United States. Harlequin, however, did not capitalize on this by including more American authors in its existing lines or introducing an American line of romances.

Harlequin capitalized on the first, early 1970s change (Presents) because it was focusing on its romance product; it didn't capitalize on its subsequent success with Dailey's phenomenal sales because management's attention was diverted elsewhere. They were diversifying into a wide range of unrelated business ventures. Distracted from its primary focus, Harlequin would be challenged on two fronts in the early 1980s that each had the potential to destroy its business empire. One was the introduction of rival Silhouette with its American authors and settings. The other was sweeping changes in the content of sweet contemporary romances produced by American houses that would lead to the "romance revolution" of the 1980s and that Harlequin was slow to respond to. The romance revolution of the 1980s was rooted to events taking place in American houses during the 1970s, and while these events did not then challenge Harlequin, they would lay the ground for the changes that would take place in the romance novel in the early 1980s that destabilized the romance publishing environment.

CHAPTER 3

The Four Phases of Love
American Romance Publishing in the Seventies

The combined output of romance novels by all American publishers in the first half of the 1970s can conservatively be estimated at between sixty to seventy titles per year, a fraction of Harlequin's yearly output. A number of small publishing companies—such as Beagle, Lancer, and Macfadden—published paperback romance reprints and some original editions.[1] Most of these publishers either went out of business or were absorbed by larger publishing houses by the mid–1970s during an intense period of reorganization and mergers that swept the publishing industry.[2]

Larger, established publishers—such as Doubleday, Bantam, Fawcett, and Dell—also produced romance novels during the late 1960s and early 1970s; however, their efforts were not concentrated on this genre and appear to have been limited to releasing only four or five titles per year. These romance novels were sweet, in the style of Harlequin. This changed after 1972, when Avon introduced highly sensual historical romances that have been dubbed "bodice-rippers," a subgenre that would be increasingly duplicated by other American publishers in the second half of the 1970s. By decade's end, romance output in the United States had increased sixfold to roughly 400 titles per year. With only a few minor exceptions, American publishers of romance novels did not challenge Harlequin head-on. Instead, they published historical romances—that is, romances that are set in a historical context, such as at Napoleon's court or in Edwardian England.

This chapter examines the response of American publishers to Harlequin's domination of the romance industry in the 1970s, especially as Harlequin's domination influenced both the growth of romance publishing and the content offered by American romance publishers. Four distinct phases of content diffusion are identified. The first began in the 1960s and extended into the early 1970s. This is the period of mystery—suspense, gothics, and sweet historicals. The second phase began in 1972 and stretched to 1975–1976. It was during this phase that Avon introduced innovations in the content of American romance novels. The third phase began in the mid–1970s with the launching of Playboy's successful romance series. Playboy was the first major imitator of the new brand of sensual historical romances introduced by Avon. The fourth and final phase occurred in the late 1970s when other romance publishers began flooding the market with sensual historical romances.

Phase I: A Miscellany of Love

Among the various sweet historical subgenres being produced in America during the late 1960s–early 1970s are those romances that are set in any historical period, such as the Regency period in England (1811–1820), the Victorian era (1837–1900), the Edwardian age (1901–1910), the Napoleonic era (1804–1815) and the Antebellum South.[3] The plots in these period romances revolve around the misunderstandings and clashes between the hero and heroine. Heroes are tall, muscular, physically fit; they box, fence, and race horses. The heroines are attractive and intelligent. Both sexes are "graciously charming, well mannered and virtuous."[4] Trappings of the period are highlighted in considerable detail: clothes are elegant, the furnishings luxurious, the social engagements, balls, and country visits glamorous.[5] The wealth of historical detail is a

Yearly Production by Subgenre, 1970–1979.

time-traveling variation on Harlequin's contemporary depiction of distant lands in its romances.

Two other popular subgenres during this period are the gothics and mystery-suspense romances. The difference between gothics and mystery-suspense romances is mainly a matter of emphasis. Romance is emphasized in both subgenres and both have strong mystery elements. In the gothic novels, the heroine is a young, beautiful, innocent girl; the hero is modeled after Heathcliff in *Wuthering Heights*. He is mysterious and moody, a strong-willed man harboring a secret. The mystery element puts the heroine in jeopardy; the hero rescues her. The endings of these novels usually have a "twist"—more often than not, the hero the heroine falls in love with, who appears throughout the novel to be "bad," actually turns out to be "good." The historical setting for this subgenre is usually earlier than the Regency (circa 1700), though some, like Victoria Holt's *Mistress of Mellyn*, are set in Victorian times. The mystery is typically situated in foreboding gothic-style structures: castles, ruins, abbeys, or manor halls. Gothic novels tend to be less rich than the Regencies in historical detail, and there is considerably more leeway in historical accuracy.[6]

A variation on the classic gothic theme is mystery-suspense romances. Because these novels are often set in the same time period against a gothic background, the distinction is a fine one; however, overall, mystery-suspense romances have fewer dark, foreboding gothic elements.[7]

Sweet historicals, gothic, and mystery-suspense subgenres dominated the product line of American publishers throughout much of the 1960s and early 1970s. They all describe the same relationships that Harlequin depicted.

Phase II: Avon Discovers Sex

Like many other paperback publishers, Avon's initial success was in the romance and mystery fields, and their offerings of the former were substantially cut back during the McCarthy era as the house adopted a better-safe-than-sorry posture. The changing social and legal climate of the mid- to late 1960s would result in less internal censorship, and while romance novels would not be immediately affected, changing social attitudes that followed in the wake of the sexual revolution of the 1960s would pave the way for more sexually explicit romance novels.

The social and legal environment, however, was not all that was changing. Conditions at Avon were distinctly different from most other paperback houses in the early 1970s, and they would pave the way for the publication of the first sensual historical romance, Kathleen Woodiwiss's now-classic *The Flame and the Flower*.

A half-dozen years before *The Flame and the Flower* appeared in 1972, the stage was set at Avon for Woodiwiss's novel when twenty-six-year-old Peter Mayer became editor-in-chief in 1964, then publisher in 1965. Prior to assuming the helm at Avon, Mayer had acquired the rights to Henry Roth's *Call It Sleep*. Originally published in 1934, the book earned critical praise initially, but the Depression ruined its publisher and the book had long been out of print. Instead of having the novel reissued in traditional paperback release, Mayer, as an Avon editor, prepared it as an original publication, with bound galleys sent to book reviewers in advance of publication—an unusual undertaking for a paperback house in 1964. Just as unusual was the front-page review by *The New York Times Book Review*, which helped send sales past the million-copy mark.[8]

The success of *Call It Sleep* proved that a paperback novel could be a commercial success without the stamp of hardcover best-seller status, and it opened up new possibilities for paperback originals. Under Mayer's direction, Avon began acquiring original manuscripts to be released in paperback; among those purchased in advance of their hardcover release were Robin Moore's *The Green Berets* and Bel Kaufman's *Up the Down Staircase*. By 1972, Avon could fill an entire month's list of twenty-six titles with paperback originals.[9] This search for original manuscripts prompted then-senior editor Nancy Coffey to read Kathleen Woodiwiss's unsolicited novel.[10]

The Flame and the Flower was not a typical romance, and not only because the content was vastly different. At four hundred-plus pages, it was also nearly three times the length of romances being published at the time. Its length, no doubt, made it more likely that the manuscript would be read, since at the time Avon was seeking "good original novels rather than romances,"[11] and a shorter manuscript would immediately have distinguished it as a romance.

Whatever the reason Coffey decided to pull *The Flame and the Flower* from the pile of unsolicited manuscripts, the novel's content held her interest. She took the manuscript home over the weekend to browse through it and, so the story goes, "couldn't put it down."[12] She regarded her own reaction as a fairly reliable barometer of the book's potential success: "I figured that if I would keep reading this story, other women would too."[13]

The book was certainly atypical in romantic content. Woodiwiss's novel was spicier and more sensual than any of the romance subgenres being published at the time. *The Flame and the Flower*—or TFTF, as it has come to be called in the trade—is a historical novel set in early nineteenth-century London; it opens with an attempted rape followed by an actual rape. The heroine, Heather, has her virginity forcibly taken by Captain Brandon Birmingham, who makes her pregnant. Her relatives force them into a shotgun wedding. Afterwards, Heather and Brandon spend almost the entire book certain of each other's hatred and resentment, only to discover, some four hundred pages later, that they are actually deeply in love. In spite of its initial violent sex and subsequent avoidance of sex, Coffey (and the readers) consider Woodiwiss's novel a sexual, sensual book because of the erotic tension the author sustains throughout.

For Coffey, the novel was a page-turner. The book not only maintained a level of romantic tension but also proved to be well written, a stylistic achievement not typically associated with the genre. Woodiwiss's opening, in fact, is far from the standard romance fare of the day:

> Somewhere in the world, time no doubt whistled by on taut and widespread wings, but here in the English countryside, it plodded slowly, painfully, as if it trod the rutted road that stretched across the moors on blistered feet. The hot sweltering air was motionless; dust hung above the road, still reminding the restless of a coach that had passed several hours before. A small farm squatted dismally beneath the humid haze.... Inside the house, Heather wearily turned potatoes against a dull worn knife that more scraped than peeled.

Not Jane Austen, perhaps, but certainly a far cry from the standard opening of many historicals in the 1970s:

> Ruth Arnold eased her feet out of her shoes and staggered over to the window of her hotel room. The view was every bit as wonderful as the brochures had promised. What they had not promised was the swarm of young men who had followed Ruth and her sister up and down every street ever since they had arrived...—Isobel Chace, *To Marry A Tiger*, Harlequin, 1972

> "Beautiful Diana, goddess of the moon," the admirer murmured in Diana's ear as they slowly circled the room. "So chaste, so remote—." They paused at the card table, and she pretended to study the play, thinking she really must get away from this gentleman. He was just drunk enough to be annoying.—Janette Radcliffe, *The Heart Awakens*, Dell, 1977

The Flame and the Flower was submitted in 1971 and published as an Avon Spectacular, or lead title, in April 1972, by an "unknown author, without any review attention, and with no extra effort from Avon to promote it."[14] Nevertheless, the book went on to sell one million copies within the year, touching what Kenneth Davis somewhat cryptically calls "a slumbering erogenous zone in the American heartland."[15]

The success of *The Flame and the Flower* surprised Coffey. She selected the novel, she says, because "I liked it. I always feel that others will like it if I do." It was positioned as a romance because Coffey perceived the book to be of interest to a female audience. Reader interest soon became obvious, and book sales led Coffey to consider other, similar manuscripts. She didn't have long to wait before the next one arrived, addressed simply to "The Editor of *The Flame and the Flower.*"

Rosemary Rogers turned to writing to supplement her meager secretarial salary, but her novel *Sweet Savage Love* remained unwanted and unpublished. It was only after she read Woodiwiss's novel that she pulled her manuscript out of the drawer and sent it to Avon.[16] It was published as another Spectacular in 1974, this time with a large advertising and promotional budget.

The eroticism of Woodiwiss's novel was surpassed by *Sweet Savage Love*. Rogers's first historical romance chronicles the torrid lust and love between Ginny Brandon, a refined, desirable lady, and Steve Morgan, a rugged, macho adventurer. Rogers's hero, Steve, seduces the virgin Ginny, and they despise each other throughout most of the book, though their mutual attraction ultimately wins out over hate and they confess their undying love for one another. However, unlike *The Flame and the Flower*, there are numerous other men in Ginny's life who force themselves on her in what some romance authors prefer to call "forced seduction," and there are frequent sexual escapades between Ginny and Steve and between Steve and other women. Rogers, more than most romance authors, leads with sexual description. By the fourteenth page, when most books are tentatively exploring even the idea of a first kiss, Rogers, in *Sweet Savage Love*, has consummated a relationship:

> At one moment her hand flailed against him, and at the next—she could not recall, later, how it came about—her hands were clinging to him instead, as if she was drowning. She felt the linen of his shirt tear under her clutching fingers and she felt his muscles tense, and then her head fell helplessly back under the onslaught of his mouth on hers.
> She felt her body bending backward, felt the length of his hard body against her, and then somehow, they had almost fallen on the rough, dirty stone floor together still kissing. Their hands found and uncovered each other, and then, without preliminaries, he was over her, penetrating her roughly and deeply and, after her first cry of despair completely satisfying.

On the next page, after a moment's anguish over the submission, they're at it again:

> "I—I'm ashamed!" she wept again. "What will you think of me now? How can I live with myself?"
> "Hush, sweet—you're a woman, remember. A live and passionate one, under that icy surface. It's nothing to be ashamed of."
> She could hardly believe that he was ready for her again so soon; but she felt the proof of it and yielded to him, letting his hands do their work while his body rocked gently against hers—slowly, teasingly, while his hands moved like burning brands over her skin, making a complete wanton of her.

Sweet Savage Love, says Hillary Ross, who line-edited the novel, was "the first book that had a lot of sex in it from a woman's point of view."[17]

Because of their treatment of sex, these books were later dubbed "bodice-rippers" by caustic literary critics. The readers certainly didn't appear to object and bought the books in record numbers, which was enough for Avon to keep publishing them. The year Rogers's first sensual historical debuted, Avon also released two more Woodiwiss romances, *The Wolf and the Dove* and *The Wildest Heart*. The success of these books led Avon to increase its romance titles. By 1975, Avon had added a third sensual historical author, Laurie McBain, and had released six books in the new subgenre, with sales topping eight million copies. The readers were waiting for more, so much so that when Rogers's *Dark Fires* appeared in 1975, it sold two million copies and went through five printings before the advertising campaign had even started.[18]

Book sales were one form of feedback that reinforced Coffey's initial belief that the books would do well. Mail was another. Coffey received between forty and fifty fan letters every day between 1974 and 1975, most asking when the next Woodiwiss or Rogers book was coming out. The letters led to the development of a fan club mailing list, to whom Avon mailed a newsletter to keep its loyal readers up to date on their favorite authors.

By the mid–1970s, the success of the more sensual historical romances was established. This new subgenre quickly took a prominent place in Avon's publishing program.[19] Nevertheless, Coffey limited the number of new authors, debuting just seven between 1972 and 1979, when she left Avon. Coffey did not enter the intense competition for sensual historical titles that other publishing houses did during the latter half of the 1970s. The reason for her self-imposed limit on the number of new romance authors was to accentuate quality writing. Because the Avon

Rosemary Rogers' *Sweet Savage Love*, an Avon Spectacular in 1974.

Ladies, as Avon's romance stable came to be known, sold extremely well, averaging between two and three million copies per book, Coffey felt that Avon "made up in staggering numbers [sales] what other people didn't make in quantity [of books released]."

Phase III: Enter the Competition

The first to enter the fray was newly formed Zebra Books (1974).[20] The founder, Walter Zacharius, had recently closed Lancer Book (1961–1973) after a bitter dispute with his partner, Irwin Stein, and was looking for a new publishing opportunity.[21] His experience at Lancer was largely with pulp-type mass-market products, and he was looking for a related mass-marketing venture. He surveyed the field, liked what Harlequin was doing, but felt he could not compete head-on with them, so he positioned Zebra in the highly popular but undeveloped historical romance field. He didn't want to do category fiction because he wanted big stand-alone titles, so he capitalized on Avon's romances and focused on the sensual historicals subgenre. He didn't appear to get much attention from other publishers, who no doubt dismissed Zebra as a new "pulp" venture, similar to Lancer, which, though many of the books sold well, such as *The Man from ORGY* (a takeoff of the popular television show *The Man from U.N.C.L.E.*), was on the margin of the "legitimate" industry.[22]

The other unlikely entry garnered a little more attention. Playboy Press, heretofore an exclusive publisher of male-oriented fiction and nonfiction, entered the romance field to cash in on the trend in the new romance subgenre. Playboy not only played a pivotal role in accelerating the subgenre's proliferation in the late 1970s, but it also influenced romance book covers, turning the illustrations from soothing pastels into blazing, passionate depictions of hero and heroine in rapacious embraces.

Mary Ann Stuart was the editorial director for Playboy Press in 1975.[23] At the time, she had been with Playboy for ten years, having started as an assistant editor. Stuart's decision to introduce romances under the Playboy label was based on the appeal of the Avon product. "I had read some of the Rosemary Rogers books," she says, "thought they were wonderful, and thought we ought to try something along that line."

Playboy management was understandably hesitant to accept Stuart's idea. It was not that management was unwilling, Stuart says, but they were concerned about introducing fiction aimed solely at women when "the company had always thought of itself as primarily in the entertainment business for men. They were just a little concerned that it wouldn't work with the Playboy name." Stuart argued that the consumer pays little attention to imprints: "I said it was very unlikely that a woman would not buy the book solely on the basis of its being published by Playboy, because it was unlikely they'd even notice."

Stuart's argument ran counter to the view of publishers and editors that lines of books are successful with consumers because, as Heisey from Harlequin put it, "one book sells another." Certainly the Playboy name had helped sell male-oriented books from Playboy Press, since it told the consumer he was getting a certain type of risqué, male-oriented publication. Stuart's argument, then, is more a rationale she used to sell management on allowing her to try romantic fiction under the Playboy label. In a compromise, Playboy agreed to release some romance novels but removed the familiar bunny logo from the book jacket.

Stuart also backed her arguments with research on romance publishing. She was one of the first to tie in the sales of Woodiwiss and Rogers with social trends, citing specifically the "grown-up" westerns then in vogue, such as Robert Altman's movie *McCabe and Mrs. Miller* (1971).[24] She felt the more adult themes in historical romances showed greater awareness of the world and were more in tune with sexual reality than either the chaste gothics or sweet contemporaries of the time. Like her other argument to convince management to move forward, she invoked the social world to sell her idea. Her reasoning was a posteriori; she had already decided she liked the books based on her own tastes and then used various selling techniques to substantiate her reasoning with management.

Stuart did sell management on the idea, receiving a tentative go-ahead that allowed her to test her theories. She was permitted to sign up a limited number of romance authors, whose books Playboy Press would release as a test to ascertain whether or not the sensual historical romances would be successful. Among the first writers signed was Barbara Bonham; her first novel, *Proud Passion* (1976), was submitted in 1975 over the transom. At an earlier time, Stuart says, Bonham's novel would have been returned as inappropriate for Playboy. However, because Stuart had just convinced management to try a few novels in the sensual historical style, Bonham's manuscript was, says Stuart, "fortuitous" for both the press and the author. The novel was reprinted several times, and more than half a million copies were in print by the end of the year. *Proud Passion* was one of the biggest books of original fiction ever published by Playboy Press.

Management's response to *Proud Passion*'s sales was extremely favorable, and shortly after the first reprinting, Stuart says, "we began expanding the whole list in terms of adding more romance writers."

To meet their production schedule of five romance titles every month,

Stuart began to actively solicit manuscripts. Some rudimentary guidelines were established to inform prospective authors about the sensual historical romance. These guidelines were very general, much like Harlequin's, sketching some content parameters and basically urging would-be writers to read existing sensual historicals such as Woodiwiss and Rogers, as well as those published by Playboy.

The number of books Playboy released monthly far exceeds the number from any other American house at the time. Playboy would have released twice this number but was constrained from doing so by its distributor, Pocket Books.

Until Playboy entered the romance field, its books were predominantly sold through mail-order to readers of their magazine. Romances, however, could not be sold in this way, since these novels were aimed at a different audience. Playboy, then, had to turn to a book distributor to get the romances into the proper outlets. A two-year contract was signed with Pocket Books, which imposed a limit of five books per month. The limit appears to have been set arbitrarily, since upon termination of the contract, Playboy changed distributors and immediately went to ten books per month; by the time Playboy Press was sold to Berkley-Jove Publishing in July 1982, it was releasing fifteen sensual historical titles monthly.

The continued success of Playboy's expanded list indicates that Pocket Books' limits on the number of books they would distribute were set too low. Exactly why Pocket Books set the number at five is unclear; however, off-the-record comments by various sources within publishing suggest that (1) Pocket Books was attempting to impose quantity control in a market that might be considered rapidly becoming overcrowded, and (2) the sensual historicals fit a distribution gap in the Pocket Books system, but Pocket Books did not want to compete intensively with its lucrative Harlequin distribution arrangement.

Even at five titles per month, Playboy was releasing a substantial number of romance novels. Their success would accelerate the next phase of romance publishing in the United States, as more and more publishers turned to this subgenre to bolster book sales.

Playboy's role is often overlooked. Also overlooked is Playboy's impact on the covers of romance novels. The cover illustrations on Avon's early sensual historicals did not reflect the content's increased sensuality. Indeed, the early covers barely depicted the heroine-hero embrace. Rather than using the cover illustrations to inform readers of the increased sensuality of the books' content, Avon employed descriptive adjectives: "The bold, tempestuous romance of a kidnapped and ravished aristocratic girl."

The adjectives helped readers identify the content as atypical of romance novels during the early 1970s. But Playboy went further. Stuart felt it was essential that the cover tell the reader what to expect from the book's content. The cover illustrations were particularly important to Playboy because, unlike Avon, it did not have a developed group of writers whose names the readers would recognize; moreover, Playboy could not spend much on advertising to promote the number of new authors it was releasing to meet the monthly production schedule. Thus, Playboy had to find another way to enable readers to identify its sensual romances from the other, tamer romances in retail outlets.

Playboy devoted a great deal of time to reviewing the artwork of other romance publishers. A group of expatriate artists living in Spain was discovered by Playboy's art director and commissioned to illustrate the covers of all its romances. The covers set the industry standard for the remainder of the decade. They conveyed with startling sensuality the content's passion, not only in the provocative embraces of heroine-hero and the plunging gowns of the books' heroines, whose ample bosoms swelled with lust (a reflection, perhaps, of Playboy's obsession with large-breasted women), but in the vivid colors and tones used by the artists to further accentuate the feeling of passion.

Covers of the "heaving bosoms" type. Left: *Savage Surrender* (Ace, 1977); right: *Bride of Fury* (Playboy, 1980).

Phase IV: Enter Everybody

At the time Playboy entered the sensual historical line of romances in 1975–1976, other publishers were beginning to look in this direction. At the American Booksellers Association (ABA) convention in 1976, Nancy Coffey remembers that she noticed almost every paperback house had a sensual historical romance on display. Many of these houses copied Avon's success. "It was," recalls Coffey, "imitative at best, almost cynically imitative without anyone trying to develop an author."[25] Stuart remembers the ABA convention slightly differently. Playboy displayed *Proud Passion*. "They [Avon] were furious, absolutely furious," she says. "They came over and said, 'You're imitating us, and have no right to.' They were very upset. It seemed to me they were saying there was nobody else competing with them."[26]

Certainly other houses appeared to be imitating Avon's success. The fact that Playboy Press was beginning to fill the paperback best-seller list in 1976 with its sensual historical romances prompted other houses to initiate or add to their production of these spicy books. It was almost as if, remembers Stuart, the other houses suddenly said, "Hey, if they [Playboy] can do it, we can too."

Almost every paperback house was publishing at least some sensual historicals by the late 1970s. Production went from one novel in 1972 to roughly 350 titles per year by decade's end. And as more paperback publishers increased the number of titles in the new subgenre, other romance subgenres faded from their lists. Contemporary romances, never a major part of American paperback romances, all but disappeared, as did the more widely produced chaste gothics and mystery-suspense romances. The Regency subgenre might have also gone by the wayside had it not been for Fawcett, which continued to produce them in some quantity. The attitude toward the various subgenres is reflected in the two following examples: Fawcett and Richard Gallen Books. Fawcett provides an example of a longtime paperback publisher of romances who phased out its contemporary line, cut back on production of gothics and mystery-suspense romances, released a few sensual historicals, but maintained a steady stream of Regency romances when few other paperback publishers were paying an attention to this subgenre. Richard Gallen Books illustrates the arrival of a new imprint entering the sensual historical romance field.

Fawcett Books

Like most other established paperback houses, Fawcett had been publishing a limited number of romance novels for some time. In the late 1960s and early 1970s, its romances were divided between sweet contemporaries (one-third) and gothic/romance- suspense novels (two-thirds). Most of Fawcett's paperback books were hardcover editions reprinted under the Crest imprint. Besides such authors as James Michener, William Shirer, and Vladimir Nabokov, there were a number of Crest women authors "in whom the feminine interest is very apparent," such as Taylor Caldwell, Nora Lofts, Dorothy Eden, and Mary Stewart.[27] These women, many of whom wrote gothic and mystery-suspense romances, never dominated the Crest imprint but were published as "women's fiction" throughout the 1970s. Their books often sold well but were released sporadically; they seldom comprised more than a few titles per year.

While its core of writers comprised the body of Fawcett's gothic/mystery-suspense romances and persisted throughout the 1970s, Fawcett's contemporary line did not fare as well. Fawcett published a number of contemporary romance titles in the early 1970s. These novels, says Leona Nevler, editorial director and later publisher, were Harlequin-like books.[28] Fawcett published one per month under the Cameo Romance imprint. Sales were modest, with runs of 50,000 copies. Then in the middle 1970s, the line encountered difficulty. "This was about the time Harlequin came out with their big advertising push," says Nevler, "and drove out all the smaller [contemporary] lines. It just didn't seem worth it. It was also a kind of publishing I wasn't that excited about doing."

Harlequin's advertising budget was large and undoubtedly affected the survival of many of the smaller contemporary romance lines in the United States. The fact that Nevler was "not that excited" about doing the sweet contemporaries is perhaps equally important, since she did not fight for their survival at Fawcett. Rather, her interest was in the Regency subgenre, and these show a steady and marked increase during her editorial reign in the 1970s.

Nevler first became acquainted with the Regencies when she picked up some British Regency romances on a trip to London in the early 1970s. In 1974, she published two Regencies. The following year she published twelve; then in 1975–1976, she increased the number to three per month. In 1977, after CBS purchased Fawcett, Nevler began publishing the Regencies under the Coventry imprint, and in the fall of 1979, she went to six books per month.

The increase to six titles was prompted by decisions at CBS. Management, seeing the booming sales of romances, wanted Nevler to take greater advantage of what they saw as a lucrative paperback market. But other than realizing that paperback romances were gaining increased attention, CBS executives were generally unfamiliar with the genre. Nevler, then, appears to have appeased management by increasing titles to six per month without altering the subgenre position of Regencies at Fawcett. Her decision to maintain Regency production was based on her belief that these books were directed toward a more sophisticated audience: "Our Regencies have a certain style and charm; the level of readership can be higher than the Harlequin or Silhouette romances. More sophisticated women [like Nevler] can enjoy them." This perception of the Regency reader affected both content and packaging, which Nevler describes as "a pretty package with the right feel; it doesn't have lusty images and it portrays a quality look."[29]

"Lusty images" were neither on the cover nor inside Fawcett's Regencies. Fawcett did publish some of the more sensual historical romances beginning in 1976. However, they were never developed into a line, nor did they match the frequency of Coventry's monthly releases. Fawcett's emphasis on Regencies apparently stemmed from Nevler's own preference for them; she felt, much like Coffey at Avon, that "others will like it if I do." By the late 1970s, she realized that "we were one of the few houses publishing Regencies" and that consumers couldn't get these novels anywhere else.

Richard Gallen Books

More typical of the increased interest in the sensual romances during the late 1970s is Richard Gallen. Gallen provides an interesting contrast to Playboy. At Playboy, the interest in sensual historical romances was introduced from the bottom up, with Stuart initiating interest at the editorial level and convincing management that an audience existed for these books. At Gallen, the interest in romances was introduced top-down, with management initiating interest in romance novels based on the success other publishers were encountering in the marketplace.

Richard Gallen is a packager of books, not a publisher.[30] The distinction is a fine one. A packager creates the idea for a series of books and then must find and "sell" a publisher on the idea, leaving printing and distribution to the publisher. A packager may or may not be involved in the marketing campaign. The packager delivers to the publisher a completed, proofed manuscript. The advantage to the publisher, of course, is that all editorial work is done by the packager. The packager's profit (or loss) depends on how well the books sell. The packager's imprint appears on the cover of the books.

Richard Gallen Books was formed in 1977, specifically to meet the apparent demand for sensual historical romances. Between 1977 and 1978, Gallen packaged a line of sensual historicals for Dell with some limited success. Desiring to enter the boom in sensual historicals, Gallen wanted to increase the number of his titles. To that end, he hired Judy Sullivan as editor-in-chief.

Sullivan had been in publishing at both the editorial and marketing-finance levels since 1972, though she was not previously involved in romance publishing. She was asked to appraise what was being done in the romance field. Sullivan read some of the books Gallen was promoting and said she didn't like them. The books were rape-orientated, in the style of Rogers's novels. Gallen told her to develop a formula she thought would work; she came up with a line of sensual contemporary romances, sans rape.

Sullivan cited two reasons for shying away from the rape-oriented historical romances popular with mass-market paperback publishers in the late 1970s. One was her own dislike of the rape theme in these novels. The other was based on her belief that the novels were out of tune with prevailing attitudes in society. Her decision to abandon the rape theme, she says, "coincided with a period in which rape had become politicized to the point that it was no longer possible to fantasize about it, like people might have done in the past. I just felt that women were reading them for other reasons, and were overlooking those parts [rape scenes]. I thought we could do something a little more intimate."

"It was about this time that Judith Krantz's book hit [*Scruples*, 1978], and I thought, 'Wouldn't it be interesting if we had the same kind of *long* sexy [contemporary] books.'" It was not, however, until April 1980 that Sullivan was able to release any of this type of novel. Until Sullivan was able to accumulate an inventory of these books, the bulk of Gallen's romances continued to be sensual historical ones.

The success of the new, longer sensual contemporary romances was inhibited by distribution arrangements. In 1978, shortly after Sullivan's arrival, Gallen's distribution agreement with Dell expired, and the packager went to Pocket Books. Playboy had just terminated its contract with Pocket, leaving a hole in its distribution system. The switch to Pocket Books was fortuitous for Gallen, since Pocket had a better distribution system than Dell. But Pocket Books also provided an obstacle, much as it had with Playboy. Pocket balked at the idea of a longer, 100,000-plus-word sexy contemporary romance; it perceived it as a "very different notion" and seemed unsure whether it would sell, since the established length for a contemporary romance had to that point averaged 55,000 to 60,000 words. When Gallen did launch its longer sexy romance line in 1980, the "wholesale distributors had never heard of anything like this and were very slow to pick it up" because they didn't think it would sell. Sullivan noted that bookstores, however, "picked it up quickly, but they were such a small part of the market that we were never able to do anything with it."

Phase IV, then, continued to be dominated by sensual historicals, mostly in the tradition of the first Avon discoveries. However a change in content, if it did not actually occur, is at least adumbrated. Numerous other editors besides Sullivan who were involved at various levels in romance publishing in the late 1970s indicate that they also were considering moving beyond the theme of the sensual historicals. Carolyn Nichols, for example, later senior editor of Bantam's highly successful Loveswept line, was at Berkley Books in October 1978, when she submitted a memo to management suggesting a line of sexy contemporary romances to compete with Harlequin; the line would eventually launch in June 1981, after the marketplace had been tested by Dell. Just as Pocket Books hesitated to debut Sullivan's longer sexy contemporary concept, Berkley failed to listen to Nichols. The problem was stated concretely by Kate Duffy, the former romance editor at Pocket Books: "The publishers started out cautiously in 1980." The track record for sensual historicals was proven, but "there was no one you could go to at that time who'd tell you whether or not they'd [the consumer] accept the change to sexy contemporaries."[31]

Dirty Books: A Note on the Content of Bodice-Ripper Romance Novels

Throughout this analysis I have used the value-neutral term "sensual historicals" to refer to the romance novels that American publishers released in increasing numbers as the 1970s came to an end. Literary critics, feminist scholars, and members of the press, when they deigned to pay attention to the sensual romances of the 1970s, had less benign labels, such as erotic historicals, horny hystericals, bodice-rippers (because the heroine had her bodice ripped off), sweet-savages (after Rogers's first book), and take-and-rapes. The reviews tended to follow the cutting edge of the labels; the novels were characterized as dirty books for women and were supposedly consumed by frustrated females who had some sexual deficiency in their lives.

The popular characterization of sensual historicals as dirty books is possible only if one has no more than a cursory familiarity with the novels' content. These novels are certainly not in the same category as male-oriented pornography, though the review reader is generally left with this impression. Male-oriented pornographic fiction is a litany of sexual escapades. Plot is subservient to sex, and romance is conspicuously absent. The novel's intent is to get the sexes together and undressed as quickly as possible and then to offer a lengthy description of the sexual act. Genitalia are described in graphic detail, often in the coarsest possible vocabulary. The woman's sexual pleasure is subservient to the man's, who treats all women as sexual objects. By contrast, sex in romantic fiction, including the so-called bodice-rippers, is anything but pornographic. Profanities and crude anatomical descriptions are generally avoided. There is little sex for the sake of sex, even in the bodice-rippers.

The sexual act described earlier in this chapter from Rosemary Rogers's first novel is a case in point. The relationship was consummated in two paragraphs, and while the couple achieved another sexual union in the next page, their "lust" was sated in a sentence. The sexual act, in and of itself, is less important in this and other sensual historical novels than the acknowledgment that women have a passionate, sexual nature.[32] Thus, after Rogers had glossed over the two sexual couplings in as many paragraphs, her heroine then spent the remainder of the chapter, some eight pages, recognizing her budding sexuality, beginning immediately after her second bout of lovemaking.

> Afterwards Sonya felt as if she had come to rest after a long and tiring journey, and she said no more about feeling ashamed. That came later, when she was alone in her room and the precepts of her rigid conventional upbringing warred against the sudden discovery of her own passionate nature.

The heroine's discovery that she has sexual needs is the major sexual theme of the sensual historical, found in ninety-six percent of the novels.[33] With this exception, hero-heroine relationships remain rooted in traditional values. Males, much like their contemporaries in the Harlequin sweets, are the sexual aggressors, have extensive sexual experience, are typically older (30), handsome, and wealthy; female heroines, on the other hand, tend to be submissive though "spirited," are younger (20), sex-typed by occupation, and virginal, though they are often depicted as more independent and worldly-wise than the Harlequin innocents.

The fact that male-female relations remain otherwise unchanged indicates that the popularity of these novels was rooted in their more sensual plotting. Exactly who read these novels was never clear. Management's condescending attitude toward the genre prohibited market research that might have identified a profile of the readers. Editors generally assumed that the sensual content appealed to younger, more sexually aware women; changes in sexual relations occurring in society were often cited as one reason for the subgenre's popularity.

The primary readers of romance have long been thought to be middle-aged married housewives. These women would have grown to maturity during the 1950s and 1960s when respectability—marriage, family, money, possessions, and position in the community—pervaded middle-class norms and values.[34] These traditional values would be increasingly challenged during the late 1960s and throughout the 1970s.

The changing attitudes toward middle-class values were born in the youth movement of the 1960s. In this climate of social upheaval, women began to reassess their place in society. Leading this new feminist movement was the National Organization for Women, founded in October 1966. In its early stages, this organization and others like it appealed to a relatively small group: primarily middle-class women with high levels of education who had the potential for pursuing professional careers and who felt themselves stymied in a "man's" world.[35] By the end of the 1960s, NOW and its ideology had made inroads among female college students, and increasingly during the 1970s, feminist disaffection with traditional sex roles would spread throughout a large segment of American society. The Women's Movement, as it became known, challenged the dominant view of women's roles, especially a woman's right to sexual pleasure, and regarded the homemaking ideal with deep skepticism.[36]

As the social ferment of the 1960s entered the American mainstream in the 1970s, social values within the wider society began to change rapidly. A 1962 Gallup poll, for example, showed that a majority of female respondents did not believe that American women were victims of discrimination. In 1970, women were divided down the middle on this question, but four years later, those responding to the same question endorsed the efforts toward sexual equality by a margin of two to one.[37]

Popular attitudes toward sexual relations also underwent a marked change during the 1970s. Studies of college students in 1959 and 1969 reveal that in both time periods, eighty percent or more of all college-aged females were virgins.[38] In 1973, similar surveys showed not only that seventy-six percent of the women in college had engaged in sexual intercourse by their junior year, but that women were appreciably more sexually active than men.[39] Another national sample in 1975 disclosed that one-third of the college freshmen endorsed casual sex based on a short acquaintance, and over fifty percent believed that a couple should live together before getting married.[40]

Changing sexual attitudes were not confined to college students. A study by Daniel Yankelovich of college and non-college young people in the 1970s confirmed a major departure in sexual behavior and attitudes, with only a minority of women disapproving of premarital sex and abortion.[41] A further indication of shifting attitudes toward sexual relations in America was the doubling of cohabitation between 1970 and 1977 to 1.3 million.[42] This behavior was not limited to the generation under twenty-five. In fact, in 1980, more than twenty percent of all unmarried couples living together were between twenty-five and thirty-four years old, and an additional nineteen percent were forty-five and over.

The 1970s, then, were marked by considerable upheaval in traditional values, especially as they related to sex roles. Younger women, and many educated middle-aged females, were confronting a different value system in the 1970s. Those who sought refuge in values of a former time would be more likely to have been Harlequin readers; they were women who, like Carol Traynor Williams, were brought up on the movies of the 1940s and 1950s during the quiescent Eisenhower years, "when a man was a man and a woman was a housewife."[43] The women who confronted and attempted to come to terms with the new morality were more likely to be younger and college-educated. The sensual romances of the mid- to late 1970s allowed women to explore their changing role in fantasy, especially as the heroines in these novels were depicted as more independent and accepting of their sexual natures. Thus, Rogers's heroine felt the awakening of her sexual needs, while at the same time fighting the restricted upbringing that told her she had no such sexual appetite.

Sexual urges were not explored in the sweet romances of this period. They assumed that sexual fulfillment came with finding the right man, the man who sends the woman's heart aflutter. Of course, the monogamous ideal is accentuated in all romantic fiction. Bed-hopping is atypical, which helps to explain the rape theme of the sensual historical: forced seduction frees the heroine from promiscuous irresponsibility by giving her a pretext to have sex.[44] It was a way for women to explore in fantasy the new sexual morality and its emphasis on spontaneous sex with no strings attached, while at the same time remaining faithful to the one man-one woman ideal.

The argument against male sexual fantasy literature and films is less concerned with the explicit descriptions of sex than the portrayal of a callous attitude toward women.[45] Many find the physical force against women depicted in these male-oriented media to be particularly objectionable because it reinforces the male-harmer/female-harmed stereotypes.[46] But in the sensual historicals, there is no harm done to the woman, and the fantasy-reality connection is more tenuous. In a real rape, there is no choice or control, as there are in female-fantasized rapes, and the result of a real rape, Sara McCarthy writes, is violence and degradation, not sexual pleasure.[47] There is choice and control in the fantasized sexual historicals, in which the man is driven "mad with desire" in a manner the woman chooses[48]; this is why the heroine can so readily rebound from an otherwise traumatic experience by jumping up, dusting herself off, saying simply, "Oh, that was terrible," and continue to go about her businesses as if nothing had happened.[49] The historical setting of these novels further removes the immediacy and threat of the "rape" by placing it in a remote time period.

The sensual historicals, then, provided a unique, if somewhat peculiar, vehicle by which women in the early to mid–1970s could explore the two diametrically opposite worlds of "free love" sexual abandon and monogamous relationships. By the end of the 1970s, however, the novels were increasingly out of sync with changing social attitudes because the rape issue, as Judy Sullivan observed, had become highly politicized. Rape was becoming a real concern in the late 1970s, and increased attention to a topic that had for centuries been hidden from view made it more difficult for women to separate fantasy from reality.[50] Editors were beginning to recognize this, and so were writers. A new theme was emerging, and when Dell debuted its Ecstasy line in 1980, the world of romance fiction would be drastically altered. The sensual historicals, like the gothics earlier, would all but cease to exist.

Conclusion

Romance publishing was not a major industry in the late 1960s and early 1970s. Nor was it a major industry during the second half of the 1970s, despite the increased production of historical romances, which at best captured twenty percent of the romance market. The primary emphasis in American publishing throughout the 1970s was on "quality" reprints of hardcover originals.[51]

American publishers have always seen themselves as guardians of the public's taste, and romance fiction was considered a tasteless, cheap, shallow genre that deserved little attention. To be sure, American publishers released some romance hardcover and paperback books, but these were offered in limited numbers to "round out" the publishers' lists.

One reason for the limited production of romance novels in the United States was the widely held belief among American publishers that Harlequin maintained organizational domain. The domain of an organization is the claim it stakes out for itself with respect to the range of products offered, the market served, and the services rendered. Domain consensus exists when an organization's claim to a niche is recognized as legitimate by both the public and other producers. By failing to challenge Harlequin, American producers acknowledged the Canadian publisher's domain of the romance market.

Harlequin was perceived as dominating the sweet contemporary romance market throughout the 1970s. American publishers made no attempt to compete with Harlequin in this market, instead providing an alternative product, notably historical romances. Even after Avon introduced changes in the content of romance novels in 1972, American romance publishers continued to view Harlequin as maintaining domain. They saw the overall market as nearly saturated, with Harlequin providing whatever novels were necessary to cater to this small audience. Thus, rather than invest the amounts required to compete with Harlequin, American publishers were satisfied with their small but cozy niche in historical romances.

The perception of a limited market for romance novels was further fostered by management's demeaning attitude toward romantic fiction in general. This helps explain not only the failure of American publishers to challenge Harlequin but also their slow response to Avon's content innovation, despite the obvious sales Avon garnered from the books of Woodiwiss and Rogers.

There were relatively few female editors in the early 1970s and even fewer women in managerial positions.[52] Male domination of the publishing industry influenced the negative perception of romance novels and those who edited (and read) them; it was, as one editor put it, generally "condescending." Because of this attitude, and the lack of women (or men, for that matter) in positions to evaluate romance manuscripts, editorial assistants, mostly women functioning as secretaries,[53] were given romance manuscripts to edit by the male editors. The feeling seems to have been, as Leona Nevler put it, "that women knew how to choose the right [romance] book."

Management's negative attitude toward romantic fiction circumscribed the attention paid by publishers to changes occurring within the genre. The fact that there were no editors—men or women—specializing in the romantic field further hampered the response of American publishers to innovations in content, since no one was monitoring the field closely. Only after the novels of Woodiwiss and Rogers had achieved substantial success in the marketplace could publishers no longer overlook a lucrative money-making subgenre, and they moved to increase their production of sensual historical romances. Playboy Press, among the first to enter the new market with a line of sensual historical books, prompted other publishers to increase their sensual historical books; the late-entry competitors seem to have felt, as Mary Ann Stuart put it, that "if they [Playboy] can do it, we can too."

The success of Avon's later romance novels (1974–1975) and the successful entry of Playboy (1975–1976) prompted other publishers to enter the romance field. The decision to increase production during Phase IV was largely top-down. Management saw other American houses making money and hired editors or promoted editorial assistants to guide the selection of romance novels. The decisions regarding the specific content of the romance novel was left largely to the editors, who, because they were women, were supposed to understand the genre. While management realized that romance novels were garnering increased sales, they were generally unaware of the reasons why; indeed, male managers were often shocked to learn from their editor that the books were replete with rape scenes.

During the second half of the 1970s, editors were charged by management with monitoring content and duplicating the success of romance novels published by other houses. This tried-and-true method of monitoring and mimicking competitors' products[54] was the primary reason cited by editors for increasing the production of sensual historical novels in this period. Few sensual historical lines were successful, however. There were simply too many hastily edited books on the market for those who liked this subgenre. When the opportunity arose in the early 1980s to abandon the sensual historicals for more liberated romances, just about everyone made the move.

The rise of female editors in charge of romance production during the late 1970s had a significant effect on the rapidity with which publishers would respond to content innovations in the 1980s. It did not affect content in the late 1970s, however.

Editors are not influenced in deciding what books to publish by their education, social background, or previous occupation, though they are influenced by the overall climate of the house.[55] Thus, the attitudes of editorial colleagues and managerial personnel—at least as perceived by the editors—can significantly affect an editor's decision regarding the types of books selected for publication.

Editorial positions are typically the most prestigious in publishing. Romance editors, however, did not, at least in the 1970s, share this prestige. The romance editors' lack of prestige is not surprising, given the general attitude within the industry that romance novels are not real books. The condescending attitude, coupled with the general inexperience of many of the new romance editors in the late 1970s, resulted in a product that was strictly imitative. Editors were not encouraged by management to develop the romance theme, nor were they secure in their new positions to be aware of popular literary trends or, if they were, to press management to permit innovations in content. All this changed in the early 1980s, when thematic changes in romance novels again took place, but this time, with most houses now having editors in place who were monitoring the field, they were quick to respond. Their response would fuel the "romance revolution" of the 1980s.

CHAPTER 4

Silhouette Books
Challenging Harlequin's Supremacy

American sensual historical romance never really challenged Harlequin's domination of the romance industry. American romance publishers conceded organizational domain to Harlequin in the 1970s when they switched their emphasis from contemporary romances to historicals. Not head-to-head competitors with Harlequin, historical sales, both sweet and sensual, climbed. But so too did Harlequin's sales throughout the 1970s. Proportionally, then, the twenty percent of the romance market American publishers held in the 1970s remained basically unchanged throughout the decade, allowing Harlequin the luxury of surveying an apparently entrenched kingdom, but wanting more.

In an attempt to broaden its market in the United States, Harlequin terminated its decade-old distribution contract with Simon & Schuster/Pocket Books. Harlequin management decided that Pocket Books was not doing enough to promote Harlequin's line of books for the lucrative sum Pocket received for distributing them. Harlequin felt it could hold on to a hefty percentage by having its own sales force, one dedicated exclusively to promoting its product. The desire for distribution control was not based solely on pecuniary motives. It was also an attempt to vertically integrate the company.

Vertical integration is an adaptive strategy of long-linked technologies—organizations that mass-produce products.[1] It is an attempt to control, as much as possible, both the input and output processing stages. Vertical integration provides the organization with greater control over environmental uncertainties by bringing heretofore uncontrolled processes under the company's control. Major American oil firms, for example, began as refining organizations but eventually integrated forward by establishing competence in marketing and distribution (output) and integrating backward by acquiring control over supplies of crude oil and marine transportation services (input).[2]

Vertical integration is a traditional way of expanding organizational domain by reducing or eliminating significant contingencies. The more a company is able to control its boundary-spanning resources, the greater its ability to maintain its operating orders. Harlequin had already exercised input-stage boundary control in the early 1970s when it merged with and later purchased its primary supplier, Mills & Boon of London. By controlling its own distribution system, Harlequin was attempting to exercise output-stage boundary control. It was a sound business decision. The miscalculation was the assumption that Simon & Schuster/Pocket Books would sit idly by and accept their losses, which at the time, Richard Snyder, president and chief executive officer for Simon & Schuster, told me, "was a significant part of our earnings."[3]

Marquess of Queensberry Rules: Harlequin Serves Notice

Harlequin, abiding by its contract, gave Simon & Schuster/Pocket Books the required three-month notice of its intention to sever its distribution arrangement. Before those three months were up in 1980, Simon & Schuster had formed Silhouette Books, and five months later (May 1980), it launched a highly successful and competitive contemporary line of sweet romances called Silhouette Romance.

Considering the disarray and confusion that pervade trade publishing,[4] it is remarkable that Simon & Schuster/Pocket was able to form a completely distinct publishing house and have books edited, printed, and in the retail outlets within nine months of Harlequin's notice of termination. Simon & Schuster, however, knew termination was an eventuality; in fact, it was forewarned as early as 1976 that such a situation was likely to occur and had almost four years to prepare. It was, after all, the second time Harlequin had terminated its distribution agreement.

In early 1976, top executives at Harlequin were engaged in regular and serious deliberations over the Pocket Books distribution contract.[5] These sessions, which often ran long into the night, eventually resulted in the decision to terminate. Fred Kerner, the newest member of management's executive team, dissented, although his objection was less to the decision than the method.[6] Kerner recalls saying,

> Look, I've worked in the New York publishing scene some twenty-five years and you're going down there with this nice "Canadian" attitude that you've got to be

gentlemen and give them as much notice as possible. You're doing the wrong thing. Number one, if we're going to cancel the distribution contract we should give them the legal three months' notice called for. And number two, we should not terminate now. Instead, we should begin to appoint regional people, people who would be looking after *our* interests. This would give us the strong skeleton for a sales staff. Then in three, three and a half years, we can go ahead and terminate, giving the three months' minimum notice. *Then* we'll be ready to move.

Kerner's advice went unheeded. The gentlemen of Harlequin management visited the street fighters of New York, met with Simon & Schuster and Dick Snyder, who, so the story goes, "foamed at the mouth and chewed the carpet" when informed of Harlequin's decision and told them they couldn't do this to Pocket Books and they couldn't do this to him. Harlequin returned to Toronto with a three-year renewed distribution agreement.

Snyder's response was less masticatory than described but is nevertheless part of the Harlequin cultural myth, which pits the hero Heisey against the nefarious and wicked New York publishing giant.[7] Snyder, however, readily admitted that he was outraged when Heisey informed him of Harlequin's decision and that Harlequin changed its plans only after "a *very* forceful conversation."[8]

Snyder did not foam at the mouth or chew the carpet but acknowledged that if he thought such tactics would have worked, "I would have done it." That was not the method he thought effective, however. His only opportunity to convince Harlequin management to change its mind was to embarrass them by appealing to their sense of honesty. As he recalled Heisey's New York visit:

> I was totally taken by surprise. And *extremely* upset! After all, they had given me an oral agreement; an okay that they were going to do it [renew]. And we had made certain plans based upon their handshake. When they [Heisey and Bellringer] walked in and said they were not going to renew it I remember looking at both of them and calling them dishonorable men—which had a major impact because, of course, they are very honorable men.

Publishing has long been characterized as a gentlemen's profession, especially when it concerns publishers of the "higher" forms of literature.[9] Harlequin executives thought no less of their profession, and by the time Snyder had gotten off the phone to his boss at Gulf + Western to see if there was any legal recourse to force Harlequin's adherence to their verbal agreement, Heisey was on the telephone from Kennedy airport, saying: "We are men of honor and we honor our agreements. We will enter into the agreement with you."[10] It is at least partially true, as Harlequin management was quick to point out in 1976 and again in 1979, that Pocket Books did not do very much to earn the tens of millions of dollars it reaped from distributing Harlequin's books. Harlequin books simply appeared on the back pages of Pocket's monthly catalogue, and when the salesman made his round to the book retail outlets, he simply flipped to the back page and inquired, "How's your Harlequin order? Is it okay? Do you want to increase it?"

"In the confusion of the publishing world," comments publishing veteran Leonard Shatzkin, "the value of a strong sales force is not readily apparent, though its cost is clear."[11] This would explain Harlequin's perceptual problem with Pocket Books. The time "selling" Harlequin might not have been all that great, though it should be noted that the time spent selling any book to retailers in the 1980s was not all that great.[12] The value of Pocket Books' distribution system was not the *time* spent selling the line, but that its system was extensive and in place. Harlequin would learn the importance of this the hard way.

Between 1977 and 1980, Harlequin did attempt to position a sales force for the eventual break with Simon & Schuster/Pocket Books, but it appears to have proceeded somewhat lethargically, while Simon & Schuster moved energetically toward developing a competitive product line. The extent of Simon & Schuster's preparation was witnessed by Fred Kerner at Harlequin, who, soon after the termination in 1979 was announced, was offered the position of president of Silhouette Books[13]:

> They wanted a president for Silhouette and they hoped to get someone from Harlequin. It was quite early on when they offered it to me. They had the manuscripts and editors in place; they were merely looking for a figurehead.
> They were completely ready [in 1979]. The covers were set. They had the manuscripts. They knew *exactly* what their first month's books would be and what their releases would be for at least twelve months thereafter. This really set me back on my heels. When I came back to Toronto, I said, "Good Lord! They're ready to go."

Copying Success: The Evolution of Silhouette

There was no reason for Harlequin to expect Simon & Schuster to enter the competitive marketplace. For nearly a decade, the Canadian-based publisher had watched its sales soar and seen most of its American competitors relinquish the sweet contemporary mass market to them. Management's ego could only have been swelled by the knowledge that the Harlequin name had, within a decade of entry into the U.S. market, become synonymous with the romance novel. This strong market position undoubtedly strengthened their belief that it would be difficult if not impossible for a start-up publisher to cut as deeply into their market share as Silhouette did (estimated at between twenty-five and forty percent), let alone be ready to launch so quickly.

Simon & Schuster's decision to enter head-to-head competition with Harlequin was exclusively managerial, based on (1) knowledge of the Harlequin product;

(2) Pocket's extensive distribution system; and (3) an astute awareness of just how much income was generated by these slim volumes of love and marriage. The decision was reinforced by research between 1977 and 1979 that clearly showed that the romance reader consumption rate in America was below the norm; Canadian consumption was 1,500 books per 1,000 women, but in the United States it was only 800, while in Holland it was 1,800 per 1,000.[14] Simon & Schuster also found growth potential among loyal Harlequin readers. A study by Rosenfeld, Serowitz, and Lawson of romance readers in Oklahoma City, Dallas, and San Diego, conducted by the ad agency for Silhouette, found that most Harlequin readers would supplement their present romance reading with a Silhouette line.[15]

One of the few in the industry to have knowledge of Harlequin's closely guarded sales figures, Simon & Schuster pumped millions into starting Silhouette Books. Management directed its staff to emulate Harlequin, to use it as their "role model"—in short, to become Harlequin competitors.[16] This strategy was clearly visible on Silhouette's pre-launch promotional material aimed at book retailers, which carried the bold-print logo: "When It Comes to Romance, Experience Is the Best Teacher." It was also seen in their early post-launch retail advertising, which simply stated: "The only *other* line you need is Harlequin."

Simon & Schuster did three other things to make the new line Harlequin-competitive. First, it hired P.J. Fennell, Harlequin's vice president of marketing and sales in North America, as the president of Silhouette Books. Second, it secured the services of Janet Dailey, who had become one of Harlequin's best-selling authors, and used her name to help promote the new line, which even subsequent CEO of Harlequin David Galloway admitted was a "good strategy,"[17] even if she was a loss leader.[18] And third, Silhouette debuted Romances with a $3 million advertising campaign, spending $1.1 million for airtime from mid–May to mid–June, when the line premiered.[19] Another $1 million was spent on other forms of advertising; this burgeoned to $22 million by 1982—a figure comparable to Harlequin's increased advertising expenditure and more than the entire U.S. publishing industry spent in domestic advertising.[20]

The Silhouette Covers: Harlequin Sues

No sooner had Silhouette appeared than Harlequin cried foul and filed a lawsuit in the U.S. District Court of New York, alleging that Silhouette's cover design constituted unfair competition. Harlequin claimed the covers of Silhouette's books were so much like their own that the Harlequin readers would be confused and purchase Silhouette Books in the belief that they were buying a Harlequin product.

4. Silhouette Books

On September 5, 1980, Judge Richard Owen issued a preliminary injunction against Silhouette. The injunction did not prohibit Simon & Schuster from shipping Silhouette volumes to which covers in the existing format had already been affixed, but it did bar Simon & Schuster from distributing new Silhouette titles with the existing cover design. The injunction was issued because Harlequin had met the criteria under the Lanham Act by demonstrating that Silhouette's design was substantially similar to the plaintiff's and that there was a "likelihood of confusion." The similarities are detailed by Madalynne Reuter in an article in *Publishers Weekly*[21]:

> In his examination of the alleged similarities Judge Owen noted that each book in both series "bears a glossy white cover, the top half of which bears a trademark and some printed information and the bottom half of which is devoted to a color illustration." Other similarities noted in the decision were: The identical size of books in both series—slightly smaller than the average mass market paperback (and, the judge commented, smaller than any other Simon & Schuster paperback); and the same placement of such data as price (in the upper right-hand corner), series number (upper left-hand corner) and identifying colophon (at the center of the top cover, with one word on each side of the colophon).
>
> Judge Owen also listed scrollwork in essentially gold colors at the top and bottom of the covers, although the Silhouette scrollwork actually reads "Silhouette Romances" and the Harlequin scroll is purely decorative, the identical layout of the author's name and the book's title, with the author listed in larger, colored letters above the title in black ink; and a similar illustration on the bottom half of the covers in both series, "a colored drawing of a man and a woman set in some scenery which suggests the story line of the book."

Judge Owens's preliminary injunction was later made permanent, forcing Silhouette to alter its cover design. But while some charges were upheld—notably the similarity of scrollwork at the top of Silhouette books—others were not. In particular, Harlequin was upset that Silhouette was allowed to continue using white covers; indeed, Harlequin continued to maintain the white covers were "quite confusing" to the reader, a point that Snyder at Simon & Schuster believed was ridiculous: "They [Harlequin] were trying to copyright the color white."

Creating consumer confusion is a widespread practice generally employed by producers of generic products to slice into established brand shopping habits: if the can of soup is red and white, it must be Campbell's; if the box of aspirin is yellow and brown, it must be Bayer. The consumer identifies these packages with the major brand and reaches for the product, often without reading the name.[22] The look-alikes are often cheaper since, if nothing else, there are no major advertising or promotional expenses. Buyers will usually realize—once the purchase has been made—that the product is not the one they intended to buy, but since they now own it, they might as well use it. The packager's intention

  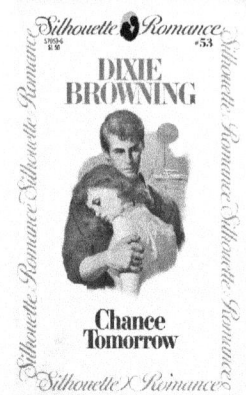

Lawsuit covers from Silhouette and Harlequin.

is to induce the consumer to try the lookalike product, find it as good as the national brand, and, satisfied with the results, repurchase the produce because it is cheaper.[23] Silhouette's books were not cheaper than Harlequin's, but they did, as Judge Owen found, look enough alike to cause the consumer to reach for a Harlequin and end up purchasing a Silhouette.

Snyder vehemently denied there was any attempt to replicate Harlequin's covers[24]:

> We were shocked at the suit. We didn't want the covers to look the same because we were selling a distinctive product.... There was no attempt to create consumer confusion. It wasn't like we were just another company that was starting up. It was *never* intentionally done.

There is no reason to believe that Simon & Schuster *intentionally* attempted to duplicate Harlequin's covers. As Snyder himself pointed out, there was not enough pull-over potential from Harlequin to justify Silhouette's intentional misrepresentation, especially given its large advertising budget to establish line identity. Nevertheless, there is good reason to believe the duplication was *unintentionally* done.

In-house advertising departments or outside advertising agencies are typically given responsibility for package design. Like writers of television dramas, journalists at newsweeklies, and television news reporters, marketing and advertising executives seldom depend on any systematically gathered audience information.[25] The primary method used to position new campaigns or designs is to survey the competition.[26] The myopic view of the audience by advertising personnel is often fostered less by the need to please the consumer than the client, who ultimately is the one responsible for approving or rejecting any proposed copy. Here, then, is a probable scenario at Simon & Schuster.

"We want you to design the cover for our new line of romances," says the publisher to their advertising executives. The new product, they explain, is to compete with Harlequin Presents, not Harlequin Romance. These are contemporary romances, not historical. "Give us something that'll tell the consumer she's getting a sweet contemporary romance."

The advertising people would have little more knowledge of the romance consumer than the widely held preconceived notion about sexually frustrated housewives. Nor would they need more knowledge about the audience. Instead, they'd gather some Presents novels and study the cover for seemingly endless hours until their subtle design variations began to look like major creative efforts. The ad people would then take the proposed design to Simon & Schuster executives, who likewise had spent endless hours examining the Presents covers, and they'd immediately see the uniqueness of the design. "Yes!" they'd exclaim. "That's it! It's distant but not too distinctive. Run 'em!"

Silhouette's Content: Subtly Distinct

The first line that Silhouette launched was Silhouette Romance. The line debuted with nine titles in May 1980, and six more titles appeared a month later. Run averages were nearly double the 200,000 norm in mass-market publishing—more comparable to Harlequin's mass printings.[27] The content, like the covers, was imitative of Presents.

Silhouette had ascertained through focus group studies of the targeted 18-to-35 age range that (1) heroines should not be too much younger than the hero—five to ten years' age difference was preferable; and (2) the "travelogue" aspect of the romance was enjoyed almost as much as the love story, and readers wanted detailed information on locales. All women in the focus group preferred—even insisted—that the heroes be bold and confident, the heroines virginal.[28]

These plot devices, as noted previously, were the same as those in both Harlequin's Romance and Presents line. But as we shall see in subsequent chapters, the American consumer increasingly turned to thematic deviations from those sketched above. Indeed, the boom in contemporary sensual romance publishing is largely the result of plot innovations almost diametrically opposite those preferred by participants in the focus groups. Silhouette's findings are readily explained.

The consulting firm hired by Silhouette did not sample romance readers, but only Harlequin readers. This was the group they were told to focus on; this was the group Silhouette wished to attract. It is not surprising, then, that the content the readers indicated they enjoyed most was similar to that in the Harlequin novels, and this helps explain the specific emphasis on virginal heroines.

The content of Silhouette was imitative of Harlequin but not the same.

Romance readers indicate some early preference for Silhouette over Harlequin because the books, (1) included slightly more sexually explicit hero-heroine relationships, and (2) it was not unusual for them to include career-oriented heroines who expected to keep their jobs after marriage, rather than give them up for home and hearth. The changes were instituted after the line launched.

Karen Solem, the pre-launch editor-in-chief for Silhouette Books, had little time initially to concentrate on content. The list for the first few months was already set when she arrived at Silhouette, and her immediate duties involved the details of positioning the new line[29]:

> I spent a lot of my [pre-launch] time working with advertising and marketing and in sales strategies; I also worked extensively with our sales force and booksellers at that time to make sure we were meeting the [projected] demand in the marketplace.
>
> My primary function was to take a close look at all the Silhouettes and bring them a little more up to date—to make sure they were really being competitive with Harlequin Presents, which was the target audience we were going for. So when the books hit the stores we wanted to find out what the people's responses were and direct the line by doing fine-tuning. I spoke with everybody and anybody that first week [mainly retailers], until the phone was removed from my ear.

Solem's fine-tuning involved slightly increasing the sensuality of the novels beyond that in Presents and filtering into the system more books in which the heroine had a career. The most important change in the novels' content, however, was in the setting.

Silhouette Romance were largely set in the United States. Harlequin, too, set some of its Presents novels in the States, but because the majority of its writers were British, Harlequin's romances typically took place in the British Isles or on the Continent. Only Janet Dailey's Harlequin novels were set exclusively in the United States, but the Canadian publisher never capitalized on Dailey's obviously successful thematic variation. Silhouette did, not only by hiring Dailey away from Harlequin but by opening the door to American authors, who wrote about places familiar to them and thus set most of their novels in the United States. One of Silhouette's new authors was Nora Roberts, whose first Silhouette novel, *Irish Thoroughbred*, was rejected by Harlequin—Roberts would go on to replace Dailey as the reigning queen of romance novelists. The floodgates opened, and manuscripts poured in. By opening the door to American writers, Silhouette had no difficulty finding American-themed romances. This was a major reason for the publisher's ability to garner manuscripts so quickly, penetrate the U.S. market, and tap a proven but underdeveloped formula with consumers. Management's decision to concentrate on American-themed romances reflected an awareness of Dailey's U.S. sales as much as their ability to quickly gain access to a wide range of heretofore untapped talent. As Kate Duffy explained[30]:

> Of course the books were like Harlequins. That's what the writers had been reading for years, and that was our competition. These were writers who'd submitted to Harlequin and were turned down on the basis of their manuscripts or the fact that they were American. We had a whole raft of writers who had manuscripts sitting on their shelves and no outlet for publishing them.

Karen Solem elaborated[31]:

> We got a lot of new writers in. There were a few Harlequin writers, and some, like Fern Michaels, who were successful in the mass marketplace. Quite a few, however, were first-time writers. And many of the first-timers didn't know there were [American] publishers that published these kinds of books [sweet sensual contemporaries]. They liked these kinds of books and they wrote them for themselves and then threw them in the closet. There were a number of authors who we had right away; they had written five or six books and [the manuscripts] were just sitting around in their closet. Some had sent their novels to Harlequin and been rejected [since] Harlequin at that time was not receptive to publishing books by American authors.

Harlequin Responds: Expanding the Romance Format

Harlequin launched Superromance in February 1981, nine months after Silhouette Romance appeared at retail outlets. It was the first new Harlequin line to launch in nearly a decade.

Superromance were distinguished by their length; they were twice as long as the traditional 55,000–60,000 word sweet contemporaries then on the market. The extended format allowed for greater subplot development, and heretofore shadowy secondary characters began to have some "flesh" hung on them, to use the parlance of the trade for character building. The new line quickly got off to a good start but soon encountered problems in the marketplace.

Superromances were secretively developed by Fred Kerner, Harlequin's first vice president of editorial. The former editor-in-chief at Fawcett assumed his position at Harlequin in 1975 and was charged with directing Harlequin's editorial product. But as we saw in Chapter 2, editorial control for the various existing lines continued to largely reside with Mills & Boon in London.

It must have been frustrating for Kerner during his first few years at Harlequin. He had management responsibility over editorial but could do nothing editorially to enhance or strengthen the lines. His editorial budget went largely unused. The budget was not wasted, however. As management, Kerner had a certain amount of leeway. An editor would have to seek management's approval to allocate time and funds to develop an unproved and untested idea; Kerner had more discretion. Stymied from developing the Romance or Presents content, he moved in another direction. The idea was to develop a new line of books—a line not linked to those books Mills & Boon continued to approve and "yet a line which would remain in the romance genre—since this was where we were successful, but at the same time, one unique to Harlequin *and* the North American market."[32]

Kerner had a clear idea of what he wanted to do: the longer mid-list romance. He did not run his idea by colleagues at Harlequin. Instead, he went to two key subordinates he had brought with him from New York: George Clay, his editorial manager, and Alice Johnson, his senior editor.

Both Clay and Johnson thought the idea of a 100,000-plus-word romance was sound and were excited at the prospect of developing a new format for Harlequin. An author who might be interested in doing such a novel immediately came to mind.

Margaret Brouse (a.k.a. Abra Taylor) was a copywriter for a Toronto-based advertising agency who had submitted some samples of her work to Clay and Johnson at Harlequin; they liked it and were going to suggest that she submit an outline and sample chapters to Mills & Boon. Instead, they decided to approach her about tackling a more substantial novel. Brouse immediately agreed.

> She liked the idea and she, George and Alice with my [Kerner's] occasional input, sat down to block in a story that could be handled in the fashion we envisioned. After a few chapters I saw no more of it.
> I had good editors so only minimally involved myself with it after passing my thoughts on what I wanted to see on to George, Alice and Margaret. The manuscript was terrific. It was a well-done job. I even liked the tile, *The End of Innocence*—very appropriate and serendipitous.

The End of Innocence was more a mainstream romance novel than a romance with one dominant hero-heroine story. Two distinct romantic subplots were involved in the novel, set in Spain. The first subplot involved the mother of the hero who had defied Spanish tradition by marrying beneath her; the subplot revolved around her pride and her struggle to carry on her husband's business. The second subplot involved a young girl, the mother's servant, and her love for a young man who helped raise bulls on the mother's farm and wanted to grow up to be a matador.

The Brouse novel was ready in manuscript form in January 1980. One thousand bound copies were run and marked "Proof Copy, Not for Publication." The covers were plain white with no artwork but labeled Superromance, since, said Kerner, "In my mind I kept thinking it was a super-sized romance, so, needing some label, and having no idea what to call it, I just put Superromance on it."[33] The first proof that came in went to Dick Bellringer, vice president of the book division and Kerner's immediate superior. Kerner recalled Bellringer's startled reaction:

> "What's this?" he [Bellringer] asked, and I told him it was going to be our new line of romances. He said, "My goodness, is it any good?" I told him: "Dick, you have at home the best critic of romance fiction that I know, and that's your wife Alma. Why don't you take this home and see what she thinks of it?"
>
> It was late in the afternoon when I took the proof to Dick and he stuck it in his briefcase. My phone rang early the next morning and he said, "How soon can you get into the office?"
>
> I was on my way as fast as I could. I didn't know whether I was going to be fired or whether Alma liked the book. I walked in and Dick put his hand on the book and said, "How soon can we start?"

The Brouse book came out in June 1980. It was not until November that the next in the new format appeared, and another few months would lapse before the official debut of the line in February 1981.

Kerner was not prepared for immediate launch approval. The Brouse book was the only one available, and the remainder of 1980 would be spent obtaining manuscripts. It was not an easy task.

The chore of obtaining manuscripts could have been easier, but Harlequin could not approach Mills & Boon's authors without upsetting that firm's management. With a main source for writers cut off, Harlequin sought authors through workshops, notices in writer's magazines, and by informing agents of their needs. It didn't take long for the word to circulate that Harlequin was seeking new talent. But manuscripts didn't pour in, like they did at Silhouette. This was not the same genre. The longer format was new, totally different, and contemporary romance authors were not sure how to write longer, more involved stories, while sensual historical authors, who had the longer format down, weren't used to writing contemporary romances. Brouse's test book was initially sent to would-be authors; later, as other books in the longer format began to appear at retail outlets, aspiring Superromance authors were instructed to read them to see what was expected in a Superromance.

Little by little, Harlequin was acquiring manuscripts. Kerner had twelve in hand when the line launched in February and immediately set out to double this inventory, anticipating the move from one to two books per month. He strenuously objected to the push to go to four books per month.

The line got off to a good start. It sold moderately well at retail outlets but did extremely well in Harlequin's direct mail-order sales. Book sales prompted them to move to two books per month at the end of the line's first year. Six months later, Kerner was asked to go to four books per month. This jump in production was urged by Harlequin's marketing people, who felt that if the firm could sell two novels per month, it could easily sell four. Kerner replied,

> Look, I understand your marketing strategy but you're making a mistake. We're putting out books that are expensive and a long read and they're going to cut into the reading of our traditional readers. But my main problem is that I don't have enough editorial material to withstand this kind of marketing plan. The books will start to deteriorate editorially.

The generalist nature of trade fiction minimizes marketing's role in the publishing industry. Harlequin, however, because of its product specialization, is more marketing-driven; marketing has substantial power within the firm and was even more influential at the time, since the then-president and chief executive officer, Lawrence Heisey, was a marketing person and used marketing effectively in the early 1970s to build Harlequin's sales. Publishers, who became involved in the romance "craze" of the 1980s, as we'll see in subsequent chapters, were likewise marketing-driven. They believed the quintessential credo of marketing: demand is not created; it is only discovered and exploited.[34]

Publishers of general trade fiction tend to view their "high" fiction products as durables, while they consider genre fiction, and certainly romance, as non-durable, throwaway books. This distinction is important because management of non-durable consumer goods considers marketing much more important in generating sales than managers of durable consumer goods.[35] The rush in the 1980s to duplicate Harlequin-Silhouette's success in the marketplace was, as we shall see in the chapters which follow, largely marketing-oriented. The marketing people at Harlequin and in the romance houses that entered the marketplace in the early 1980s knew little about the content of romances. The pressure to "market" these novels would be decried by editors. Kerner's marketing diatribe, then, is worth detailing, since it was to be repeated by many editors of romance lines in the 1980s, with similarly disastrous results:

> I'd always lose any augments with the marketing people. I'd talk of editorial quality and they would say, "You have editorial quality." To them editorial quality was that we could get the right number of words in the book and the story followed a basic storyline. They had no idea what acceptable writing was. They couldn't understand that writing was difficult *at all*.
> I tried to tell them that while the package might look the same, every box contained a different cereal, a different soap. They couldn't understand that every single title had different ingredients, and sometimes these ingredients were going to satisfy more than other times. They just didn't understand the word quality. To them, quality was that the books were copy-edited well, that the typesetting was acceptable, and that the package looked the same. They knew nothing about the stories.
> The problem really was that when marketing said something and came up with

a strong case by manipulating whatever numbers they wanted. I too could manipulate numbers any way I wanted, but they wouldn't be marketing numbers.

I could use any language I wanted; they never understood me. They couldn't even understand basic English. I would sometimes deliberately insult them by using language they didn't understand. I'd say that their idea is meretricious, and they'd say, "See, there it is, it's a good idea; it has merit." It was a petty, childish game, but it was my only satisfaction. I had to come away from those meetings saying, "My God, I haven't got a chance in the world but please let me get a little satisfaction by sticking a pin in somewhere."

Marketing in today's consumer-driven society is based on updating an old adage: you can lead a horse to water *and* get her to drink. The revised adage is good as far as it goes, but if the water is foul, the horse won't drink it after the first sip; hence the often-repeated industry slogan: "Good advertising kills a bad product."[36]

Forced to go unprepared to four Superromance novels a month, Harlequin's editors saw the quality of the books deteriorate, and sales soon slumped. Marketing's response was that they had a lousy product on their hands, despite the earlier success of the line. They decided the problem was not poor writing or editing but that the novels were too long for people to read and therefore were unappealing. The decision was to cut the books from 100,000-plus words to 80,000. Kerner objected that this would ruin the concept and that the loss of 20,000 words would inhibit character development and sub-plotting. Marketing didn't see how 20,000 words would make any difference in content. The customer did.

Battle Royale

A multiplicity of publishers followed Silhouette into the romance market. Nevertheless, it was primarily a battle for market share between Harlequin and Silhouette, which contributed to the proliferation of romance lines during the first half of the 1980s. These two publishers alone accounted for ten romance lines. The rapid succession of these lines between 1980s and 1984 was a duel for market position. Managers and editors for both houses vehemently deny that any product mimicking occurred. The launch dates indicate the contrary. There was seldom more than a year or two lapse between the time one house launched a new line and the other house debuted a similar one. For example, Harlequin launched Superromance in February 1981; Silhouette responded with Special Editions in February 1982; Dell Ecstasy appeared in December 1980, Silhouette released Desire in May 1982, and Harlequin countered with Temptation in May 1984.

It takes approximately twelve months to launch a new line. This includes the acquisition and editing of manuscripts, designing covers, and developing a marketing and sales campaign. With only minor variations found in product movement, the launch dates of Silhouette and Harlequin's lines indicate each line followed by about one year the introduction of another house's line.

The first new Silhouette line after Romances was First Love. First Love was positioned to fill a gap in Harlequin's product niche (teen romances); it was developed by Silhouette after Scholastic Books, a longtime publisher of young people's fiction and nonfiction, had tested the waters with its Wildfire teen romance line (see Chapter 9). Silhouette's longer 100,000-plus-word romance line was Special Editions, positioned to go head to head with Harlequin's Superromances. This was followed by Desire, Silhouette's answer to Dell's Ecstasy line of liberated romance novels. Then came Intimate Moments, a romance series focusing on career women. This may be Silhouette's only unique line of romances, though it fit within the movement occurring at the time among other publishers to concentrate on a particular romance theme. Silhouette's Inspirational Romances, a line of books that depicted divinely inspired love, resembled Zondervan's Serenade Books. Both Harlequin's late-entry American Romances and Temptation were developed as a response to Silhouette's American-themed romance line and their more sensual Desire novels. Intrigues, a romance mystery series, was Harlequin's one unique line. Silhouette did not have a line of romance mystery books, but there was movement afoot in early 1983 that indicated consumers wanted this type of romance, so Harlequin launched its romance mystery line only a month after Avon introduced a comparable line, Velvet Glove.

Keeping up with the Joneses became a very expensive proposition for both houses. Had the market not dramatically shifted after Dell introduced Ecstasy Romances in late 1980, Silhouette would have remained a viable romance publisher. The dramatic entry of a potpourri of American publishers into the mass market romance business after 1980—and the resulting confusion in the marketplace over just what consumers wanted—forced both Silhouette and Harlequin to intensify their competition. Without this competition, at least five of the lines, positioned to remain competitive with other houses, would not have happened: Desire, Intimate Moments, Inspirational Romances, Temptation, and Intrigues.

The romance market, as we'll see in the next chapter, burst from its decade-long lethargy after 1980, and both Harlequin and Silhouette had to keep their lines competitive. It was a fairly even match. Both publishers had the financial might to back their commitment in the romance field. In Silhouette's favor was its extensive distributing system, which Harlequin management, by their own admission, could never improve on. In Harlequin's favor was its widespread consumer name identification, which Silhouette management admitted they could never quite overcome. The contest, though not apparent at the time, was tilted in favor of the specialist publisher, Harlequin, over the generalist publisher, Simon & Schuster/Silhouette.

Organizations are specialists when they engage in a narrow range of activities, such as romance publishing, while others are generalists because they cover a much broader range of activities.[37] Specialists do well when they can focus their activities; generalists do better by using a shotgun approach, publishing, for example, a wide range of books in the hopes that one or two will hit their mark, become best-sellers, and thereby sustain the failures. Generalists have more flexibility in shifting their product emphasis to take advantage of changing market conditions,[38] while specialists have more at stake within their given niches—failure for them is devastating and may well result in the disintegration of the organization. Harlequin was thus fighting for its very survival, while Simon & Schuster could sustain itself whether or not Silhouette succeeded.

Silhouette initially did well with its one line, Romances. Its early product differential expansion, First Love, was likewise successful, filling a gap in Harlequin's product offering. Profits for the first two years met projections, but increasingly after 1981, the profits began to erode as they tried to keep up with a market that had seemingly gone mad. "We never really cared about the other people [in the romance field]," said Richard Snyder, president of Simon & Schuster, "only Harlequin. But the others took enough of the market to take the profit out of it, or at least the significant profit."[39]

The intensified competition after 1981 was largely responsible for shrinking sales, both at Harlequin and Silhouette. Generalist Simon & Schuster was able to shift to a more lucrative area, the educational market, and management decided to sell Silhouette. As Snyder noted to me:

> The leading reason for the sale obviously was the marketplace; it was too crowded. Secondarily, and more importantly, was that this [sale] was tying in with the restructuring of Gulf + Western, which was going on simultaneously. And unbeknownst to Harlequin, Simon & Schuster was going to be the primary vehicle for major entry into educational publishing. Silhouette became ancillary to us and got in the way of things we had to do. That was the *major* underlying reason for the sale.

The decision to sell was easier than the sale itself. There was no love lost in the early 1980s between management at Simon & Schuster and Harlequin. A fortuitous note from Heisey to Snyder would open the door.

Heisey, now chairman of the board at Harlequin, sent Snyder a newspaper clipping on P. J. Fennell, who had been with Harlequin and left to become

Silhouette's first president, though he remained there only a few months. There was no letter and only a few scratched words across the edge of the clipping, "Could you believe?" Innocuous as it was, the note gave Snyder an excuse to write Heisey, thanking him for the clipping and suggesting a breakfast. As Snyder recalled the meeting[40]:

> We got together over breakfast and danced around. Eventually we got to the point where one of us should buy the other. I told him I *definitely* wanted to be the seller. He then suggested I contact Dave Galloway [president of Harlequin], which I did, and we set up over a longer period various meetings. Slowly but inexorably things moved forward.

The sale was approved by the U.S. Department of Justice in August 1984. It was, according to Snyder, "the best deal I ever made." Galloway also was pleased with the outcome: "We got what we wanted and they got what they wanted; all around, a very good deal."[41] If a good deal is one in which both parties are satisfied the outcome, this was, indeed, a good deal. Silhouette walked away from the bargaining table with $10 million in cash, the potential of generating another $25 million in the years to come, based on Harlequin's profits, and a renegotiated twenty-two-and-one-half-year distribution agreement. In return, Harlequin gained control of its major North American competitor and, as things began to fall apart for the smaller romances houses, soon reassumed the romance throne, though it would never regain it to the degree that it maintained at the outset of the 1980s.

Conclusion

At the outset of the 1970s, Harlequin integrated backward by purchasing Mills & Boon and thereby assuring itself of a continued source of pre-tested, successful novels for release in North America. In the latter part of the 1970s, Harlequin decided to integrate forward by distributing its own books. It was a sound business decision, but Harlequin made two mistakes. First, when they did make the decision to cut ties with Pocket Books in 1980, management had not taken sufficient time—no doubt distracted by all the peripheral acquisitions going on at the time—to adequately develop a sales force and a distribution channel. The other mistake was to inform Simon & Schuster of their decision to terminate three years earlier and then allowing themselves to be talked into renewing their contract. This gave Simon & Schuster management more than sufficient time to prepare for the break when it did occur. They were one of the few within publishing not to snigger at Harlequin's product, knowing exactly how lucrative the romance field was. They were ready to launch

Silhouette within months of a termination notice when it occurred the second time.

Silhouette was an immediate success. This was helped by consumer product confusion since Silhouette books looked so much like Harlequin's. The real success was based on development of a proven formula at Harlequin that Harlequin never capitalized on, and that was to publish more American novelists who set their romances in the United States, places to which the women readers could relate. They got off to a good start by signing Harlequin's star American novelist, Janet Dailey. They also had a stream of books available that they could not believe—all those women who had written a contemporary romance and had no outlet for them. And with the financial clout of Simon & Schuster behind them, they went head to head with Harlequin in advertising expenditure, thus ensuring the consumer knew their books were widely available—and, of course, they were widely available because Pocket Books had the distribution channels solidly in place.

Harlequin did not sit idly by. They were already at work developing a more competitive product. Silhouette appears to have nudged this product forward. Superromance was the first major content variation in the Harlequin line in a decade. It appears to have met with some initial success, but the press to release more books on the market—which, we'll see in Chapter 5, plagued many late-entry competitors in the United States—resulted in a deterioration of the quality of the novels, and readers responded by curtaining purchases. The difference was that this push was made by marketing personnel at Harlequin rather than by management. Since marketing was what made Harlequin in the first place, marketing had more say at Harlequin than is typical of the department in other publishing houses. Indeed, marketing's attitude seemed to have been that *they* were the ones responsible for Harlequin's success; they appear to have limited understanding of the publisher's product, which led them to ignore input from editorial.

The Silhouette-Harlequin battle between 1980 and 1984 was contentious and resulted in (1) too many books being introduced to vie with one another, resulting in an oversupply of romances on the market, and (2) an intense and very expensive advertising campaign. Harlequin ultimately emerged the winner if only because their very survival was at stake, while Silhouette was but one dimension of Simon & Schuster's publishing empire, and one that was beginning to be viewed internally as a very expensive one. They were ready to call it quits when Harlequin made them a buyout offer.

How Harlequin co-opted Silhouette into its empire and emerged in the 1990s to reclaim its romance throne is addressed in Chapter 8. The next chapter appraises how the introduction of Dell Ecstasy would radically change the content of romances and complicate the Harlequin-Silhouette battle for market share in the early 1980s. The changes that occurred within Ecstasy were much more complex than those introduced by Avon a decade earlier, and this caused considerable confusion within romance publishing. The next few chapters examine how some lines successfully co-opted changes at Dell and why so many others failed. The lesson learned during this period would contribute to the successful positioning of romance lines after 1990 and their current genre domination of the mass-market field.

CHAPTER 5

The New Dawn
Romance Publishing Comes of Age

Silhouette Books competed with Harlequin on its own turf: sweet contemporary romances. Silhouette's success was achieved at immense cost. A new book division was formed, and vast amounts of capital were invested in the line. Other publishers probably would have abandoned the market to the two giants because they neither could nor would match the capital expenditures of Harlequin or Silhouette.

Soon after Silhouette romances first appeared, a unique development in the market changed the face of romance publishing for the remainder of the 1980s. A new content form was introduced, giving rise to a whole new subgenre, which, for clarity's sake, we'll call contemporary liberated romances. The new subgenre was introduced rather cautiously at first by Dell, but sales soon prompted an increase in the production of Dell's new Ecstasy line. Other publishers were soon scurrying to cash in on the new subgenre's popularity among consumers.

The rush by publishers to take advantage of the new romance market helped to create what has been called the romance phenomenon of the 1980s. It was indeed a phenomenon. Dozen of separate romance lines appeared in the first half of the decade, crowding the market with thousands of new titles yearly. As early as 1983, mass-market romances, once relegated by publishers to the back burners of their list, accounted for up to fifty percent of all mass-market paperback books published in the United States.[1] Two years later it was all over, or at least had settled down. This chapter examines how it began.

Dell's Romances Grow Up

Six months after the launch of Silhouette Books, Dell debuted a new line of romances called Ecstasy (December 1980), which had considerable impact on romance publishing. The innovations in content introduced in Ecstasy were rooted in the existing Candlelight line.

The Candlelight Romance line first appeared in July 1967. The line went through numerous thematic changes over the years similar to content shifts occurring elsewhere in the romance industry. Its first romance was *Ellen Matthews: Mission Nurse* and reflects the nurse-doctor theme popular in romances at the time. A mix of gothics, mystery-suspense, and sweet contemporary romances peppered Candlelight's list in the early to mid–1970s. Like many of the other American romance publishers prior to the surge in sensual historical romances of the late 1970s, Candlelight's success was not pronounced; indeed, the line appears to have been in jeopardy of being discontinued near the end of the decade.[2]

Candlelight was unaffected by the upswing in sensual historical romances during the late 1970s. In 1980, its level of production remained the same as it was in 1967: six romance novels per month. The division of these novels was different from their American counterparts in that four of the six releases were sweet contemporary romances similar to Harlequin's; the other two were Regencies.

It is uncertain why Dell did not enter the sensual historical marketplace with everyone else in the late 1970s, but it probably reflected management's attitude toward the genre. Dell, like many other American publishers, did not concentrate on romantic fiction but produced some novels in the genre to meet what was perceived in-house as a limited demand. Dell's romance novels were not expected to generate significant profits. Thus, referring to her position as editor of Candlelight Romance in 1979 soon after she came aboard, Vivian Stephens could say, "The line wasn't really looked at to make any money or make a statement for Dell. It was just there."[3] For this reason, inexperienced personnel were promoted into editorial positions, since genre publishing, Stephens goes on to say, "is usually done by people who are just starting in publishing. It is used as a stepping stone to get into mainstream fiction."

Dell's failure to enter the sensual historical market in the 1970s, coupled with management's indifferent attitude toward the line, would prove significant in the 1980s, since the sweet contemporary Candlelight line provided the base upon which to inject change into contemporary romances. Stephens was not locked into the same tradition as Harlequin, or forced to compete with Harlequin, like Silhouette. In fact, her biggest asset was probably her total publishing naïveté.

5. The New Dawn

Vivian Stephens came to Dell as an associate editor in the fall of 1979. Her previous publishing experience was negligible: she had been a researcher at Time-Life Books prior to accepting the position with Candlelight.[4] To prepare herself for the job, Stephens spent the summer of '79 reading romance novels. She was forty-six years old when she started at Dell, nearly twice the age of most other romance editors, and the only African American editor in romance publishing.

Stephens was given responsibility for the Candlelight line. She was under no direct instructions to develop the line, nor did she feel any pressure to alter the Candlelight format: "I was very happy to do just that [edit the books]. I had no desire to do anything else. I just wanted to do something I could enjoy without any competition." At best, Stephens's plans were modest: "What I tried to do was just increase the quality of the work, to kinda stretch the line, to try new people."

Realizing she had limited editorial experience and only a general idea of what the romance genre entailed, Stephens was at a loss as to how to accomplish even this modest goal. With no bank of research available to her at Dell on romance readers, Stephens did something unique in romance publishing at the time—she went into the field. Her experience is worth citing at length:

> I guess the first thing I did, speaking of the genre in general, was to go to Woolworth's. It was the Wednesday before Thanksgiving. The store was at 42nd and 3rd; it was huge, and had a huge paperback section. The Harlequins took up one whole wall. It was evident the salesman had just stacked the bins.
> At lunchtime I really watched women come in and buy books. They never bought less than two. They would buy eight, six, five. They didn't touch a Candlelight. Not one!
> (I hadn't had the chance to get many books out; I hadn't worked there that long. Actually, none of my books were out. I'd only been at Dell two months.)
> Finally, I saw a one woman go over and pick up Candlelight. It wasn't a contemporary; it was Regency. So I went over and spoke to her and asked her why she didn't like any of the Candlelight contemporaries. She said the heroines were too insipid, that no one was that innocent [the book content at the time reflected values rooted to the 1960s when the line launched]. But she liked the Regencies. Of course, if you know anything about the genre, you know you can't take too many liberties with the Regencies because you're locked in time. You really can't deviate too much because you must use the Regency language. And she liked that.
> In talking to her I found she had a master's degree in Greek, of all things. She was an executive secretary to a broker on Wall Street. She was buying books—and the other thing she let me know, which I knew all along, but it was wonderful to hear someone say it—for her larder, the way you'd stock canned food. She knew she'd like it but she wasn't in the mood to read it right then. When she got in the mood, she wouldn't have to go out and buy anything; she'd just go to her cupboard and pick up a book.
> So without me being conscious of it, I decided that I'd try to increase not ... the

quality [of the Candlelight contemporaries]—which I thought were quite good, because they were being written by English teachers—but the interest.

Stephens made one other observation while at Woolworth's that would guide her decision on changes in content:

> People kept saying young girls read these books, but I never saw young girls there at lunchtime. There were some young ones, some nineteen-year-olds; the majority of women, however, were in their thirties and forties.

Stephens's firsthand observation confirmed her opinion that the Candlelight novels needed to be updated:

> The books didn't really interest the women I thought wanted to buy the books. I was in my mid-forties and I rather enjoyed them. But they had nothing to do with my fantasies. So I consciously decided to make the books a little racier. I didn't ask anybody anything. I just sorta had it in mind. But I didn't have writers I could talk to.

Still, exactly what was needed remained unclear. Her ideas began to coalesce with the submission of a manuscript she found in the slush of unsolicited novels:

> Then one day I got in a book. It was very sensuous. I realized right away the style was like a Harlequin Presents. So I wrote the woman—whose name was Joan Hohl—and asked if she could send the balance of the book.
> (I really cannot judge a category romance unless I have the whole thing. If I have the whole manuscript, I can see how it can be fixed.)
> She sent it in and it was very sensuous. I never read anything as sensuous without being explicit. I bought it.
> She said she had sent it to Harlequin and that they had refused it. The book was called *Morning Rose, Evening Savage*. That was the book that preceded the line. I thought, "What the hell. I'll put it out. And if I get *any* negative feedback saying it's too sensuous, then of course I wouldn't do any more books [like it]."
> The book came out in August of 1980. I didn't really hear anything. That's all I was waiting for. I was waiting to hear a negative. But I didn't hear anything at all.

The lack of negative reaction reinforced Stephens's decision to put out another sensual contemporary. Two manuscripts crossed her desk at the time: another by the author she had just published, and an unsolicited manuscript submitted by Jane Castle. This latter book, *Gentle Pirate*, surpassed the merely sensual and ultimately liberated the romance novel.

The hero and heroine in Castle's romance more closely resemble real 1980s people than those in other novels of the genre. The hero lost an arm in Vietnam. He is twenty-eight, not perfect, not extraordinarily handsome, but with a keen sense of humor. The heroine is the widow of a Marine killed in combat. The heroine's relationship with her deceased husband had been less than ideal: he was a wife abuser. Stephens published the novel, she says, "because all the things that are in it are right now, the world today." The novel sold out of its first printing within weeks and paved the way for the growth of the Candlelight Ecstasy line.

5. The New Dawn

There was no resistance at Dell to publishing these two titles under a new imprint. Nor did Stephens, like Mary Ann Stuart at Playboy, have to "pitch" the novels:

> I went to my editor-in-chief [Kate Duffy] and said, "I have two books that I think are better than the Harlequin Presents. What do you think?" And she said, "It's all right with me, but I think that you should speak to the sales department." So I went down and spoke to one man, Bob Avery, who was president of sales, and I said the magic words, "I think I have something we can pit against Harlequin Presents," and he said, "Let's do it!" It was that simple.

Stephens could not completely explain her success, but she suggested that her "magic words" had at least something to do with it. This may be true, but there are at least three other reasons why Dell was so willing to introduce a new line.

First, the Candlelight line's performance in the marketplace had been lackluster to this point. Thus, Dell had little to lose by introducing a new line. Second, little capital investment was needed to produce another line; no money was spent in advance promotion. The only launch change was to add the word Ecstasy after the Candlelight imprint name to distinguish between the two lines. Third, the new line would be distributed along with the old. If the line failed, it could simply be killed. If it succeeded, the other Candlelight romances would not be affected. As Stephens remembered it:

> I thought it was obligatory that if I were going to do something more sensuous, I should warn the reader. I wanted to call them Ecstasy Romances. My editor-in-chief said, "It sounds too orgasmic." Everybody promised, but no one came up with a name. On the day they came to me and said, "Vivian, copy is waiting," I said to go with Candlelight Ecstasy Romance. I thought if anybody screams we can always change it.

The line took off, to Stephens's surprise and delight. Its success can be seen in the overall production figures. Between 1980 and 1982, the sweet contemporary and historical (Regency) line faded away. The Ecstasy books took over. The initial release of two books per month (1981) rose steadily to peak at eight Ecstasy novels every month in 1983–1984, along with four Supremes. In 1985 the trend started to reverse itself.

Romance aficionados and industry sources credit Dell's Candlelight Ecstasy line with changing the content of the romance novel in the 1980s, much as Avon is credited with initiating changes that affected the content of romance novels in the 1970s. However, unlike Avon, whose success was built on a few select romance authors, Candlelight Ecstasy's success was built on a conscious and consistent editorial policy.

Immediately after Candlelight Ecstasy debuted and the continuation of the line was ensured, Stephens formulated written guidelines by which to judge subsequent manuscripts. The guidelines incorporated the elements of the first two Ecstasy novels. The semi-conscious awareness of a disparity between existing content and the social world, which guided Stephen's initial decision to publish the two manuscripts and thereby unwittingly marry the sensual historical romance with the sweet contemporaries, was now more cogently expressed. As Stephens noted:

> The tip sheet said the heroine had to be American, older than twenty-five, and upwardly mobile. I took this from society as it was in 1979. I felt she [heroine] should be upwardly mobile on the job, that she could meet a man who was not necessarily rich but who was a winner; who was upwardly mobile himself, though he might be a step or two ahead of her on the job but was compatible with her. That's really the basis of the Ecstasy line.
>
> I wanted it [the line] to be sensuous because, as I said at a meeting once, men and women do go to bed with one another without the benefit of clergy. And so far as we know, they don't go straight to hell. The other thing was that I wanted them [Ecstasies] set within the United States or its territories because—and I still feel this way—the average American woman will never get to the south of France or to the Greek Isles. However, she most certainly can get to the most celebrated spot in her town, or in her state, or in the country.
>
> A lot of people who had the traditional American wedding in the 1940s and 1950s went to Niagara Falls. That is an attraction for lovers in this country. I can see people saving to get there better than I can see them getting to the Isle of Rhodes.

The content variations that Candlelight Ecstasy introduced were widely adopted by other romance publishers. In the next few years, production of historical "bodice-rippers" fell dramatically, while sensual contemporary romances, invoking the liberated criteria introduced by Candlelight Ecstasy, rose sharply.

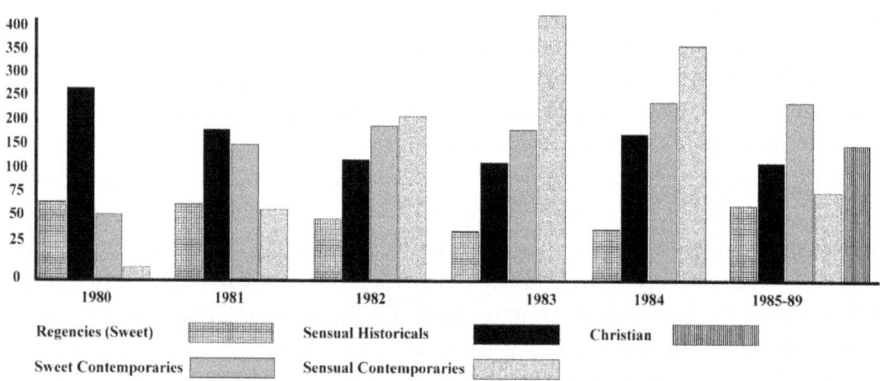

Yearly American Romance Production Estimates by Sub-genre: 1980-1989

Yearly Production by Subgenre, 1980–1989.

In the novels of the 1980s, the man is still older than the heroine, but the age differential has diminished, more in keeping with that existing in society; there is seldom more than a few years' difference, not the ten-to-twenty-year gap which separated seventies heroes and heroines. The heroine has gotten older, too: more are in their late twenties or early thirties; some are in the forties. The innocent and doe-eyed, naïve nineteen-year-old heroine became passé. Divorce is a recognized fact of life, and many heroines find their perfect mate the second time around. Women with careers in other than sex-typed occupations are in the new novels as well. So is sex sans marriage.

In 1980s romance novels, both women and men have been liberated, adumbrating the third feminist movement that didn't emerge for another decade. The new heroine was no longer the innocent flower who languishes unfulfilled without a man. Instead, she is a savvy, accomplished, attractive woman who knows how to appreciate a good man when she finds one, but she's not daydreaming her life away waiting for Mr. Right to magically appear and sweep her to home, hearth, and motherhood. These and other characteristics that distinguish the new heroine are noted by Rosemary Guiley.

Hero and Heroine Characteristics: Coming of Age in the 1980s

HEROES		HEROINE	
Traditional	*New*	*Traditional*	*New*
Antagonistic	Appealing	Fragile	Accomplished
Arrogant	Assertive	High-spirited	Assertive
Brutal	Athletic	Idealistic	Attractive
Domineering	Attractive	Inexperienced	Capable
Enigmatic	Aware	Intelligent	Experienced
Masterful	Caring	Likable	Independent
Moody	Dynamic	Passive	Intelligent
Quick-tempered	Masculine	Petite	Mature
Rich	Sensitive	Pretty	Resourceful
Rugged	Sexy	Proud	Sensitive
Tall, dark & handsome	Strong	Self-assured	Successful
Virile	Successful	Virginal	Vivacious
Worldly	Witty	Vulnerable	Witty

Source: Rosemary Guiley, *Love Lines* (New York: Facts on File, 1983), 100.

Ready, Set, Imitate

Harrison White takes issue with the economists' neoclassical theory that markets are defined by a set of buyers or that producers respond to markets based on an amorphous demand.[5] Rather, White argues that firms develop a market by watching their competitors' observables. These observables include volume and payment, not qualities or their valuations, and the firm acts on the basis of these observations. The more interrelated or "cliquish" the firms, the greater the ability of producers providing similar products to monitor one another.

Publishing, like many forms of mass entertainment, is a "cliquish" industry. Eighty percent of the major trade publishers are geographically concentrated within a dozen square blocks in New York City, an area euphemistically called Publisher's Row.[6] This does not mean that everyone knows everyone else in publishing. Nevertheless, editors at one house generally know the editors at other houses, if not personally, then at least by reputation.[7] This knowledge of the activities of other publishers is facilitated by the mobility of editors[8]; certainly, romance editors (as editors in general) changed houses with some celerity in the 1980s and, with only a few exceptions, had worked in at least one other firm editing romance novels.

White's monitoring theory suggests that when one firm or organization is viewed by competitors as successful in the marketplace, the other firms will copy its success. This copying is especially pronounced when the firms are geographically localized and produce similar products, such as genre fiction. Indeed, the similarity of products has been found by DiMaggio and Powell to result in a startling homogeneity of form.[9] They refer to this product homogeneity as mimetic isomorphism; it goes beyond White's monitoring theory by suggesting how "new" products first appear[10]:

> While there certainly are those who consciously innovate, there are those who, in their imperfect attempts to imitate others, unconsciously innovate by unwittingly acquiring some unexpected or unsought unique attributes which under the prevailing circumstances prove partly responsible for the success. Others, in turn, will attempt to copy the uniqueness, and the innovation-imitation process continues.

Stephens's "unwitting" acquisition of Castle's novel with its "unique attributes" proved "partially responsible for the success" of the Dell Ecstasy line; it was the major reason cited by editors of romance lines in the early 1980s for launching new liberated contemporary romance novels.

Romance producers of the 1980s certainly imitated Ecstasy, but publishers in the 1970s also imitated Avon's sensual historical. The distinction is less a matter of kind than of degree: barely a year passed before publishers responded to content innovations in the 1980s, while it took almost three years before anyone imitated Avon's lead and another two years before Avon's new sensual historical theme was widely adopted as the industry standard. The rapidity with which publishers responded to Ecstasy's new romance theme was largely

the result of management's changing attitude toward romances in general and their promoting women to fill editorial roles in romance publishing in the late 1970s.

Until the mid–1970s, when sensual historicals began to be produced in increasing numbers, romance publishing was not a major industry. Female editors were in the minority in publishing. Many editors had assistants who were—and often still are—no more than glorified secretaries.[11] These "assistants," often female, were generally given romance manuscripts to "edit." Even female editors tended to receive romance novels for publication consideration, regardless of the type of books they were editing.

The growth in sensual historical romance publishing in the United States pushed many of these female "editorial assistants" into editorial slots. Management believed that female editors could identify with the romantic theme of these novels and hence understand the consumer. The same women had been "editing" romance novels for years, but because of production increases during the late 1970s, the assistants could not handle all the editing chores and still perform their secretarial duties. Frequently, these "secretaries" were promoted to editors of romance novels. Five of the ten women in this study who worked in publishing prior to 1979 advanced from assistant editor to editor or senior editor in charge of romance novels; three others moved from editor to senior editor or editorial director of romance lines.

Within the houses, the prevailing attitude toward the women who filled these new editorial positions was, according to Kate Duffy, "condescending ... [because we] were publishing 'those books.'"[12] Vivian Stephens remembered the editorial meeting at Dell before Candlelight Ecstasy was introduced in this way[13]:

> [They treated me] with humor [when] I did my presentation. Category books are always last. After they finished the major [mainstream] list, then science-fiction, westerns and mysteries, it was my turn. I spent the same amount of time doing my presentation—mainly because I was new to publishing and didn't know any better: I'd give the plot, background of the book, background of the author, and they would laugh. It was like, "Come on, Vivian! Yours are not real books."

The explosive growth in romance publishing of the 1980s muted this "condescending" attitude. Editors indicated that they were suddenly treated with more respect, if only because publishers realized the amount of profit generated by romance novels. Yet the editors remained evenly divided as to whether this new respect reflected a change of heart toward romances. Half would agree with Stephens's assessment that romance publishing "has nothing to do with real writers and real writing. But everyone accepts it and makes money, saying 'Oh, how vulgar.' They think the money is very nice." The other half are more optimistic and tend to agree with Ellen Edwards, who felt that once publishers began to realize the money-making potential of romance novels, "category [romances] are treated better; [they're] more important to the company."[14]

The changing attitude toward female editors and the increased number of women in editorial positions are important to understanding the reason for the dramatic growth in romance publishing in the 1980s. In the early 1970s, few women (or men, for that matter) were responsible for observing trends in romance publishing. This is why it took three to five years before Avon's innovations were copied by other publishers. Once management recognized that the Avon product was garnering considerable success in the marketplace, they became interested in it. Female "secretaries" were promoted to editors. The prevailing condescending attitude by management toward the genre and the general inexperience of many of the new romance editors resulted in a strictly imitative product.

The increased number of women in editorial positions in the late 1970s, and management's growing awareness that these books were making money, enhanced the ability of editors and managers to understand and respond to changes in the field. Thus, when Dell introduced the sensual contemporary theme in 1980, editors were in a better position to monitor content changes, and management was more closely monitoring the genre's sales. The money-making potential of romantic fiction resulted in pressure from management to duplicate Dell's success. And because editors were in a position to more closely observe trends, they could quickly build on Dell's initial innovation by marginally differentiating their products from one another. The first line, and one of the most successful at competing with the Ecstasy line, was Second Chance at Love. Second Chance differentiated itself from Ecstasy by its focus on love refound. Carolyn Nichols, the editor of the line, had been ready to introduce the concept of Second Chance some years earlier but was rebuffed by management, who now suddenly told her to get it out.

Second Chance at Love

The idea for a line of sensual contemporary romances featuring a divorced heroine who finds love the second time around was originated by Carolyn Nichols. The Berkley-Jove editor conceived the idea for the Second Chance line in mid-1978. On October 24 of that year, shortly after her arrival at Berkley-Jove, she presented a memo to management for the series, which she perceived as a contemporary line that would compete with Harlequin Presents.[15]

> There was something in the air at about that time. Completely unknown to me, Vivian Stephens started thinking about bringing more sensuality into the books. It

seems to me both of us were on that track. It was probably intuitive. [I think we sensed that] since women had bought the hot [sensual] historicals that they were ready for more sensuality in the category of contemporary books.

The concept for Second Chance did not evolve, or at least it evolved ploddingly over the next few years. As the publisher, William Grose, interpreted the idea, "It would take an enormously successful romance formula to bring it into the twentieth century."[16] Apparently, Grose was not ready to try the Second Chance idea when it was proposed; nor did newcomer Nichols press the idea beyond the memo stage, perhaps unsure herself about the validity of the idea since, despite a solid background in television, she was relatively new to publishing.[17] The concept, after all, was based on personal taste[18]:

> Carolyn [Nichols] had been a fan of Harlequin for years and she realized she wasn't satisfied with them.... They [Harlequin] were dated in their approach. She got the idea of something that would appeal to her as a reader when she realized it wasn't otherwise available.

The idea resurfaced two years later, at the behest of the president and publisher of the firm. "I think that Dell Ecstasy had just been launched," Edwards recalls, "and that they [president and publisher] saw this as a market." This impression was confirmed by Grose in an interview with Giusto-Davis at *Publishers Weekly*: "Judging from how well some of our competitors have done, it seems that the market for romances just keeps growing and growing. Women who read these books do so in enormous quantities."[19]

Ellen Edwards, who later served as senior editor of Second Chance, was an associate editor under Nichols and helped write the guidelines by which to judge manuscripts[20]:

> The line was created by Carolyn Nichols, and she had very definite concepts in mind. She wanted to deal with older heroines that had experience and were getting their second chance at love; they were either divorced, widowed, or had spouses but it didn't work out. We formulated the guidelines around that and an understanding of what category romances are. We wanted to make the guidelines as specific as possible so that they would answer some of the [writers'] most frequently asked questions.

The guidelines were indeed specific: they ran five single-spaced pages and detailed elements of plot, setting, sexuality, point of view, type of description, and manuscript preparation, as well as composites of characteristics for the hero, heroine, and "other" characters in the novel. The guidelines for the "new" heroine and hero are worth noting:

> HEROINE: Aged 26–40, and an American, the heroine is not naïve and virginal, but rather a mature young woman who has already had a serious love relationship. (The first relationship has ended before the start of the novel.) She should be

attractive, appealing, and spirited, yet a vulnerable person the reader can admire or like.... Although the failure or loss of her first love has made her suffer, she must never be portrayed as depressed (or depressive), and even in the beginning of the story, she has a vivacious personality. She should have either a profession, a great interest (sports, the arts, etc.), or a demanding job in or out of business. She should not be a typing-pool level secretary, but executive/administrative assistant positions are definitely acceptable—she may be an aide of the top executive she falls in love with, or she may replace someone else on an important assignment. If she does not work, she must have a serious interest that shows her to be a well-rounded person. Such a career or interest helps to provide plot elements. Often it is the means through which the heroine meets the hero, or the reason she is in the place where the novel is set. The SECOND CHANCE AT LOVE heroine rarely crumbles in a confrontation, blushes, or runs away. She does not tell outright lies, although she may hedge in order to spare someone's feelings.

THE HERO: The hero is virile, masterful, and attractive—though not necessarily handsome in the conventional sense. He is tender and sensitive. He is generally not more than five to eight years older than the heroine, from late twenties to mid-forties. He can be American or foreign, and while he need not be rich, he must be successful at whatever he does. He can possess a complex personality, but serious problems such as alcoholism, impotence, or addictive gambling must be avoided. He need not be "brooding," the "strong, silent type," or any of the other stereotypes found in traditional romances. He may be open, honest, and amusing. In short, he should be the kind of man *you* would want to fall in love with. In addition, as stated above in the description of the plot [not detailed], there cannot be "gothic" elements associated with him. By the end of the book, the reader should be sure that, with her second chance, the heroine is getting Mr. Right. However, the hero can be the same man the heroine was previously in love with, especially if they parted through a misunderstanding or circumstances beyond their control.

Category Romances in the New Age: The Need for Editorial Direction

The term category romance has been used a number of times in the above comments by editors. Category publishing is the trade term used to distinguish formula fiction from noncategory or "mainstream" fiction. Category is used because the type of genre fiction has prescribed parameters, conventions that are adhered to. With the imposition of rigid guidelines in the early 1980s, the term category romance took on a new, distinctly pejorative connotation.

Almost all trade publishers, as we have seen, have tip sheets for would-be-authors. They are not really guidelines but advice on manuscript preparation and submission. At most, the tip sheets reiterate the genre's conventions and urge the would-be authors to familiarize themselves with the novels by reading other books in the series. But in the early 1980s the guidelines began to specify in excruciating detail exactly what the writer should do. These guidelines reinforced the negative perception by trade publishers of romance writers—and hence romance readers and editors—because they implied that women submitting manuscripts didn't know how to write.

It wasn't that the writers didn't know how to write, but merely that no one, including the editors, was sure what to write. Dell had turned the romance field topsy-turvy by introducing a multiplicity of new themes. There was nowhere to turn for content direction. The need for guidelines was the result of confusion in the task environment—which consisted of romance readers and writers—and editors attempted to deal with this uncertain environment by establishing directions for writers. This was necessary because of the rapidity with which editors responded to the new content form, and the need, fostered by management, to release not just five or ten books over the next year but five or ten books each month.

Most romance writers are romance readers,[21] and for decades they were dichotomized between reader-writers of sweet contemporaries and reader-writers of historicals. Sensual historical writers were familiar with the sensual aspect of romances, but not the contemporary formula; sweet contemporary writers were familiar with the contemporary aspect of romances, but not the sensuality, which was a notch more explicit than that available in the Presents line. Had the Ecstasy line been a blend of sensuality from the historicals with the contemporary theme of the sweets, writers could have read both types of books on the market and imitated the new line. However, the liberated contemporary novels introduced by Stephens were more than a mere blend of these two types: they depicted a world totally different from the one portrayed by either the sensual historicals (with their rape theme) or the sweet contemporaries. Guidelines were necessary to "guide" the writers in developing the "liberated" format of the Ecstasy novels. This need for direction was heightened by management's decision to produce the new books as a line, thereby obligating the editor to acquire a certain number of books every month, not just good novels as they became available.

Dell introduced a heroine who was older, divorced, sexually experienced,[22] and career-oriented. Love was still the *sine qua non* of the novel. Dell's content variations were more dramatic, and the more unique "the recombination of existing factors of production," wrote the economist Joseph Schumpeter, the greater the amount of disruption that will occur in the task environment as producers scurry to imitate the latest innovations.[23] Thus, Dell, unlike Avon a decade earlier, "recombined" the existing romance theme by introducing more than one content variation: divorce, careers, older heroines, and so forth. Many editors appeared unsure exactly which innovation appealed most to readers, or even who the readers now were. The result was a potpourri of lines over the next few years that attempted to marginally differentiate themselves by focusing on a different dimension of the new themes; for example, Second Chance at Love featured divorced women; Intimate Moments and Finding Mr. Right, both discussed in the next chapter, focused on other thematic variations: Intimate Moments homed in on career-oriented females; Finding Mr. Right pivoted around the heroine's choice between two suitable males.

The rapidity with which publishers responded to Dell's innovations did not allow editors or writers time to grasp the reasons for Ecstasy's success, yet the editors were required to publish from two to eight romances per month in the new liberated style of Ecstasy. At the same time, few books in the new subgenre were available. Editors in the 1980s, then, could not point to other writers—as Mary Ann Stuart at Playboy did by simply telling her writers to read Woodiwiss, Rogers, and McBain—and say merely, "read so-and-so; that's what we want." Editors resorted to detailed guidelines to help delineate the new content for authors so that they would be able to fill their lists, while, at the same time, marginally differentiating their product from other lines.

Editorial guidelines diminished in number as the task environment began to stabilize in the second half of the 1980s. As more and more romances in the new subgenre appeared in the market, editors and authors began to understand what the audience wanted and return to the more traditional role of gatekeepers. Forcing editors into the uncomfortable role of gatemakers would be a costly learning process for many publishers; it resulted in the demise of many romance lines because the new editors were forced to act precipitously. Guidelines returned to their more innocuous tip-sheet stage as the liberated format introduced by Ecstasy became established. By 1985, guidelines in the detailed, eight-page 1981 style of Second Chance had ceased to exist. Author names began to emerge as early as 1983, names that readers of the new subgenre recognized as providing consistent quality writing. One of the first romance lines to exploit the emergence of author names was Loveswept: it is one of the few non–Harlequin/Silhouette lines that continued to thrive during the second half of the 1980s. The new line was built on the ashes of Circle for Love.

From Circle of Love to Loveswept: Repositioning a Romance Line

After Second Chance at Love proved successful in following Ecstasy's lead, the next contemporary romance line to launch was Bantam Books' Circle of Love. The line débuted in March 1982 with sweet content in the dated style of

Harlequin Romance. It immediately encountered difficulty in the marketplace and was discontinued within eight months.[24]

The decision to enter the category romance business was derived from management's perception that there was a market for that kind of product.[25] This judgment was based in part on a survey of other romance publishers and in part on Bantam's success over the years with single-title sweet romance releases, especially the popular romance novels by Grace Livingston Hill and the 150-plus Barbara Cartland titles, which they distributed in the United States.

Before embarking on its Circle venture, Bantam hired a reputable firm to conduct market research to determine content directions, since there was no romance specialist in-house to whom management could turn to for input.[26] The research firm's results were both ambiguous and dated. One of the firm's findings, which Bantam attempted to incorporate into the line's content, was revealed by Louis Wolfe, president and chief executive officer, in a pre-launch interview: "We learned that women who make multiple romance purchases a month have indicated they want better-written, more suspenseful and more fulfilling stories."[27] An example of the ambiguity of the research is cited by Bantam's Loveswept editor, Carolyn Nichols:

> Some of the questions in the study were ambiguous and could be interpreted in many ways. The chief example is [that] a random sample of women indicated they would like better-written romances. To consumers, well written means creative, but to people in publishing, it would mean the prose, vocabulary and the expertise with which the books were edited. My impression was that there was a gap of understanding between the respondents and those who were interpreting the information.

The ambiguity of the research was not the only problem. More germane to Circle's difficulty was that the market had shifted. In the months between the time the research was fielded and the line debuted, Candlelight Ecstasy and Second Chance at Love had dramatically altered the direction of romance content. Nichols nicely summarized the problem:

> The decision to enter the business was based on a very big market survey. [But] the market research was obsolete when it rolled out of the typewriter. The market researchers had not considered what was happening in the market. They didn't know about Ecstasy, which was about to debut, or about Second Chance at all— and these two lines changed the face of romance publishing in the United States. Prior to that, Harlequin had been a monopoly; Silhouette was born only to compete with Harlequin in the sweet romance area.
> Ecstasy and Second Chance at Love were the first lines of books to present older, more sensual, heroines; more appealing stories, which were primarily set in American locations. So the Circle of Love research was obsolete and they [Bantam] did not know it. And so they went ahead with books in the style of the sweet Harlequins, sweet Silhouettes, and the market was already saturated.

Nichols, who had been the editor at Berkley-Jove responsible for formulating the successful Second Chance line, was hired by Bantam in April 1982, "to get the publisher in the romance business." She arrived having already decided the fate of Circle: "It wasn't my intention to continue Circle of Love; it was my intention to bring out Loveswept."

Nichols's a priori judgment sealed the fate of Circle. The line continued to be released until Loveswept was ready. No attempt was made to salvage it, and printings were substantially reduced to minimize losses. The decision to discontinue Circle was based on its poor positioning; sweet romances had been replaced by contemporary liberated romances. Thus, Loveswept, a line of sensual contemporary romances, was born, based on Nichols's assessment of the market: "What was selling, what the consumer indicated she wanted." But while Nichols believed the sensual liberated contemporary romances were continuing to garner audience appeal, she felt category romance publishing was already passé because "market conditions were already glutted. We were expecting further, larger gluts on the market. So it seemed to me that only the best would sell. [It was] the survival of the strongest."

To Nichols, the best could only be achieved in the gatekeeper tradition, where editors sift though manuscripts looking for unique stories and do not force writers into a pre-established format. This approach to romance publishing differs from the one she established at Berkley-Jove, where the Second Chance category was positioned to compete with Candlelight Ecstasy. However, market conditions had changed by 1983. Second Chance had been the second category sensual contemporary line to debut and quickly positioned itself in the market for the new liberated format initiated by Ecstasy. Between the time she had spent at Second Chance (1982) and her arrival at Bantam (1983), sensual-liberated category publishing was gaining increased attention from romance publishers, making it more difficult for a new line to find a niche. Nichols's "educated guesses" and "informed instincts" as to the future of category romance publishing changed her attitude toward this type of publishing.

> I have a very different view than that espoused by Harlequin and Silhouette, namely that this is a brand name game; I don't think so [anymore]. I think that in a glutted market, the consumer, the reader, will choose the way she always chooses, has chosen, and the way readers of other genres choose, and that is by what is tried and true. And what is tried and true is the author's name.

Increasingly toward the latter part of 1983, trade sources indicated that consumers were complaining about inconsistency in the various lines. In part, these complaints reflected a decrease in quality in the content as publishers rushed to get more and more books on the market; in part, they also reflected a greater demand by consumers for quality books. Consumers were beginning to look for certain authors, rather than the overall line. By mid–1983, readers were complaining of the declining quality of romantic fiction on the market. Typical consumer attitudes were the following quotes from a survey conducted by the romance newsletter *Boy Meets Girl* in September 1983[28]:

> I dropped them [Harlequin subscriptions] about eleven months ago. The quality was going down and I was getting more picky about what I bought.
>
> The [Silhouette] authors I really liked weren't always there. If I bought them in the stores, I could pick those I wanted. Even though [with the subscription service] I was getting one book free, I still preferred being able to choose.

Nichols correctly assessed the needs of writers, who were being stymied by length restrictions and other guidelines, and of consumers, who increasingly were looking for favorite authors. To address both of these problems, Nichols created Loveswept as "the author's line." This was Loveswept's niche. She responded to the authors' complaints by removing guidelines and giving established writers more latitude in developing themes; she capitalized on the consumer's increased attention to favorite authors over brand names, providing the reader some assurance of quality writing.

> I conceived of it [Loveswept] as the author's line. [I thought] we'd find the brightest new stars we could and show their faces on the inside front cover and include autobiographical sketches on them—that rather than an editorial letter in front of the book just like everybody else. I decided to do an editor's corner, where I could give little anecdotes and preview the books for the next month, and just have a little more chatty kind of approach to the reader.

To bring Loveswept to the attention of the public, Nichols put out a sampler.

> Probably the best thing I did to get the line off to a good start was to put out a sampler. It included the first chapters of the first six books, pictures, and biographies, and I told the consumer what our intentions were. We gave away almost 200,000 free of charge. Another [competitive] line is now [1984] going to launch with a sampler first; it's never been done before, but it looks like it's going to be emulated a lot from now on. So, I think that attests to how successful we were. The week we went on sale we had sellouts all over the country.

The success of the sampler can be gauged by the following selected comments from romance readers in a sample conducted by *Boy Meets Girl* shortly after Loveswept launched.[29] The reader comments also indicate the diversity of content in the line, freed from the guidelines, as well as the market trend for consumers increasingly to identify romances by author over brand name.

> C.D. is a 30-year-old, single career woman.... She has read all six Loveswept launch books. She could not recall their titles, but identified authors Sandra Brown, Helen Mittermeyer, and Dorothy Garlock without assistance. "My favorite was Sandra Brown's. The characters were very human. The humor was good and

the love story was very strong. All the books were very real, and some very humorous.... I enjoyed the author sketches in the books, too." She was influenced to try Loveswept by the introductory sampler, "but the authors were more important," she said.

B.L. is a 34-year-old, single career woman.... She has read all six Loveswept launch books, though with unaided recall could name three authors ... and not titles. "The titles they use make them hard to remember," she said, "and that is true for all the lines." She liked Sandra Brown's story best. "The first chapter got you hooked. It was a real kicker. I think the line is promising. There were a couple of unique story lines. I liked the conversations, the backchat. I wish they'd concentrate on more dialogue and substance and less heavy breathing, though. She was influenced to try Loveswept by the introductory sampler [but] also liked the authors. "That's the number one reason I bought."

M.R. is a 73-year-old widow. During the first week the Loveswept titles have been for sale at retail, she has read four of the six launch books.... "I really liked Dorothy Garlock's book. It was my favorite.... Sandra Brown's book was funny.... So far, if they keep up the quality, the line should do well. There was plenty of sex—not as much as Ecstasy—but with Ecstasy and Desire they kind of beat you over the head with it. [Loveswept] is better in this respect." She was influenced to purchase Loveswept by the introductory sampler and the authors.

A number of readers in the *Boy Meets Girl* survey commented on two developments: humor and realism. Both these aspects of Loveswept's content are noted by Nichols. The first indicates a personal preference by the editor, reinforced by audience feedback; the second underscores Nichols's awareness of trends emerging in romance publishing; it is worth citing because it also goes to the heart of another matter: the genre's unrealistic depiction of life and love.

I personally enjoy humor, and I think humor is the saving grace in this crazy world. And I love books with humor. So I look for that. And lots of readers write to me and say they love the humor in our books.

I [also] look for *believable* characters and situations, but that isn't realism. These books ought not to be realistic. Realism is harsh; believability is creativity. More people have gone wrong on this matter than anything else in romance publishing. One [line] has bombed, another's about to go out of existence for this very reason; that is, the editors thought the readers wanted more realistic books when what they wanted was more believable books.

Realism, as Nichols points out, is harsh, and fantasy readers, regardless of the genre, want to escape life's realism, if only for a little while. This was indeed a problem with a number of lines, as we shall see in the next chapter. Another problem, one hinted at above by M.R., was sex. Ecstasy and Second Chance, as well as Loveswept later, dealt with sex, but dealt with it sparingly and in context. However, many of the editors in the 1980s did not appreciate the multiple themes found in Ecstasy and Second Chance novels and focused on the sex angle, going overboard and insisting on page after page of sexual description. It proved to be the downfall of many lines.

Conclusion

Vivian Stephens had two traits that helped her "appraise" the Candlelight line she was hired to monitor. One of these is shared with many of the other successful editors of the 1970s and 1980s[30]—she was older than the typical right-out-of-college editorial assistant,[31] so she looked at things with a more mature eye. She was also new to publishing, so she wasn't locked into any preconceived notions of how things should be done.[32] She didn't feel the sweet contemporaries were in sync with the social world of the 1980s. She wasn't sure what she wanted to do, but she was looking for something more in keeping with current social attitudes. This meant she was open, at the very least, to adding a little more spice to the line, which led her to pluck a more sensual novel from those submitted, and she very tentatively filtered it in to the existing Candlelight series. When no readers raised any objection, she was encouraged to try another.

This one was also sensual but had a multiplicity of other dimensions—a handicapped hero and an older, divorced heroine were certainly different from anything being published at the time. She was not dissuaded by management when she approached them with the idea of a new line, that ended up, like Superromance, being dubbed Ecstasy for lack of a better name when the line was about to go to press. Stephens has gone on to romance "stardom," like Nancy Coffey at Avon after discovering Woodiwiss, for introducing a radically different content to the romance format.[33] Stephens's contribution would be more "upsetting" than Coffey's, if only because there were so many thematic variations in the Ecstasy product. Other editors that followed had to decide just what it was about the Ecstasy product that attracted consumers.

Two lines immediately followed. They were both successful; coincidentally, they were both helmed by the same editor, who also shared with Stephens a more "seasoned" eye. One line, Second Chance at Love, as the name implies, focused on a divorced heroine finding love the second time around. Carolyn Nichols had wanted to do something along this line a few years earlier but was rebuffed by management, who now, surveying the uptrending romance market, encouraged her to develop her ideas. Because the line was so new, and so unique, Nichols formatted detailed guidelines for budding authors since the would-be authors couldn't find similarly themed novels on the market to emulate.

Nichols would be subsequently hired away from Berkley-Jove by Bantam specifically to get the publisher into the romance business. She arrived with every intention of killing the dated Circle of Love sweet line and debuting Loveswept. The market had changed drastically in that one year between the launch of Second Chance and Loveswept, however, so Nicholas now felt she could abandon guidelines, there being an abundance of sensual liberated romances now on the market, and return, in the Avon tradition, to focusing on quality writing and limiting the number of monthly launch novels. Her astute decision to move from guidelines can only be appreciated after ascertaining what went wrong with so many other lines that launched in the aftermath of Ecstasy's success.

Chapter 6

Risky Business
Rushing to Cash In on the Romance Craze

Monitoring the success of rival firms may lead to product imitation; it does not necessarily lead to product success. The innovator captures the market first and gains recognition among consumers for its new product, building a loyal customer base. Such was the case with Avon's romances in the 1970s and Dell's Ecstasy line in the 1980s. Later Avon-Ecstasy imitators often do not fare as well.

The first competitor to follow the innovator's lead frequently takes a respectable share of the "new" consumer market, mainly because there often are not enough innovative products available at that point to fulfill consumer wants. Both Avon and Dell Ecstasy released relatively few of the new romances, leaving an opportunity for Playboy in the 1970s and Second Chance at Love in the 1980s to slice into the as-yet unsated demand for the new product. But as others moved to capitalize on the "obvious" market demand—seen first in the innovative product and then in the success of the imitator—competition became stiffer, the field grew increasingly crowded, and the consumer market began to shrink, or at least was sectioned into smaller and smaller market shares. This is one reason for the failure of many of the post–Ecstasy lines that began to crowd bookshelves between 1982 and 1984. Few would survive beyond 1985.

The failure of many of the late imitators was not due simply to an overcrowded marketplace. It was compounded by confusion regarding consumer demand. Management's rush to release competitive lines gave editors little chance to appraise consumer likes and dislikes, and, as a result, they were unclear about what plot elements most appealed to consumers. Seeing how Second Chance capitalized on the Ecstasy story line by concentrating on one dimension of the plot, divorced heroines, editors attempted to develop nuances within the Ecstasy theme by focusing on specific plot elements. Some, like Rapture and

Love and Life, just didn't have enough marketing vigor to create consumer identity; others, like Inspirational Romances, were never able to garner a substantial readership, owing largely to the truncated romantic theme; still others, such as Finding Mr. Right, went too far astray from the essential romance theme and were rejected by readers.

Crowding the Market

David Galloway at Harlequin bemoaned the glut of titles flooding the market during the first half of the 1980s. He was incorrect, however, when he said the glut was due to "everyone trying to copy Harlequin."[1] Indeed, no one was following Harlequin because its product was dated. If anything, Harlequin was trying to catch up by adding more sensuality to its novels.

By mid–1982, the success of the new liberated contemporary format was firmly established. Candlelight Ecstasy, Second Chance at Love, and another Ecstasy imitator, Silhouette's Desire, convinced other houses that there was a market for the new liberated themes. Other romance publishers began to copy the success of these three lines. Some, like New American Library's Rapture Romances and Ballantine's Love and Life, were strictly imitative. Others, like Zondervan's Serenade Books, Berkley-Jove's To Have and to Hold, and Avon's Finding Mr. Right attempted to fine-tune the contemporary format to tap previously unoccupied niches within the contemporary marketplace. In all cases, editors agreed that the decision to enter the contemporary romance game after 1981 was based on the observation of how well Ecstasy and the Ecstasy imitators were selling; American publishers had finally woken up and realized that romances were, as Dell vice president Ross Claiborne exuberantly exclaimed, a "license to print money."[2] The industry soon turned and started instead to bleed money.

Rapture Romances

Following current trends, New American Library (NAL) launched Rapture Romances in January 1983 and struggled until February 1985 before the line disappeared from bookshelves.

"We started the line because romance publishing is one of the most profitable genres in publishing today," said editor Robin Grunder. "We wanted to have a part of that. We looked at what was selling the best and patterned ourselves on that."[3]

NAL, like many other publishers, had been publishing romances all along. The firm had an existing line of Regencies and some sweet contemporary romances, though the latter were published sporadically and not under a particular program. Following the success of other contemporary lines, management expressed an interest in developing their existing sweet contemporary authors. Grunder, who had functioned as an editorial assistant in the romance area after graduating from college a year earlier, was promoted to editor. She first surveyed the competition and says she "talked to agents to get a better idea of what our competitors were doing, what's upcoming. After all, agents are looking at stuff upcoming a year from now."

She suggested to NAL management "that if the publisher was going to put a lot of money into it [the line], then sweets were not the direction to go." Instead, she recommended sensual contemporaries. After submitting guidelines for the line, Grunder received permission to proceed. The guidelines, excerpted below, show a marked similarity to existing sensual contemporary romances of the period.

> Since the emphasis in Rapture Romances will now be placed heavily on the physical expression of love, it is important that each love scene (a love scene can be something as simple as the look two people exchange, the unexpected electricity that flares between strangers, a quiet moment of unspoken sharing) be an integral part of the plot development and contribute something new to the relationship, that it have its own mood. Foreplay and afterplay, with descriptions of what the heroine thinks and feels, what the hero says and does, before, during and after making love can provide this, as can a change in setting (i.e., outside in the afternoon rather than in the bedroom at night); a switch in the seducer/seducee roles; a change in the level of experience or attitude of one of the participants: an infinite number of distinctions can be made. And the love scenes should be described in full and lavish, though not clinical, moment-by-moment detail. We don't want to know that he is handsome, we want to know that he has crispy curling black hair with just a touch of gray at the temples. We don't want to know that the sky was romantic, we want to know that the sky was a dark velvet canopy over their heads, and as they walked barefoot at the edge of the ocean the cool water tickled their bare feet and the rush and roar of the ocean seemed to echo their own heartbeats. We don't want to know that his touch aroused her, we want to know that the rough feel of his calloused finger-tips as he wonderingly explored the outline of her face with feather-like caresses set her trembling as no arrogant and inescapable embrace could have. It is important that the reader at all times feel the strong mutual desire of the hero and heroine, their constant awareness of and fascination with each other.

Grunder's emphasis on sexual description was imitative of Ecstasy Romances, and her detailed description seemed aimed at neophyte writers who were unfamiliar with the genre and who themselves wanted to cash in on the romance bonanza. The Rapture line was just another line like Ecstasy; management appears to have felt that if they just put the books on the racks, they'd sell. This strategy might have worked in the past, but Rapture appeared during the peak of the Ecstasy imitations in 1983 and simply got lost in the shuffle.

Meager sales and the proliferation of similar lines prompted management to increase the number of titles per month from two to four in July, and then to six in October, as if more novels would somehow solve the problem of poor sales. The jump in production was fostered by management's belief that they must hold rack space in order to maintain a visible presence among the crowded shelves. But management recognized that rack space in itself was no longer enough and strengthened its commitment to the line, but not the novels. The publisher allocated $500,000 for advertising and promotion during the second half of 1983, increased Rapture's visibility at national and regional conventions, and attempted to "hook" consumers by offering a $1.00 rebate with four proofs of purchase.[4] It was too little, too late.

Having gotten off to a weak start, Rapture was never able to capture a significant share of the romance market. The enhanced promotional budget was offset by deterioration in the quality of the novels, caused by the increase in monthly titles.[5] NAL acknowledged this problem when it decided in December 1983 to scale back from six monthly titles to four in March 1984. The increase, however, had forced Grunder to accept manuscripts that should never have been published, and subsequent attempts at "quality control," the catchphrase of the industry in 1984, would prove futile.

Grunder parted company with NAL in December 1983, undeservedly taking the lioness's share of blame for the line's weak market position. Her editorial assistant, Mary Ann Gartland, replaced her as editor. She assumed that the reduction to four titles per month would be sufficient to allow Rapture "to bring our strongest authors to the readers," so she turned her attention to shoring up NAL's two historical romance lines, Signet Regency Romances and Scarlet Ribbon.[6]

Susanne Jaffe, executive editor for NAL/Signet, articulated NAL's commitment to Rapture, saying Gartland "is symbolic of this commitment," and acknowledged her cutting-edge contribution to their new project: "historical bodice-rippers and sexy gothics."[7] The infiltration of these dated books into the ongoing Regency and Scarlet Ribbon lines resulted six months later in the replacement of Gartland by her assistant, Jeanne Tiedge, who made her mark by introducing the ill-fated "Adam" books into the Rapture line—contemporary romances told from the *male* point of view—and who left NAL with the line's eventual termination in February 1985.

To Have and to Hold

Berkley-Jove Publishing Group, which published Second Chance at Love, launched its second romance line, To Have and to Hold, in October 1983—and killed it in December 1984. To Have and to Hold departed from the traditional romance theme of an unmarried woman finding love and marrying the hero. In To Have and to Hold, heroine and hero are married at the outset; the romantic interest evolves as the couple encounters some obstacle in their lives that they surmount and, in the process, develop a deeper understanding of each other. The original proposal for the line promoted the relationship as "my love and my friend."[8]

The concept for the line was originated by a staff member of the romance trade newsletter, *Boy Meets Girl*. The idea was proposed to Bantam Books but was turned down, since Bantam at the time had allocated its resources to the Circle of Love line. Berkley-Jove picked up the idea shortly thereafter, based in part upon the recommendation of Carolyn Nichols, at the time senior editor for Second Chance at Love. The concept was turned over to her assistant Ellen Edwards to develop when Nichols jumped to Bantam in April 1982. One cannot help feeling that the seasoned Nichols might have made something of the idea, which her newly promoted and largely inexperienced assistant was unable to do.

To Have and to Hold was conceived as a fresh, new product for the romance reader. Berkley-Jove bought the idea because Nichols believed it had potential to reach a broader romance audience. No market research was involved, and there was limited audience input. At best, Edwards said, "we did get some mail that said they [readers] would like to know what happens after they [heroine and hero] get together. I think that was an indication that we thought the line would work."[9]

Within the publishing house, editors' interest in the line was enhanced because they knew that their competitors had nothing similar on the market. "New" was the byword of the day, which is reflected in Edwards's comments on the line's launch[10]:

> Basically we feel it's going to have a wide appeal.... In society at large, marriage is coming back into vogue; you see articles and books about it. I sometimes compare the interest in books like *How to Make Love to Each Other* as a trend toward romanticism in nonfiction category books. There is a certain correlation there. Basically, I just think they'll be very different and they'll appeal to people for that reason.

It took two years for the concept of matrimonial love to evolve into a line, mainly because no one was writing about it. The first four books released received mixed reviews from retailers across the United States.[11] Robin James's *The Testimony* was the most favorably received of the four, with Ann Cristy's *Tread Softly* also garnering a lot of positive response; the other two books received practically no attention.[12]

While a few books did well, To Have and to Hold never took off. By April 1984, no sales for any title in the line exceeded 50,000 copies,[13] a fraction of the typical 200,000-print run. The slow sales were a puzzle to editor Edwards.[14]

> Obviously, we feel there's a problem with To Have and to Hold, and we're looking at it very closely. The numbers are not what we want, but we're definitely publishing through the end of the year [1984].
>
> I don't think at this point we've isolated specific reasons. You have to consider all the factors: the crowded market; the unusual concept; maybe distribution problems; maybe there were too few (sales) people out there; maybe the quality of the first books wasn't as high as it needed to be, or, at least, maybe they weren't slanted quite right to be the ones to introduce the line; or maybe the consumer had seen one too many new lines and was less willing to try another one. I think in the early [launch] days there may have been some confusion about what they [consumers] were getting. Was it clear enough among consumers that it was a non-realistic depiction of marriage? Or did they expect it to be another very serious, realistic treatment?

More likely, the problem was the concept itself. There may be love, sharing, and caring in marriage, but the romantic element is strained, lost in the drudgery of everyday routine and the familiarity of cohabitation. Perhaps this is why great works of literature tend to focus on the strains and conflicts of marriage. More fantasy-oriented artistic works emphasize the courting process. Popular music, for example, has been found to contain three major types of love lyrics: the "happy in love" ballad, the "frustrated in love" song, and the "novelty song with sex interest."[15] Songs of marital love are scarce. Three ballads of pining love, for example, were sung by Paul and Paula, a young college duo in 1963: "Hey Paula" and "Young Lovers" cracked the Top Ten list; the other, "First Quarrel," posted a respectable twenty-seven on the music charts. The couple wed that summer and returned to extol their marital bliss in song. The song bombed.[16] Shortly thereafter, Paul and Paula faded into rock and roll history, much as To Have and to Hold passed into publishing history.

Love and Life

Ballantine launched Love and Life in July 1982 and published its last title in the line in December 1983. The line was conceived as a series of contemporary sensual romances that would be in keeping with recent developments in romance content. Because the line was perceived by Ballantine staff as competitive with other contemporary liberated lines, Ballantine never really addressed content as a possible problem, focusing instead on the books' physical appearance and making numerous packaging changes in hopes of salvaging the line.

These changes were unsuccessful for a number of reasons, but the problem with the line began at its inception.

The idea for Love and Life started at the editorial level. The editor for Ballantine Books' historical romances, Pamela Strickler, began actively seeking longer contemporary women's fiction in 1981. Strickler was, in essence, looking for romance novels similar to those she had worked on as an assistant editor under Nancy Coffey at Avon, only she now sought manuscripts in the contemporary rather than historical genre. Her editor-in-chief, however, overruled the idea, instructing Strickler to submit a list of shorter, category-type books. Strickler had neither the interest in nor experience with this type of book, but complied by putting "the same kind of [women's] mainstream author line of ideas into the shorts."[17]

The rationale behind management's desire for a category line of romances, suggested Strickler, was the prevailing belief within publishing that middle-of-the-road paperbacks (mid-list books) could help a house if they were packaged as a series. This belief was reinforced and perpetuated by successful category lines such as Harlequin, Silhouette, and Second Chance at Love, all of which did an excellent job of packaging but also concentrated on quality content.

But while management perceived Love and Life as a category line, Strickler continued to view it as a shorter version of mainstream fiction:

> The uniform packaging we did placed the list in the wrong position. It positioned it [the line] wrongly in the minds not only of the audience and booksellers, but even our own sales force. They were never formula books; they are not even really romances.

Here, then, lay the initial problem for Love and Life. While management presented the books as a category line of romances, the editor selected manuscripts that fit management's demands for shorter works but maintained her initial mainstream idea. Thus, the content of Love and Life was never a category in the sense of having clearly defined guidelines, but management packaged the line as a category romance series. As Strickler pointed out, this internal confusion also caused confusion for readers.

> These lists [e.g., Harlequin, Silhouette] are very successful. They answer a need in the audience. But we weren't doing that and it was never possible to make anybody understand that, including the audience. We never got the audience. What happened was that the category audience identified us as noncategory; the noncategory audience identified us as category.

Strickler eventually got her way when management threw in the towel and basically let her pursue her original concept, but by then it was too late.

There were other problems besides the category/noncategory confusion, notably content, packaging, and cover art. The shorter length—just as it did when the marketing department forced editors to shorten Harlequin Superromances by 20,000 words—made character development difficult, if not impossible.

Unlike other romance novels, Ballantine also radically changed the design of the book; it was designed with a distinctive, magazine format: the name Love and Life was carried at the top, like a masthead, and there were big photo portraits of women on the cover rather than illustrations. Strickler thought these innovations were "a brilliant idea." It didn't work, so the covers were changed. "We still stuck to photographs, but did 'soft focus' scenes," said Strickler. "That didn't work either." A new editor-in-chief reappraised the books with a fresh eye and concluded "the covers just look cheap." They were modified again, but by this time the line had already been resoundingly rejected by the consumer, and the decision was made to discontinue it.

The "cheap" look of the books no doubt had little appeal to romance consumers. Part of this look was created by the early magazine format; it was further aggravated by the use of photographs, even though they were well done. At the time, illustrated covers, not photographed ones, had a special appeal to women romance consumers. In contemporary teen romances, photographic covers are widely used; this still holds true today (circa 2000s) though those teen covers that depict another world, as the paranormals do, tend to rely more on illustrative covers. The cover shots in contemporary teen romances lend credence to the more "real life" stories depicted in these novels, where teenage heroines confront not only the doubts of young love but also such everyday problems as bringing a boyfriend home or coping with curfews imposed by parents. Illustrated covers, on the other hand, are more

Love & Life launch cover.

suggestive of fantasy. Illustrations have been found to appeal to adult romance readers because the consumer "doesn't want to read about someone just like themselves, teens do."[18]

The difficulties encountered by Love and Life, then, were due to a concatenation of factors. Two of these, content and cover photography, were duplicated by Finding Mr. Right, with disastrous results.

Finding Mr. Right

Avon launched Finding Mr. Right on Valentine's Day 1983 and terminated it eight months later. The line encountered immediate difficulty in the marketplace. The problems began, as with Love and Life, with divergent perceptions in-house as to the nature of the line.

Finding Mr. Right was a packaged line similar to those provided to publishers by Richard Gallen in the 1970s; that is, the packager formulates content, selects manuscripts, and does all editorial work, "selling" the books to a publisher, who provides promotional expenses and distributes the novels. The packagers for Mr. Right were Denise Marcil and Meredith Bernstein.

Marcil and Bernstein formatted the concept for Mr. Right by surveying the field with a view toward filling an unoccupied niche.[19] They believed the market was moving toward a more realistic approach to romances. The packagers interpreted this trend—considering also what was being done by other houses—to mean that women often had to choose which hero they wanted. "We had to come up with something that would be unique in an overcrowded market," said Marcil. She went on to detail the uniqueness of her line:

> There isn't one hero, but two, and the question is: how do you find the man who's right for you? They're not like category romances in which one man is the red herring, obviously inappropriate from the beginning.[20] The men in our books are both likable and appealing, but they have flaws—they're human beings. The heroine isn't perfect either. The suspense that keeps the reader turning the page is, which one will she choose at the end? The reader doesn't know until the heroine knows.
>
> The heroine goes through a marvelous self-exploration deciding which man is appropriate for her. In some cases, it'll be a man who's wealthier and more successful than the other, but in some cases, she'll choose the other man because money isn't important to her. The books aren't predictable. Our writers have to make her choice believable and sympathetic.

The idea for Mr. Right originated in June 1981, and by the end of October the packagers had two complete manuscripts and several partials to show romance publishers. They approached all major publishers, but only two houses were interested. Avon came up with the best offer.

Page Cuddy, editorial director at Avon, bought Mr. Right; it was the house's first venture into category romances. The move toward category publishing was not enthusiastically received by Avon's editorial staff. "I have never been interested in stories that authors write to specs [like Mr. Right]," said Cuddy. "I am interested in stories they [authors] want to tell."[21] Why, then, did Avon purchase a category line of romances? According to Cuddy, house management wanted to stay competitive with other romance publishers.

> I think all publishers have a responsibility, regardless of the area you're working in, to try new things. We don't do much contemporary romance [publishing], so it [Mr. Right] was out of that impulse and the notion that it was a little different from anything else....
>
> This is a small house, one that has been called an eccentric house [because] we published Rosemary Rogers. We try very hard not to be typecast; we try things that [might tap] different segments of the market. It [Mr. Right] was competition for Harlequin.
>
> The decision [for Mr. Right] was a purely internal thing. We were not doing anything in contemporary romances; this was an idea that seemed different. I and people I work for are not doing their job if we do not explore new segments of the market. This doesn't mean we necessarily go into all of them, but it's a crucial part of what we do.

Here, then, lay the in-house misconception that subsequently gave rise to poor market placement. Avon purchased Mr. Right, perceiving it to be a category line of romances. Yet while admitting that the line was sold as an identifiable (category) package physically, "so that people would go for them one after another," Marcil denied that the books were category romances: "We were going not after the category romance market but an upscale market of people who read best-sellers or Danielle Steele or any contemporary popular women's book, not just romances."

Thus, Avon encountered the same problems that afflicted Ballantine's Love and Life. "Avon marketed to the wrong market," said Marcil. "It wasn't supposed to go to the category market. It was for an upscale reader, for people who were picking up books that are on the best-seller list, people who are more sophisticated, a little more modern to contemporary in their thinking. I don't know what went wrong. Avon botched it."

Unlike Ballantine, Avon made no attempt to salvage its foundering line. Poor sales are the primary reason. Avon's decision to cancel rather than salvage the line was triggered by the results of a focus group survey, which revealed a mixed audience reaction to the line and its thematic triangle.[22] According to the survey, many readers found the heroine too self-centered. Some found the notion of sexual intimacy with more than one man "immoral." Others dismissed the books as not romantic. "We received an incredible amount of mail on Finding Mr. Right, both pro and con," recalled Coleen O'Shea, senior editor at Avon.²³

> The complaints were as varied as the writers. People either didn't like the packaging or they didn't like the stories, or they didn't like [the heroine] having two men, and so on. It really was a range of responses. On the other hand, we received material [from readers] that said, "Yah! It's terrific to see a woman who goes out and knows her own mind."
>
> It's really hard to pinpoint [the problem].... At this point in time we're casting a wary eye on the whole romance area. We're looking around to see what's happening, what's coming out, what's not working, what the market is leaning towards, what the readers are looking for, what we are hearing form our readers, and what we're hearing from readers of other lines.... We're just watching.

The content of Finding Mr. Right was certainly a source of difficulties. From the outset, readers had problems with the heroine's sexual escapades with two men. This is typically *verboten* in romantic fiction, at least until fairly recently. Even when the heroine is divorced (and thus sexually experienced enough to make comparisons regarding her present lover's bedroom abilities) the former husband is never brought into the picture; for example, the guidelines for Second Chance at Love stated that the heroine was to be "a mature young woman who has already had a serious love relationship [though] the first relationship has ended before the start of the novel." The readers' rejection of the heroines' choice between two sexually compatible males is cogently explained by Freud in *Civilization and Its Discontent*: "A love that does not discriminate seems to us to lose some of its value, since it does an injustice to its object."

There are two other reasons for the failure of Mr. Right. One is suggested by the ease with which Avon could extricate itself, having devoted little time or money to its development. The second was the less-than-wholehearted support from within that Cuddy expressed. This apparent disinterest seems to have affected the number of books published and the promotional efforts of Avon. Only one Mr. Right romance per month was released, far below the four to six titles per month released by other romance publishers. And while some promotional activities were undertaken, they were not as extensive as those of other romance houses. "We just had an informal agreement [regarding promotion with Avon]," said Denise Marcil, one of the line's co-packagers.

> As situations came up we'd say we'll match you dollar-for-dollar, or we'd say—looking at the budget—we'll take care of x, y, and z. And then we went to the romance conference in Sacramento to help launch the line, and for which Avon didn't pick up the tab. And we arranged with the person who was putting on the conference to give away a trip for two to Hawaii as part of the promotion, which [again] was totally on our own.

Give Me That Old-Time Love: The Christian Romance Market

Harlequin Romance and Presents and Silhouette's original Romance line were all sweet contemporary stories of love. Most of the historical lines of the late 1970s and early 1980s were sensual; Ecstasy and its imitators simply shifted the sensual to contemporary situations. Even Harlequin found it necessary to stay product-competitive and introduced Temptation in 1984 to compete with Dell's Ecstasy and Silhouette's Desire lines. But advance trade copies of the first Temptation book, *Spring Fancy*, received a huge thumbs-down from readers because the content contained "explicit sexual scenes, crude double-entendres, unlikely sexual euphemisms, and a brief allusion to necrophilia."[24] This response did not move Harlequin to return to sweetness; rather, it prompted the house to make a "few prudent editorial changes" to the version which subsequently appeared in retail outlets, and "lovemaking, while still rampant, no longer took place in a hearse."[25]

Sexuality in the first half of the 1980s replaced sensuality, and it appeared to many romance readers that the only difference among the titles they saw in book bins regarded the degree of sexuality: sex, more sex, and nothing but sex. The increased level of dissatisfaction with the apparently insatiable sexual appetites of romance heroines was beginning to be voiced by readers. Some typical reader comments[26]:

> I really like the books with humor or a gripping plot. It seems like some of the lines are just sex. What I want is romance. I'm no prude. I've been married twice. But there's too much beating you over the head with the sexual scenes. I want romance as fantasy.
>
> I'm no longer buying full lines. They spend so much time on the love scenes that there's hardly any story.
>
> The sexual relationship doesn't ring true. It's like it's required that within the first ten pages they're into a physical relationship whether they really know each other that well or not. They call them romances, but where's the romance?

The negative reaction to this growing emphasis on sex was especially pronounced among Christian women readers. They revolted against the sexual excessiveness in romances, and they wrote letters to Christian publishers asking them to publish romances with less sex in them, since secular publishers were not responding to their needs. These same publishers also heard from Christian romance authors who complained that they felt forced to depict "lust, not love."[27] One of the first to respond to Christian romance readers was Zondervan, and their successful entry into the market soon prompted a dozen other Christian publishers to follow suit with various evangelical series. Some, like Thomas

Nelson's Cherish, were never adequately marketed and soon folded, while others, such as Bethany House and Harvest House, continued to release Christian romances long after many secular lines collapsed.

Zondervan, a religious publishing house, introduced a line of Christian romances in April 1983 called Serenade Books. According to Anne Severance, then editor of the line, the concept for Serenade was originated at the editorial level and was an attempt to provide an alternative to the growing sexuality of the secular romance lines.[28]

Zondervan introduced a line of evangelical romances. This stemmed partly from perceived market demand, based on mail received from readers, and partly from the theological orientation of the house. Management, said Severance, believed "the secular publishers were portraying lust in the guise of love. We tried to turn that around and present the real truth, that there is far more to it [love] than two bodies meeting.... We try to go at it from the totality of the personality as opposed to just that one dimension. After all, God is love."

Love in the Serenade inspirationals revolves around two people who meet and share not only an emotional union with each other but a spiritual union with God. The basic plot was sketched in Zondervan's guidelines:

> In addition to the developing love relationship between the protagonists (one of whom must possess strong faith), there should be an underlying spiritual theme which evolves naturally from the storyline. As the relationship deepens, the weaker character should be brought to a realization of his/her need for or growth in Christ, and this problem is then resolved along with the dénouement of the plot. Since the practice of Christian principles provides the resources for resolving conflict, these principles can be easily integrated.

The guidelines offered no description of Christian principles, but the "evangelical spirit" was defined in a footnote. This footnote would provide little information for the aspiring non–Christian writer/reader, but it would be readily understood by any Christian.

> The evangelical spirit is the inward, passionate, and zealous personal commitment to Christian faith which is born out of deep conviction that faith in Jesus Christ, who died and was resurrected, produces life-changing affect in man and his [sic] culture. It is this Good News which gives meaning [to] life, has the power to heal broken relationships, to sustain marriages, and to resolve conflict. Christian characters, while they may be struggling to attain Christian maturity, should reflect the Christian lifestyle in dress, conduct, and philosophy.

Zondervan and many of the other larger religious publishers continued to release their evangelical romance lines throughout the 1980s. Monthly titles rose initially but soon peaked and then returned to a normal level. Zondervan, for example, launched with two monthly titles and then went to eight; after 1985, however, the norm dropped back to two to four titles per month. There was not enough demand to sustain the higher production figures, but enough to keep most houses afloat long after many secular houses disappeared.

The continued success of Christian publishers of the romance novels is largely the result of their specialized audience appeal and channeled distribution through Christian bookstores. Parallels with the Christian publisher's success with romances can be found in Glenn Carroll's study of the newspaper industry.[29] Carroll found that generalist (mass circulation) newspapers create the conditions for the success of specialized newspapers. He pointed out that large newspapers are characterized by strong economics of scale (e.g., low cost for mass advertising), which force them to contain a variety of news and features to appeal to a wide range of reader tastes. The net result, Walter Powell points out, is that "by pursuing large audiences, generalists neglect many specialized pockets of consumers."[30]

Carroll called the split into general and specialized markets "resource partitioning," with generalist and specialist organizations operating in entirely distinct resource spaces or partitions. Powell found the term "an apt characterization of the current state of the book trade," and suggested that "small publishers driven by social, religious, or political causes" are likely to develop in increasing numbers in the future because the large trade and college textbook publishers are less willing to take on books that have only modest sales potential due to economics of scale—they apparently share the increasing expectation about the number of copies that a book must sell in order to be considered successful.[31]

The successful entry by Christian romance publishers resulted from the prevailing generalism in the field; generalist romance publishers had neglected the Christian reader's religious orientation. We might extend and validate Carroll and Powell's respective discussion of specialist niches by observing how Zondervan, the specialist religious publisher, failed in its attempt to enter the secular market and how Silhouette, the secular publisher, likewise failed to bring specialist romance novels to the generalist market.

Seeing the boom in secular romances, Zondervan attempted to move beyond its own retail outlets in 1983–1984 and to enter the secular market with its specialist line. The house negotiated with B. Dalton and Waldenbooks to carry some of its romances on a trial basis. The two major chains agreed to place the line in selected outlets to determine sales potential. But sales never met the large retailers' expectations, and Zondervan gave up its attempt to penetrate the secular market. One problem with secular distribution of Christian romances involved confusion over where the book should be placed in stores. The secular outlets never really knew where to display them. "Mostly," Severance said, "we were in the romance section, [but] some of the time we were in the religious section and some of the time they were pulled out of the display dump [special romance racks] and placed on the shelves, and of course they get lost there." Another problem concerned the shopping habits of Christian book readers, who tend to frequent Christian bookstores for Christian-themed literature and neither looked for nor expected to find the books in the secular outlets.[32]

The problem with secular distribution of Christian romances was also discovered by Silhouette, which followed Zondervan's lead with a line called Inspirational Romances. Silhouette, like the religious publishers, had received mail critical of the high level of sexuality in romance novels. Seeing the increase in Christian-themed love stories in specialist religious markets, Silhouette perceived a "new" niche in the secular market. Management thought they could avoid the acceptance problems encountered by the religious houses, since Silhouette titles were already a familiar sight in secular outlets. In this they were correct, and Inspirational Romances soon appeared alongside the other Silhouette lines. Sales, however, remained flat. To its dismay, Silhouette discovered that Christian romance readers purchased their novels at religious book outlets; moreover, those women who might have otherwise objected to the level of sexuality in the secular romances, but who were not devoutly religious, were not enticed by the heavy Christian overtones of these novels. The line was killed after a little over a year on the market.[33]

Identifying a New Market: The Movement Toward Romance Mystery-Suspense[34]

During the peak of 1983, it appeared that the thirst of romance audiences was unquenchable. Few lines had yet to fold, though most publishers acknowledged that the market was overcrowded as a result of too many novels that were too thinly differentiated from each other. On the other hand, consumer reaction to Loveswept was often cited by those in the industry as proof that a late entry into the field, if well written and positioned, could still find its niche and succeed.

Since 1980, the romance market had grown beyond anyone's expectation. Publishers no longer considered romance readers to be a small, isolated segment of bored housewives. The pendulum had actually swung in the opposite direction, and by 1983 all women were perceived as potential romance readers.

The popular press played a critical role in portraying the ubiquity of what was labeled the "romance phenomenon of the 1980s." Most editors said this publicity made non-romance readers aware of the genre and prompted at least some women who had not read a romance novel to purchase one. Some became hooked; they found that their preconceptions of the novels as too sweet or characterized by insipid, out-of-date heroines were invalid. The extent to which media attention actually fostered reader growth is unknown, but the editors' belief that this attention was a factor in extending the romance audience led to the idea that the audience could be further increased by crossing over—marrying the romance genre with other genres, such as mysteries, science fiction, and westerns.

The genre most talked about by editors in 1983 as the perfect partner for Miss Romance was Mister Mystery. The couple had previously been married twenty years earlier in a former incarnation but had experienced irreconcilable differences and divorced. The new marriage was not to be a simple renewal of vows but one better suited to the new liberated heroine: foreboding gothic heroes frightening flustered young heroines in castle ruins would not play well in the 1980s.

The new paring of romances with mysteries, however, was not so much a revival of their original association as it was an attempt to take advantage of the current vogue in the mystery genre. *Remington Steele* (1982–1987) was a popular television show that appeared in the early 1980s—along with others, like *Hart to Hart* (1979–1984) and *Scarecrow and Mrs. King* (1983–1987)—and was frequently cited as a favorite of romance readers. Like other television mystery-dramas, *Remington Steele* had a strong heroine-hero romantic angle, which would be eclipsed by the romantic antagonism between Bruce Willis and Cybill Shepherd in the television series *Moonlighting* (1985–1989).[35]

The liberated heroine Laura (Stephanie Zimbalist) was caught in a man's world, struggling to identify herself and her career but not abashed at finding the right man. The scenario for the show is aptly conveyed by the heroine in the show's introduction:

> Try this for a deep, dark secret. The great detective, Remington Steele (Pierce Brosnan)—he doesn't exist. I invented him. Follow!
> I always loved excitement. So I studied, and apprenticed, and put my name on an office. But absolutely nobody knocked down my door. A female private investigator seems so—feminine. So I invented a superior. A decidedly masculine superior. Suddenly there were cases around the block. It was working like a charm. Until the day *he* walked in, with his blue eyes and mysterious past. And before I knew it he assumed Remington Steele's identity. Now I do the work and he takes the bows. It's a dangerous way to live, but as long as people buy it, *I* can get the job done. We never mix business with pleasure—well, almost never.

Each episode focused around some mystery and a client who required the services of the Remington Steele Detective Agency to solve it. The mystery was ultimately solved by the heroine, who somehow managed to look smart but still a little klutzy and vulnerable next to the hero—who reflected sartorial elegance, was immaculately groomed, and exuded a suave sophistication even under fire.

The romantic tête-à-tête in *Remington Steele* was not unlike that found in romance novels of the period. A typical example of the humor element of the show is captured in the opening of the episode "Signed, Steeled, & Delivered."

Laura is shown packing paperwork to take home over the weekend. Meanwhile, Steele's in his office detailing to his secretary how he intends to spend his Friday night: "Front row center for the Bolshoi, dinner at Andre's, a leisurely drive back to my place for...." At this point the secretary breaks in to announce that his date called and is sick.

Undaunted by this news, Steele immediately goes to Laura's office. "You look exhausted," he says to her and proposes a night on the town. Laura, in the best romantic heroine tradition, looks delighted and stutteringly says, "You and m-me, me on a date?" Then, guessing that she was a spur-of-the-moment substitute, Laura flings, "Tonight! You wait until 5:45 on a Friday night to ask me out. Let me guess. Sheila has mumps. Susan got hit by a car. Mary cancelled. Doris has diphtheria." Steele coolly admits the truth and asks, "What difference does it make, so long as you're free?" "What in the world," Laura angrily retorts, "makes you think that I'm free? It's Friday night. *Friday night!*" She grabs her bag and storms out of the office, goes home, and eats pizza.

Later that night, of course, she is "rescued" from home by Steele, who knocks on her door with a client in tow. Laura's hair is wrapped in a towel, and she looks less than glamorous in a plain, unalluring, white cotton robe. But before opening the door, she rushes to her bedroom closet and takes an evening gown out, placing it in plain sight in the living room. Steele and the disheveled client then are admitted, and the mystery begins.

Remington Steele and many of the other 1980s mystery-dramas had strong leading heroines. Along with the mystery, there was also a certain amount of humor. Judging by ratings, the mixture appealed to a wide range of viewers. Editors felt this romance-mystery-humor combination would help attract non-romance women readers if it could be applied to the romance genre.

There was a general feeling among romance editors in 1983 that "anything different will start attracting readers,"[36] which helps explain the movement toward romance-mysteries. At the same time, few editors envisioned that this subgenre would become a distinct line, mainly because "it's really tough to [write] romantic suspense; it has to be *awfully* good."[37] Thus, while almost all the romance houses considered filtering romance mystery-suspense novels into their line, few saw the return of these novels as a separate category; instead, they tended to agree with Carolyn Nichols's assessment[38]:

> The hunger is for stories that are like the old Mary Stewarts, those marvelous Dorothy Edens ... the one-of-a-kind books. You can't create a crop of authors who can write romantic suspense. You have to look for the individual authors with the right touch, the right combination. It's a book-by-book decision. And they're not category books. They go onto the general list as lead books.

The introduction of romance mysteries as a distinct line was, however, attempted by two publishers, Avon and Harlequin. Avon began soliciting romance-mysteries in mid–1983. Like most other houses, Avon editors did not envision the subgenre as a distinct line because, as Coleen O'Shea said, "these books are ... more complicated than a category romance, though they build on a category romance structure.... It's a double-pronged story, in which the heroine stands at the very centre of both the romance and mystery, and she must participate actively in each. This is what we're looking for now."[39] The perfect combination of content envisioned by Avon was 60 percent romance, 40 percent mystery.

Avon editors intended merely to add single titles to the houses' list. Management, however, overruled Page Cuddy's objection to category mystery-romances and pushed for the development of a line of novels in the emerging subgenre.[40] Management believed that romance lines continued to be a viable means of generating sales, and they replaced Finding Mr. Right with Velvet Glove.

Velvet Glove, like Mr. Right, was packaged by Denise Marcil and Meredith Bernstein. The problem with the new line was similar to those encountered with Mr. Right. Avon's editorial staff was not enthused with the category move, and management failed to allocate sufficient resources to back the line. Marcil's lament over the results of Velvet Glove echoed her complaint about Avon's handling of Mr. Right.[41]

> We were never pleased with the packaging that Avon did. I think that was one of the problems. I don't think it stood out as something that was particularly distinctive in terms of romantic suspense. They look more like romances [which, of course, they were].

Velvet Glove was launched in July 1984. The original publishing schedule called for one book per month, which didn't give them much presence on the bookshelves. To fix this, management increased the quota to two books per month, which made it more difficult for the packagers to obtain enough manuscripts, especially given the fact that few were writing in the subgenre since it was so new. Sales remained small, and in March 1985, Avon cut production back to one title per month. By the end of the year the line was killed, after the post–March inventory of Velvet Glove titles was exhausted. Carin Cohen, who replaced concept editor Coleen O'Shea, explained in early 1985 that while Avon initially received "great reader response" to start the line, "this was not being reflected in sales."[42] The dearth of sales, combined with the ease with which Avon could extract itself from yet another packager relationship, no doubt hastened the line's demise.

Velvet Glove represented a serious attempt to achieve the precarious balance of romance and mystery.[43] However, the line was never given time to build an audience, and the packaging, as Marcil pointed out, did not sufficiently distinguish the books from the potpourri of general romances on the bookshelf, which hindered the line's ability to attract women mystery readers.

Harlequin had more success with Intrigue, at least initially. Intrigue line consisted of attenuated mysteries: 80–20 romance-to-mystery-suspense. Harlequin introduced Intrigue the month after Velvet Glove appeared in retail outlets. The line launched with four books per month and continued thereafter with two books per month. Hilari Cohen and Debra Matteucci, co-editors for Intrigue, like many other editors, noted the parallels between the books and popular television mysteries and suspense-laden films, such as *Indiana Jones and the Temple of Doom* and *Romancing the Stone*.[44]

These television programs and feature films all had "an element of danger that is specifically excluded from the Harlequin Intrigue product."[45] Indeed, the initial Intrigue guidelines state: "There should be no murder, traditional kidnapping, drug-smuggling, or gun-running." Such an exclusionary clause would have prohibited any of the television programs and movies mentioned by the editors from being published as an Intrigue.

The line received such a poor initial response that *Romance Times* declared it dead shortly after its launch.[46] It didn't die, but it did not live up to expectations at the time, though it continues as a separate line today with modest success.[47] The line's initial survival in the 1980s may be attributed more to the Harlequin name than to the appeal of its content, and it seems that Intrigue was sustained by loyal Harlequin readers rather than, as originally intended, by slicing into the audience of women mystery fans.

Why was reader response initially so poor? For one thing, Intrigue, in fact, held little intrigue; as one reader complained, "the intensity isn't there."[48] The mystery/suspense element is likewise thin, about the level of any romance— just enough to keep a plot evolving so there is some reason for heroine and hero to be thrown together. The line specifically excluded murder, one of the main ingredients of a mystery-suspense novel, because, said the co-editors, they doubted that women romance readers could fantasize murder. In this, they seemed to be referring to blood and gore murder mysteries and ignoring the tameness with which good murder novelists deal with the subject. Dead bodies pepper the novels of popular mystery authors, such as Dick Francis and Sue Grafton, but the mystery, not the bodies, drives the plot.

Mysteries generally have a strong romantic element, typically 60:40 mystery-suspense to romance ratio. Single-title romance-mysteries have apparently done well by reversing this balance. Harlequin, by emphasizing the romantic (80 percent) over the mystery-suspense, essentially nullified the mystery-suspense aspect, which is why they pulled in existing Harlequin readers but didn't tap women mystery-suspense readers. The need to publish two complex stories per month and the failure of Harlequin editors in the 1980s to appreciate the ability of women to fantasize about murder on the same level as they are able to fantasize about romance effectively minimized expanding the subgenre as a viable line and capturing a share of the female audience who were not already Harlequin aficionados.

Conclusion

The major problem many newly launched lines encountered in the aftermath of Dell Ecstasy's success lies at the feet of management, who precipitously rushed to capitalize on what they suddenly saw as a lucrative market. Their response is understandable: often the first imitators, like Second Chance at Love, do well by slicing into the growing demand for the initial product. Management, however, didn't fully support the move into romances. First, management did not have sufficient respect for its editors by finding qualified people. This is due to management's continued denigrating attitude toward the genre. It was felt that sharp editorial work was not necessary for a line of books that were viewed as pretty much the same, so administrative assistants with limited editorial experience were simply promoted to editor. This relates to the second problem that management fostered, and that was to release too many books, saturating the market with romances that were poorly written on the assumption that the romance reader was not discriminating in her reading habits and just consumed these things en mass.

Perhaps the best illustration of these issues can be seen in developments at New American Library, which launched Rapture Romances specifically because it wanted a part of "the most profitable genre in publishing today." To that end, NAL promoted editorial assistant Robin Grunder, with her newly minted college degree, to the editorial ranks. With only one year of experience and now responsible for a line she had no background in, Grunder had to quickly assess the market. She correctly advised management that sensual, not sweet, contemporaries were the way to go. The problem was that she copied Ecstasy's success but overly relied on the sensual aspect of the novels, ignoring its other thematic dimensions. Rapture didn't take, and the line, with little support from management to position it, got lost among all the other novels then on the market. Management's solution to weak sales was simply to increase the number of titles, as if more books would make more money. This would later be recognized as a mistake by management, but by then the line was floundering. Grunder was let go. She was replaced by her young, inexperienced editorial assistant, who was charged with doing *something* to salvage the line. The new editor didn't want to go where the old editor had gone astray, so looked backward at the formerly successful (but now dated) bodice-rippers to get NAL into the romance game. She was terminated six months later, replaced by her young, inexperienced editorial assistant, who tried something else and introduced the "Adam" series of romances into the Rapture line, which told the story from the male point of view. She left a year later when the line was terminated. Variations of this scenario happened at other houses, sometimes with experienced editors.

Some mistakes were made because management and editorial were on different pages. Management at Ballantine conceived Love and Life as a category romance, but the editor, Pamela Strickler, who as an assistant under Nancy Coffey was more comfortable sifting mainstream novels, wanted to continue with longer books in the mainstream tradition. Forced to do category, she compromised by looking for shorter versions of mainstream romance novels. It didn't work. A similar disjunction took place between management and the packager for Avon's Finding Mr. Right and later with Avon's Velvet Glove.

The fault for the failure of many lines does not rest solely with management, however. Editors must bear their share of responsibility. Even some experienced editors misread the market.

The idea of a market niche is a valid one. It only works, however, if the path not taken by others is one the consumer wants. This worked nicely with Second Chance at Love, as we saw in the last chapter, and also with Christian romances in the 1980s, and to a somewhat lesser degree with Harlequin's Intrigue romance-mystery series. These niches continue to be vital today, and we will come back to them in Chapters 8 and 9, along with the potpourri of successful new lines filling market niches today. But before appraising the more insightful positioning of lines at the outset of the new millennium, it will first be instructive to ascertain why so many qualified editors failed to listen to the input they received that might have helped them niche their line more successfully.

Chapter 7

The Editorial Ear
Selective Listening

There is little doubt, surveying the thinly differentiated post–Ecstasy romance lines and talking with trade sources, that romances during the first half of the 1980s were patterned after Ecstasy's liberated contemporary novels. But so too were post–Avon romances of the late 1970s patterned after the content of Avon's sensual historical novels. The distinction is less a matter of kind than degree: barely a year passed before publishers responded to content innovations in the 1980s, while it was three years before anyone followed Avon's lead in the 1970s and another two years before Avon's sensual historical theme was widely adopted as the industry standard.

As management in the early 1980s became increasingly aware that romance novels were making money, and as more women filled editorial positions in the late 1970s, managers and editors were better able to respond to changes in the marketplace. Management's rush to cash in on Dell's Ecstasy sales success forced editors to move precipitously. Editors, however, were somewhat myopic in their evaluation of the field. Editors asked romance readers to tell them what they wanted from the novels of the 1980s, but by and large they turned a deaf ear to the input they solicited. Editors also tended to ignore the creative inclinations of seasoned writers, instead telling them what to write, thereby creating a new corps of complacent neophyte writers who provided soporific romances to an increasingly dissatisfied readership.

Sifting Reader Input

In the 1980s, editors were caught in the maelstrom of events: they were pressured to expedite the publication of new lines of romance novels and did not have the time to identify exactly who was the new romance consumer, let alone find out what she liked about the Ecstasy novels or her expectations for competing romance lines. Editors had to act, and their actions were generally predicated on their observation of competitor line sales. Their first major action was to move from sensual historical to sensual contemporary romances. The second decision was to increase the sensuality of contemporary romances. And finally, the editors concluded that the success of Second Chance at Love—which had found a niche by focusing on a specific theme in Ecstasy's content, divorced heroines—meant that they could make their own house's romances successful by further fine-tuning one of Ecstasy's multi-faceted story lines and adopting it as their leitmotif. These three major decisions were all made not by attuning themselves to the new market but by observing the competition. Limited input was sought from the reader, despite protestations that the reason decisions regarding content were made was based on listening to the romance consumer.

A major reason why editors stereotyped genre fans in the 1970s was their lack of interaction with romance readers. The editors sat behind their desks and didn't know, or seem to care, who read these books; after all, the books were released by the publisher only to round out their lists. Neither Coffey nor Stuart, nor even Nevler at Fawcett—the one house which continued to release sweet Regencies—based their editorial decisions on direct reader input but on their own tastes and preferences, while most late 1970s editors based their sensual historical selection on other houses' sales. This did not change in 1980–1981. When Karen Solem monitored Silhouette's launch, she did not concern herself with the readers; she was on the phone constantly to retailers, who let her know how the books were selling, not who bought them. Even Stephens, who went out and talked to the woman at Woolworth's, based the introduction of Ecstasy less on this input than on her feeling that the novels released by Candlelight were dated because they didn't appeal to her.

The editors of the post–Ecstasy 1980s lines actively sought reader input. They might have been satisfied with sales, but even in mass-market publishing, where category books are turned over in the retail outlets within thirty days, it could still be nine to twelve months before firm sales figures became available. By the time sales figures became available, the house would not only already have published a year's worth of books but have contracts for another six- to twelve-month supply. Editors couldn't wait for sales to trickle in; they needed input immediately so that plot adjustments, if required, could be expeditiously addressed. They actively solicited letters from readers, and lines carried notes such as the one below in the front of the book.

Dear Reader:

Silhouette Special Editions are an exciting new line [1982] of contemporary romances from Silhouette Books. Special Editions are written specifically for our readers who want a story with heightened romantic tension.

Special Editions have all the elements you've enjoyed in Silhouette Romances and *more*. These stories concentrate on romance in a longer, more realistic and sophisticated way, and they feature greater sensual detail.

I hope you enjoy this book and all the wonderful romances from Silhouette. We welcome any suggestions or comments and invite you to write us at the address below.

Input was almost immediately forthcoming, and it was invariably pleasing to the editors.

Those who write regarding product quality typically represent the extreme ends of the consumer spectrum: the highly satisfied or the high dissatisfied. Most people respond in a quieter, less direct, but nonetheless effective manner, either by purchasing the product again or ceasing to use it. Letters to those who produce goods are seldom representative of consumer likes and dislikes, in part because input is often carefully sifted by the recipient of the letter.

In his seminal study of the selection of content for television news programs and weekly newsmagazines, Herbert Gans found that the majority of letters sent to the network or magazine were critical.[1] They were often fired off by conservatives who perceived a liberal bias in the treatment of a specific story; liberals, or those who agreed with the stories' point of view, were less likely to respond. Among letters to romance publishers, the opposite pattern occurred. The majority of letters were favorable, with an abundance of praise for the new "liberated" heroine and her thoroughly-modern-Millie willingness to experience meaningful sexual relations outside the bonds of matrimony. Certainly one reason for the positive feedback was that the printed solicitation gave romance readers an opportunity to praise the genre of their preference. In addition, the carefully couched language of the editorial request, with its abundance of superlative adjectives ("exciting new line," "written specifically for our readers," "heightened romantic tension," etc.), tended to foster positive reader response.

Despite the contrasting responses of letter writers to the news media and letter writers to romance publishers, the results they produced were the same. The editors of neither media form were influenced by audience input. News editors, concluded Gans, "had a vague image of the audience [and] paid little attention to it; instead, they filmed and wrote for their superiors and for themselves, assuming ... that what interested them would interest the audience."[2] This was also the recurring assumption by romance editors, most of whom, like Nancy Coffey, believed, "If I like it, they [readers] will, too."

Their line position decision already made, romance editors did little more than nod sagely with satisfaction at the letters received that agreed with them. Critical letters were ignored, in much the same way that Gans found news editors responded to unfavorable comments: "These [crucial] letters can be disregarded because most journalists believed the writers to be unrepresentative of the total audience and therefore need not be taken seriously."[3] Yet, as both Gans and this author discovered in the present study, when editors received praise from their audience, these letters suddenly were regarded as perceptive and representative of the public's view. The fact that most letters to romance editors were positive led may editors to conclude they knew what they were doing. Kate Duffy at Pocket Books comments on the input: "When Silhouette first began [the readers] weren't saying anything at all; they [consumers] weren't encouraged to say what they wanted. As editor-in-chief, I wanted to hear, and asked for input in the front of the books. A lot said they liked the books."[4]

The "lot" who liked the new romance novels of the 1980s appears to be demographically distinct from the "few" who didn't, at least in the early years of the sensual contemporary subgenre. The dichotomy is perhaps best illustrated by the age split observed at a Harlequin Party.

Throughout the 1980s, starting in 1979, Harlequin hosted four to six "Harlequin Parties" every year in different cities across the United States. The parties were advertised in advance in the local newspaper. Harlequin readers could request an invitation by sending their name to the corporate headquarters. From the thousands who responded, one to two hundred were invited to these luncheons, which featured a Harlequin author and other members of Harlequin's team. The parties were billed as a sort of thank-you to loyal Harlequin readers; in fact, they were more of a public relations endeavor, since media coverage was always extensive in the cities in which the parties were given.

In 1983, I attended a Harlequin Party that was held in Nashville, Tennessee.[5] After the formal noon luncheon presentation by author Flora Kidd, who talked of her books and how she came to be published by Harlequin, Harlequin's editorial vice president, Fred Kerner, spoke on "how you too can be a published Harlequin author." In the discussion from the floor that followed, the subject of sex in romance novels was raised. One elderly, sixty-something-year-old woman objected to any detailed discussion on this topic and praised Harlequin for its adherence to "decency." She was applauded by other older women in the audience, who similarly seemed drawn to the Romance and Presents line. There were, however, murmurs of dissent heard from young women scattered throughout the dining room, such as "Oh, come on!" and "Join the world." Their comments would suggest that they were drawn to Harlequin's more risqué Superromance line.

The younger, twenty- to thirty-year-old woman of the late 1970s and early 1980s accepted premarital sexual relations as a matter of course; as one young personal romance acquaintance somewhat crudely, but nonetheless succinctly, put it, "People fuck!" The sixty-five-plus 1980s woman was brought up in another era—an era when, as Carol Trevor Williams put it, "a man was a man and a woman a housewife," and sex before marriage was a sin.[6] These women had a different slant on sexuality and were more likely to concur with the aging, displaced queen of romances, Barbara Cartland, when she announced at a 1983 romance conference in New York that romance novels should depict "pure love," and sex of any kind was "disgusting and very, very immoral."[7]

In one of the few public-domain surveys of romance readers conducted in 1983, younger, under-thirty readers were found to be more willing to accept the sensuality of 1980s romances: just shy of eighty percent (78.8 percent) said the amount of sex depicted in romance novels was "about right." Only 10.6 percent said they would like to see more sexuality.[8] By and large, the group of women readers between the ages of thirty and sixty-four found the treatment of sex in romances "about right"; a quarter of the respondents, distributed almost evenly across age groups, said that there was too much sex in the novels, and most of these women were alluding to the persistent but decreasingly prevalent rape themes of the sensual historicals.

Since the younger readers in the study were the most receptive to sensuality in romances, and since two-thirds of the editors during the 1980s were also thirty years of age or younger, it is not surprising that most editors of the day felt the amount of sexual activity in the novels was appropriate, if not inadequate. Letters that expressed divergent opinions were often dismissed out of hand: they were ostensibly sent by "old ladies," who obviously didn't appreciate the brave new world the young editors inhabited, or they were younger women "out of touch" with the world after the sexual revolution of the 1970s. The initial complaint about the level of sexuality in romance novels eventually swelled to a roar of protest by mid-decade, not so much because readers objected to sexual description but because that was often the primary theme of the novels. In 1982–1983, however, when the new lines for the coming year were being developed, it seemed to many editors that sex sold, and input from readers tended to reinforce this, though the readers were largely applauding the move to sexuality from the sweets. It was only logical, therefore, that if a line with sexuality was selling well, then a competitive line should sell even better if the sexual bar was raised. As a result, the market was deluged with new sensual lines by the middle of the 1980s that tended to overemphasize the sexual, to the subordination of plot. The editors were not assessing reader comments critically; they were simply hearing what they wanted to hear. They soon discovered, however, that sex simply for the sake of titillation did not sell; at least it didn't sell when it was presented in poorly written books without plots.

The Search for Authors

By and large, romance writers come from the ranks of romance readers, who tend to be white, middle-class, married females thirty to forty-five years old, college graduates, and relatively affluent.[9] These characteristics remain relatively constant today, though with the advent of more African American romances between 1990 and 2010, there are naturally more African American female authors.

Money is certainly one reason why women turn to writing romances, and tales of riches to be made in the romance field prompted many women who previously might have only flirted with the idea of writing a romance to sit down and pen one. The booming romance market of the day also encouraged an indeterminate number of neophyte novelists to look toward this ostensibly lucrative field. Their interest was solely pecuniary and they had limited familiarity with the genre.

At one time or another, most fiction readers (regardless of genre) have probably toyed with the idea of writing a novel. More often than not this is likely to occur when one reads a disappointing book and thinks, "I can do better than that." The readers' imagination then leaps to six-figure incomes and million-copy sales generated by the luminaries in the field. This is often the only monetary point of reference the would-be author has. Few readers realize how little remuneration is actually generated by writing, and most would have been surprised to learn that the median year's income of a full-time, committed writer around this time (1979) was only $11,000 a year,[10] which would be comparable to $35,000 today (2013), a respectable income but nothing earth-shaking.

Most women who take up the romance pen might strive to achieve Kathleen Woodiwiss's or Nora Roberts's level of success, but few realistically expect to duplicate their fame and fortune. Their monetary goals are more modest. Employed women, like Rosemary Rogers in the early 1970s, initially seek only to supplement their meager salaries, which continue, even at the outset of the new millennium, to remain substantially below those of their male counterparts. Similarly, the housewife who tries her hand at romance writing does not anticipate displacing her husband as the primary contribution to the family income, but only to add to that income.

It should be remembered that while eighty-plus percent of all women are employed today, it was not until 1979 that, for the first time, there were more women working full-time (50.8 percent) than non-working.[11] It should not be surprising, then, that the majority of female romance writers in the 1980s, both published and aspiring, were married women with at least one child, often of preschool age, who elected to stay home and raise their children. They may have been housewives, but they did not fit the "brainless" stereotype of the housewife; indeed, the romance reader of the 1980s was likely to have a college education and to participate in a wider range of cultural activities.[12] Given her educational attainment, the monotony of housekeeping was not likely to fulfill her. The married woman romance reader was likely to be transformed into a writer. "I have a friend in a writing group," a budding romance author told Catherine Kirkland, who did a study of published and aspiring romance writers in the first half of the 1980s,[13]

> and she told me about Barbara and how much of an advance she'd gotten for writing her first book. I knew I could do it; my husband used to always tease me and say, "You should write those." But I didn't know how, or where to go—how even to begin. It was just a thought that was always there. But when I heard that Barbara had gotten a $6,000 advance, and at the time I was wondering what I was gonna do when my youngest son went to first grade, I thought, "That's it. I'm gonna do that." My husband travels a great deal and I'm alone with the kids, and I don't want to go back into newspaper work because I knew that it would take me away from home even more, and I thought that the kids really needed one of us there. So I was trying to think of something I could do in my home, basically. And I thought, "This is perfect! That's it! I know I can do it!"

Kirkland's reader-writing typology can be broken into two basic classifications: those entering the genre without any real interest in it, and those who are avid readers and who want to contribute something to the genre.

The first, pecuniary-motivated writer can be broken into two subgroups. One writes solely for the money. There were plenty of these, lured by stories in the media about the popularity of romance novels in the 1980s. The other group is those women with general literary ambitions, who entered the romance field though the "back door." She has "great" literary pretensions but has not succeeded in getting one of her masterpieces published; she sees romances as a means of entry into the publishing world. This individual tends to have a surprisingly deprecating attitude toward the romance genre and an inflated opinion of her own writing talent. Neither group are serious romance writers and are easily spotted by the serious reader-writer. "You could hand me a book and I could guess whether or not the writer really enjoyed romance," one reader-writer in Kirkland's study said. "You have to like the fantasy yourself before you can recreate it on paper. And there's a certain flatness to the books in which all the pieces may be there, but it lacks spark."

The other group of aspiring authors is devoted romance readers. They are conscious of the financial rewards, but are motivated as much by the desire to contribute to the genre—they are driven to create. These women, in the "I can too" tradition, are stimulated to write by their reactions to specific stories, hoping either to emulate a well-written book, or, more often, to improve on a poorly written novel. Disappointment with a story, Kirkland found, is the result of an author's failure to arouse specific emotions in the reader that she expects and anticipates. Kirkland quoted two writers to show how this act of mental rewriting transforms a reader into a writer as she reads an unsatisfying novel. Both have subsequently gone on to be best-selling romance authors, and the first one had been writing romances for seven years before a manuscript was finally accepted[14]:

> I think [the reason I became an author] was mostly [that] the stories never quite went the way I wanted them to and I started rewriting them in my head. I had that feeling that I could do it, that I could write a more satisfying story than what I was reading.
>
> And then I found myself … putting words in. I was two pages ahead. And of course it never came out the way I thought it was going to. But I kept doing the situation myself, I kept evolving the plot. And I thought, what the heck; if I'm going to be doing this, I'll do it myself, give it a whirl.

The surge in romance publishing in the early to mid–1980s opened the doors to both the disinterested and the serious romance writer. Editors, hungry for manuscripts, read—and often accepted—anything they could get their hands on. Authors who wrote purely for crass financial gain made a quick buck, and many editors admitted taking bad manuscripts simply to fill the monthly quota that management had arbitrarily set. Authors of dubious talent sought to grab their fifteen minutes of fame by turning to a host of quick-read how-to-books for guidance in romance writing, such as *Love's Leading Ladies* (1982), *Write a Romance and Get It Published* (1983), *Writing Romance Fiction—For Love and Money* (1983), *You Can Write a Romance! And Get It Published!* (1983), *Your First Romance* (1983), and *The Romance Writers' Phrase Book* (1983). Longtime romance readers didn't need to be told about nuances of style, content and character development. They did make use of these how-to books, but for an altogether different reason.

The world of publishing is shrouded in mystery to most would-be writers. Publishers seem to prefer things that way and make little attempt to enlighten the uninitiated. They tend to believe that determined, committed writers will unravel the secrets of manuscript submission. By keeping their world close to their chest, they avoid being deluged by a host of untalented amateur writers. Maxwell Perkins, for example, the dean of American editors (who discovered Fitzgerald, Hemingway, and Wolfe, to name but three) gave a rare interview in the 1940s; afterwards, he not only was overwhelmed by bad manuscripts, but because he said in the interview that "one can tell as much by seeing an author as by reading the manuscript," he was besieged by would-be authors queuing up in front of his office demanding to be seen.[15]

The need to fill their romance lists brought many editors out from behind their desks to actively solicit material. As might be expected, they received a lot of material from people who didn't know anything about the genre. Besides some "absolutely terrible stuff" that went nowhere, there was a flood of extremely mediocre material, some of which was filtered into a house's line simply to meet production quotas. There were also some treasures, and more than a few good romance novelists were discovered.

The vagaries of the submission process can be illustrated anecdotally by the response of one aspiring author to an article on romance publishing that appeared in *Nashville* magazine by this author; the feature-length article addressed the romance revolution taking place in the mid–1980s.[16] A middle-aged woman who read the article called me, wanting to know how she could get a romance published. The woman read romances in moderate amounts and wanted to write a teen romance because she knew the age group well, having taught junior high for fifteen-plus years. She was no longer teaching because of a disability but wanted something constructive to do with her time; she also readily admitted that she was not averse to supplementing her meager disability income. She did not ask questions about romance content, bur rather wanted to know pragmatics surrounding manuscript submission. The discussion revolved around the details of manuscript preparation: margins, page length, sample chapters, a book outline or synopsis, a cover letter of introduction to the editor, and so forth. The aspiring writer called back a number of times over the next few months to clarify these points and later, after her first novel was accepted, phoned to talk about her expectations regarding print runs, royalties, and such. She has since written regularly for the teen romance market and has branched out into the general romance field.

For the serious reader-turned-writer, the booming romance market of the 1980s was a blessing in disguise. On the one hand, it opened the gates to many writers who previously had only toyed with the idea of writing a romance novel, and some of these authors have gone on to gain renown within the field and earn a decent income from their writings. On the other hand, readers and writers alike sometimes felt shortchanged: (1) editors had less and less time to spend polishing the writing of authors, and (2) authors were increasingly dissatisfied with the rigid editorial guidelines.

Not Enough Time in the Day

Initially, romance editors found themselves following the tradition of mainstream editors. They actively sought out and encouraged new talent. They did not merely accept or reject manuscripts but spent considerable time working with promising authors to help them polish their novels. Many authors in the early boom years received this kind of treatment and, like Jan Cunningham (a.k.a. Chelsey Forrest), sincerely appreciated it[17]:

> "The writing was fun," Jan says, "but the waiting was hard. It took Silhouette only a month to respond, but as every writer knows, even a month can seem endless." It was for Jan, who checked her mailbox daily. "I didn't know what they'd say," she says.... "It was very, very difficult—the waiting, I mean."
>
> Then she received an answer. "I couldn't believe it," she smiled. "I was thrilled."
>
> There were some changes suggested, however. Mostly, fleshing out her characters. For a while she was on the phone regularly with her editor in New York, working things through. "They were absolutely wonderful," she says. "It's like the old kind of publishing, where you work real close with your editor. I doubt if many first [non-romance] novelists get that kind of help."

The amount of editorial help writers received declined precipitously with raised production quotas. Even the best authors suffered when editors were forced to go from two to four to six and even eight books a month with no corresponding increase in editorial staff. The decline in quality of writing, widely lamented by readers by 1984, was primarily the result of the editors' inability to keep up with management's pressure to publish more and more books. Editors no longer had the time even to proofread the novels going to press, let alone polish the works of new writers. Kirkland cites one author's lament[18]:

> At one point in our book, we had a passage where the heroine turned to the hero and said, "The Attorney General [instead of Surgeon General] said that smoking is dangerous to your health." That was our slip, but nobody caught it. I only hope that since we put a lot of humor in the book and the hero and heroine are forever saying funny things to one another, that the reader will see that as being funny. The big mistake they made in the book was I said that the population of this city in Brazil was 600,000 and somehow that came out to 6,000,000 in the editing process. I think that since these books are read in forty-five minutes, nobody much cares, but I care. Mistakes can go through. You don't see the galleys, which is why mistakes are made. Somewhere along the line the copy editor gets hold of them and they go back to the editor, and she has twenty books to look at, so you know ...

Mistakes that normally would be caught by editors increasingly found their way into print, and the poor quality of many of the books raised the ire of consumers, who began to turn away from romance lines in search of specific authors on whom they knew they could depend. This was as much of a problem as the sexuality, both of which hastened the demise of many lines by mid-decade.

The Learning Process

Kirkland, in her study of the writer, found that most published authors did not even mention editorial guidelines in their discussion of the writing process. The few that did bring up the subject emphatically dismissed them[19]:

> "I don't read tipsheets," said one prolific romance author. "I've looked over some that [a friend] has received. I was very amused by them. I thought, 'Oh, Lord, if I'd read this before I started, I never would have done it.' It was really confining. NO, I don't read tipsheets and I don't seek out advice because I think it's going to inhibit my writing..."
>
> "I write the same story," another writer of category romances said. "I don't write according to what they [editors] want. I write … exactly what I like to read."

The animosity toward tipsheets was less evident in 1981–1982 than later. The newly launched Ecstasy novels were different from predecessor romances, and the editors rightly felt writers needed guidance in order to supply novels. The internal decision by Dell's staff to release one Ecstasy per month forced Stephens to devise guidelines, since she needed authors and few were yet familiar enough with the new subgenre to provide her with novels. Editors of other lines found guidelines even more necessary, since they were looking for specific themes to fit their pre-established market position and had *no* books on the market. Thus, there was no time, as there had been in the post–Avon years, for authors to grasp nuances of the new subgenre and submit manuscripts as they naturally evolved from the reading process.

In late 1980, only one book was published in the new sensual, liberated contemporary subgenre. By late 1983, more than 150 romances a month were rolling off the presses. By then, guidelines were no longer necessary as the sensual liberated theme had become established and standardized. Other than Harlequin and Silhouette, the only successful contemporary romance line to launch between 1983 and 1984 was Bantam's Loveswept. The line was well received by the readers, and editors at other houses generally applauded editor Nichols's absence of guidelines amid the guideline craze. Nichols could do away with guidelines for Loveswept because she picked only the best authors, those who knew what constituted a good story in the liberated contemporary format. In addition, by 1983 the majority of writers were now familiar with the subgenre; in 1981, when Nichols launched Second Chance at Love, this was not the case, and Second Chance, Ecstasy's first major competitor, had the most detailed and stringent guidelines of all the romance lines.

Editors of other lines went to guidelines because they needed books in a new format that was otherwise not available and had little time to wait for "the right" manuscript to cross their desks. Most lines that remained by mid-decade—and there weren't that many—followed Loveswept's lead and abandoned guidelines altogether. They could do this for two basic reasons. On the editorial side, the editors had learned what readers wanted by observing successes and failures of other lines, and they used this hard-learned knowledge to judge manuscripts. On the writer side, writers no longer needed the guidelines of the early years because, except for the neophyte writers who were never committed to the genre in the first place (and who needed the guidelines because they didn't read the books), romance aficionados now knew what they liked, and if they decided to pick up the romance pen, they could simply look to the existing line to ascertain thematic variations. The "guidelines" that now exist, with a few exceptions that will be examined in subsequent chapters, have reverted to very general suggestions pertaining to manuscript submissions.

Conclusion

The customer was the buzzword of the 1980s romance revolution: listening to her wants, meeting her needs. There was precious little listening, however, which explains why so many lines failed. Even the ones that succeeded were predicated more on the editor's "feelings" than on consumer input.

When Silhouette launched, Karen Solem fretted. She was on the phone constantly to try to evaluate how the books were faring. Her input was solicited almost exclusively from retail outlets. Even Vivian Stephens, who walked across the street to Woolworth's to see what the consumer was purchasing, only asked one woman why she was buying the novel she was purchasing and what she thought of Dell's Candlelight line. One woman! And that person confirmed Stephens's already-formed opinion that the Candlelight line was dated and needed to be updated to account for contemporary tastes. Still, that's one consumer more than Carolyn Nicholas at Second Chance at Love asked. And while others touted that they were desperately seeking consumer input on likes and dislikes, few listened.

The deaf editorial ear is fairly typical and has been found in a wide range of consumer-orientated organizations. It seems that people just want confirmation that their choice is correct and will ignore countervailing input in favor of that which confirms their taste preference. This is even more applicable in publishing, where a manuscript's fate depends almost exclusively on the editor's assessment of its value.

The biggest mistake some of the post–Ecstasy lines made was to overaccentuate the sensual. Heightened sensuality was, in fact, what Stephens was looking for at Dell. The fact that she was fortunate to find this mixed with a multiplicity of other socially relevant themes helped make Ecstasy the success it was. Some lines, notably Second Chance at Love and later Loveswept, kept the sensual aspect but made sure they incorporated other elements in the book. Most of those that failed simply notched the sexuality to the next level, so much so that one sexual escapade seemed to follow another without any romantic tension. By mid-decade, readers were turning their backs on these novels, even those who had no problem with sexuality in the novel as long as it was a dimension of the romantic theme. Authors themselves sometimes felt pressured by editors to include more sexuality than they were comfortable with. Zondervan responded to both reader and author complaints by launching Serenade, a Christian line of books. This might at first appear as if Zondervan staff was listening, but in reality they were doing what everyone else was: surveying the competition and looking for their niche. Their niche was already predetermined—they are a religious publishing house, so it was a natural fit to capitalize on the romance "craze" by launching a line of Christian romances. Other Christian lines followed but entered the business much as subsequent secular lines did, with little knowledge of the romance field or halfheartedly. Like many post–Ecstasy lines, late-entry Christian romance imprints met with a similar fate; most were gone or had greatly reduced print runs by the end of the 1980s.

The guidelines Vivian Stephens formulated for Ecstasy were very general. They became much more elaborate with Second Chance. Despite the widespread criticism of these guidelines, Second Chance had to formulate details to meet the editor's expectations since there were few books on the market that she could direct would-be authors to read and emulate. When Nichols launched Loveswept the following year, guidelines were no longer necessary, the new liberated romance format being well established in the year since she had launched Second Chance. Others relied more extensively on the guidelines, but since they did not allow much deviation, many authors felt stymied. The guidelines also prevented the editors of these category romances from looking outside the box at potentially new themes. The guidelines didn't just lock the author in; they locked the editor in.

By the time guidelines were abandoned mid-decade, it was too late to save many of the floundering category lines. The same cycle took place with many Christian houses entering the market after Zondervan in the second half of the 1980s. Zondervan's guidelines were very general, in the same broad style as Ecstasy when it launched. Subsequent Christian houses imposed more rigid guidelines, with similar ill-fated results. The so-called romance revolution was close to over for most secular publishers by the mid–1980s; it was sustained through the late 1980s by the entry of Christian romance publishers, most of whom had a brief fling before greatly reducing production or discontinuing their line by the close of the decade.

Romance publishing in the aftermath of the 1980s, both secular and Christian, continues to thrive. Romance publishing doesn't get the same public attention today as it did in the 1980s. The field is not as turbulent, even if it is more vibrant than ever. Most romance publishers today have settled into comfortable niches that provide a wide range of thematically differentiated products. These romance niches, and how they were identified and developed, are the subject of the next few chapters.

Chapter 8

Alive and Kicking
Harlequin Regains
Market Supremacy

The purchase of Silhouette by Harlequin in 1984 ensured the return of Harlequin to the supremacy of the romance market since these two giants vied with one another for domination of the industry. The resurgence of Harlequin to supremacy over the market was augmented by the fallout of smaller competitive lines, which began to occur as early as 1983–1984 and which would accelerate through the remainder of the decade, by which time many publishers of romances in the United States had thrown in the towel and, once again, acceded dominance over the romance market to Harlequin. This does not mean American publishers did not continue to produce romance novels; romances were just not pushed to the degree they were in the late 1970s and early 1980s. It was not a return to the placid 1960s through mid–1970s, however, when few publishers in the United States even bothered with the genre. Publishers in the 1990s became more aware of Harlequin and Silhouette's financial successes and were monitoring the market more closely to ascertain their competitive niche—finding an area left vacant by Harlequin and tapping it, rather than trying to go head-to-head thematically with Harlequin. And Harlequin, less complacent than it had been earlier, was similarly monitoring the market more astutely to ensure that either (1) they had socially relevant thematic lines positioned before competing houses did, or (2) they were quick to capitalize on the success of newly launched competitive lines by launching their own.

The contemporary history of Harlequin begins in the 1980s with the formation of Silhouette books, which prompted Harlequin to survey the market more closely and ensure new, Silhouette-competitive lines. Staying line-competitive has been their mantra ever since. The story of Harlequin today is the story of its position vis-à-vis competitive houses. Heuristically, however, it is more illustrative to focus on Harlequin in this chapter and then, in the next, the competition, before appraising the impact of all these developments on the market in Chapter 10. This avoids jumping back and forth between lines at different houses and getting lost in just who did what when. These competitive lines are, of course, incorporated into this section; they are just not fleshed out until the next chapter. It is simply a matter of emphasis. The rationale for this emphasis can be appreciated in Table 8.1, which illustrates the complexity of line developments at Harlequin without interweaving all the non–Harlequin lines into this matrix.

Line Development at Harlequin/Silhouette

Harlequin Romance
1961*/1964†–present
↑
Silhouette Romance
5/1980–1/2007

Harlequin Presents
5/1973–present

Harlequin Mystique
8/1977–2/1982

Mills & Boon Masquerade
9/1977–9/1993
↓
Mills & Boon Legacy of Love → Harlequin Historical
10/1993–6/1996   7/1988–present

Mills & Boon Doctor Nurse Romances
11/1977–7/1989
↓
Mills & Boon Medical Romances+
8/1989–12/2000
↓
Harlequin Medical Romance
1/2001–present

Gold Eagle
1980–present

---

* 1961: Imprint name débuts.
† 1964: First year dedicated to romance novels.
+ Mills & Boon Medical Romances were re-titled Mills & Boon Love on Call between 1993 and 1995 before reverting back to Mills & Boon Medical Romances in 1996.
The specific month some lines were launched or discontinued is not always clear. In those cases only the year is specified.

Harlequin Superromance
6/1980–present

Silhouette First Love
10/1981–5/1987
↓
Silhouette Crosswinds
6/1987–10/1988

Silhouette Desire
6/1982–7/2011
↓
Harlequin Desire
8/2011–present

Silhouette Special Edition
2/1982–2/2011
↓
Harlequin Special Edition
4/2011-present

Silhouette Intimate Moments
6/1983–1/2007
↓
Silhouette Romantic Suspense
2/2007–3/2011
↓
Harlequin Romantic Suspense
4/2011–present

Harlequin American Romance
4/1983–present

Silhouette Inspirational
2/1984–12/1984

Harlequin Temptation
3/1984–6/2005
↓
Blaze
9/2001–present

Harlequin Intrigue
8/1984–present

Worldwide Library
1986–1988

Silhouette Shadows
3/1993–7/1996

8. Alive and Kicking

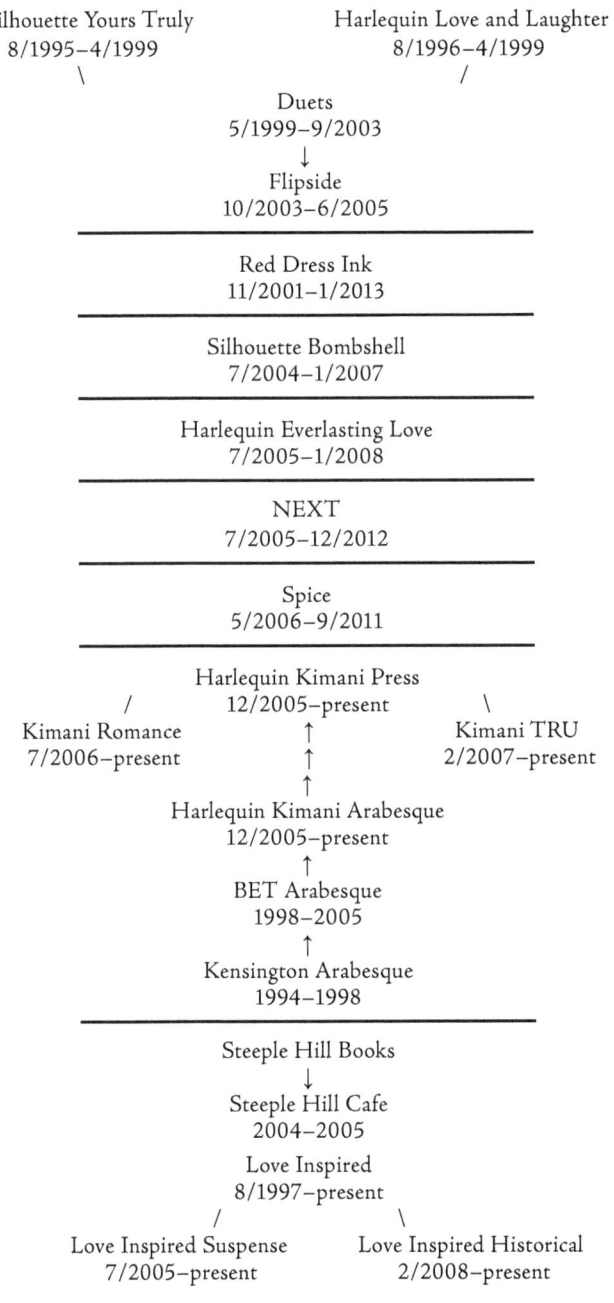

Heartsong Presents 10/2012–present
Silhouette Nocturne 10/2006–11/2010 ↓ Harlequin Nocturne 12/2010–present
Harlequin NASCAR 2/2007–12/2010
Harlequin Teen 7/2009–present
Carina Press 2/2011–present
Harlequin Heartwarming 4/2011–present
Harlequin Kiss 2/2013–present

The story of Harlequin today begins with newcomer David Galloway, who took the helm from W. Lawrence Heisey in 1983. Heisey grew the firm during the formidable 1970s, and his significant contributions were sketched in Chapter 3. It is apropos that we begin with this transition, because it marks the shift in the company from a fly-by-the-seat-of-your-pants upstart to a corporate giant, and the rules change, or at least the way of doing business changes, when a growth organization transitions to a major corporation.

The Changing of the Guard

Torstar is a Canadian newspaper conglomerate. Its media group owns a wide range of newspapers across Canada, but its flagship paper is the *Toronto Star*. Torstar purchased controlling interest (52.5 percent) in Harlequin in 1975 and got an incredible bargain: shares sold for $3.67. Torstar increased its holding by 17 percent in 1980 ($17 per share) and the following year paid $30 per share for the remaining shares. Torstar received a good return on its investment: Harlequin pumped millions into Torstar's bottom line during the newspaper wars in Canada during the 1990s.

Harlequin was already moving toward a more complex organizational structure with its purchase of Mills & Boon in the early 1970s and its subsequent international expansion in the mid-to-late 1970s. Torstar simply raised the organizational bar at Harlequin. Harlequin demanded, for example, that Mills & Boon stop publishing authors who were not selling and held the writers more rigidly to their contracts. They "purged," according to Dixon, some English authors in 1994 and replaced them with Silhouette authors who were selling much better.[1] The driving reason for this, according to Dixon, is because Torstar followed a "capitalist ideology," while in the same breath acknowledging that Mills & Boon's financial and political ideology are also capitalistic. Dixon, a writer and copy editor with Mills & Boon, nostalgically misses the personal quality Boons brought to the firm. This is no doubt true. Large firms are more impersonal. The eminent organizational sociologist Max Weber would hold that the impersonality of modern corporations is a good thing because business decisions should not be made on personal likes and dislikes. Indeed, Dixon gives a number of instances where Alan Boon's paternalism was not always in the best interest of the company. Large, in itself, is not necessarily bad.

New organizations, especially large corporate entities, bring changes. They are not all negative, as Dixon admits: for one thing, authors at Mills & Boon, for the first time in the firm's history, were given regular updates of their sales figures. These changes also involve new people. David Galloway took the helm at Harlequin in 1983 and was its chief executive officer until 1988, when he was promoted to head the Torstar Corporation (1988–2002). He was followed at Harlequin by Brian Hickey (1988–2001), who was succeeded by Donna Hayes (2002–2013), the first woman to head Harlequin and the first to come from a publishing rather than a marketing background. She was followed by Craig Swinwood in 2014. Swinwood, like Hayes, has a publishing background and had worked at Harlequin in various capacities before becoming its CEO. A brief history of each of these executives is sketched before detailing some of the developments that took place under their tutelage in subsequent sections of this chapter. These executives, like most corporate executives in large-scale contemporary organizations, were less hands-on than Heisey or the Boons in overseeing line developments: when Heisey took the helm at Harlequin in 1971, sales were $7.9 million[2]; when he retired as chairman in 1989, Harlequin sales topped $300 million.[3] At the close of the first decade of the new millennium (2010), sales were approaching half a billion dollars ($468 million).[4]

Bureaucratic organizations tend to delegate specialists within the organization to ensure developments in their area. This is because it is impossible for one person to oversee the potpourri of departments in a large-scale organization, let alone one that has a strong international presence. The Harlequin line flow chart on pages 141–44 shows the complexity of book divisions and line developments at Harlequin: each book division (e.g., Kimani Press, HQN,

MIRA) or free-standing line (Presents, American Romances) will have an editorial director or a senior editor, who, in turn, supervises an editor and any number of associate/assistant editors, depending on the number of books they are responsible for releasing. There were twelve imprints and twenty-three lines listed on the Harlequin site in 2014, with acquisitions editors in Toronto, New York, and London. Allowing just one editor and one assistant and associate editor for each line, there would be over a hundred editorial personnel overseeing fiction, and this is without taking into account all the other areas that keep Harlequin functioning, such as its international editorial staff, marketing personnel, and a burgeoning computer workforce that monitors e-books, Internet blogs, and related electronic developments that have become such an integral part of modern publishing.

The size of the organization makes it impossible for the CEO to be as hands-on as Heisey was when Harlequin was still a relatively small organization and when Heisey, before acquiring Mills & Boon, could sit down once a year at the Ritz bar in London and over a handshake with Alan Boon renew their agreement for another year.[5] The complexity (and legal machinations) of large-scale modern organizations prohibits such informality. The classic role of a CEO in a large corporation is to provide overall direction to product development but leave the day-to-day operations necessary to achieve these goals to key divisional/departmental personnel while they concentrate on the "bigger picture."

The complexity of modern organizations also tends to hide from public view internal workings that do not shed a favorable light on the corporation. In short, it is in the best interest of organizations not to publicly air their dirty laundry. David Galloway put this quite succinctly when a squabble took place between Torstar and Sun Media, and Paul Godfrey at Sun Media cast some aspersions toward the way he felt Galloway was conducting business: "I never in my business career," said Galloway "seen [sic] one business executive trash another business executive."[6] Speaking ill of someone within the firm would be especially abhorrent to the gentlemanly Galloway.[7] I mention this because I am making certain assumptions in the following CEO assessments that otherwise have not received public scrutiny and are based solely on my interpretation of events. These assessments are based on modern business practices and in no way detract from the contribution of the various executives.

David Galloway

Galloway is a Toronto native who obtained his master's in business administration (MBA) from Harvard in 1968. He spent three years in the marketing department at General Foods before partnering to form a highly respected Toronto consulting firm (Canada Consulting Group) in 1971. He was hired by Torstar not long after it purchased full control of Harlequin in 1981. He served six months as Torstar's executive vice president of corporate development before being moved to Harlequin (June 1981) as its executive vice president responsible for all operations—effectively their chief operations officer (COO). His rapid accession would indicate he was destined from the start to take over the reins at Harlequin.[8] In 1983, Galloway was promoted to president and CEO of Harlequin, and Heisey was "kicked upstairs" to become chairman of the board, a position he held until he retired at sixty in 1989.[9] "David was asked to join Harlequin to try to straighten things out," said Murray Cockburn, Torstar's CFO at the time. "And he did a terrific job."[10]

Heisey shepherded Harlequin through a significant period. His foray into the United States would substantially increase sales, and his marketing campaigns would make Harlequin's name synonymous with romance publishing. But he was also responsible for the decision to go it alone and terminate Harlequin's distribution contract with Pocket Books, which resulted in the formation of Silhouette Books and significantly undermined Harlequin's market share. "We should never have left Simon & Schuster," Galloway said in hindsight. "It was not a good decision at all."[11] The old ways of doing business were over at Harlequin, now a Torstar subsidiary, and Heisey was part of the old guard. Galloway, with his freshly minted Harvard MBA[12] and business savvy, represented the new corporate world. Heisey was promoted to chairman, where his knowledge could be tapped, but the running of the business was left to Galloway, and Galloway faced a daunting task—to return Harlequin to market supremacy.

Galloway said that there were three steps he had to take in order to nurture Harlequin back to profitability.[13] First, he had to move forward and finalize the purchase of Silhouette, which was accomplished in August 1984. He basically "stole" Silhouette for a purchase price of $10 million; it was still a bargain even if one includes the $25 million in potential payout from subsequent Harlequin sales, since Simon & Schuster's real profit on the deal was made with the return of the distribution contract for Harlequin's product in the United States. Galloway's second task was to get costs under control. He did this by slashing overhead by twenty-five percent between 1982 and 1984, saving the company some $30 million over this three-year period. His necessary executive decision would have been hard for the amiable patriarch Heisey to make: fifty employees in the United States and thirty in Canada were let go. The third step was to build direct sales. Direct sales had been pioneered under Heisey, but they were substantially developed by Galloway, who recognized them for their magic at generating sales.[14] Selling four to six books every month through the Harlequin book club would help to generate fifty percent of Harlequin's profit by the mid-1980s.[15] Not mentioned in Galloway's self-imposed tasks were two other considerations. One was to clean up some of the secondary products Harlequin had acquired in the second half of the 1970s under Heisey: *Antiques World* magazine was sold, as were the forty Scholar's Choice retail stores that were mostly operating at a loss.[16] Another consideration: gain control over Mills & Boon's independence. The first step in this process, which would unfold over the next two decades, was initiated by Galloway as a cost-cutting measure: he moved the center for overseas operation from London to Toronto in 1984, effectively wresting control from an area traditionally under the preserve of Mills & Boon.

Galloway turned Harlequin around, and in the four years after his arrival at Harlequin, he moved sales from a low point of $11 million to $52 million.[17] When Galloway left Harlequin in 1988 to become the president and CEO of Harlequin's parent, Torstar, he had accomplished his formidable task and returned Harlequin to supremacy of the romance market. Harlequin's return to organizational dominance was achieved largely through organizational tactics rather than line (product) innovations, since most of the lines were in development or in place when Galloway took over as CEO.[18]

Brian Hickey

Hickey graduated with an MBA from the University of Toronto. He worked at General Foods in Canada for three years after graduating, where his first boss was David Galloway; he then took a position with S. C. Johnson in Wisconsin, where he worked for eight years. He was a marketing executive at Johnson Wax in 1981 when a headhunter contacted him with a job offer from Harlequin—the headhunter, Grescoe reveals in an interview with David Galloway, was prompted by Galloway, who didn't want to approach Hickey directly because he didn't want it to look like he was bringing a friend aboard.[19] Hickey initially balked at the idea, having no publishing experience, but also because he appears to have shared the widely held corporate view of Harlequin in the early 1980s that it was a "little" company of no real consequence. The headhunter sent Hickey Harlequin's annual report and, so the story goes, he was impressed by their business structure.[20] This shows an astute reading of Harlequin's business, since at the time it was beleaguered by an onslaught of competitors in the United States. He accepted the position, which at the time was to develop Harlequin's international sales, an area he had some experience with at S. C. Johnson.[21]

He oversaw Harlequin's entrance into Japan, and after taking the helm at Harlequin, he was responsible for significant market entry into Eastern Europe after the fall of the Berlin Wall; he also made overtures to enter Russia and China, though the China market would not come to fruition and the Russian market was filled with distribution pitfalls.[22] The international development of Harlequin's sales will be critiqued in greater detail in the international section later in this chapter. Harlequin has always had an international presence and international developments continued under Hickey's successors, but it is important at this point to recognize that Hickey made a significant contribution in this area, especially given some of the "bumps" that he would encounter elsewhere. Hickey would have to take responsibility for these bumps because they happened on his watch, even if they were not necessarily his fault. Some ventures that didn't work out would include a failed attempt to purchase Zebra Books in 1992,[23] an aborted foray into television movies in 1993,[24] and a joint venture with women.com between 1999 and 2000 to promote Harlequin books online that ended a few million dollars later, not long after it began.[25] His most significant "bump" would not become obvious for a while, but Hickey would take responsibility for its subsequent difficulty since he was the one instrumental in moving Harlequin into the children's educational arena and away from its primary market.

Hickey's interest in the children's education market was prompted, like so many gatekeeping decisions, by his personal interest in this area: he was unable to find educational material to help his son at school. And so, Children's Supplementary Educational Publishing (CSEP) was born in 1993 as a division of Harlequin. CSEP would subsequently acquire Tom Snyder Productions for $24 million in 1993. It was a good fit since Tom Snyder Productions was a well-established producer of educational material for schools. Other acquisitions followed, including the purchase of Los Angles-based Frank Schaffer Publications for $56 million in 1994[26] as well as the purchase of Troll for $140 million[27] to directly challenge Scholastic Canada "at its own game."[28] CSEP's primary market was teacher products; it had 500 employees at its peak in the mid–1990s. The move appears to have met with the approval of Torstar, which was "looking for a so-called 'third leg' for its overall corporate profile to complement the newspaper division."[29] It did not live up to promise, at least in part because Hickey was overoptimistic about its potential: CSEP offered a 10–15 percent return on sales, which is slightly lower than the 15–20 percent that books generate; Hickey suggested, however, that profits would be much larger, even better than for books.[30] In a passing comment, Hickey shrugs off responsibility for CSEP's failure and lays the fault at Harlequin's doorstep, saying that despite the boom in the supplementary education material industry, Harlequin never went far enough and did no more than some basic "homework."[31] Whoever was responsible, CSEP did not fair well. In 2000, Torstar decided to "get out of the money-losing business"; it wanted out so badly that it took substantial write-downs.[32] By 2001, all divisions except Tom Snyder had been sold[33]; Snyder Productions would eventually be sold to Scholastic, its primary product rival.[34] CSEP also "drained" some of the resources that would otherwise be utilized at Harlequin, which no doubt contributed to weak sales toward the end of Hickey's tenure at Harlequin: Donna Hayes came over from the North American Direct Marketing Division at Harlequin, as did Mary Abthorpe, Harlequin's marketing manager of new acquisitions; Amanda MacLennan, Mike Muldoon and Trace Brown all transferred from key roles at Harlequin to one of CSEP's new divisions.[35]

An executive is responsible for the company's profits or losses, in much the same way a coach in professional sports ultimately takes the credit for the team's success or bears responsibility for the team's losses. Hickey's contribution was substantial. During his tenure, revenues grew from $200 million to $579 million.[36] But often one's last quarter is the one that counts, regardless of how good or bad former years were. The dismissal of a highly respected sports franchise coach is public laundry after a losing season. It is less public, though no less common, in the corporate sphere. Hickey's unexpected early retirement at fifty-six was treated by Galloway in the following corporate-speak manner after one quarter of profit losses and another quarter of flat earnings,[37] and after Torstar had decided to takes its losses and get out of the supplemental educational market: "Harlequin has enjoyed steady growth under his leadership and he has built a wonderful team."[38] Support for my assessment that Hickey was moved to take early retirement is the lack of his presence in news releases toward the latter part of the 1990s: in the first half of the 1990s Hickey was often cited as Harlequin's CEO who announced that Harlequin was doing this or that, but after 1997–1998, most statements about Harlequin did not come from Hickey but from David Galloway at Torstar. This is particularly telling since the late 1990s and early 2000s were marked by the so-called "newspaper wars" raging in Canada[39] and Galloway, as Torstar's CEO and the *Toronto Star's* publisher, had other issues that he needed to attend to besides being Harlequin's spokesperson.

It is important to point out that most (though not all) of the difficulties that Hickey encountered occurred when he moved beyond Harlequin's primary product, which represents 85 percent of Harlequin's business.[40] Harlequin did introduce a number of new book divisions and lines while he was president, including MIRA, which strengthened Harlequin's entry into women's mainstream fiction (shepherded to fruition by Donna Hayes), as well as Red Dress

Ink, a line strategically positioned to capitalize on the new wave of "chick-lit" that was prompted throughout the publishing industry by the phenomenal success of *Bridget Jones's Diary* in 1996. Red Dress Ink launched after Hickey's retirement, but it was developed during his tenure as Harlequin's CEO. Steeple Hill's inspirational line of books was also born while Hickey was president, and while the name would later be dropped, the Love Inspired books continue to be released. There were also a number of line issues during Hickey's reign. Silhouette's Shadows was born and died under Hickey (1993–1996), and their humor series, both Silhouette's Yours Truly and Harlequin's Love and Laughter, born in the mid–1990s while Hickey was president, were rolled into Duet in 1999 as his tenure came to a close, and then into Flipside in 2003, where they remained on life support for two more years before they were allowed to finally pass into oblivion in 2005.

Donna Hayes

Hayes, a Montreal native, graduated with an honors degree in literature and communication from McGill University in 1978. She worked for a number of years at Doubleday Canada and briefly at the advertising agency Ogilvy & Mather before taking a job with Harlequin, where she worked for sixteen years before becoming its CEO at age forty-five in 2002. Her accession was foreshadowed by her promotion to COO the previous year.

The press was quick to headline her as the first woman to run Harlequin. Some went on to imply that this promotion fit since she was a Harlequin devotee: "Harlequin CEO Fell in Love with Books When She Was a Teen," proclaimed the *Daily Press*, which immediately qualified her love of books to mean romances: "Donna Hayes remembers exactly when she read her first Harlequin romance novel. She was in Grade 7...."[41] More significant is the fact that during her time at Harlequin before becoming its CEO, she worked in direct marketing, which included the book club that accounted for one-third of Harlequin's business.[42] She was also the driving force behind the development of both Red Dress Ink, to tap the young, twenty-something female audience,[43] and MIRA, whose single-title mainstream novels grew during the late 1990s to account for up to twenty-five percent of Harlequin's business.[44] The MIRA move was significant and was one of the key attributes cited by Galloway for her promotion to CEO: "Donna can take credit for bringing Harlequin into the single-title business."[45] Her promotion hinged on her knowledge of line development, rather than marketing strategy. She was the first CEO to head Harlequin who came from a literary background. This would be far more significant than her gender in moving Harlequin forward.

Development of the company's primary product had not been significant under Hayes's predecessors. Only one new line, Presents, was debuted in the 1970s. During the tumultuous 1980s, Galloway had little time to worry about line development and devoted his time to (re)stabilizing the company: most of the new lines that appeared in the 1980s were to ensure product counter-positioning with Silhouette. During Hickey's tenure as CEO, the company moved away from its primary product, and while MIRA (1996) and Red Dress Ink (2001) debuted during this period, it was Hayes who was largely responsible for their development. Her job as CEO would focus on the literary aspects of Harlequin's product. She was, in Galloway's terms, perhaps more than any previous CEO, "a real publisher, in every sense of the word."[46] It was during her tenure that Harlequin took a different course from the one Hickey plowed, a direction that Torstar was similarly moving toward: building, not buying.[47]

One primary growth area was MIRA. There was tremendous potential here since Harlequin only maintained a seven percent share of the women's [noncategory][48] fiction market in the United States.[49] Harlequin also developed an African American line of books and expedited their entrance into this field by buying an existing line of African American romances. They looked at the younger market with some success (Red Dress Ink) but were less successful, as we'll subsequently see, at developing a line of romances for an older market called NEXT. A major rebranding took place while Hayes was CEO, and the Silhouette moniker was finally terminated, nearly thirty years after it had effectively been subsumed by Harlequin. International developments would naturally continue during her tenure. E-books and related electronic means of delivering and marketing novels would become more imperative as publishing stepped into the twenty-first century, and Hayes would ensure that Harlequin would be at the forefront of these developments—in 2010, a weak U.S. dollar and economy negatively impacted Harlequin's retail print sales, but this was offset by a 73 percent jump in digital sales.[50]

Craig Swinwood

Swinwood grew up in the same neighborhood on the South Shore in Montreal as Hayes. He too spent his career at Harlequin, some twenty-six years, ten more than Hayes when she became CEO. He began as a district sales manager, where he worked with distributors getting books into grocery stores and Wal-Marts across Eastern Canada. More recently, he worked on developing strategies to appeal to teens and developing Harlequin's newer nonfiction books before becoming COO of North America. He assumed the CEO mantle at age fifty on January 1, 2014, when Donna Hayes announced in December 2013 that she had "decided to retire"[51] after twenty-six years with Harlequin. Torstar CEO David Holland considered the new CEO to be Hayes's "natural successor" and expected him to continue developing teen products, growing the single-title business, and expanding digital publishing.[52] It is a given that he will continue to oversee Harlequin's vast international publishing venture.

Swinwood's role as CEO soon became obvious. He shepherded to fruition the sale of Harlequin to HarperCollins. The deal was announced on May 2, 2014, and was finalized in August. Harlequin will be a free-standing house within HarperCollins, with headquarters remaining in Toronto. Swinwood will be instrumental in ensuring stability within Harlequin during the transition process. He will also bring invaluable insight to HarperCollins in the management of romance novels, particularly in the international arena, which was one of the key reasons HarperCollins wanted to acquire Harlequin.

Harlequin Staples

Romance and Presents are clearly *les grandes dames* of Harlequin's lines. Indeed, the distinction between Romance and Presents, at least initially, was thin since they were both being published under the Romance series by Mills & Boon in the U.K., which is one of the reasons the two lines continue to be edited out of Harlequin's London office. The ever-so-slightly heightened sensuality of some of the books was behind the rationale for debuting them as Presents in North America in 1973. This still differentiates the two lines. The Romance series continues its travelogue focus and consequently has more non-romantic elements than Presents; indeed, the Australians demark the difference between the two lines in their titles: the sweeter Romance line is renamed Cherish, while the more sensually charged Presents line is called Sexy.[53] This is not to suggest that the degree of sensuality is the only thing distinguishing these two lines, or that the novels have not thematically changed with the times. Vivanco found the Presents heroes to be much more intensely alpha,[54] and Jensen found the Harlequin hero and heroine had evolved into more balanced individuals as early as the 1980s.[55] The heroine in both types of novels today is a thoroughly modern woman and reflects the changing role of women in the wider society that has continued to unfold over the last thirty-plus years. It is not surprising, then, that today Presents goes into the bedroom, whereas when the line debuted, the novels' only intimated sexual intimacy occurred behind the bedroom door. The sensuality of Presents now falls into the group Dianne Moggy, Harlequin's vice president of series romances, refers to as "passion."[56]

The passion cluster would also include Harlequin's Desire and Blaze lines. Indeed, Moggy says that some of the titles within Presents are sexually quite explicit. It may simply be a matter of emphasis. The sensuality of Presents is definitely there, but the line itself is nowhere near as erotic as Blaze, which Moggy acknowledges is unquestionably at the upper end of the passion (erotic) scale.

The success of these lines, both locally and globally (see the international section below) is based on audience demographics. Twenty-five percent of romance readers are over 54 years of age: 11 percent, 55–64; 6 percent, 65–74; 8 percent, 75 and older.[57] This suggests that the reader of these two lines is slightly older. Moggy concedes that this is certainly the public perception. But she goes on to indicate that another key readership group for these lines is the sixteen- to eighteen-year-old female: the 14–17-year-old group composed 6 percent of romance readers; those 18–24, 9 percent.[58] That's because "they enter romance at a very young age and then life happens: they go to school, get married, have families. During that time period, they perhaps are not reading as much, and then [they] return to the [Romance/Presents] category" later in life. These books may be attractive to these younger females because they do not overly exploit the sensual, which they are likely to graduate to as they move into their own twenty-something sexually active years. This suggests that the Romance line should do well in the years to come with older women because the Baby Boomers (born 1946–1965) are a demographically strong group (80.2 million) and twice the size of the typical fifty-plus group. On the other hand, the Millennials (born 1986–2005) rival the Boomers in size (79.4 million), but they are moving out of their teen years and into their twenties. This demographic shift suggests the Romance line might generate less sales, though some of the other, more sexually explicit lines may see some growth for those Harlequin readers who want to "graduate" to more risqué romances.[59]

The Mills & Boon Medical Romance line from the 1970s is also sexually "chaste," though a little less so today. Medical Romances took some time to reach the North American shore. Medical themes, we saw in Chapter 2, were popular in the 1960s and 1970s and peppered romance titles of the day. Mills & Boon lifted this from an occasional single-title release under Romance or Presents and launched Doctor-Nurse Romances in 1977. The theme was broadened in 1989 to be more encompassing and was retitled Mills & Boon Medical Romance. It transitioned to Harlequin Medical Romances in 2001 and continues to remain popular.

The medical world appears to have a fascination for television viewers and romance readers. There is always at least one popular medical show dominating the television ratings: in the 1960s and 1970s, it was Dr. Kildare, Ben Casey, and

Marcus Welby. In the 1980s, St. Elsewhere (1982–1988) topped the prime-time ratings; in the 1990s, it was Chicago Hope and ER. At the outset of the new millennium, medical television shows are more popular than ever, with Scrubs (2001–2010), Gray's Anatomy (2005–present) and Doc Martin (2004–present). The popularity of television shows is one indicator that romance novels revolving around medical themes would also do well. This is because the medical world is, by its very nature, dramatic, revolving as it does around life and death issues. The shows also give a behind-the-scenes peek into a world that most people don't get to view. The romance aspect, Moggy suggests, also has appeal because it provides an emotional "softness" to a sometimes harsh world where people are often struggling to hang on to life and is something that is only tangentially depicted in television shows.

The medical line itself, while generally healthy, has a mild infection. The infection is limited to North America since the line does quite well in the U.K. (and France). Medical romances also do well as single-title releases in Harlequin lines. They just don't do well as a stand-alone line: Harlequin Medical Romances do not do well in bookstores in North America, though they are very popular in both the direct-to-consumer market and in digital space. The success of Medical in these non-print markets may be because it is easier to identify the line, while the print format may get lost in the racks. Moggy acknowledges the racks may be an issue, but more likely the packaging has not been the most appealing, which, in turn, affects its desirability in the racks. Attempts to repackage the line have not been successful, and no one who has examined this issue within Harlequin knows "why it [print format] has not resonated with readers." And it is not that Harlequin hasn't endeavored to solve the problem: "We're constantly trying tests and other strategies," Moggy says. The print success in the U.K. and France is not clear either, though Moggy suggests it may simply be due to its longevity there. This is logical since "in any market, the programs that are the longest standing are the ones that tend to do well." While Harlequin insiders are puzzled over print failure in North America, it is not of undue concern since Medical sells well in the other mediums.

Another somewhat sensually toned-down romance line that has also been in existence since the 1970s is Mills & Boon's Historical series. The historical line was originally called Masquerade, then, briefly, Legacy of Love, before it was folded into its present Harlequin Historical imprint in 1996. Historical romances have traditionally been sweet, except for the bodice-ripper historicals that dominated American romance lists in the 1970s. Harlequin never produced any of the Mills & Boon historical romances during the 1970s and, because it did not then have a historical line, never produced any bodice-ripper-themed novels. It did release a line of historical novels in North America for the first time in the late 1980s, and a few bodice-rippers did find their way into the Harlequin oeuvre.

In 1988, Harlequin filled a product gap by producing historical romances in North America for the first time. Unlike other Mills & Boon existing lines (Romance, Presents), Harlequin did not filter books into the North American market from the U.K. There was a good reason for this. One of the minor but nevertheless persistent complaints by Harlequin readers in the United States during the 1970s was the heavy "British tone" in the Romance and Presents books. Harlequin Historical novels were original novels that were acquired by editors in North America. The novels did not have to be set in North America, and some authors with roots in North America wrote Regency or Gothic romances, but in general the books written by North American authors tended to focus on historical periods in the United States and Canada, leaving American Romances to concentrate on contemporary settings in North America. The Mills & Boon historical line—the poorly positioned, renamed Legacy of Love—would be combined into Harlequin Historical in 1993 and continues to be popular among those women who straddle both ends of the age continuum.

Historicals, then and now, and regardless as to whether they were Mills & Boon or American-themed historical novels, remain a popular romance subgenre and nicely complement the contemporary travelogue aspect of Romance by taking the reader on a journey back in time. It is a logical extension for Harlequin to fill out its North American romance list by publishing these tried and true novels. The shift away from the Legacy logo in the U.K., Moggy suggests, is simply because Legacy does not have the widespread name recognition that the historical label does. It is unclear exactly why Mills & Boon dropped the Masquerade label for Legacy. It may be that, initially, the masquerade logo, which hints at the harlequin character who attended the masquerade ball in Italian commedia del'arte, conveyed a historical setting that became more remote over the years. Mills & Boon appears to have tried to update the nomenclature by renaming the books Legacy of Love, with the legacy suggesting something set in the past. It is obvious that this name never really resonated with the readers since it was replaced in short order by the Historical label that clearly conveys the time period of the novel.

Most of the other lines have their origins in the early 1980s and consequently have a heightened degree of sensuality. There are three exceptions to this.

One exception is the Historical line produced by Harlequin in the 1980s; this is because historical novels generally tend to have a muted level of eroticism, the focus instead shifting to historical details. Another exception to eighties sensuality is American Romance, which tends to hover at the lower end of the erotic scale: American Romance's thematic underpinning was less the sexual than the Americanization of the novels. The American Romance line, of course, continues to exploit the American setting: fifty percent of its novels today revolve around the modern cowboy.[60] Moggy says the western theme is "incredibly popular," perhaps because "there isn't anything more quintessential than the American cowboy." Romances with American settings, it will be recalled, were the driving reason Silhouette was initially so successful since Harlequin never capitalized on the success of Janet Dailey and turned a blind eye to American-themed romances. The third exception to the heightened eroticism of the period was in Harlequin Intrigues, which launched in 1984 in response to Silhouette's Intimate Moments series of romance suspense books.

Silhouette's Intimate Moments (1983) and Harlequin Intrigues (1984) were both born during the romance wars of the early 1980s, though Intimate Moments transitioned to Silhouette Romantic Suspense in 2007 to more accurately convey the central theme of the books. The line took the Harlequin Romantic Suspense moniker during the rebranding in 2011. Romantic Suspense and Intrigues continue as separate lines because, while they may "look alike on the surface," says Moggy, they have different tones and distinct themes. Intrigues is geared to the romance reader who also gravitates toward mystery novels. This is a key demographic group since the mystery genre is the second largest category of fiction, which helps explain why Intrigues is consistently among Harlequin's top-selling global lines. Romantic Suspense is also a key category and one that garners a following. It focuses on action adventure, an element in some of Harlequin's other lines, but in Romantic Suspense the central crisis pivots on the woman-in-jeopardy theme, "so saving the situation is saving the heroine." Moggy acknowledges that some of the writers could be placed in either category, which is why there are sometimes internal discussions about combining the two, especially given the shrinking rack space in brick and mortar bookstores. The surface similarity is, however, only apparent to the nonreader. Moggy indicates that reader input and sales figures supports maintaining them as separate entities because the reader clearly differentiates between them: "If you want the adrenaline rush, you read Romantic Suspense; if you favor the whodunit, then you go with Intrigues." The romantic side of the novels today may be tinted with sensuality, but the reader gravitates to these books for their mystery-suspense element.

American Romances, Harlequin's "late" (1983) entry to compete with Silhouette's American-themed novels, like most of the lines from the early 1980s that still exist, including the Medical and Historical series as well as Romantic Suspense and Intrigues, keep thematically close to their original intention. This, in itself, moves the sensual to a secondary role in the story. Harlequin's Superromances and Silhouette's Special Editions and Desire lines, however, tend to be more sensual.[61] Superromance, it will be recalled, was developed as longer romances to allow the author to explore more nuanced stories. The longer format (80,000–85,000 words) allowed for more subplot developments and provided the room for secondary characters to gain some depth. Superromance heightened the sensuality of the Presents books then being released, which is heightened further in Special Editions, Silhouette's answer to Harlequin's Superromance; it is raised another notch by Desire, which was developed by Silhouette to compete with Dell's Ecstasy line. All these lines seem to have found a snug niche with readers, depending in part on the level of sensuality the reader wishes to explore, and in part the thematic focus of the various lines, which gives each of them a unique position in the market. Silhouette's Special Editions and Desire continue but are now folded into the Harlequin family name as part of the long overdue rebranding that took place in 2011. It seems that when the romantic element is the raison d'être of the novel, the sensual moves to the foreground.

The length of Superromances continues, and this alone makes it one of Harlequin's most nuanced romances in the category field; indeed, it remains among the longest of Harlequin's category lines. Special Editions and Desire too seem to have found a comfortable niche, having neither too little nor too much sexual activity, though they are nowhere near as sensual as Blaze. We might simplistically rank the various lines according to their level of sensuality, something the cover art tends to hint at.[62] The scale devised is an approximation of the level of sensuality that normally would be found within the line. It should be pointed out that there may be some books within a line that may vary the sensuality in the series, in much the same way the word count for a novel is a general guideline, even though some books may be lower or higher than the norm for the series. It is also difficult to clearly point out the level of sexuality in a series, so the lines are put into a numerical range, with 1 to 3 being low levels of sexuality, 4 to 7 being an intermediate range of sensuality, and 8 to 10 being highly eroticized.

Harlequin's Romance, Historical, and Medical lines are at the lower level of eroticism, though they are slightly more erotic than the Harlequin adolescent line and Harlequin's inspirational series, both of which would fall at the lower-lower range (a 1 versus a 3). Intrigues and Romantic Suspense are erotically "weakened" because of the heavy suspense/mystery plot, so they tend to fall at the mid-lower (level 2) erotic range. Most of the others fall somewhere in the intermediate range: American Romance and Superromance seem to fit into the lower intermediate level; Presents in its current form and Special Editions

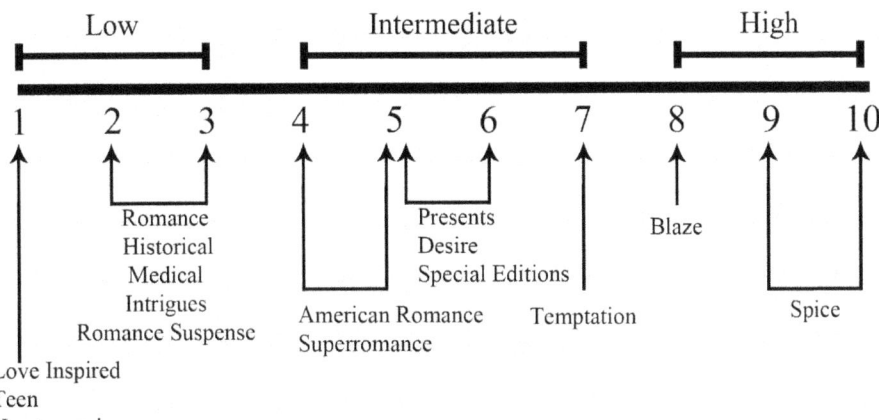

Harlequin Erotic Scale

straddling the middle of the intermediate scale, with the extinct Temptation weighing in at the upper intermediate level. Blaze is Harlequin's steamiest extant line and falls into the higher range of eroticism, though closer to an 8 level than the short-lived, highly charged Spice line that crossed the threshold and weighed in at the upper end of the erotic scale. It is not too surprising that the sensuality of Blaze, addressed in the next section, is a fairly late entry and more geared toward contemporary sexual mores, while overly charged 9- and 10-level books border on the pornographic and may be a little too far along the erotic scale to be classified as "romance" by many Harlequin readers—9- to 10-level novels often depict graphic sexual scenes depicted in some detail that may not be related to a romantic tryst.

Strategic Line Developments

A romance from an earlier period, say the 1950s or 1970s, tends to reflect the values of society at that time. This is just as applicable with historical novels: a novel set in the eighteenth century that was written in the 1990s will reflect the values that were widely shared by the writers and readers of the 1990s. The social changes that have taken place in the romance novel have been traced by a number of critics. One, covering nearly a hundred years of content, was undertaken by Jay Dixon, who successfully shows how Mills & Boon romances have changed over the years.[63] These changes are fairly subtle from year to year, which is why the non-romance reader doesn't see the changes, even though the reader is likely to appreciate them. The changes only "stand out" when one looks

Harlequin covers representing degrees of eroticism. From left: A cover from the 2014 Love Inspired line—low eroticism; a cover from the 2010 Harlequin Presents line—intermediate eroticism; a cover from the 2010 Harlequin Blaze line—high eroticism.

at discrete historical periods in lieu of year-to-year variations; for example, 1950s novels compared to 1970s ones versus those released in 1970, 1971, 1972. That is why new lines are such a good indicator of social changes. They are filtered into the system by editors who share the sensibilities of the world they inhabit, and the success of the lines is an indicator that their editorial eye is in sync (or not) with the world the reader and author inhabit. This section addresses some of the new lines that introduce changes. These changes reflect the modern social world and would, to varying degrees, subsequently be incorporated into more traditional lines.[64] The changes stand out in newly launched lines precisely because they do not slowly unfold over time but spring full-blown from Zeus's head. Character developments that shape heroine and hero relationships in the romance novel at the dawn of the new millennium are first quickly sketched since they are quintessential features of romances today.

The modern heroine is anything but a spineless doormat sitting by the window pining away her life until Mr. Right happens by. Like most women by the close of the twentieth century, the modern woman is out there, actively pursuing a career, and is not "searching" for a man, though like most women (and men), she is not averse to finding someone to share her life with. Because the heroine has more depth, the novel has more depth, which refutes the contention by Barash and Barash that most romance novels "deal with the trials and tribulations of finding the right man."[65] Besides, quipped Nora Roberts quite succinctly, "weak, passive people don't make good characters."[66] Other than becoming a much stronger, take-charge woman, the heroine has not dramatically changed. This is because the focal point of the novel is the man, which explains why the heroine is seldom described in any physical detail.[67]

As early as the 1980s the hero had changed. The "New Man," Carol Thurston wrote in her analysis of eighties romance fiction, "is sensitive and vulnerable ... with an ego and masculinity secure enough to seek a relationship based on quality and sharing."[68] The modern hero is typically referred to as an alpha male, which demarks his difference from the traditional hero of romantic fiction (see table on page 91). Pamela Regis, leaning on Jayne Ann Krentz's work, *Dangerous Men and Adventurous Women*, explains[69]:

> Krentz describes the romance novel hero as a "source of emotional and ... sometimes physical risk.... He is an "alpha male," not the sensitive, understanding, right-thinking, "modern" man who is part therapist, part best friend, and thoroughly tamed from the start." Instead he is ... "tough, hard-edged, [and] tormented...." This hero, Krentz asserts, "is not only the hero, he is also the villain." He is "the most dangerous creature on earth" ... and he must be conquered. The heroine must "force him to acknowledge her power as a woman." As the villain, the hero provides the heroine with the primary source of conflict. She must tame him in order to complete the courtship.

The hero as villain has posed some puzzlement to critics of the genre. To proponents of evolutionary psychology, the hero as villain makes perfect sense. Men, they'd argue, often start out as cads in romances, as Fisher and Cost explain. They are often rude, independent, and aggressive, but they metamorphose into "loyal, devoted men who are in love with the heroine." This desire for a mate who encompasses both a "cad" and a "dad," Fisher and Cox conclude, is a beneficial mating strategy for women because "evolutionary speaking ... cads may have high gene quality and dads may provide high paternal investment."[70]

The evolutionary explanation is rejected by some in the industry.[71] Indeed, critics of the evolutionary perspective would argue that the term alpha male simply came into use "because some authors were engaged in a struggle with editors about a certain type of hero and needed a vocabulary for the discussion."[72] Be that as it may, the term alpha male is widely used within the industry today to describe desirable characteristics in the hero.

The alpha male as described by Krentz encompasses four of the five heroes found in the romance novel. The other, the sentimental male, is only slightly different, though he too has alpha qualities. The sentimental hero "is strong, virile, manly ('a lion among men'), but he is wounded physically, psychically, or emotionally." Instead of the heroine having to tame this hero, "the heroine must cure him."[73] Other social characteristics remain relatively constant and are in sync with those that are widely adhered to in society: if not wealthy, he should at least have a job with a stable income, is slightly older, typically more sexually experienced, is often someone the heroine knows, and, perhaps stepping beyond reality but not desirability, he should be honorable and have integrity.[74]

Blaze: Sex and the Modern Reader

Premarital sexual activity has not greatly changed in nearly a half-century. Lawrence Finer found that "almost all Americans have sex before marrying" and have been doing so since the 1950s: 82 percent of the women turning 15 between 1954 and 1963 had had premarital sex by age 30; 91 percent of those turning fifteen between 1964 and 1993 had had premarital sex by age 30.[75] Though it fell outside the scope of Finer's study, I suspect that the majority of those at the earlier points in time were in a committed relationship and were less likely to publicly acknowledge their activity because there was greater social stigma toward having sex outside marriage before the so-called sexual revolution of the 1960s. Casual sex today—hooking up, in contemporary parlance—is more common: 60 to 80 percent of North American college students have had a hook-up experience; related research found that while two-thirds of those in seventh, ninth and eleventh grades had not experienced sexual intercourse, the third that did were most likely (61 percent) to have engaged in casual sex outside a dating relationship.[76] In short, more young men and women are sexually experienced today and are less likely to find their behavior meeting with opprobrium, at least among their peers.[77] It is hardly surprising that romance novels reflect these changing sexual mores, especially given that nine percent of romance readers fall into the 18–24 age range, while another 19 percent are between 25 and 34 years of age.[78]

Silhouette launched Desire with heightened sexuality in June 1982 in response to the contemporary sensual dimension found in Dell Ecstasy's new books; Temptation, launched in March 1984, was Harlequin's foray into the sensual romance market and was positioned to compete with Desire and Ecstasy. What might have been considered erotic in the 1980s, however, appears to have lost some of its fire in the ensuing years. This became apparent when Blaze, a once-a-month miniseries within the line (referred to as a continuity in the trade), started to outsell the line itself. Blaze was thus spun off of Temptation, and the reader gravitated to it rather than staying with the original books. "There was so much demand for Blaze titles, with their higher level of sensuality," Moggy says, "that it was just a natural evolution to turn it into a separate line. It was a case where the baby ate the mother." Temptation struggled on for a few more years after Blaze spun off but was eventually terminated in 2005 so the company could focus on the smoldering Blaze series.

Blaze was developed for the younger twenty-something age group who were raised in a more sexually liberated society. The success of Blaze can be seen in the number of miniseries that have appeared within the line. Most lines today have miniseries, though Blaze has more than its share. Some miniseries feature one author; others revolve around a specific theme. Some miniseries have only two to three books; some a dozen or more. The miniseries might be generated by the author, who might wish to write a number of books revolving around a set theme, while others are formulated in-house based on reader input or the feeling by an editor that a niche is not being filled. These are continuities that gain special reader favor, but the sales are not sufficient enough to warrant a separate line. There have been over fifty miniseries since the debut of Blaze in 2001. The titles of some of the miniseries suggest their heightened sensuality: The Bad Girls Club, eXtreme Blaze, and Lust in Translation, to mention just three. One of the more popular at the moment is Blaze's Uniformly Hot series that features men in the military. Uniformly Hot was launched in January 2009 with one book per month, though at the outset of 2014 this was decreased to one book every other month, indicating this continuity is running out of steam but still maintains a level of interest among readers, at least enough to warrant continuing to publish them for the time being and not to fold them back into the Blaze line. It is worth a small aside to note that while the wars in Iraq and Afghanistan found increasing disfavor among Americans after 2005, this continuity is justified because the negative attitudes toward the war did not spill over to taint those serving.[79] Not too surprisingly, the number of titles featuring Navy SEALS increased exponentially after they stormed bin Laden's compound in Abbottabad, Pakistan, on May 2, 2011.[80] Navy SEALS are often visited in the Blaze series, and by reading about them in this series, the reader can anticipate getting a book about the SEALS that smolders around an 8-level of eroticism. More "toned down" stories about the Navy SEALS can be found in other lines, however: *Sign, SEAL, Deliver* in Superromance and *The SEAL's Stolen Child* in American Romance drop the sensuality into the intermediate range, and it plummets to a level 1 in *SEAL Under Siege* in the inspirational Love Inspired Suspense book.

Gold Eagle: Harlequin's Rogue Line

Gold Eagle is a Harlequin anomaly since it is male-oriented action-adventure fiction aimed at a male audience. It slipped into the fold during the late 1970s, when Harlequin was in its outside-the-box acquisition phase. There have been a number of spinoffs from the initial series, the most recent of which is the adventuress heroine in Rogue Angel.

In 1986, Harlequin launched Worldwide Library. It was a half-hearted attempt to compete in the single-title market that was soon abandoned (1988). The Worldwide imprint survived, however; it was conveniently used to place books that didn't snugly fit Harlequin romance lines, like the French romance

Mystique series and Worldwide Mystery. It was the perfect place to put the action-adventurer Executioner series when the opportunity presented itself. And so Gold Eagle was born under the Worldwide imprint. It fit Harlequin's list, says Dianne Moggy, the first editor for Gold Eagle, simply because it was a continuity—a trade term for a continuing series. The Gold Eagle books continue to be published out of the Duncan Mills office in Toronto, but one would have to know the Duncan Mills address is Harlequin's address on the inside copyright page. There is no Harlequin identification on the book jacket or on the title page. The rationale appears to be the same as Playboy's in the 1970s, though in the opposite direction. The Playboy name was so strongly identified with male-oriented material that the Playboy logo was removed from the romance line in fear that it would be off-putting to women readers. Here it worked in the opposite direction: the Harlequin name is so strongly identified with women's fiction that the name was removed from the books so potential male readers would not think they were romance novels.

The initial acquisition went smoothly but soon became contentious. Paul Grescoe details what happened.[81] Don Pendleton created the Executioner series at the bequest of Pinnacle Books for a new paperback imprint in 1968. The first book in the series appeared in 1969. In 1980, Pendleton was in ill health and sold the rights to the series to Harlequin for an overpriced guarantee of $200,000 per year for life.[82] Pinnacle sued for breach of contract but lost: it could not claim the name but retained the rights to residuals from the old titles.[83] Harlequin continued to produce Executioner under Pendleton's highly identified action-adventure name but used hired writers to pen the novels. His health improved, and Pendleton began to write a series of action-adventure novels for Warner Books. Harlequin sued but this time lost: Judge Gerald Goettel of the U.S. District Court in Manhattan found that Pendleton did not breach his exclusionary contract because his new character in no way resembled his hero in the Executioner series. Grescoe argues that the series never made much money for Harlequin since it never regained the $200,000 yearly payout that was guaranteed Pendleton. That changed in 1995 with Pendleton's death, since the contract was only payable during his lifetime. The series, like the action-adventure genre itself, Moggy says, has had its ups and downs over the years. It might not be doing as well for Harlequin has hoped, but it is a consistent seller among action-adventure aficionados. The fact that it is still in existence thirty-five years after Harlequin published its first title is sufficient to attest to this. Like any continuity, "the storyline has changed though Matt's hair remains the same color regardless of who is writing it." In this, Mack Bolan in the Gold Eagle series is much like James Bond novels that persist long after Ian Fleming's death. Instead of fighting Russians during the Cold War, Bond and Bolan are now fighting international terrorists: in one of the new releases, *Pirate Offensive* (May 2014), the always intrepid Bolan is now battling pirates on the high seas. Executioner has also enjoyed a number of line spinoffs. Some of the early ones, notably Mack Bolan and Stony Man, were directly tied to the Executioner series.

More germane to this analysis of the romance novel is the recent Gold Eagle continuity Rogue Angel. This line debuted in July 2006. The idea was conceived in-house by Randall Toye, a history buff, who envisioned the heroine as a modern-day Joan of Arc. The novels are produced the same as other action-adventures in Gold Eagle. The author's name that appears on the cover is a house name, Alex Archer, regardless of who actually writes the novel. Mel Odom and Victor Milan wrote the first eight novels for this bi-monthly series, after which other writers joined to pen the further adventures of Annja Creed, "a world-traveling archaeologist with a penchant for adventure, lost cities, mysterious codes and puzzles ... [and who is] heir to Joan of Arc's mystic sword."[84] She is the female version of Harrison Ford's Indiana Jones in *Raiders of the Lost Ark*, which first appeared in 1981; a different female version of Indiana Jones, Lara Croft, would appear a few years later in the highly successful video game *Tomb Raider*, which was released the same year Rogue Angel debuted. The romance in Rogue Angel is overwhelmed by the action-adventure aspect of the story, but it is noteworthy that it is the only Gold Eagle Worldwide series that is prominently displayed on the Harlequin website.

Beyond Whiteness: The Birth of Kimani Press

The first African American line of romances from a major publishing house was launched by Kensington Press in 1994. Kensington, a major player in the romance publishing industry, will be returned to in the next chapter, where we will also delve further into the growing market for multicultural romance novels. Kensington sold its Arabesque line to BET when the well-known African American television network launched BET Books in June 1998. At BET, two related series were born after the acquisition of Arabesque. Sepia (October 2001) was developed to publish mainstream commercial fiction in the wake of Terry McMillan's highly successful 1992 book that was made into a blockbuster movie in 1995, *Waiting to Exhale*; New Spirit was introduced in 2002, according to Glenda Howard at Harlequin, "to tackle contemporary issues such as love, temptation, and infidelity, but with a spiritual element."[85] Arabesque, New Spirit, and Sepia all came to Harlequin when it bought BET Books in December 2005. Howard goes on to indicate that not long after the purchase from BET, Harlequin discontinued both New Spirit and Sepia. New

Spirit's sales were declining as the market shifted to more explicit urban fiction in the style of Sister Souljah's *The Coldest Winter Ever* (Pocket Books, 1999); Sepia became redundant with the introduction of Kimani Press, which was launched to convey brand strength and give the books focus.

Harlequin was prompted to look more closely at the African American market by big-box retailers, such as Wal-Mart and K-Mart, who indicated there was a need for books for that demographic.[86] This is why Harlequin was already acquiring manuscripts for an African American series of romances when the BET opportunity "fortuitously arose," said Moggy. It was, indeed, fortuitous for Harlequin because it helped to jump-start the line and immediately gave them a strong presence with, Moggy says, "not only an incredible author base but real talent in terms of editorial knowledge since we were just getting into that market." Novels published by Kimani Press and Arabesque are single-title—which is to say, neither is a category line—and because of that, the novels tend to be longer, 75,000–85,000 words, and there is no preset number of books released every month. Kimani Press, however, is considered Harlequin's flagship multicultural imprint and publishes only established authors who have a strong fan base in women's fiction, whereas Arabesque novels are contemporary romance—*not*, the writer guidelines clearly emphasize, women's fiction. Nevertheless, Arabesque has a number of "rules" in its guidelines that are more detailed regarding what should not take place than is spelled out in the other Harlequin lines. The detailed guidelines are atypical for a single-title program. They appear to be, at least in part, a carryover from New Spirit's spiritual element without explicitly bringing in the Christian theme.

- The hero and heroine should be single—recently divorced (not just separated), widowed, or coming out of a relationship. They should not be sexually or emotionally involved with anyone else at the beginning of the novel.
- Ideally, the heroine should not be pregnant before marriage. Some story lines do allow for premarital conception, as long as the couple eventually marries.
- The hero and heroine should exhibit good character and not be dishonest, unethical, or otherwise morally corrupt.
- Unless the story line has been approved by the editor, the hero and heroine should not be married to each other at the beginning of the novel. We also strongly discourage having the characters live together as a couple.
- In general, the hero and heroine should be role models—upwardly mobile and educated individuals that our readers can admire.

- Explicit and excessive profanity in the text is not permitted. Also, please limit the use of mild profanity in dialogue as well.
- In general, condoms should be used in intimate scenes where the hero and heroine are not married.
- Drug use by the hero and heroine are not permitted. Use by secondary characters should be limited as well. Descriptions of violence should be kept to a minimum.

If the reader wants a *sexy* love story that features minorities, they can turn to Kimani Romance, which is a typical category romance that allows a level of sexuality that can range from "moderately sensual to super sexy" and where the contemporary urban theme appears stronger than in Arabesque. Its only real category distinction is that it features African Americans. The line was ensured a strong launch because the first few novels were by Brenda Jackson, a well-known and highly regarded writer of African American romances who published her debut book with Kensington's Arabesque line in 1994. Not long after launching Kimani Romance, sales prompted an increase from two to three books per month, and not long thereafter, the line went to four books per month. Title increases of this type underscore the success of the line. Nevertheless, there has been some reader disenchantment with Harlequin's Kimani novels because African Americans are overrepresented to the exclusion of other people of color.[87] These concerns have not been aimed solely at Harlequin and will be returned to in the next chapter. It is important at this point to mention that Harlequin's original guidelines for the line specified that the characters depicted be African American exclusively. This was modified in 2014 to say "African American and multicultural heroines and heroes," though Moggy says the African American focus was never rigidly enforced and there had been multicultural heroines and heroes before it was officially changed in the guidelines. This may be true, but it is unlikely that multicultural characters would be found in many of the novels, if only because the African American stipulation in the guidelines would discourage would-be writers from submitting novels that featured minorities other than African Americans. Still, Moggy is correct when she goes on to mention that the increase in multicultural characters is a trend across the industry, underscoring how "both our author base and our readership [are] actually helping to change the guidelines of our series." This, she qualifies, is a good indication as to how "the series really do reflect both the authorship and the readership."

Kimani TRU was added in 2007; it is aimed at teens and was Harlequin's first venture into the young adult (YA) market. Marva Allen at the Hue-Man Bookstores in Harlem gave the line a positive review when it launched: "There is nothing like what Kimani TRU is doing."[88] Moggy says it is a very small part of the Kimani program. Its primary market is libraries, and the library market, especially when compared to the mass market, is relatively small. Still, the idea is to make these books accessible to teenagers in the hope that they might enjoy the books and subsequently buy them. It is one of the standard "defenses" in the industry, and it is a very apt one: romance readers are voracious readers and read across genres. They are not wed only to romance novels. They read! TRU, therefore, while it is not generating any substantive income to Harlequin's bottom line, is an admirable program geared toward getting minority young people to read and if, by chance, they like the books and subsequently buy them, so much the better.

Finding God: Harlequin Gets Inspired

With the exception of Silhouette's brief excursion into the Christian romance market at the height of the romance wars of the early 1980s, the inspirational field has been largely left to Christian publishers. They initially entered the fray in the mid- to late 1980s in response to the overwhelming eroticism found in secular romances. Christian romance author Janette Oke put it quite succinctly: "A lot of people [are] growing tired of where secular romances [are] leading them. People in general are tired of smut."[89] They too suffered from a glut on the market during the late 1980s, and there was considerable fallout in the early 1990s. Nevertheless, Christian publishers have continued to release evangelical romances with considerable success.

Christian fiction is a vibrant market: at the close of the twentieth century, Christian fiction accounted for 5.25 million books and generated $43 million in sales.[90] This is relatively small when compared to the $1 billion dollar romance industry, and Harlequin no doubt felt that if the smaller Christian houses could do $43 million, they might be able to duplicate this success in the mass-market industry, which is their area of specialization.

Harlequin did not jump in like Silhouette haphazardly did two decades earlier. Management spent two years closely examining the market before deciding to launch Spring Hill Books and introduce Love Inspired in September 1997. After the Love Inspired romances were established, the line was broadened to include other Christian-themed niche romances: Love Inspired Suspense (2005) and Love Inspired Historical (2008). Steeple Hill books also did some Christian single-title novels under Café, "mainly at the height of chick-lit's popularity" (circa 2005), says Moggy. Chick-lit, however, often filters some sexuality into the plot, à la *Sex and the City*, and this wouldn't do in an inspirational line. Steeple Hill editor Krista Stoever explains the niche for Café: "The underlying theme of the books is how young, single women stay true to their Christian beliefs in the modern world. For example, a protagonist might struggle with avoiding sex while dating. It's a different set of troubles for a heroine."[91] Since single-title Steeple Hill Café inspirational chick-lit books were a small part of the Steeple Hill imprint and were positioned primarily to capitalize on the brief popularity of chick-lit category books, it was discontinued after a few years as chick-lit itself started to fade in popularity. The Steeple Hill Imprint soon disappeared as well: Moggy says the market research clearly showed that the Steeple Hill name "didn't resonate with the readers the way Love Inspired did."

Moggy is correct in identifying Harlequin's mass-market expertise as a driving reason why the company decided to enter the Christian romance market. The readers for their mass-market books are the Wal-Mart shoppers, and this is an area where Christian publishers do not have much of a presence. On the other hand, Harlequin tried but was unable to break into the Christian retail outlets. They seem to have entered the Christian market half-heartedly, since the line launch was not accompanied by the traditional marketing campaign: "It's difficult to market these types of books," said Kathryn Orr, Harlequin vice president of public relations. "People are very private about their religious beliefs. We're just going to put the books out there and leave it to readers to discover them on their own."[92]

Though Love Inspired launched without a strong marketing campaign, Harlequin was proactive and attempted to get the books into Christian bookstores. They attended some of the conventions held by the Christian Bookstore Association (CBA) but made little headway. The rumor is that CBA members didn't want anything to do with Harlequin, when in truth, one CBA industry insider confided, it had more to do with the CBA stores, which are set up for trade-sized hardback and paperback books, not mass- market paperbacks. This meant that the Love Inspired books simply got lost in the stores. This did not improve even after Harlequin offered to provide mass-market racks to display their novels. This didn't appeal to CBA members, whose retail stores tend to be smaller than the large chain bookstores, and the racks simply ate up too much floor space. In short, Harlequin was right to publish Christian mass-market paperbacks because the mass-market is their specialty, but this same specialization kept them from recognizing how to break into Christian bookstores. Moggy admits that "we are definitely not a player" in Christian bookstores, but she fails to mention that they would have liked to have been one.

The degree to which Harlequin conveys the Christian message is open to debate, despite the tagline for the series, "Life, Faith, and Getting It Right."[93] Some readers of the line feel that they are not as thematically strong as the message conveyed in Christian romances published by Christian publishers. The authors of the Love Inspired series are Christian, but it may be that Harlequin editors "tone down" the spirituality more so than Christian publishers, who accentuate that element of the romance. Laura Clawson touches on this in her comparison of secular and Christian romances, though it is important to point out that her secular comparison is limited to other Harlequin lines (Silhouette Romance, Harlequin American Romance, and Silhouette's Desire).[94] She finds the only real distinguishing feature between Harlequin's secular and Christian lines is that the latter are more oriented toward domesticity. Clawson concludes her analysis by suggesting what I have intimated: that there is some (perhaps unconscious) watering down of the Christian message in the Love Inspired series:

> Christian romances' [from Harlequin] very lack of conflict between the aggressive, worldly, and highly instrumental masculinity and highly expressive femininity found in [Harlequin's] secular romances, however, may reveal an unwillingness on the part of the authors and publishers of [Harlequin's] Christian romance to employ plots in which the heroine triumphs over the hero, pushing him to substantially change his outlook on life and, particularly, love.[95]

The Harlequin guidelines specify just what the Christian message is. In rudimentary form they are "contemporary romances with a Christian worldview and wholesome values … that emphasize emotional intimacy rather than sexual desire." Moggy clarifies the Christian element: "The importance of family and community, and of giving back to both of these." This is certainly an important element in Christian published romances. Missing from her discussion of the inspirational line, however, is the centrality of God in the budding relationship between heroine and hero. God is mentioned in the Harlequin books, but one Christian reader pointed out that references to Jesus Christ are largely absent, and that is certainly not the case with Christian published romances. Their take on the Christian romance is discussed in greater detail in the next chapter.

Harlequin may have found a way to convey the Christian message more forcefully. Harlequin purchased the Heartsong series in 2012 from Barbour, an Ohio-based Christian house that publishes over 150 books per year. To ensure continuity in the transition from Barbour to Harlequin, the two companies shared management for a twelve-month period so that readership followed when the changeover to Harlequin was finalized. The only change appears to be that it is now called Heartsong Presents, which suggests that it has been folded into the Harlequin family, though it only says on the inside copyright page that it is a Love Inspired Book and does not otherwise identify it as a Harlequin product. "It is managed," Moggy says, "just as Barbour managed it. It goes to direct-mail customers, though we offer it digitally as well. There is no retail print distribution. There are two contemporary and two historical every month and the books are shorter, 50,000 words, compared to [longer] Love Inspired [Historical] books."

Though no content analysis of these books has been conducted, it is assumed that coming from a Christian publishing house, the Christian element is stronger than in Love Inspired, and perhaps that is why their most Christian-themed romances are delivered in a distinctly non-mass market way.

Entering the Mainstream: MIRA and HQN

MIRA recently celebrated its twentieth anniversary. It was launched in 1994. It is unquestionably one of the most significant developments in Harlequin's long history because it made Harlequin a major player in non-category, mainstream women's fiction. HQN developed slightly later: it has a somewhat shorter word count, 10,000 to 20,000 words less than MIRA, and is promoted as its author line. "No one," Moggy says, "goes out to buy an HQN book. They go out to buy the next novel by Diane Palmer or Linda Miller." Still, the distinction is thin, admits Moggy, since one could argue that some authors could be published in either MIRA or HQN. The main difference is that MIRA is "really looking for commercial literary fiction."

This is not Harlequin's first step into mainstream fiction. Worldwide Library (1986–1988) was a short-lived attempt to move in this direction. Worldwide released a wide range of men's and women's fiction, but therein lies the problem. It had no focus and was hastily developed when Harlequin was shotgun-blasting new ventures. It helped Harlequin think things through this time around and, if nothing else, gave some insights as to what not to do. The main reason for moving beyond category romances was that Harlequin was losing too many good writers who wanted to move beyond the limits of category fiction. "We needed an opportunity for our authors who wanted to write bigger books—under the Harlequin umbrella," said Moggy. "And up to that point they actually had to go to the competition." To make sure it worked this time, a "great deal of time was spent speaking to authors, agents, and [retail] accounts."

It is clearly a success. By 2001, just six years after launching MIRA, single-title sales represented 25.6 percent of Harlequin's revenue.[96] A little over a decade later (2014), it is now "almost half of the company's revenue," Moggy affirms. More proof of its success lies in the number of MIRA and HQN books that now regularly dot the best-seller lists. The name (pronounced Mirror) refers to refers to one of the biggest stars in the constellation Cetus. It's also a woman's name, so it refers to the brightest star in women's fiction. It is certainly a bright star for Harlequin and puts the company in a league with other major publishers who once snubbed Harlequin for producing trashy category fiction.

MIRA and HQN, along with LUNA, which focuses on other-world fantasy fiction, are all 100,000-plus words, which move them beyond category publishing. Harlequin's mainstream efforts work the same as any publisher of mainstream fiction. There are author tours and advertising campaigns for established authors. Some multi-*New York Times* authors have "an incredible fan base, so you can directly reach them." It is tougher to get information out on a new author, but this problem plagues all publishers. Moggy gives an example of how this worked for one of their new protégés.

Jason Mott's debut MIRA novel was *The Returned* (2013). It is about a couple in the 1970s who lost their son. Skip forward a few years. They get a knock on the door from an FBI agent who has a little boy with them. And the little boy is their son at the same age as when he disappeared. This is happening all over the world. People's loved ones are returning at the same age as when they left the world. "It is not quintessential women's fiction, but it resonates with women," Moggy explains:

> We did very traditional support for *The Returned*: Galleys [pre-release copies of the book] went out to get reviewers excited—and in this case we were helped because his agent sold the movie rights, and that got a lot of buzz. We did a big campaign in various newspapers and magazines. For debut authors it's all about getting people to talk about the book. The digital world is big today, too. It gets people blogging [about the book]. The digital world has played a huge role in getting author recognition. In the case of *The Returned*, the author wrote some prequels that we published for free to get people excited. There was also a price promotion. The books sold for 99 cents for a period of time in digital space.

This kind of single-title promotion is unnecessary with category publishing. As former CEO Lawrence Heisey pointed out long ago, once marketing acquaints the consumer with the line, little else is needed because no matter who is writing the books, the reader knows what they are getting from that particular series of books. Mainstream books are each independently judged and marketed. Harlequin has proved very competent in this area, and this seems to have surprised a lot of people in the business who thought Harlequin was only competent at publishing "cheap [category] romances."

A Line Miscellany: Embracing Some Themes, Shunning Others

Like any publisher, Harlequin seeks opportunities to position new lines when there appears to be an interest in a new topic. The company has two specialties, so it tends to be top-heavy in these areas: mainstream women's fiction now and category romance novels traditionally. It sometimes steps out of this box in mainstream fiction, as we saw with *The Returned*, when it is a story that is viewed as "resonating with women," but this is atypical.

Harlequin Teen was launched in 2009 and is a mainstream line of books aimed at teenagers,[97] where TRU is a category line and focuses on minority teens. The teen market is a key demographic, and it is a bit surprising that Harlequin waited so long to tap it. The hesitancy was probably owing to the view that it published adult romances. This is understandable because the young adult (YA) market, which in the publishing world means teenagers, not twenty-somethings, is a whole different world.

It has been a learning process. In this case, they learned from their failure, Silhouette's First Love. First Love was launched at the height of the romance wars in an apparent attempt to expand the romance format into the young adult market. Silhouette, however, had no expertise with the distinctive YA market. The line lasted as long as it did (1981–1988) because Silhouette was shotgun-blasting lines to stay competitive, and this prevented management from critically examining this one line of books. It continued to linger after the merger because Harlequin was busy reorganizing. It would appear that when the dust settled in the mid–1980s, First Love was looked at more critically. Sales weren't there, which is why First Love was reborn as Crosswinds—rebranding a line is inevitably an indication that the initial line is not doing well and another tactic is being attempted to salvage the line. It only took one year to figure out that the rebranding wasn't going anywhere, and the line was discontinued in short order. The YA market was nevertheless a lucrative one that Harlequin wanted to crack. A lot more planning went into it this time, however.

Dianne Moggy explains some of the problems they had to overcome introducing Harlequin books to the young adult market. YA books are either trade paperback or hardcover, which is not Harlequin's strong suit. And while Harlequin has been very successful with its adult line of MIRA and HQN trade paperback and hardcovers, YA books are aimed at a different account. They are filtered through a different set of buyers from those Harlequin typically deals with, and the books go into different sections of the bookstore. This has not changed in the digital age as it has with some of the other books Harlequin publishes online. Surprisingly, teens do not read digitally.

Young people are very passionate about their books, primarily because it is for show, a status symbol indicating to other teens their coolness. In short, the books are accessories. This phenomenon may have been there in the past, but it seems to have become more pronounced since the Harry Potter books first appeared in 1998.[98] The success of the first *Hunger Games* (2008) book published by Scholastic and the popularity of Veronica Roth's trilogy, which was launched when HarperCollins published *Divergent* in 2011, ensured that YA adventure books remain cherished among adolescent females. Owning the books is an indication of cultural elitism, but it is important not just to own the book but to be seen with it, an indication, Moggy says, that announces to your peers that you're in the in-group. It doesn't matter whether this is true or not; it matters because this is what the YA buyers at retail outlets believe, and their belief shapes their purchase and placement of the books. This means the buyer doesn't want to see too many books flooding the market too soon. They would be resistant to the mass-market pattern of a book per month because they feel that the higher price point would be resisted by teens who supposedly cannot afford the books if they came too frequently.

KISS is one of the new lines that might appeal to teenagers but is aimed more at the currently voguish New Adult (NA) category: young twenty-somethings who like the television show *Ugly Betty* or movies like *Crazy Stupid Love* or *500 Days of Summer*, which opens with the catchy disclaimer that would appeal to Millennials: "Any resemblance to people living or dead is purely coincidental.... Especially you, Jenny Beckman.... Bitch!" The "B" word and other crudities are not atypical among contemporary urban teenagers; they are nevertheless typically frowned upon in YA fiction, as is sexual activity, a mainstay of KISS that would appeal to young urban women, the primary market for KISS novels.

The same twenty-something age group is also the target market for Nocturne, a longer (80,000–85,000 word), mainstream novel line, although it has strong category elements. Its longer format is largely owing to the need to develop the paranormal world that is central to the plot. Harlequin has done a lot of research with the paranormal genre over the years and one of the key things that, Moggy stresses, is *crucial* to reader enjoyment is that the paranormal world be fully developed: "So whether it's vampires or shape-shifters, or werewolves or fairies, readers unanimously wanted longer books so the paranormal world is fully created for them. That's quite different than many of the other genres." The closest subgenre that emphasizes the "other" world as much as the romantic one is romance suspense and mysteries, where the suspense-mystery aspect is just as important as the romance, which is why Harlequin recently raised Intrigues from 50–60,000 words to 70–75,000. Nocturne, which launched in 2010, capitalizes on the success of the *Twilight* films, the first of which appeared in November 2008. Two paranormals are released monthly, one in print and one in digital format, which is embraced more fully by twenty-somethings than teenagers. Harlequin has recently (2014) replaced Nocturne Bites, their paranormal short stories that were released digitally, with Harlequin-e. Bites tended to support specific titles or authors that were published in the Nocturne series.

8. Alive and Kicking 175

Paranormals have come and gone over the years, and it is likely that at some point down the road the fad will again burn itself out and the line will be discontinued, but that happens with many consumer products. In the meantime, to keep consumer interest alive, Harlequin is building on the popularity of two-in-ones, where two novels are combined into one print edition, which makes them more attractive to the consumer because the books cost only slightly more than a single category romance: around $6.50 compared to $5.00 per novel. The two-in-ones are also attractive to retailers because they have only so much shelf space.

Harlequin-e is Harlequin's new digital format. It was being tested in 2014. The test revolves around twelve books called *Thirty-six Hours*: each book focuses on the next thirty-six hours in a different person's life after a devastating storm strikes a small Colorado town. In digital space, Harlequin divides each book into three parts. The first part is free; there is a nominal charge for the second and third part: the second and third Kindle parts sell for $1.99 on Amazon. This may sound like a good value, but it is pretty close to what the books go for at big-box retailers like Wal-Mart after they've been discounted by twenty-five percent from the normal list price of $4.99.

The one place Harlequin has not gone, or has ventured into rarely and cautiously, is explicit sexuality. When management at Harlequin talks of erotic tales, they do not typically go to the far end of the spectrum, what has here been categorized at the 9–10 level on our sensual Likert scale. Level-8 sexuality is quite explicit and even some secular readers may construe these novels to border on the pornographic. This concern would likely increase if the novels go beyond the eight level that may depict casual sexual activity with a number of partners—which is in some Harlequin lines—but where the sexual act itself is described in graphic detail and typically is the unending storyline: two people (or more) meet, clothes immediately disappear; the sexual act is lingered over and unfolds for some time, and upon completion, the chapter/scene ends and the next chapter/scene begins with another sexual escapade. Many Harlequin readers might say sexuality at this level borders on the "pornographic." This is why Harlequin, as well as most mainstream romance publishers, strays no further than an eight level of eroticism in print, and that rather tenuously.[99] Even Blaze, where body contact is fairly common, the focus still pivots on "the emotions [which] are the real turn-on."[100]

In the 1970s and 1980s, there was considerable hue and cry over the "pornographic" element of romance novels and much of this focused on the sexuality in the bodice-rippers. Harlequin only infrequently published a few of these books in its late-1980s historical line. One would never know this if the popular press is relied upon for insight: *U.S. News & World Report* in 2009 listed the "10 Winners of the Recession" with bodice-rippers by Harlequin garnering the number three spot, while *Time* magazine lead with the headline, "The Global Boom in Bodice-Rippers," and then went on to talk about Harlequin's domination of the market, implying they are one and the same.[101] The level of sexuality of the bodice-rippers of the 1970s and 1980s did not translate well to contemporary novels, so Harlequin, which at the time did not publish historical novels, never went there. In today's more sexually charged social world, the bodice-rippers seem rather tame in their graphic depiction of sexuality, which is one reason that, except for a few popular writers, they have largely disappeared from the shelves.[102]

Today, the pornographic is more likely to be found in BDSM novels. These have gained a certain amount of favor among mainstream publishers since *Fifty Shades of Grey* and its offspring appeared at the top of the best-seller lists in 2011. But as Moggy points out, BDSM in fiction does not have to be a ten; it can fall at the 6, 7, or 8 level. She is absolutely right. This is why *Fifty Shades'* love dots some of MIRA's fiction, as well as the fiction of other mainstream publishers of women's fiction. Most in this lifestyle, however, scoff at *Fifty Shades* as BDSM-lite.[103] BDSM devotees get a little more "down and dirty" when they beat their submissives: serious bruises and contusions are not uncommon, and blood is often drawn.[104] This would not be considered "erotic" to the average romance reader, which is why BDSM books published at the upper range of sexuality, as well as more explicit ten-level sexuality, is either self-published or published by some of the smaller independent presses outside the mainstream.

And Then There Were

Harlequin has had relatively few discontinued lines, all things considered. Indeed, many of Harlequin's lines have existed for decades. This longevity is more of an anomaly than lines that have been discontinued. Some lines were looked at as short-term projects and were launched knowing that the current social craze would run its course and when that happened, the line would be discontinued. Others were to take advantage of joint opportunities that came Harlequin's way. Some of these worked out, others didn't, or at least didn't work out in the long run. And some were looked at as filling a product niche but were poorly positioned or had internal problems that, try as they might, could not be satisfactorily resolved.

Red Dress Ink is a good example of a line that was launched because of the chick-lit craze that followed the publication of *Bridget Jones's Diary* in 1996. Most major publishing firms jumped aboard this bandwagon and rushed to

publish chick-lit novels as part of their mainstream press; a few even had dedicated chick-lit imprints, such as Kensington (Strapless) and Simon & Schuster (Downtown). "Everyone is trying to find the next Bridget Jones," said Irwyn Applebaum, president of Bantam Dell Publishing.[105] *See Jane Write: A Girls' Guide to Writing Chick-lit*, followed to help wanna-be writers. The books went beyond the traditional romance where the happy ending is ensured. The novels appealed to younger women. Weddings and babies, the mainstay of traditional romances, went by the wayside. The theme centered on everyday struggles, not necessarily related to men. The new heroine, writes Elena Cherney, "has to struggle with mean bosses and has issues with [her] mother and sisters."[106] And when it comes to men, that too is not a given. "There's not necessarily a Mr. Right," said Laura Morris, product manager for new business development at Harlequin, who was involved in the Red Dress series. "She has to kiss a lot of frogs."[107]

Harlequin, whose expertise at the time was in category fiction, is the only house to develop chick-lit as a category line, which means that while most houses were releasing a few novels every year in the chick-lit format as part of their overall program, Harlequin was publishing a new title every month. It was a contentious in-house issue because it didn't fit snugly into the Harlequin oeuvre. Hayes found the brand strategy "fascinating. Discussion in-house raged long and loud. Do we make it part of the Harlequin brand or launch a new brand?" But it worked out because "when you read about [the line] in the media," Hayes continues, "inevitably the story is [about] Harlequin [who] has always published these wonderful traditional romances, and now they're doing this other hip fun line for young women."[108] Their concession was to remove the Harlequin logo from the cover and replace it with the Red Dress Ink moniker under a dress on a hanger. The proof is in the pudding: the line lasted from November 2001 to January 2013, a pretty good run for a steady diet of books that, Moggy says, was a program that was not sustainable: "It was really a victim of time." She goes on to elaborate on a point that has been visited before—with the bodice-rippers in the 1970s and Ecstasy knock-offs in the 1980s: "Like any trend, once it becomes popular, everyone gets on board. Soon quality diminishes. Everybody tries to write [it] because they think it is what's selling, and publishers get on board to sell [it] because they think there's a market, which leads to a glut and quality issues. You can have only so many books that are about firsts—first date, first job; it gets very repetitive." And so Red Dress Ink was discontinued at the same time most publishing houses were moving beyond chick-lit. Most publishers still publish an occasional chick-lit novel by a well-known author who has a strong reader base, but there is no frantic search for new authors that marked the early years. Harlequin likewise continues to filter an occasional chick-lit book into its MIRA line by some of their established chick-lit authors, but most of the others who have stayed with Harlequin after the line was discontinued have moved to other subgenres.

Red Dress Ink cannot be construed as a failure; it had a fairly long life for a short-lived trend. Even short-lived lines that stretch over only a few years cannot be considered disappointments. Harlequin's NASCAR series and Mills & Boon's Rugby novels lasted only a few years (circa 2007–2010) but capitalized on popular themes and sold fairly well.

The popular press had some fun with the NASCAR-Harlequin relationship: the headline at USA Today blurted, "NASCAR, Harlequin Gear Up for Love Stories"; the New York Times declared, "In Harlequin-Nascar Romance, Hearts Race."[109] Both feature stories acknowledged, however, that it made sense, even if it joined odd bedfellows, by acknowledging it was economically sound since NASCAR fans buy $2 billion in licensed products annually and that women account for forty percent of the sport's fan base. It was a natural fit since Harlequin's key distribution channels are discount stores such as Wal-Mart, and these stores, Wal-Mart in particular, license an incredible number of NASCAR products. One of the purposes for proposing this relationship was mentioned by Mark Dyer, vice president of licensing for NASCAR: "It's probably more of a brand-building and P.R. bonanza for us than a financial windfall.[110] One romance aficionado, commenting on the reader post for this series, would confirm that this was a success. She said that she thought car racing was just about driving around in circles and that she learned from these novels that there was much more to the sport than that. The Harlequin-NASCAR relationship fostered the idea for a similar romance-sports hookup in the U.K., and so Mills & Boon forged a similar alliance with the Rugby Football Union and released The RFU International Billionaires series. The results were probably similar for the non-sports enthusiast who read romances. "You don't have to like rugby to like the books," said Clair Somerville, Mills & Boon's sales and marketing director. "They've got all the elements of a quintessential Mills & Boon romance: jet-set locations, hunky alpha male heroes and hot sex, but in a rugby context."[111] The launch was greeted with a similar lighthearted headline in The Guardian, which announced the launch of the series under the headline "Mills & Boon Whisper Sweet Nothings in Cauliflower Ears."[112]

A somewhat more traditional alliance was forged between Mills & Boon and the National Trust in the U.K. Harlequin has a long history of publishing historical romances, particularly in the U.K. These books are based on romances that took place in a National Trust historic property: think Downton Abbey before the hit PBS series debuted in 2011.[113] The main difference in the National Trust novels, besides the historic setting, is that the books, while sold traditionally,

8. Alive and Kicking

can also be found at the retail shop at the historic site. Despite the relative success of this association with the National Trust, Moggy indicates that Harlequin North America has never seriously considered establishing a similar relationship with historical properties in Canada or the United States. The rationale is that Harlequin already releases any number of books that feature historical locales or houses in its other lines. Moggy illustrates this point by referencing a book in progress (mid–2014) that revolves around a house that was built before the Civil War and the house serves as a device for traveling back into time and into the present day…. "It's a story of the house! Through the events that have taken place there."[114] Be that as it may, if a series is a success, à la Blaze, this would not stop Harlequin from launching a line to capitalize on its success. This would suggest the hesitancy in extending the National Trust venture in the U.K. and situating a similar series in North America would owe at least as much to its limited (sales) success in the U.K.[115]

In the case of the Harlequin-National Trust association, Harlequin approached the co-brander. A more recent venture occurred the other way, with *Cosmopolitan* magazine, the co-brander, approaching Harlequin. This relationship will no doubt be successful because it is romance fiction aimed to tap an existing audience base, the female readers of a young woman's magazine. "Cosmo Red Hot Reads" features two monthly 30,000-word titles, designed for reading on mobile devices.[116] The young, tech-savvy Millennial female audience that is attracted to *Cosmo* should enhance the potential for a longer lasting relationship than some of its other ventures.

Bombshell (2004–2007) also fits into this short-term niche. It was seen as a short-term venture to capitalize on a trend, in this case "The Lara Croft thing," says Moggy. The action-adventure angle would prove more appropriately positioned in the Rogue Angel series under Gold Eagle since the imprint focuses on action-adventure heroes, and now heroines, and this made Bombshell redundant.

Some short-term series, however, were more problematic. They were designed to survive, at least for some period of time, but never lasted long. Shadows (1993–1996) was, Moggy thinks, just ahead of its time, "before paranormal really caught on." It might just as likely be that it wasn't strictly paranormal but also included heavy dosages of romance suspense and gothic elements. Moggy is correct to say that Shadows was not just before paranormal fiction caught on; it was significantly ahead of the curve. Her assessment is substantiated by the success of Nocturne, launched in 2010, which wasn't that much different but debuted after the paranormal craze hit on the heels of *Twilight* in 2008.

Spice was not so much ahead of its time as it was a tad beyond the level of sensuality that is generally accepted within romantic fiction.[117] This, in itself, is instructive. Those in romance publishing, including authors and readers, often talk about the various levels of eroticism in the novel, saying this book or that line is more or less sexually explicit or erotic than another book or line. Spice suggests that there is an upper level that is off limits, at least to many Harlequin readers.

Spice surpassed Blaze in its level of eroticism, if only because sexual activity was more casual and unfettered since the heroine often had sex with a number of men during the course of the novel. Indeed, Clair Somerville, the marketing director for Mills & Boon said to a reporter when the line debuted in the U.K. that the Spice paperbacks are "more about sex for enjoyment. It doesn't have to be linked to an emotional connection,"[118] which typifies most romantic fiction. The first sentence of the back-of-the-book blurb for Spice's *Rampant* (May 2012) revels in the sex-for-sexual pleasure that characterized the line: "The moment she arrives at her rented vacation cottage in Scotland, Zoe Daniels feels it—an arousal so powerful she's compelled to surrender to the unusually forceful carnal desires—with nearly anyone who crosses her path."

When casual sex is unconnected to emotional bonding and is graphically depicted, it hovers at the 10-level on our sensual Likert scale and at that level can cross over into the pornographic.[119] The books never connected with the readers, probably because it crossed an imaginary sensual threshold. A few of the more toned-down, level-8, authors who wrote some of the Spice books continue to publish with MIRA, and one of the MIRA books, *Dirty* by Megan Hart, was rated in the number-one slot in *Publishers Weekly* Valentine's Day "10 Dirty Romance Novels" in 2014.[120] Some authors, however, went elsewhere. Some may have gravitated to writing more evocative sensual romances for Ellora's Cave or Siren Publishing; others drifted into the world of self-publishing, where, Moggy suggests, a lot of those writing more explicit romances tend to go.

It would appear that Harlequin is again dipping its toe into the higher end of the erotic scale with, surprisingly, the Presents series. When Presents debuted in 1973, it simply acknowledged that people in a committed relationship engaged in sexual activity outside marriage, but the chapter ended at the bedroom door. Presents is now clearly in the middle range of eroticism, with some books a notch or two on either end of the five midpoint. In mid–2014, Harlequin moved some of the Presents novels to the far end (level 9 to 10) of the erotic continuum with a trilogy called Fifth Avenue. It fits into the Presents line because it revolves around betrayal and revenge. It steps outside the Presents tone because it goes beyond Blaze: "It is our edgiest," Moggy proclaimed. Because this steps outside the boundaries that typically demark the line—and therefore can be off-putting to some readers—Harlequin is not putting the novels on the series rack but releasing them within the single-title MIRA books. This is a bit confusing since "it's under Presents branding but with mainstream trade paperbacks." This may pose problems for the reader identifying the books. Mainstream readers of MIRA books will see the Presents brand and think it is a category book, while Presents readers, who might appreciate the heightened eroticism within the betrayal and revenge theme, won't be able to find it within other Presents novels, even though it's a Presents book. Moggy indicated that the summer 2014 release of Fifth Avenue was favorably received, but those involved with editing a book or launching a line tend to be optimistic. The proof, as always, is in the pudding—sales! Whether the series continues and how it is eventually branded will suggest the degree of success or failure of Fifth Avenue's eroticism. One can only wonder, as Tom Peck and Sophie Mills did when the Spice series debuted in the U.K., how the books would "register on the Mills & Boon social barometer...."[121]

The sales clearly were not there for NEXT, though its theme looked promising. NEXT was a line that focused on the next stage in a woman's life.[122] It could be her next love, but it could also be her next job, her next residence, her next adventure. This emphasis made the thirty-something heroine slightly older than the norm in romance fiction; Moggy even acknowledges that an occasional forty-something-year-old might be featured. NEXT bears a resemblance to Second Chance at Love, one of the few successful series from the early 1980s that was critiqued in Chapter 5. Second Chance focused on a woman's next chance at a relationship. The distinction is mainly that NEXT went beyond the relationship and dealt with other "nexts" in a woman's life. The problem was not the premise, the age of the heroine, or the writing; the problem was an internal one of positioning.

NEXT was positioned as a category romance. Moggy was satisfied with the level of writing, but felt the line was published as a category line but the actual content was much more mainstream and single-title. This caused reader confusion. "Readers who come to the series section in a bookstore," Moggy explains, "have a very definite idea of what she's going to find there. And while romance is in all the [NEXT] books, the focus isn't always on the romance, so the reader didn't know what it was." This was compounded by internal confusion as to how to market and package the books. This is similar to some of the problems for lines from the 1980s: if the book is a category romance, it goes one place with a distinct look; if it is mainstream women's fiction, it goes another place with an altogether different marketing plan and look. When the two overlap, as happened here, it is difficult to place the book, and if it cannot find its "voice," it cannot find an audience.

Another line that didn't find its "voice" was First Love. Moggy points out that publishing is a business and that at some point hard business decisions have to be made so the resources devoted to that program can be reallocated more fruitfully to other programs. This is the primary reason for the ending of many lines discussed in this section: most lines have a lifespan that is tied to demands in the marketplace and when the marketplace interest shifts, the line is not going to produce any longer. Some lines may linger beyond their lifespan because the line escapes close scrutiny. This happened with First Love. Silhouette launched it when it was tossing everything into the market. Then Harlequin purchased Silhouette and the consolidation overshadowed a close scrutiny of line sales. As soon as events settled and Harlequin took a closer look at the sales figures, First Love was discontinued since it was not producing.

There is one line, however, that was watched closely at Harlequin and that Harlequin believed so strongly in that it did any number of things to try and make it successful. It remained on life support well beyond its natural life.

Silhouette launched Yours Truly in 1995, and Harlequin countered with Love and Laughter exactly twelve months later. By the mid–1990s, Silhouette had been firmly folded into the Harlequin family. Nevertheless, the two houses still acted independently of one another in the 1990s, and a friendly rivalry existed between them. Both lines centered on the humorous element. This makes perfect sense since a recurring feature romance readers favorably comment on is the humor found in the books. That women readers found the humor in romance novels attractive should not be surprising, because this is one of the attributes woman cite that appeals to them in a prospective partner.[123] If readers like the humor in the books, why not have a line of books that feature humor? This is the reason the line lasted as long as it did. The logic was there, if not the sales.

The two separate humor lines were combined into one line in 1999 called Duets. This too makes sense because it focuses the organization's resources. The fact that it was rechristened Duets, however, suggests a rebranding "save-the-line" issue. The line was already on life support, however. This is suggested by the fact that Duets only lasted four years. The name probably didn't help since it did not convey the humorous slant of the novels. Harlequin's commitment to the premise lingered on and the line was reincarnated with another non-definitive name, Flipside, in 2003, with a chick-lit humorous twist. But chick-lit has, ipso facto, a humorous thread that runs through it, and chick-lit was more specifically developed in Harlequin's Red Dress Ink series. A year later there was evidence, even to the most optimistic at Harlequin, that, try as they might, the humor line, by whatever name given it, was going nowhere. It was officially discontinued in June 2005, ten years after its birth.

The rationale for staying with the idea is logical. Why the problem took so long to diagnose is more problematic. The problem is clear now, in hindsight. Moggy explains why the line had difficulty finding an audience. One of the problems was reminiscent of NEXT: "We tried too much to convey the humor and forgot that the romance should be front and center. Of course, the romantic element was part of every story, but sometimes the humor took over." More problematic was the ability to sustain the humor:

> Romantic comedy in general has been incredibly difficult to publish. There are some individual authors who have been very successful on the single-title side. But even then there aren't that many authors who successfully publish it in single title. In terms of the series, we found it very, very difficult to find authors who could sustain the humorous element.
>
> Humor is so subjective, so what's funny to you is not funny to me. And it's incredibly difficult to write. If [for example] you look at the romantic comedy on television [or film], the most comedic parts are often the initial setup and lead. Then there is some humor spread throughout. You can set up a very cute and fun first meeting and conflict between the heroine and the hero [re: *When Harry Met Sally*]. But to carry it through the course of a book is very difficult. Plus humor has an *incredibly* visual component to it, which is much harder to convey in the written word [re: the orgasm scene in *When Harry Met Sally*].
>
> We tried to rebrand it and did a couple of things [with Duets]. We moved them into two-in-ones, so it was a great value for the price. This worked because they're short novels to begin with, so by combing two in one it was a great value that might appeal to the reader—this has worked well in some of our overseas markets. We also tried a different type of packing. And, of course, a new name and different branding. Three fairly large differentiating factors. But at heart [it remained] very similar editorially.

Not everything gets off the drawing board. There is a lot of brainstorming that goes on. Some of the ideas that have emerged from these sessions, like Red Dress Ink, have moved to fruition. Others may yet, and thus Moggy is understandably reluctant to discuss them. There are two she raises, however, that crop up with some regularity. Since they are outside the Harlequin market for women's fiction, they have not been pursued. One is classic Western novels—not romances set in the West that ekes its way into a number of romances, particularly in American Romances—but old-school male-oriented westerns. Many of these old-school Westerns, though male-oriented, have a strong female slant and are worthy of genre consideration from that perspective, such as *High Noon, Shane, The Man Who Shot Liberty Valance,* and *Rooster Cogburn*. The other genre often talked about is original hard-boiled mysteries. The mysteries Harlequin presently publishes under the Worldwide Mystery series are reprints of hardcover originals for the North American market (despite the Worldwide logo with its suggestion of more global distribution). The Worldwide imprint is a carryover from an earlier point in time. This imprint, as well as Gold Eagle, would not likely be done today under the current focus on women's fiction. But it was not that long ago that Harlequin only published romance novels, not "women's fiction." The current focus on women's fiction is a major reason these male-oriented genres keep getting turned down as a new opportunity. The new relationship with HarperCollins might mitigate these developments with Harlequin since there are other HarperCollins venues for Westerns, hard-boiled mysteries and male-oriented fiction, such as Gold Eagle, that otherwise don't really have a place within the Harlequin romance oeuvre.

The International Arena

Harlequin has long had an international presence outside North America. The purchase of Mills & Boon opened this door since Mills & Boon romances were widely distributed not only in the United Kingdom, but also English-speaking Australia and New Zealand. Mills & Boon also had a small presence in Western Europe, specifically France, Germany, Greece, and the Netherlands.[124] By 2000, Harlequin novels could be found in 94 countries in 24 languages; by 2010, its romances appeared in 111 countries in 31 languages.[125] Its international presence has long contributed to Harlequin's bottom line: about a million novels were sold each year in Australia and New Zealand at the time Harlequin acquired Mills & Boon in 1972.[126] As early as 1982, sales outside North America accounted for more than half (54 percent) of all Harlequin book sales. This may have dropped recently (2012) with Canada (5 percent) and the United States (47 percent) now generating the lion's share of revenue, but international sales still contribute a hefty 47 percent to Harlequin's bottom line.[127] International sales account for one-third (36 percent) of all Harlequin books sold,[128] and that alone accounted for over one-fourth (28 percent) of Torstar's operating revenue.[129] Overseas expansions provide Harlequin with its greatest opportunity for growth. Its largest international markets outside of the United States are the U.K., Australia, Germany, Scandinavia, France, and Japan,[130] which is why these countries are the focal point of this analysis.

Despite Mills & Boon's international presence, it never really made much headway besides reprinting the books in Australia and New Zealand. Paul Grescoe reports Heisey's assessment of Mills & Boon European sophistication: "[T]hey never really had a sense of what they could do.... Alan [Boon] thought about being in other countries, but he didn't know enough about business to figure [out] how it could be done."[131] Mills & Boon simply licensed the rights to their books to local publishers who reprinted them under their own logo, which explains why they only reaped one to two percent of the cover price of the novels when the industry standard was ten to fifteen percent.[132] Harlequin soon ended this licensing arrangement and began publishing the books themselves. By the late 1970s, Harlequin had started its true international expansion, mostly by setting up joint ventures with local publishers. These alliances allowed Harlequin to quickly expand its product in the global arena. These alliances are now looked at as a key means by which an organization can expand its market.[133] Harlequin was ahead of the curve when they embarked on these ventures in the 1970s. Most of these ventures were mutually satisfying; some were not.

The successes and failures enumerated in this section only scratch the international surface. It is meant solely to show how Harlequin has managed to enter some markets and some of the problems it has encountered in others. More important to the central tenet of this book, it shows how their product offerings are selected and modified in the best gatekeeper tradition to fit local social exigencies.

The most straightforward transmigration transformation is, unsurprisingly, English-speaking Australia, where Harlequin, via Mills & Boon, has long had a presence: Harlequin Enterprise Pty Ltd. has some forty staff members and currently achieves between AU $5 to $10 million in revenue.[134] We also see that, despite this presence, the same reader hesitancy surrounding the genre continues. It is less pronounced here than in many other global expansions, but it still persists. A focus group study of romance readers in Australia undertaken by Glen Thomas at the outset of the new millennium shows the persistent reticence of readers to acknowledge their attraction to romance novels.[135] Nevertheless, the editors at Harlequin Australia filter pretty much all of the romance lines into the country that are available in Britain, Canada, and the United States—some 900 titles per year. The Australian books and readers also seem to reflect issues, both pro and con, that occur in the other English-language countries. MIRA's mainstream fiction, for example, sells particularly well. Thomas also found that the readers in the focus group study who gravitated to Medical Romances tended to be somewhat older on average (52) in comparison to those who were attracted to the more risqué Blaze series (39). The parallels in Australia are not surprising, since the books are similar to those in other English-language countries and have undergone little editorial tampering. Thomas concludes that the texts change with the times and are constantly being updated to incorporate changes taking place in the wider social world. A fitting postscript to Thomas's study is the fact that Western-themed romances travel well,[136] which is not surprising given that the cattle driving (droving) tradition is strong at ranches (stations) in the outback and is as much a part of the Australian mythos as the cowboy is in the United States.[137]

Thomas mentions the strong sales for MIRA's mainstream novels in the Australian market. Most of these are filtered from those published in North America, but the independence of the Australian office can be seen in its willingness to move beyond existing books and introduce novels more attuned to Australian tastes. *Hard Jacka* (2007) is an excellent example of an original MIRA novel published in Australia primarily for the Australian reader. It has strong parallels with Jason Mott's *The Returned*. Both are male-authored mainstream novels that are not romances, but the subject matter has strong appeal to women readers. Captain Albert Jacka, Hard Jacka to his superiors, is a legendary figure in Australia because of his heroism at Gallipoli. He would go on to become mayor of St. Kilda in 1930 and would die two years later at Caulfield Military Hospital from complications from his many war wounds. The book would become a MIRA best-seller in Australia.[138]

The shared socio-cultural traditions of the United States, United Kingdom, and Australia help Harlequin novels to travel. Western Europe, more so than Eastern, shares similar socio-cultural traits with the United Kingdom, Canada, and the United States. In many of these countries, Harlequin, initially via Mills & Boon, also had a presence. In 1973, shortly after purchasing Mills & Boon, Harlequin established Mills & Boon Limited in Australia. It launched Harlequin Holland in 1975, set up a joint venture in West Germany in 1976, and established Harlequin France in 1977. Harlequin had a particularly productive year in 1979: it set up a joint venture in Greece, launched Harlequin Japan, set up joint venture romance publication firms in Central and South America, and entered the Scandinavian market. In 1981, Harlequin launched Harlequin Italy.[139] In many of these countries, Harlequin encountered the typically condescending attitude toward the genre which, at least initially, impeded Harlequin's international expansion. Sales would help to overcome these negative attitudes.

Paul Grescoe sketches the early years of Harlequin's entry into Germany.[140] Mills & Boon already had a relationship with Axel Springer Verlag in the early 1970s, after Springer, a highly regarded publisher of "literary" books, had set up Cora Verlag to move into the mass-market field. In 1974, Mills & Boon, with Harlequin now behind it, negotiated a new two-year contract and pushed to increased their titles to two every two weeks. Since romances were considered "trivial literature" by the snobbish editorial hierarchy at Springer,[141] they naturally balked at the idea. Sales within the year established within Springer that this unprecedented release schedule was, one Springer insider quipped, "the idea of the century."[142] Its success prompted Harlequin in 1976, the year its contract with Cora Verlag expired, to purchase a 50 percent stake in Cora Verlag. A large part of Harlequin's success was in adapting its format (rather than its content). In Germany, the novels were published in the there-popular magazine style with color photographs on the cover instead of illustration. Cora Verlag also had a distinct distribution advantage in Germany that helped Harlequin novels reach their intended audience. Cora Verlag controlled the newsstands, which gave Harlequin wider distribution than it could garner in bookstores, and newsstands provided higher profit margins than bookstores. Harlequin's German market was broader than just Germany because Cora Verlag also controlled distribution channels in German-speaking Austria and Switzerland. Harlequin continues to be a strong presence in Germany today, and in 2010 it acquired full ownership of Cora Verlag from Axel Springer,[143] which will add substantially to Harlequin's profit since Harlequin releases roughly 700 titles per year and sells over 10 million books in Germany every year,[144] which is comparable to the number of books sold yearly in the U.K.[145]

Harlequin was similarly plagued with a condescending attitude toward the genre that hindered its entrance into France. Grescoe quotes Heisey, who summed up the French attitude: "Our women don't read these kinds of books." His response was apt: "Well," Heisey recalls saying, "the reason they don't read them is that they've never been offered them."[146] And given the chance in 1978, Harlequin sated their pent-up demand. By the early 1980s, Harlequin was selling thirty million books and had captured three-quarters of the French romance market.[147] Harlequin accomplished this by relying on an astute marketing campaign, which it updated in 1992 when it learned that its slogan, "Harlequin, a whole world of escape," was negatively perceived, so it was Francophiled to "Laisez-vous prendre au jeu de l'amour" ("Let yourself be carried away by the game of love"). The ad campaign that followed clarified how to play the game by French standards: "Harlequin books are like men—it would be too bad to try only one."[148]

At the same time Harlequin was entering Germany and France, it was also introducing its books in Scandinavia, where it relied on tried and true marketing techniques adapted to local exigencies. In Finland, for example, Grescoe reports that Harlequin broke the Finnish book distribution monopoly by introducing its own racks in supermarkets; in TV-commercial-free Sweden, it gave away 250,000 (remaindered) books and advertised heavily in magazines and billboards.[149] The Scandinavian market is particularly illustrative, as seen in a study done by Eva Hemmungs Wirtén, which shows the intricacies involved in transforming a Harlequin English-language book into a commodity that is culturally relevant in a non–English-speaking culture.

Editorial transformation should not be surprising since staff in each of the overseas branches has long made decisions about what they think is right for their list.[150] The editorial transformation is remarked on in passing by

Grescoe, who mentions how the Anglicized names in Harlequin novels were initially (and unnecessarily) Germanized in German and how some of the more sensual aspects were downplayed in France: one translator told Grescoe that one of the guidelines she was to adhere to was to "shave the bearded ones"; crude love scenes were Latinized "by replacing a detailed anatomical evocation, too sordid for us, with a description of strong feelings—or to take out some shocking scenes."[151] Wirtén's study shows just how the editorial process works in a non–English-speaking country.[152] She also successfully shows how meaning travels.

I have referred to the process of taking a Harlequin product and adapting it in another culture as transmigration transformation. This term takes into account the complete transformation of a transnational product, which includes not just adapting the text, but also other culturally relevant strategies, including packaging, and marketing and distribution transformations that help to sell the book in another culture. Wirtén, who focuses on the editorial transformational process, shows how local editors transform the text to local sensibilities, a process she calls transediting—localizing a global text. She shows that the Stockholm editors at Förlaget Harlequin, the primary people responsible for sifting manuscripts for the Scandinavian market, function in the classic gatekeeper tradition, and with only a few exceptions—books Harlequin insists be published—the Stockholm editors selectively screen manuscripts and solicit the "right" translator who will capture the flavor of the book while simultaneously adapting it to local social exigencies. Racial, colonial, and violent allusions are socially sensitive issues that are forthrightly expunged. Textual violence, for example, was noted by Jensen in her study of Harlequin.[153] She found that even in the Presents novel *The Devil's Mistress* (1982), Harlequin tended to "romanticize violence in 'love' relationships."[154] Contemporary (2012–2013) comments from readers on this novel on Goodreads are appalled today at these vicious Heathcliffian outbursts.[155]

The overly sexual is also forthrightly addressed in Stockholm. The sexual is not a particular problem with those books that are translated from the "sweet" Romance series or some of the toned-down Presents novels, though some of the more recent sensual Presents novels are likely to undergo greater editorial scrutiny than more staid Presents novels. The same holds with Superromance, published as *Exklusiv* in Sweden, since the sexual is more problematic, if only because the line itself raises the sensual bar by one or two levels. Crude anatomical descriptions have to be addressed. Penis is inevitably deleted for a more metaphorical reference. "Slept with" in one book becomes "made love" with; "spread her legs" was changed by the translator to "opened her legs," which the editor felt was too clinical and re-edited to "received him."[156] It is important to recognize that we are not dealing simply with sexual terminology but cultural sensitivity, which is why one editor added a sentence not found in the original to make clear that there are consequences to sexual activity and one has to take responsibility for one's actions: "'But it can lead to children,' Robert continued. 'And children need parents who can take care of them.'"[157]

What editorial transformations took place in Eastern Europe and Russia remains a moot point because distribution issues overshadowed Harlequin's entrance into these countries. At first, Harlequin appeared successful in gaining entry into Eastern Europe after the Berlin Wall came down in 1990. As it did elsewhere when it entered a country, it relied heavily on marketing techniques to familiarize locals with its product.

In November 1989, when the wall was first breached,[158] Harlequin employees in then-West Germany rushed to the border crossing and gave away one million German-language romances to East Germans[159] who poured into the West just for a taste of their new-found freedom. Initially, Brian Hickey downplayed the importance of Eastern Europe: "It's only 110 million people, one-third of the Western European market."[160] He soon had second thoughts. After entry into Czechoslovakia and Bulgaria, he optimistically forecast the move into Poland and Hungary would account for nine percent of worldwide sales in 1992.[161] There were two reasons for Hickey's subsequent enthusiasm: (1) a highly literate population, and (2) a fascination with all things Western.[162] It was a short-lived enthusiasm, even though Polish-translated Mills & Boon books did fairly well in the England, which has a growing Polish immigrant population.[163] Hickey put a brave face on remarks in a media analyst's report that the Eastern European "ventures were not contributing as much as hoped for yet," and said "We're doing business profitably."[164] In one sense they were successful while in another not so. There real success came in picking up Eastern Germany, which composed 30 percent of reunified Germany's population.[165] Harlequin would be less successful in some of the other former eastern-bloc countries, where the distribution channels were rather antiquated. The economic conditions in Eastern Europe didn't help. The economy there was strained, Moggy points out, long before the recessions that opened and closed the first decade of the new millennium.[166]

The planned, long-anticipated move into Russia never went far either, in part also owing to a similar lack of a book delivery infrastructure.[167] Galloway shook his head at the way books were distributed in Russia, since bookstores are rare and most people buy novels from street vendors. "There's got to be a better way," quipped Galloway.[168] Harlequin has made some recent headway in Russia, however. In 2010, Harlequin formed an alliance with Izdatelstvo Centrepolygraph (ZAO), one of Russia's leading publishing houses. ZAO acquired worldwide rights to publish Harlequin books in the Russian language and indicated it would filter 100-plus novels yearly into the Russian market, mostly under the Harlequin logo.[169] This relationship may not be as fruitful as initially hoped, given the continued tension (and sanctions) between the West and Russia because of events unfolding in Ukraine.

Going across the Atlantic (or the Channel) is not without its cultural problems, and it seems that the further inland into Europe that Harlequin goes, the wider the cultural rift. Going across the Pacific is a whole other matter, both organizationally and thematically.

Harlequin's first Eastern venture was in Japan; subsequent attempts to enter China have not been fruitful. There was an attempt with a potential partner to test market books in China, but it never moved forward.[170] One problem, Moggy indicates, revolved around the distribution issue; another was the multiple dialects. Harlequin (and others) continue to eye this market for obvious reasons.[171] Presently, however, they only license their books there.[172] Their print presence in China is limited, though there is a fairly vibrant digital presence,[173] which has the ability to circumvent the closed, hardline political system in China that continues to pose an obstacle to market entry for many Western countries. Japan, of course, is much more open, so the political situation did not hamper entry. Other factors did, though only temporarily.

Harlequin carefully studied its first Asian foray. It conducted two years of market research in the late 1970s. The results, Paul Grescoe reports, were promising, and so Harlequin entered the Japanese market in September 1979. In typical Harlequin style, it was preceded by a large advertising and promotional campaign that targeted the female audience—ads in women's magazines, for example.[174] They appeared to do well initially, selling over 1.2 million books within six months, but sales soon stalled and the momentum would not be regained for nearly a decade.

The initial problems were multiple. One was that supermarkets, a key distribution source frequented by female shoppers, did not appreciate the benefits of selling romance novels. The books lacked curb appeal: the covers were simply reprints of North American covers. The covers often showed, in the North American tradition, Anglo couples embracing. Expressions of love were culturally off-putting: Grescoe cites a 1979 survey that revealed that Japan's romance quotient—expressions of love—was among the lowest of the fourteen industrial nations polled. Happy endings were cited as a problem as well: Japanese, it was said, prefer unhappy endings where everyone parts in sorrow and tears. These explanations appear to be self-serving justification for early market issues, because Harlequin made headway in Japan throughout the 1980s and is doing very well there today. Indeed, Japan by 1989–1990 was one of Harlequin's more

8. Alive and Kicking

successful overseas markets. It just takes time, Moggy explains, referring to *any* new market entry: "Nothing becomes successful overnight." But once it became established, Harlequin did well, exceptionally so, says Moggy, since the Japanese "readers are incredibly loyal." So loyal, in fact, that for a number of years Harlequin ran contests for readers, the prize being to come to North America and visit corporate headquarters in Toronto and the editorial offices in New York. The Japanese market was already a success before Harlequin novels went manga, and since moving into this format the novels have gained even wider popularity.

The average American traditionally reads a newspaper or pocket book at an airport terminal or on a subway, even if today that paper or book is on a Kindle. In Japan, they would more likely be reading a comic book. The Japanese comic book is unlike comics in the West, and their graphic artists, who also excel at film animation, are highly regarded. The comics are storyboard illustrations, but the stories are much more complex than the short comics read in the United States, and it is not unusual for them to run 350 pages. The comics in Japan are refereed to as mangas and have been called "the [most] dominant force in Japanese pop culture"; they compose over one-quarter of all books and magazines printed in Japan, and the most popular ones sell 1.5 to 2.5 million copies per week.[175]

Mangas can be of any genre. Harlequin manga covers appear with the Harlequin name next to their former diamond logo; should one miss the association, the cover also promotes the book as a "Pure Romance." There are two color-coded series, Harlequin Pink for teens and Harlequin Violet for a more mature audience.[176] Their success is seen in the numbers. In 1989, there was only one manga romance; production was erratic over the next few years (1999–2006) and averaged about four books a year. This started to change in 2007 when 35 books were released; the numbers have steadily climbed since, from 49 books in 2008 to 92 in 2013.[177] Harlequin Japan has kept abreast of the market: it released *Monthly Harlequin* in January 2009, a Japanese magazine of one-shot manga stories that runs roughly 60 pages[178]; in December 2009, eight Harlequin mangas appeared on eManaga.com at the bargain rental rate of $2.00 (U.S.), which was half the price that Amazon was charging for the Kindle versions of the same titles.[179] In 2013–2014, Harlequin entered into an agreement with SoftBank, one of the largest cell phone companies in Japan, to distribute their manga romances on cell phones. This test will give them an entry beyond Japan into neighboring Asian countries. Mangas are less familiar to North American audiences, and this no doubt is one of the reasons the books didn't fare well when they appeared as Ginger Blossom books in North America.

A cursory examination of online cover images shows that the female is typically a white Westerner while the man appears to have Japanese features, though they are not particularly strong.[180] In manga style, the covers are "cartoonish" illustrations. The hero and heroine on the covers are shown in various embracing poses, indicating that this aspect of Japanese society that executives bemoaned as a problem that hindered Harlequin's initial entry into Japan two decades ago is not really an issue; the quintessential happy endings seem to be less problematic as well. The stories are typically reprints of Silhouette/Harlequin novels, even though the author's name is prefaced with "original text by...." *Women in White*, for example, is by well-known romance novelist Diana Palmer; it was originally published unnumbered as a promotional novel in the Silhouette Desire line in 2000; the manga release date is 2010.[181] As is characteristic of manga books, the illustrator's name also appears prominently on the cover. The books, then, carry traditional Harlequin themes that have been written by Westerners but illustrated by Japanese manga artists. In light of Wirtén's Swedish study, the success of the themes of manga romances might be due, at least in part, to the editorial selection and editing process in Japan. Part of the editorial filtering process is seen in a study conducted of romance novels that appeared in India.

India similarly has a unique, non–Western cultural heritage, tempered somewhat by the long period of British colonialism. Harlequin had almost immediate success with this market. It has relied on "older" themes, romances more in tune with contemporary social exigencies in India.

Jayashree Kamble con-

Harlequin manga cover of *The Andreou Marriage Arrangement.*

ducted a study of the romance reader in India in 2005.[182] She found the romance readers, like romance readers elsewhere, are reflective of Everywoman: they ran the gamut of women in age and social background. The readers in her study were twice as likely to have a college education as compared to those who read romances in the United States (87 percent versus 42 percent). Her sample bias is likely the result of the women being surveyed in urban areas who are fluent in English. Nevertheless, it is this educated group of women which is most likely to be influenced by the latent feminist message of these novels—college-educated women were initially the most receptive to feminist message in the West. The Indian reader also shares similar rationales for reading romances: some felt the novels made them more accepting of others, and most simply enjoyed them as light, easy reading; a few found them monotonous and stopped reading them. Kamble categorically rejects the popular misconception that the readers in India read the books only for escapism or sexual gratification. It is interesting to note that the novels the women read in her study were from the more staid Romance and Presents series and that half of the romances examined were published in the 1970s.[183]

One has to appreciate that the feminist movement in India is in its infancy and has not made the inroads it has in many Western countries.[184] This helps explain why the novels selected are less erotic books than found in English-speaking countries. Many were also published in the 1970s when the feminist movement was just beginning to make inroads in England and the United States, when many Western romance readers had yet to embrace the feminist ideology.[185] And like the romances read by non-feminist women in English-speaking countries in the seventies, Kamble argues that they are emancipating, though, like the criticism by feminists of these novels in the 1970s, the books don't go as far in promoting a feminist ideology as some might like.

Indian society is strongly patriarchal. It also promotes the idea that women have little say in selecting their husbands. Kamble argues that while arranged marriages in India are beginning to be challenged by some, "many [women] have been raised to believe that [such a challenge] ... is morally suspect." Indian women have been taught that marriage has next to nothing to do with love, passion, or personal fulfillment. These seemingly staid novels, then, Kamble argues, are really quite ground-breaking. If nothing else, they promote the radical (Indian) idea that a woman has the ability to choose her sexual and emotional partner. We might anticipate that, much like what happened in the United States, once the feminist movement makes more inroads in India, the women will gravitate to another level of even more liberating romantic content.[186]

Conclusion: A Vibrant Twenty-Five Years, 1990–2014

Harlequin was becoming increasingly bureaucratic during the 1970s. This was necessary to monitor Mills & Boon and to oversee its expanding international market. Torstar simply accelerated the bureaucratization of Harlequin. One of Torstar's first direct interventions was to appoint David Galloway its CEO and move Heisey into the honorary position of chairman of the board. Galloway took Harlequin over during one of its most turbulent times and was responsible for stabilizing Harlequin and the romance environment when Harlequin acquired its major rival, Silhouette. In 1988, he was promoted to head Torstar, but his ideological stamp on Harlequin would long be felt: both Brian Hickey and Donna Hayes would become Harlequin CEOs during Galloway's tenure at Torstar. Hickey seemed like he would be a good choice, coming as he did from a marketing background, but he moved too far afield of Harlequin's primary product with his venture into educational products. He would be replaced by Hayes, the first CEO of Harlequin who had a strong publishing background, most in various positions at Harlequin. She would be critical in developing Harlequin's product line and was responsible for the successful movement outside category romance into women's fiction. Craig Swinwood succeeded Hayes in January 2014 and within months had finalized the sale of Harlequin to HarperCollins. The implications of this sale will be addressed after first surveying Harlequin's American competition in the next chapter.

Considering the number of lines Harlequin has developed since its inception a half-century ago (1964–2014), there have not been many failures within the romance genre. Harlequin's initial romance staples, Romance and Presents, have had a long history at Harlequin, and though Presents has ventured further into the sensual than Romance, it remains, for the most part, at the tamer end of Harlequin's product line. Teen and Love Inspired, more recent lines, also fall into the more chaste arena, largely because the market for these novels necessitates a more muted sexual tone. Also fitting snugly into this early, somewhat chaste period are Mills & Boon's Historical romance and the medical line, both of which debuted in the 1970s. The sensual was stepped up in the 1980s during the romance wars between Harlequin and Silhouette, both of whom were vying to incorporate the more liberated dimensions of the novels introduced by Dell Ecstasy. Harlequin's Superromance was countered by Silhouette's Special Edition; Silhouette launched Desire to compete with Dell's Ecstasy and Harlequin countered with Temptation; Harlequin's American Romances debuted to offset the American-themed novels that were Silhouette's launch trademark line. Silhouette's somewhat more sedate Intimate Moments was countered by Harlequin Intrigues.

It was a surprise to some in the industry that Harlequin did not discontinue duplicate Silhouette lines after the purchase. But Harlequin realized that Silhouette romances had a loyal following that might not return to Harlequin if Silhouette was discontinued as a separate house, so it published under both house logos for the next thirty years. The only surprise in the eventual "rebranding" was that Harlequin waited so long to finally merge Silhouette and Mills & Boon into the Harlequin fold, though it was clear it was moving in this direction in the 2000s because this line or that was being collapsed under the Harlequin imprint before the official rebranding swept the remaining free-standing lines under one unifying name.

Hickey's tenure was distracted by his venture into the educational market. Nevertheless, two critical content innovations did occur under Hickey, both of which were pioneered by Hayes, which certainly was a factor in the decision to promote her to CEO. She introduced MIRA and Red Dress. MIRA moved Harlequin into women's fiction and helped keep many good authors who grew tired of the restrictions imposed by category lines but to that point had to find another publisher for their outside-the-box romances. It was a successful move, since MIRA today (2014) composes a quarter (25.6 percent) of Harlequin's revenue. HQN spun off of MIRA. Two other major imprints that would launch under Hayes's subsequent tenure as CEO, and that continue to thrive, are Harlequin's African American/multicultural series and its inspirational romances.

Success is measured in the business world by sales. Some products have a long shelf life, like Romance, Presents, and Superromance. Others are successful, but it is recognized that their life span is limited. Red Dress is a clear example of this phenomenon. The line capitalized on the popularity of chick-lit, which took off with a vengeance. Not to take advantage of this market trend, which every publishing house in the United States was rushing to emulate, would have been fatuous. The only thing Harlequin did was to launch a separate chick-lit line while everyone was publishing chick-lit novels. But lines, not novels (outside MIRA and HQN) are Harlequin's forte. Going in this direction made perfect sense for Harlequin. Red Dress had a long run and the line was eventually discontinued after ten years as chick-lit ran out of steam. Other lines were seen as even more limiting, but lucrative. Harlequin cross-branded with NASCAR to tap the large group of female racing devotees; Mills & Boon did the same with rugby in the United Kingdom. The popular media had a lot of fun with these alliances, and while the books did okay, the press coverage was a gold mine for the publisher.

Mills & Boon also tapped into the National Trust in the U.K. but with limited success. On this side of the Atlantic, Harlequin struck up a relationship with *Cosmopolitan* magazine to release digital Red Hots to the young, savvy *Cosmo* readers. The degree of success of the Red Hots is problematic. The true yardstick for success is not what the editor says—they *all* say the new line is wonderful, simply wonderful—but the line's longevity, since no publisher is going to keep publishing something that is not selling. An early benchmark of how well the line is doing is whether production schedules are increased or decreased. If Red Hots go from two to three per month, it can be considered a clear success; if it gets cut from two to one per month, it's only a matter of time.

So many lines can only mean there will be some inevitable failures. There haven't been that many, all things considered. In every case, the rationale for launching the line made perfect sense. Bombshell was an action-adventure romance series that was better served by Rogue Angel. Rogue Angel is a Gold Eagle series, but it is the only Gold Eagle book promoted on the Harlequin website. Bombshell simply became redundant with Rogue Angel. Shadows was also more successfully served a few years later by Nocturne. Shadows, like Nocturne, is a paranormal romance line which is almost de rigueur in the romance category today. Shadows was a decade ahead of its time—before the *Twilight* saga hit, which is what Nocturne capitalized on. Nocturne was more successful because *Twilight* helped set the parameters for the paranormal genre, so, unlike Shadows, its focus was clearer and it didn't wander afield into the romance suspense and gothic categories. NEXT just didn't work. NEXT also made thematic sense, revolving as it did around the "next" step in a woman's life. It got lost, however, because the next step didn't focus, like Second Chance at Love a few decades earlier, on the next romance adventure but added too many "nexts" that often didn't revolve around the romance.

Temptation was successful, but Blaze, initially a variant within Temptation, raised the erotic bar, and did so quite successfully. Blaze, as Dianne Moggy so nicely put it, "ate the mother." So it made sense that if Blaze kicked the erotic up a notch, that Spice, kicking it up even further, would be successful. It wasn't, proving that, at least for many Harlequin readers, erotica only goes so far. Ironically, as we'll see in the next chapter, erotic at the extreme is quite successful—just not within the Harlequin oeuvre. A humor romance line also seemed to make perfect sense since one of the recurring aspects of the romance novel enjoyed by many devotees is the humorous slant of the novels. This is one line Harlequin struggled mightily to make work, but finally threw in the towel after a decade of tinkering with the theme and rebranding the line. Humor, it seems, works well within the romance novel, but is hard to sustain in and of itself when it is made the thematic linchpin of the romantic novel.

The international arena has similarly witnessed its share of successes and failures. It also has had more positives than negatives. Harlequin's long international arm has been a major factor over the years in shoring up Harlequin's profits. The successes were more copious in the 1970s and 1980s when it expanded into English-language countries or those more "thematically attuned" Western European ones. More recent (1990–2010) moves into Eastern Europe (and China) proved more difficult because of (1) antiquated distribution problems and (2) a stagnant economy that was not suddenly energized simply because it was no longer shackled to Soviet (or Maoist) socialistic principles. Harlequin did make significant inroads into Japan, but only after adapting the novel to the manga-style format that is popular there. It has put a good face on its moves into Japan (and South America), and rightly so. This analysis, however, suggested that their success is limited because they persist in "forcing" Western themes upon non–Westerners. This myopicism is reminiscent of the romance industry in the 1970s and 1980s when it persisted in "forcing" minorities in North America to read about blue-eyed, blond-haired heroines and heroes. This matter will be returned to in Chapter 10 after first addressing changing thematic variations taking place in the United States during this period of time.

CHAPTER 9

Line Diversification
The Byword of the New Millennium

The romance revolution of the 1980s is a misnomer. It was called a revolution in the popular press, which tended to headline the slew of romance novels being produced. There might have been a lot of romances on the shelves, but they weren't selling, which is why so many secular lines drastically reduced the number of monthly releases, if they did not do away with the line altogether. The parade of titles kept coming during the second half of the 1980s, but these were mainly Christian romances, which kept the notion alive that the market was awash with romances, even though many of the Christian lines met the same fate as their secular sisters by the end of the decade. The number of lines on the market in the 1980s is misleading since by the end of the decade, it had been whittled down to a handful. The real revolution did not take place in the 1980s but unfolded over the next two decades. The number of lines in existence today far surpasses that which existed at the height of the so-called romance revolution of the 1980s. The fact that they remain in existence underscores their sales success.[1] Harlequin is still the dominant player in the publishing industry, even if it is now under HarperCollins, but its previous eighty-plus percent share of the market, which it recaptured with the purchase of Silhouette, is closer to fifty percent today.

One might argue that the real revolution of the 1980s was in the sensual liberated novels. This seldom garnered much attention since industry outsiders rarely recognized thematic distinctions between lines and simply scoffed at their overt sexuality without noticing their liberated format. But even if we acknowledged that the liberated theme of 1980s romances was, indeed, "revolutionary," it was nevertheless fairly restricted, since even many industry insiders failed to appreciate the liberated format and focused on the sexual (versus the sensual) aspect of the novels. The real thematic revolution started to occur in the 1990s and continues to unfold today. This is clearly seen in the potpourri of divergent lines and themes in existence today. The multiplicity of Harlequin lines delineated in the last chapter underscores the wide diversity of themes today, but Harlequin, which remains the dominant player even if it is now subsumed by HarperCollins, is just one among many. This chapter examines some of the successful houses that compete in the current romance market and how they position themselves to capture a slice of the romance pie by debuting lines different from Harlequin's.

Mainstream Publishers: Vying with Harlequin

John Thompson, tracing the history of contemporary publishing, identifies three publishing phases, two of which we've already seen.[2] The "synergy" phase lasted from the 1960s through the first half of the 1980s and replaced the entrepreneurial phase (1940s–1960s).[3] The synergy phase was characterized by large corporations, such as Gulf + Western, purchasing media organizations. When the hoped-for synergy failed to live up to its initial promise, corporations divested themselves of those acquisitions not directly tied to their main products. The third and current "growth" phase in publishing began in the 1980s but gained momentum during the 1990s. This is the era of media behemoths. The distinction between the synergy and growth phases is that corporate ownership in the synergy phase was unrelated to the media enterprises, while today they are interconnected media-related conglomerates.

The outcome of the present publishing phase at the outset of the twenty-first century is that there are only a handful of large publishing groups. Bertelsmann (Germany) acquired Bantam Books in 1980 and Doubleday in 1986, then Random House. Penguin Random House now has the following imprints: Bantam, Delacorte, Dell, Doubleday, Berkley, New American Library (NAL), Crown, Knopf, Pantheon, Anchor, Vintage, Ballantine, and Modern Library, among a host of others—thirty-four in all, just in the United States.[4] Penguin Random House alone publishes over forty percent of all trade titles.[5] Hachette (France) owns some seventeen houses in the United States, including Grand Central Publishing (formerly Warner Books) and Little, Brown & Company. HarperCollins is a subsidiary of Rupert Murdoch's News Corporation (British) and controls twenty-five imprints in the United States if we add their recent acquisition of Thomas Nelson, which along with Zondervan, now forms HarperCollinsChristian, and its 2014 acquisition of Harlequin, with whom it no longer has to vie because it now owns them. Rounding out the Big Five are Simon & Schuster, with ten imprints in the United States, and Holtzbrinck

(Germany) with nineteen, including Faber and Faber, Henry Holt, and St. Martin's. To this list we should add three large independents, which the Big Five lust to add to their roster—Kensington, Scholastic, and Sourcebooks,[6] all of whom produce a significant number of romance novels.

The melding of all these once free-standing houses into a handful of publishing conglomerates is of concern to media analyst Ben Bagdikian because of their potentially monopolistic powers.[7] Oligopolies would be a better word. It is not that the market is dominated by one large company, which allows it to control prices, but rather that a few companies control the market. This is still of concern because while Americans have an aversion to monopolies, oligopolies seem to allow for competition because there are a number of them, but in reality, some have argued, the end is the same: market control shared by three or five rather than one. These conglomerates, though independent of one another, are nevertheless interdependent.[8] A firm operating in a market with just a few competitors must take the potential reaction of its closest rivals into account when making its own decisions. This makes them inherently conservative—they are hesitant to act differently because they might upset the apple cart.

Albert Greco rebuts Bagdikian's thesis. He argues that after a "careful review of the empirical data" there is little to support Bagdikian's fears. He cites data from the U.S. Department of Justice that indicates there is no such control by the conglomerates because book prices do not greatly exceed the Consumer Price Index and "market entry into book publishing seems to be, at best, a relatively easy task with more than 53,000 publishing houses releasing 150,000 titles annually."[9] His point is well taken, but, as we'll see in this chapter, there are a lot of self-published romance authors and digital romance publishers, and a potpourri of small houses that produce romances—but this hardly makes them competitive with the Big Five, or even the Big Eight. Siren, for example, is a small electronic publisher that releases considerably more romances every month (100) than many of the Big Eight do per year and appear to be doing so profitably, but this hardly gives them the market clout or financial muscle of any of the Big Eight.

The mainstream publishers are facing a new world: "What used to work is not working any more," said Monique Patterson at St. Martin's in a recent *Publishers Weekly* feature.[10] It is not St. Martin's that is having a problem adapting; all the mainstream publishing conglomerates are having difficulty figuring out the romance market today. Diane Patrick at *PW* summed up the problem: "[M]ost professionals we contacted acknowledged that ... all the old rules [are] crumbling." And to move ahead publishing houses have to "ignore former 'set-in-stone' publishing conventions, categories, and strategies."[11]

The "action" today, at least thematically, which is the heart of keeping the romance novel current and sales robust, is taking place stage left. Mainstream romance houses have been watching each other, which is why they produce a lot of similarly themed romance novels. Sociologist Harrison White argues that the more interrelated or "cliquish" the firms, the greater the ability of producers providing similar products to monitor one another.[12] In an oligopolistic world, they tend to lose sight of smaller competitors whom they don't view as "players" and therefore think they are remaining competitive, which they are, but only with like-sized and like-minded corporations. Mainstream publishers are now suddenly finding that they are not competing with each other but with smaller companies that have not been on their radar; they now find themselves trying to adapt, but they are reacting too slowly and losing ground to the smaller upstarts. The three big independents that round out our Big Eight are also reacting to the upstart romance houses, but they are not as bogged down by a cumbersome bureaucracy and so are doing better than their larger counterparts because they can move more swiftly: the complex bureaucracy of large organizations, while necessary to organize the multifarious divisions within the company, tends to slow down decision-making, which, in turn, makes changes difficult to implement.[13]

This chapter underscores the changes that are occurring in the industry today. There are more successful romance houses and thematic variations than ever on the market (mostly outside the Big Five) and they are generally being well received by readers. Mainstream publishers only have to turn their attention to their upstart rivals to see what is working. They are doing this, but not doing it very well. Yet! They may be slow learners, but they are learning, as we will see in this chapter, which examines what is being done in the romance field outside the mainstream and how mainstream publishers are attempting to compete.

Small, independent houses do not try, like most mainstream houses, to be all things to all people, but have carved out their own comfortable little niches. Mainstream publishers that compete in these various niches are examined when the category is appraised: HarperCollins, for example, has made a strong presence in Christian romance publishing by buying into existing Christian publishing houses; it is one of the few Big Five that is represented here, but it is competing less with like-sized conglomerates than with a mix of small religious publishers that have a strong market presence. All the mainstream publishers talk about erotic publishing in the same vein that Harlequin does, which means their level of eroticism seldom passes into the upper erotic level. The real heat in this category is filled by niche erotic digital publishers. The same holds for young adult romances, which all mainstream publishers dabble in, but where Scholastic tends to dominate. It also holds with African American/multicultural romances, which most large houses release in limited numbers and which some in the Big Eight even specialize in, but few stray into interracial love, which some of the smaller African American houses tend to embrace. Few mainstream houses venture into another delicate area: Gay-lesbian (GLBT) romantic fiction is left largely to small independent GLBT houses and digital publishers to sate demand for male/male romances. Only one mainstream house has a strong presence in all these areas except Christian romance fiction, and that is Kensington Publishing, which, while part of the Big Eight has always been a maverick publisher. Its independent status allows it to make prompt decisions and go where others are hesitant to tread. Kensington is the true rival to Harlequin because it is the only house that is releasing mass-market romances in some number. Sourcebooks, too, is an independent publisher. Sourcebooks' line diversification is not as broad-based as Kensington's, but it has a strong line of romantic fiction that rivals most of that released by the Big Five.

The digital age has posed a real challenge to mainstream publishers, and while all have a growing digital presence, their lackadaisical venture into this area has flung the doors open wide to authors who have been cut out of the traditional houses by allowing them to self-publish, and some are doing extraordinarily well, much better than they could do with traditional publishers. This is not to suggest that mainstream publishers sit idly by on the sidelines. They are taking steps to compete with or co-opt their upstart sisters. They are often behind the curve, however, more reactive than proactive—going to Amazon to find authors is a reactive, not a proactive, strategy.[14] They are catching up, with varying degrees of success, as we'll see when we examine each category in turn.

Young Love: Young Adult Romance Publishing

Scholastic, a specialist publisher of young adult (YA) fiction, was the first to identify YA as a potential romance market. It launched *Wildfire* in 1980 after market research indicated that books with romantic themes were the most frequently ordered in its teenage book club. The first ten titles in the series sold 250,000 copies and led to two other Scholastic romance lines: Wishing Star and Windswept.[15] The success of Scholastic with these lines, as well as the hot adult romance market of the 1980s, soon prompted others to join the fray, including Dell with Young Love, Bantam with Sweet Dreams, and Silhouette with First Love.[16] By the middle of the decade there were twelve YA romance series in existence.[17] The problem was the market was not as hot as it looked to publishers and could not sustain all the novels flooding it. Only First Love could still be found in retail outlets by the 1990s, before it was finally discontinued in 1994.[18] A content analysis of YA romances declared that the books pivoted on the importance of the hero in giving meaning to a young girl's life and were "a necessary part of their growing into womanhood."[19] This is likely the reason for their failure. A related study by Bereska found that YA novels in the 1980s were curiously devoid of sexuality. The books, then, did not reflect the reality of adolescents in the 1980s and "consciously denied" the sexuality of adolescent females at the height of the sexual revolution. Bereska concludes that while the novels are fantasies, "a dose of 'reality' is also required," and failing that, the books didn't appeal to YA readers.[20]

YA romances continued to be produced, but there are relatively few category YA romance lines. There's Harlequin Teen (2009), of course, and Kensington, always at the forefront of pacing trends, introduced kTeen Dafina (African American) in 2006 and k-Teen in 2008. Most publishers do not have a dedicated romance line, which doesn't exclude them from a strong YA showing: Little, Brown and Company was responsible for the four-book *Twilight* series. Some have a general teen line, like Viking Juvenile, Walker's Young Readers, and HarperCollins's Harper Teen, which had a successful ten-book run with *The Princess Diaries* (2000 to 2009) that ended when the heroine turned eighteen. In either case, both publish romances as part of their lists.[21] There is also Scholastic Books and Sourcebooks. Both houses release single-title teen romances on a regular basis in some number.

Scholastic Books is the preeminent publisher of YA fiction and nonfiction and tends to dominate the YA market in much the same way Harlequin dominates the romance market. The house may be best known for publishing the *Harry Potter* series and the *Hunger Games* novels. Its specialist YA niche gives it a strong presence and considerable muscle in the YA market. After all, it is the largest publisher and distributor of children's books in the world. This is the rationale for focusing on Scholastic in this section. Sourcebooks serves to illustrate how some of the other mainstream houses of general fiction address the YA romance market.

Aimee Friedman, executive editor at Scholastic, could not identify the percentage of fiction titles at Scholastic that fall into the romance category, since the company does not have a dedicated romance line. She does indicate that "a significant portion of our YA titles [at Scholastic] have a romantic element."[22] Most mainstream publishers of YA romances say pretty much the same thing. The difference is that Scholastic, because it is a YA publisher, probably publishes twice as many YA novels as the other generalist houses combined, simply because all it releases are YA books. Sourcebooks illustrates the approach of Scholastic's competitors in the YA romance field. Sixty percent of Sourcebooks releases are in fiction. Of the books published in fiction, approximately one-third are adult romances. Todd Stoke, editorial director at Sourcebooks, estimates that from the fiction list, about ten percent are YA books, of which roughly half have a romance theme.[23] YA is, then, a relatively thin slice of Sourcebooks' overall output, even though it releases approximately twenty-five books per year in the genre and have well over a hundred novels in the YA category on its website.

In some of Scholastic's YA novels, the romance is a subplot; in others, it is a core part of the storyline and thus can be said to constitute a true romance novel. An example of the former would be Katie Alender's *Marie Antoinette, Serial Killer*, a contemporary mystery suspense with the subplot tagline, "Paris, France: a city of fashion, chocolate croissants, and cute boys"; examples of the latter abound and would include Elizabeth Eulberg's *Better Off Friends*, Maggie Stiefvater's bestselling Shiver series, and Kim Culbertson's *Catch a Falling Star*, "a deliciously charming novel about [seventeen-year-old Carter Moon] finding true love ... and yourself."

Friedman feels we are in the golden age of YA literature. The market has exploded in the past fifteen or so years. At the same time, she sees a slightly softer market today. This may by due more to demographic trends than reading habits: Millennials (1985–2005) in their adolescent years would begin to decline after 2000.[24] This birth bubble coincides with the "golden years" of YA fiction. The softening in the market that is starting to take place (2014) is when Millennial adolescents are in decline.

The changes Friedman notices in thematic variations in YA romances follow basic trends in the adult market. YAs followed the chick-lit craze with Hailey Abbott's Summer Boys series (2004–2007). As chick-lit waned, so too did YA chick-lit. It was "replaced" by dark paranormal romances in the wake of the *Twilight* saga, and more recently by dark dystopian romances à la *The Hunger Games*. The YA market appears to be in full recycle mode, as it moves back toward "more straight-forward love stories." This is likely to be hastened along because it is a kind of self-fulfilling prophecy. If Friedman, as executive editor, feels more straightforward love stores are of interest, Scholastic editors are likely to filter more of these stories onto the market. If this occurs at Scholastic, other YA publishers are apt to do likewise; it would not be long before adult romance editors would take notice of the "hot new YA trend" and start filtering similarly themed classic romances into their lists. And the cycle begins anew, which is why contemporary romances, redubbed realist fiction in the YA market, are vibrant at Sourcebooks. One cycle that does not seem to reverberate with young people is the historical arena. Sourcebooks did have some modest success with a "historical" YA novel a few years ago that was set in the 1980s, but that seems to be the far reaches for historical fiction for a generation who looks forward, not backward, in time.

YA books are aimed at different age groups; one set is aimed at those young adults in grades six through eight, another is geared toward those in grades nine through twelve. All books come with an age recommendation. The first *Summer Boys* was designated for those in grade nine, but it was kicked up thematically in subsequent novels that were designed for those in grades ten through twelve. The same can be said for *Boy Meets Boy* by David Levithan (Random House Children's Books, 2003) where a gay-straight alliance was formed to help the straight kids learn how to dance. As might be expected, those at the upper grade levels deal more forthrightly with sexual adventure and are more sexually explicit.

The fact that so much media is sexually saturated—television shows like *Sex and the City*, movies, music, music videos—makes it much more acceptable today to filter sexual dimensions into YA romantic fiction than was tolerable in the 1980s. The sexual thematic dimension would be akin to a four to six on our adult erotic scale. It is fairly common, Friedman says about YA fiction in general, to have "frank depictions of sex and intimacy, particularly in terms of first experiences and early sexual discovery." This also includes acknowledgment of adolescent gay and lesbian relationships.

There are, on average, ten to twelve YA novels released yearly by YA publishers that portray gay and lesbian characters in a positive manner, according to a feature story in *Publishers Weekly* that appear in 2003.[25] Friedman is proud to be part of this industry-wide trend and cites the recent publication of Bill Konigsberg's novel, *Openly Straight*. (Scholastic, 2013). The acceptance of those who are GLBT has gained ground in recent years and has filtered over into adult fiction. Part of the YA appeal is that it is different. Libraries and booksellers, says Friedman, are always on the lookout for books that go beyond the "status quo teenage experience." The books also appeal to those who are coming to terms with their sexual feelings, in the same way teen heterosexual romances address this same issue. This is addressed by Sara Farizan in *If You Could Be Mine* (Algonquin Young Readers, 2013), which examines a lesbian relationship between two young girls, one of whom is being forced into an arranged marriage in her native country of Iran. Friedman is cautious to say why GLBT romances are resonating at the moment. Her goal as an editor is simply to reach as broad an audience as possible. By releasing books about GLs (more so than BTs) that goal is achieved.

Crude expletives are also no longer shunned, replaced with fill-in-the-blank asterisks: "F***," he said. F-expletives dot the narrative of Mark Haddon's 2003 award-winning teen novel, *The Curious Incident of the Dog in the Night Time* (Vintage Contemporaries). The central character is of interest because he is a teen math prodigy with Asperger's syndrome who imitates Sherlock Homes by trying to solve a mystery surrounding the killing of a neighbor's poodle. The book was on the reading list for a number of honors-level high school classes in middle Tennessee. It was banned by a school board after one individual complained because of the F-word. The decision is noteworthy because the school board rescinded its ban within 48 hours after intense criticism by residents in the greater Nashville area. One local editorial writer commented: "This generation has been desensitized ... to both violence and profanity [and sex], so this book would not have as much of an effect as it would have in the 1980s or 1990s. The board even said that they know that children are already exposed to this kind of stuff...."[26] Indeed, one publisher even said in a *PW* interview about YA romances that "most publishers have seen little pushback for the genre," considering some of the content.[27]

The foregoing changes in YA fiction suggest that YA romances would also have changed, certainly from the rather insipid "puppy love" depiction that appears to have been an earmark of YA romances in the 1980s and is, at least in part, a reason for their failure to garner an audience even then. The novels today are more cutting-edge. *A White Romance* (Scholastic, 1989), for example, deals with the integration of a formerly black high school and the disruptive influence of drugs on a relationship. This is a much more complex story of friendship and love than is suggested by Naomi Johnson in her recent analysis (2010) of best-selling teen romance novels, who concludes that "heroines no longer ... become women through romance, they now become empowered and feminine through consumption [of appropriate fashion items: clothes, lipstick, hairstyles, etc.]."[28]

Johnson's conclusion is based on an analysis of romance novels primarily from the successful *Clique* series (2004–2011) by Little, Brown and Company, which, she goes on to say, is based on books by Alloy that, "to my knowledge is the only company consistently producing best-selling young adult romance novels...."[29] This alone taints her analysis, since the YA book publishing industry is much more dynamic and goes far, far beyond Alloy Entertainment. There are at least two other important issues that suggest a more detailed analysis of YA romantic fiction needs to be undertaken. The first is that the Clique books are aimed at girls in the fifth grade,[30] so some of the "depth" expected from those assessing romances is not going to be there. The other is that one series is not reflective of YA romance content, and some of the books mentioned in this assessment of YA romantic fiction in this section that are geared toward older teens shows that young love is much more complicated than many surmise and the books are addressing some cutting-edge social issues that young people themselves are confronting, like love and sex.

One curiosity of YA fiction, mentioned in the previous chapter when

Harlequin's YA line was appraised, is the desire of young people for print books. The YA publishers agree that print is the preferred format and yet they are well represented in digital space. In other words, YA novels do equally well in print and digital, but they are aimed at a different market. Young adult books are not just for young adults, as the label would tend to imply. YA publishers recognize that a large portion of their books are purchased by adults. In fact, twelve of the twenty-five best-selling titles in the first half of 2014 were aimed at teens, which itself suggests an adult audience, according to Carol Fitzgerald at The Book Report Network, because "teens alone cannot drive these numbers."[31] "Young people don't have Kindle, don't have a Nook; they have an iPad or their phone. They're just not interested in e-books," said Stocke at Sourcebooks. In the same breath, Stocke, who lives by his metrics, sees this changing, not so much because young people are going to suddenly embrace digital—though this is likely to happen at some point down the road—but because the demographics are changing.

Readership demographics, Stocke points out, indicate that as readers age they shift to e-books: "The audience is shifting. It's aging toward collegiate and post-collegiate." This may suggest the "golden age" of YA fiction has peaked, not because it has lost favor, but simply because this age group is shrinking. It perhaps foreshadows a new dawn and explains why New Adult (NA) themes are gaining in popularity. The growth in the New Adult titles (and the foreboding decline in YA sales) suggests an artificial statistic. Sales will increase, but not because the audience has suddenly embraced New Adult fiction; it is artificially driven by the growth of this market segment. It promises to be short-lived, if only because the twenty-something market segment is already close to its peak size. In the meantime, everyone is getting in on the act, so the number of NA titles makes it appear all "the rage." Even Sourcebooks is eyeing NA, albeit reluctantly: "New Adult books all tell the same story [sexual awakening]." And yet, Stocke has put out the word to Sourcebooks agents that a New Adult "refreshing spin" would be welcome at Sourcebooks. He anticipates he'll have trouble with New Adult in print. That shouldn't be a problem; sales will be in e-books because that's where new adults have migrated. Scholastic, on the other hand, because its key audience is YA not NA, will see a decline in sales because the "aging" twenty-something-year-old reader is outside their market.

God Is Love: The Christian Romance Market

Christian romance publishing may be a relatively thin slice of the romance market, but it is nevertheless a vibrant one. Christian houses initially entered the romance field in the mid- to late 1980s in response to the overt sexuality of secular romances flooding the market during the height of the romance revolution in the early to mid–1980s. This is still their raison d'être, perhaps even more so than in the 1980s, since the erotic bar is even more pronounced today, both socially and fictively. For those seeking "tamer" romances, the secular field is relatively lean. It is not always necessary to give all the details of a romantic relationship. One can get the picture without having to enter the bedroom. After all, sex, a number of Christian editors said, was created by God, but that does not mean one has to wallow in it. The trinity is also important in Christian romances: God, the hero, and the heroine. This order is important. God is what bring two people together and unites them in their life quest.

The major Christian houses that publish fiction include Thomas Nelson, Bethany, Zondervan, Harvest House, United Methodist, David Cook, WaterBrook Multnomah, and Revell. Most were doing some Christian romance fictive titles in the 1980s. Bethany may have been among the first with Janette Oke's *Love Comes Softly* in 1979. Bethany's openness to the romance theme was more proactive than the industry's reactive response to the overt sexuality of secular romances in the mid- to late 1980s. The reason Bethany debuted a Christian romance novel ahead of some of its competitors, David Long at Bethany suggests, is because its vice president of editorial at the time, Carol Johnson, was one of the few women working in the industry and so brought a different perspective to the books filtered into the system.[32]

More Christian romance novels appeared in the second half of the 1980s, but it would not be until the mid- to late 1990s that a wider range of Christian romance genres would begin to percolate. Chick-lit has since run its course in the Christian market, much as it has in the secular one, and romance suspense is a popular category today, just as it is in the secular market, though it is of interest to note that romance suspense with a Christian theme does better online and at Christian bookstores than at the big-box stores like Wal-Mart,[33] more than likely because the secular publishers have a stronger romance suspense presence at these outlets. Bethany, which is top-heavy in the historical field, is seeing an uptrend in English Victorian and Regency historical romances, while HarperCollins Christian, though light in the historical field, is releasing more Edwardian and World War II love stories. The upswing in these historical periods followed the popularity of the PBS television series *Downton Abbey*.

Zondervan and Thomas Nelson are both under HarperCollins and illustrate how a secular conglomerate is filtering Christian manuscripts into the market. Bethany and Revell are both under Baker Publishing today but share similarities with Christian purveyors of other evangelical romances, like Harvest House, Summerside, and WaterBrook Multnomah. David C. Cook and Barbour have a vibrant fictive program but put out only a smattering of romance novels, though it is worth noting that, small as the programs are, Carla Laureano with David C. Cook was awarded a 2014 RITA at the RWA for best inspirational romance, *Five Days in Skye*. Tyndale and United Methodist Publishing are smaller Christian houses that have both discontinued their romance lines though they continue to filter romances into their general fiction lists. All Christian publishers are differentiated from Harlequin's Love Inspired line of Christian books since most Christian romances are not published as mass-market books but as trade hardback and paperback books. This means, if nothing else, that Christian publishers are more open to accepting books that don't fit a rigid, preconceived formula, even though most are nevertheless formulaic. As one Christian writer told her editor, "Christianity is the core of my life. So no matter what I do as a writer that is going to come through. I don't have to be pushed; I don't have to be twisted into a certain formula—it's part of who I am as a person."

Zondervan and Thomas Nelson are well-established Christian publishers. Zondervan was purchased by HarperCollins in 1988; Thomas Nelson was owned by a number of private equity firms (2006 and 2012) before it was acquired by HarperCollins in July 2012. Both are now under the umbrella of HarperCollins. In contrast, Bethany and Revell are owned by Baker, a Christian publishing group of some size. Revell became part of Baker in 1992; Bethany joined the Baker family in 2003. The association with Baker provided financial stability to both Revell[34] and Bethany.[35] A key distinction, however, is that while Zondervan's imprint is thematically different from Thomas Nelson's, there is no thematic difference between the novels published by Revell and Bethany, a concern, David Long at Bethany acknowledges, that is a frequent matter of (understandable) discussion in-house.

Both HarperCollins Christian imprints are edited out of the Nashville headquarters of Thomas Nelson. It makes sense to consolidate the editorial process; at the same time, the two imprints maintain their separate identify. One reason for maintaining distinct imprints is that there is a thematic distinction. Zondervan is more old-school evangelical, and this, in itself, sets it apart from most other Christian houses. Books with a more overt Christian message are published by Zondervan while those that are more subtle in their "preachiness" tend to be filtered into Thomas Nelson's books.[36] Editors in Christian houses today acknowledge that there was a more overt salvation message in Christian romances of the 1980s and that this is less distinct today. Zondervan, one of the few that had a heavy presence in romance fiction from the 1980s, seems to have kept this emphasis, but even then it is less blatant today than it was in the late 1980s through the early 1990s.

HarperCollins's means of publishing and acquiring authors is fairly common among contemporary Christian publishers. They all emphasize that they are not category romance publishers and focus more on author-driven novels. Mainstream secular publishers are just as likely to state this. And like most mainstream secular publishers, many of the Christian publishers do not accept unagented manuscripts, so the number of submissions is greatly reduced, and those that are filtered into the editorial system are more likely to have been pre-screened along some preconceived agented notion of what this or that house wants in a Christian novel. In any event, guidelines are not really necessary because the genre itself maintains certain elements that writers and editors embrace, the primary one being that the novels should unite a couple in a relationship through Jesus Christ.

The Christian message aside, Christian editors function in the classic gatekeeper tradition. They select novels that appeal to them. The *Quilting* series released by Abingdon Press at United Methodist is an excellent example of the personal sifting in filtering manuscripts.

A series of once-a-month quilt books ran for a little over two years and was terminated in 2015 after inventory was exhausted. The rationale for the line was based on the "incredible obsession Americans have for quilts."[37] This makes sense, but it was not the *driving* motivation. Rather, it was the editor's own fascination with quilts that prompted the series.

Quilts of Love editor Ramona Richards inherited her mother's quilts. Her mother had taken a lot of time and effort to write the story behind each quilt and sew it to the back of the quilt, including the date it was made, what it was made of, and what the pattern was. This was all "fascinating" to the editor who then, after the fact, justified the line by connecting the dots to social trends: "People with quilts.... They love quilting and the stories behind the quilts, so being a writer and an editor I put together this proposal, and everyone [at Abingdon] was very excited about it." The problem was just bad timing: "The industry was in upheaval and we were just coming out of the recession. People weren't buying print books as much as they had been."

It was more than just bad timing, however. There were at least three other issues. One was that the books were 60,000 words when most of Abingdon's fiction was 80,0000 to 100,000 words, so the reader might not have viewed the books as worth the cost in much the same way Pocket Books was concerned that the reader would think they were getting "cheated" on the smaller-looking paperback books when they were first released. Another issue is that while the books were designated romances, not all the books had a romantic theme, so readers who turned to the series for a romance story might be disconcerted by not finding one; conversely, those who might have been intrigued with the quilting angle may have identified it as more of a romance novel, which they might not have been interested in. Yet another issue is that Abingdon was never able to get the line into quilting stores since they don't typically carry fiction. The result of this exclusion is that they never reached the audience that was most likely to embrace the novels. In short, the people most interested in the quilting angle seemed not to have been aware of the series. This is more a marketing and distribution issue than an editorial one, though they tend to feed off one another. Abingdon is, like many publishers, addressing the marketing issue more directly today than when *Quilts of Love* appeared. United Methodist Publishing is moving to a new facility from its somewhat shabby downtown Nashville location and has recently hired some "savvy digital people" to ensure their novels have more of an online presence and reach a wider audience.

A similar marketing-distribution problem affected the HeartQuest romance line at Tyndale House: "These days, of course, we're capitalizing on social media," said Kathryn Olson. "But back in the day of HeartQuest [1997–2004], we used primarily [expensive] print advertising in magazines that catered to romance readers, such as *Romantic Times*, or to Evangelical Protestant women, such as *Today's Christian Woman*. There was also, then, a healthy network of small independent Christian bookstores. They were our primary customers since we could never get the large secular chains like Barnes and Noble and Borders to shelve our books in with the other [secular] romance novels." That problem still exists in secular bookstores for Christian publishers of fiction but is less pronounced simply because brick and mortar stores are themselves less of a presence today. The distribution issue at Tyndale for HeartQuest was complicated by the competitive marketplace. The line was launched in the mid- to late 1990s because, as Olson points out, other Christian publishers were doing some romance-type fiction, "but I don't think anyone [at the time] had a 'pure romance' line, one that followed the tried-and-true romance story formula but without graphic sex." Coincidentally, alas, other Christian houses were listening to Christian authors who were dissatisfied with the secular sexual emphasis and responded in like manner. Right around the time HeartQuest launched, "just about every Christian publisher [suddenly] got into the romance market." One in particular posed a significant challenge not only because it had a strong mail-order romance books club, but because it was releasing significantly more romances than the relatively thin HeartQuest line, and so HeartQuest got lost in the racks.

Most Christian publishers are, like their secular colleagues, trying to establish more of a digital presence. Bookstore attrition is not limited to the secular market: United Methodist Publishing closed all of its seventy-plus Cokesbury outlets in 2014; this included closing its Dallas store, which was among the largest bookstores in the United States. Most Christian houses had a presence in the religious section of secular bookstores like Barnes and Noble and could be found prominently in the fiction section of Christian bookstores. These fast-disappearing outlets are changing the way books reach their intended audience.

Books-a-Million is one of the few large brick and mortar retail bookstores that is growing today. Books-a-Million has a heavy presence in the South, where Christian fiction does particularly well. The success of Christian books in the South is not particularly surprising since Southerners (and Midwesterners), David Long at Bethany House observed, are particularly open to hearing the evangelical message. Small, independent bookstores tend to push more literary fiction and often don't have a religious section, or if they do, it's a very small one. The other outlet tapped by Christian publishers is big-box retailers such as Wal-Mart, K-Mart, Sam's Club, and Costco. Rack space in these outlets is relatively small, however, if only because books are just one product among the host of products stocked. Nevertheless, these retail outlets remain important because their presence is strong throughout the United States and this ensures, even with limited space, that those books carried are likely to reach a mass audience, not just those who frequent Christian bookstores.

The Christian Formula

There is a lot of room for an analysis of Christian romance fiction. It may well be the most misunderstood category of romance publishing, in part owing to the lack of critical analysis of the field. One of the more problematic studies was conducted by Peter Darbyshire,[38] a professor of English literature who brings his humanist judgment to bear on Christian romance content. He focuses on Harlequin's Christian romances and does not seem to appreciate that Harlequin's brand of Christian romance has been taken to task on some sites and blogs because its Christian message is somewhat attenuated, at least compared to other Christian publishers. His "analysis" is further hindered because his "assessment" is based on a selective skimming of only *one* Harlequin Love Inspired novel, *Heiress*. This alone taints his conclusion that Christian books promote the message of the Christian Right because the Harlequin books [sic] advocate the sanctity of marriage and promote traditional family values (i.e., gender role divisions). This can be said of the content of most secular romantic fiction, not just Harlequin's Christian line, since romantic fiction, by definition, is about finding a soul mate to spend one's life with, and marital relationships, for better or worse, still tend to pivot on gender divisions, though they are less pronounced than they once were, both in the real world and in the fictive one.

A closer reading of the Christian romance field reveals books with complex themes akin to some of those found in the secular field; Christian romances have delved into such themes as sex slavery or an unwed woman having to cope with having a child out of wedlock. The complexity of Christian romantic fiction is not encapsulated in just one novel. Darbyshire's analysis might have been totally different had he read *The Edge of Grace* (Abingdon, 2011) by Christa Allan, whose novel treads respectfully into the issue of homosexuality. The plotline refers to the book's title while simultaneously enunciating the book's central premise:

> The early morning call shatters Caryn Becker's world. Unable to cope with her brother's news that he is gay, Caryn rejects him and disappears into her own turbulent life as a young widow and single mom. But when David is attacked and nearly killed, Caryn is forced to make hard choices about family, faith, and her own future; choices that take her to the very edge of grace.

The Edge of Grace, Ramona Richards emphasizes, is not about redemption— a gay man turning his back on his sexual predilection and undergoing a lifestyle change by reverting "back" to heterosexuality. The book is about the heroine and her having to deal with her brother's lifestyle. The reason Richards felt the novel was appropriate for a Christian audience is because thousands of Christians are forced to confront this type of issue every year and have to come to terms with it.

The analysis by Rebecca Kaye Barrett about what women take from a Christian romance novel is more instructive than Darbyshire's, relying as it does on interviews with Christian romance readers and writers.[39] The salvation message she finds readers take from Christian romance is not the same as those found in 1980s novels that pivoted on redemption. The salvation discourse she refers to is where "the church is the bride of Christ, and just as Christ loves his church, so ought husbands love their wives." By talking to readers, she finds the Christian message was important to their appreciation of the romance. She quotes one reader, for instance, who is reminded of her faith in a Robin Lee Hatcher book: "Boy! Did this book make me utterly ashamed of myself. I realized, to my dismay, that I don't anywhere near lean on the Lord as I should."

An instructive comparative study of Christian and secular romances from Harlequin's more Christian-comparable, less erotic lines was conducted by Laura Clawson.[40] Clawson found that while there were some minor differences, they were not pronounced.[41]

> Overall, differences between Christian and secular books do not create a clear picture of cultural difference.... A few statistically significant differences do exist, however. Secular books are more likely to feature characters—heroes or heroines—who work in managerial or entrepreneurial professions.... Characters in Christian books are [also] more likely to have both friendships and close kin relationship[s] prior to entering into the romantic relations.

Clawson tentatively suggests these differences may be simply the result of a more secular preoccupation with worldly success than that which embraced Christians.

As for marital history and sexuality, Clawson found that the heroes and heroines are both equally likely to have been previously married, when they are not never-married singles. Their reason for their current nonmarital status is attributed to different causes: previously married "Christian characters are significantly more likely to have been widowed [while] secular characters are more likely to have been divorced, abused, or cheated on." As for sex, not surprisingly, Clawson found secular characters more likely to have sexual experience while Christian books simply avoid this and don't give information about their characters' sexual history. A separate analysis by Rebecca Barrett-Fox of the characteristics of the hero in Christian romances found that he was an alpha male.[42] The alpha traits she describes are not much different (except for his faith) from those found in secular romances.

The Christian message mentioned by Clawson and Barrett-Fox was the primary focal point of discussion when talking to editors about the Christian message in the novels.[43] Christian publishers of romances are largely Protestant, and while some houses emphasize the evangelical element more strongly than others, most don't push any denominational point of view. This is because they want to spread the word of Christ. Indeed, the digital age has placed the books in the hands of the general romance reader, not just the Christian romance reader. The general reader is likely to trawl Google and other electronic sources for romances that they would otherwise only find in unfrequented Christian bookstores or the religious section of secular bookstores. This may have helped legitimate them in the eyes of the Romance Writers Association (RWA), which, more than one Christian romance editor felt, has not been all that embracing of Christian romances at their annual conference until recently. This is an interesting perception since not long after its inception the RWA awarded a Golden Medallion[44] for the best inspirational romance between 1985 and 1986. It was discontinued because there were so few entries since the inspirational romance market was just beginning to percolate. The inspirational category was reinstated as a RITA in 1995 and has been awarded every year since. It appears that the feeling of exclusion by some Christian editors is based on the relegation of Christian romances to the inspirational category and that those who write and publish Christian romances are not considered part of the wider romance field. This, one Christian editor indicates, is changing. The fact that the RWA had a panel discussion entitled "God and Sex" at its 2014 annual conference is considered by this editor to be a step toward respectability in the romance field, not just in the Christian sector of the marketplace. The toned-down evangelical message also seems to be helping these books garner greater acceptance in the broader romance field.

Amish Wonderland

The cowboy is sacrosanct in romance fiction, and most publishers of secular romances have romance novels about cowboys, if not a dedicated line. The Amish man is the substitute for the cowboy in Christian romance fiction. Both nostalgically recall simpler times, a mythologized ideal period located in the past. The key distinction is that the Amish lifestyle is, by definition, Christian. It is particularly evangelical since the Amish lifestyle pivots on scripture. Amish believe in the importance of individual Bible study and the necessity of living a life free of sin after adult baptism; they do not believe in using anything that is not found in the Bible, hence their rationale for using horses and buggies as a means of transportation rather than the automobile.[45] Most Amish romances are set in the present but nevertheless hark back to the past, which is why they can sometimes be found filed under contemporary romances and at other times under historical romances.

The wheels were greased for Amish novels with the success of *Witness* (1985), starring Harrison Ford. Amish romances might have peppered some Christian lines after the film debuted, but they would not garner substantive attention until Bethany House published Beverly Lewis's novel *The Shunning* (1997) about the Amish in Lancaster Country, Pennsylvania, which, coincidentally, was the locale for the film *The Witness*. Coming out of the chute first, Beverly Lewis remains one of the top Amish romance authors. After *The Shunning* appeared and received accolades, Barbour released Wanda Brunstetter and WaterBrook published the first of Cindy Woodsmall's Lancaster-set Amish romances. All three authors leapt to best-seller status and continue to write Amish-themed romances that generate strong sales for the houses that launched their careers. The success of these novels, David Long says, parallels almost exactly the heavy entrance into stocking Christian fiction at Wal-Mart. It wasn't long before "everyone started chasing the Amish books because they were hot; Harvest House [soon] devoted almost their entire list to Amish."[46] Every editor today acknowledges what no one foresaw: Amish is an entire category unto itself. Christian publishers all have Amish novels and most have an entire line devoted to the genre. In fact, Barbour, which sold its Christian Love Inspired romance line to Harlequin, still maintains a separate series of books devoted to the Amish and their romantic entanglements.

The market is glutted with Amish romances. The editorial demand for these books has led, like it inevitably does, to people writing about a topic they don't know much about but have gleaned from other Amish books. David Long elaborates: "Some authors do a fantastic amount of research: they spend time with families, have personal connections. Then there are writers who are basically spinning off what they've read. They're retelling an almost fantasy version of what the Amish lifestyle is." Those familiar with the Amish lifestyle are more persnickety about the accuracy of Amish life depicted in the novels and are even less tolerant of incorrect "Amishisms" than the Amish, who find the books rather silly.[47]

In the end, it doesn't really matter whether the books accurately portray Amish life or paint a fantasy wonderland of Amish life because the books are not about the Amish; they're about a simple Christian-lived lifestyle, which is why they resonate with Christian women romance readers. These novels, Ramona Richards suggests, are the logical outgrowth of the prairie romances from the 1970s and 1980s.[48]

It may be a crowded market category, but it is still growing. Considering that there is a new Amish settlement founded every 3.5 weeks and the number of Amish people doubles every twenty-one years,[49] there are still a lot of stories to tell.[50] Amish romances remain a popular romance category among Christians because they tell a simple tale about Christian life and love. It looks like Amish love will be around for quite some years to come.

The focal point of this analysis has been on the Christian dimension, but secular readers, whom the Christian market is trying to attract, may constitute an expanding audience since the Christian message is not the overriding theme of the book. The novels appear of interest to those romance readers, secular or Christian, who want a nice story about good old American values that doesn't beat them over the head with sex, sex, sex.

Cover for *Finding Love at Home*, an Amish-themed book (Harvest House, 2014).

Love at the Xtreme: Erotic Romance Publishers

The Christian publishers are at the sweet, sweet end of our erotic continuum. For those who want sex, sex in the extreme, sex at the nine and ten level of eroticism, where few mainstream publishers go, there are the erotic romance houses who specialize in love spelled S-E-X. Mainstream publishers are involved in erotica, but attention tends to surround the upstart e-book publishers of erotic romance fiction, mainly because they are the ones who are publishing the body of romances at the upper end of the erotic spectrum, which we'll label xrotica. Of the twenty books noted on two separate top-ten lists of recommended erotic romances,[51] Ellora's Cave had five, followed by Harlequin with four; Grand Central Publishing, Samhain, and Kensington each had two; the five remaining were split among Bantam, Berkley, newcomer e-book publishers InterMix Books (Berkley/NAL), Open Road, and one self-published author.

It is not surprising that Ellora's Cave had the most "dirty books" since they were one of the erotic trailblazers. Samhain, one of the three that tied with two books apiece, is a relatively new house that was founded specifically to publish erotic romances. It might be a bit surprising that Harlequin had so many given the discussion in the previous chapter that Harlequin is not known for erotica at the extreme. The four books Harlequin published were split between their two mainstream imprints and are not category romances: two were published as MIRA books, two as Carina e-books. Reviews of the four Harlequin books on Goodreads all indicate the four books were all solid, well-written stories with believable characters. The various reviewers all found the books erotic but qualified them at around the six to eight level of eroticism on our erotic scale. "It's not a book littered with hardcore sex," writes one reviewer of *The Siren*. "[S]ure, there is sex but I've read books with way more," said another. A reviewer commenting on *A Shot in the Dark* says that the "story has *elements* of BDSM and D/s with *moments* of *light* bondage..." (author's italics). One found that the BDSM element of *Theory of Attracting* to be hot, but hot was qualified by another reviewer who also enjoyed the story but dismissed its eroticism as "BDSM lite, no clubs, no edgeplay...." The same qualifiers tend to shade the erotic novels by many of the mainstream publishers on the top-twenty lists, such as Bantam and Berkley's Heat. Other mainstream publishers who release some erotic novels, mostly in the six to eight ranges, include Crown, Knopf Doubleday, Random House; St. Martin's, and Avon Red,[52] as well as Sourcebooks' Casablanca line, Grand Central's Forever, Berkley's Sensation, and Kensington's Brava and Aphrodisia.

Eroticism lies in the eyes of the beholder, so a five-level depiction of sexual activity can be found to be quite "hot." Our erotic scale, however, defines eroticism at the upper end (xrotica) to be graphically depicted and often occurs outside a committed relationship; it is also, more often than not, with multiple partners over the course of the novel. This is also the definition of male-oriented pornography. The key distinction is that male-oriented pornography focuses *solely* on the physical attributes of "the other," while erotic romances tends to parade the personal emotional experience of both characters along with the physical. The xrotic romance also tends to end in traditional fashion with the heroine settling down with one man, though this is not always the case. Xrotic romances include BDSM, of course, various co-minglings (ménage-plus), along with fetish, kink, and taboo themes besides more traditional romances nudged into the xrotic world, such as paranormals, sci-fi, historicals, and interracial lust. The xrotic publishers all tend to have some form of disclaimer that is in an obvious attempt to distance themselves from "questionable" (sexually explicit) material—see, we don't publish *that* kind of stuff. A composite of romantically inappropriate activities among xrotic publishers includes anything to do with sex acts that cause serious physical damage, genuine tragedy, or anguish; incest, which some feel necessary to qualify meaning incest in any form; sexual activity with children under 18, and that means, one publisher specifies, not 17.9999; rape presented in a positive light or for titillation; sex or sexual intimacy with animals; bondage that endangers life; abusive relationships; and aberrant sexual behavior, such as necrophilia.

Many erotic authors at this end of the xrotic spectrum are self-published, such as Meredith Wild, K. Bromberg (JKB Publishing), and R. K. Lilley.[53] Most publishers of xrotica specialize in e-book publishing. Twenty-three independent, non-mainstream publishers of erotica are noted on RomanceWiki. Frequently cited xrotica publishers include Ellora's Cave, Siren, Samhain, Totally Bound, Grand Central, Entangled, Phaze, Crimson, Mischief, Red Sage, Loose Id and Changeling Press, whose submission guidelines indicate they have only one heat level, "over the top hot." Of these, only Grand Central is part of the Big Five (Hachette), though Entangled is now affiliated with St. Martin's. Many xrotic publishers were launched by women who found the romances on the market too tame for their taste or were frustrated romance writers whose books were rejected by mainstream houses because of their steamy content.

Ellora's Cave is probably the best-known xrotic publisher of e-books, in no small part because it was one of the first to enter this field. Ellora's Cave may not have "invented" the erotic romance, but the company certainly "ramped it up."[54] EC continues to maintain its focus on xrotica though its list, like most of its competitors, is peppered with more traditional romances. Ellora's Cave also proved the training ground for two of its competitors, Samhain and Changeling. It has published countless authors who have since moved on to mainstream publishing houses.

Tina Engler launched a website in 2000 to sell her self-published erotic romance e-books, which she penned under the name Jaid Black. Ellora's Cave was an outgrowth of that venture. It was officially incorporated in 2002 in Ohio and like many small, start-up companies, it was a family affair: her mother, Patricia Marks, has served as its chief executive officer since the company was formed. The company releases an average of ten books per week. It has five imprints with twenty-four lines. Its bread-and-butter imprint is Romantica, a trademark name owned by Ellora's Cave.

Romantica is Ellora's Cave's main imprint and publishes the majority of the house's titles (3,914 e-books/1,250 paperback books)[55] under seventeen lines, including Branded (marital heat, 17/3), Fusion (multicultural/interracial, 13/6), Shiver (erotic horror, 19/1), Sophisticate (older women/younger men, 75/22) Spectrum (gay/lesbian, 189/48) and Taboo (BDSM, 341/108). The Romantica line delivers a classic romance story because it's a love story with a happy ending; it's just sprinkled heavily with lots of sex, "described in graphic detail, using the kind of language regular people use, rather than flowery euphemisms"; the novels usually end with a mate-for-life, but, to use the parlance of xrotica, one has to fuck a lot of frogs to get there. Kink (sexual fetishes) moves beyond the traditional romance and focuses on no-strings attached sexual adventures; it is the only line under the Exotika (234/34) imprint. There are six lines that appear under the Blush imprint (527/326) which tones down the erotic element. Just as MIRA was a means of keeping Harlequin category writers with Harlequin, Blush is a way to keep those writers with Ellora's Cave who want to write "regular" romances, and for those readers who like a more traditional, less sexually explicit, but still erotic romance.

The other xrotica publishers share similar start-up histories: They have similar imprints and lines and use digital as their primary method of distribution.

Christina (Cris) Brashear was an IT worker who struck up a relationship with Tina Engler at Ellora's Cave when Ellora's Cave was just starting.[56] Engler brought her to Ellora's Cave because of her IT background. A falling-out between the two women led Brashear to start Samhain because she didn't want to go back to the corporate world. She was encouraged to do this by some of the authors she worked with at Ellora's Cave, who went over to Samhain after she started her own company, which further aggravated the rancor between the two publishers. Samhain is also strongly familial: Brashear's sister and daughter both work for her. Samhain has a full-time staff of seventeen, of which twelve are editors, another few dozen part-time associates, and around 800 authors. There are a range of romance categories and she has released well over 2,000 books in the romance genre, thirty to forty percent of which are "Red Hots" or xrotic novels. One of the more interesting lines is Retro Romances, which more mainstream publishers are moving toward by taking advantage of their inventory. Retro Romances re-releases romances that have been published by another house but have not been published in digital form, and the copyright has reverted to the author. These books constitute only about fifteen percent of Samhain's sales, but they have a higher profit margin since the books have already been edited and all Samhain has to do is scan them and redo the cover design, which the author doesn't hold the rights to. But even this is fairly straightforward because her artists can use the original design for inspiration and quickly devise an appropriate cover to convey the content of the novel.

Samhain is primarily a digital publisher, doing some print-on-demand (POD). Brashear realizes there may be more opportunity in the print format, but like many small new publishers has too much on her plate at the moment to worry about how to reach them. Her IT experience is both her strong suit and her weakness. When we spoke in mid-2014, she was just about to launch a new website that she was quite excited about—and with good reason after examining its post-launch debut. Rather than buying a prepackaged web program, she designed her own, "completely custom coded." She chose this route because there was only a modest ($10,000) difference between setting her own up and buying a prepackaged one, which now allows her to sell her program to others. The IT upside is offset by her downside: she is not organizationally savvy, though she is learning. She cannot, for example, after ten years in business, track sales by genre and category so is unable to identify, and take advantage of in-house trends: "It's something we're trying to puzzle out." She hopes the new program will help her identify sales more clearly. She is aware of her business issues and is attempting to rectify them, which itself is saying a lot because many young entrepreneurs don't recognize their weaknesses. To this end, she is planning over the next year to launch a major marketing campaign to attract readers and is putting together an outside marketing team to help develop a marketing strategy. She is also moving toward a more traditional time frame and is trying to schedule books six to nine months out so there will be more time to build them up.

Margaret Riley, who co-founded Changeling Press in 2004 with retired Air Force husband Bill, was also affiliated with Ellora's Cave. Riley was one of the first three authors published at Ellora's Cave. They were erotic novels, "before it had a name, at least within romance publishing," she quipped.[57] During a February snowstorm when the power was out at the house for a week, she and her husband discussed starting a small press. They had some small business experience, and Riley, who had been writing for a number of years, was less than satisfied with her existing publishing relationships. By the time the power came on they had a business plan and a name. She took a number of fellow Ellora's Cave authors with her to form Changeling, which aggravated her relationship with EC. These authors gave her a strong launch base. She says that she knew she made the right decisions because within three weeks of launching the website, sales were clicking. As so often with the smaller digital houses, many of the authors affiliated with Changeling have moved on to careers with houses in the Big Five, even if some still publish with Changeling.

Changeling started publishing science fiction and paranormal novels, which were Riley's interest, albeit with a strong erotic bent. Back then "you couldn't find sci-fi under the romance category at Amazon. Now you can." The endings were relationship driving and had a happy ending, which is where "we crossed over into the romance genre, though [we initially] didn't put the tag on it. As time went on and more [romance] stuff started coming in, we changed our genres. We now classify everything as romance." Changeling drifted into male/male because "some of our authors wanted to write male/male but couldn't find a home for it, so naturally we said, 'sure, we'll do it.' It's done very well for us." Changeling presently publishes about two percent of the material submitted: an average of four books per week, a number of which are re-releases. The company didn't start selling its digital books off-site until 2008, so a fair amount of its rereleased books have never found their way to traditional sites, like Amazon, Barnes & Noble, and allromance.com.

Siren is a slightly different story. It too is familial: David DeBalko, the company's CEO, says his wife Diana started the company in 2004. She was a devout Harlequin reader her whole life but couldn't find erotic romances, so as an outlet she started Siren for her first (and only) erotic romance, *Vision of Light*. The novel was nowhere near the xrotic level the books are today, nor were any of the other initial ten Siren releases.[58] The company graduated to xrotica because that's where the market was moving.

Amanda Hilton is listed on the site as the publisher. She still uses her pen name, Amanda Hilton, because, DeBalko says, "she is in the adult industry." Hilton has an English degree with a strong IT background, which stood her well in establishing Siren as an e-book publisher in the early days of digital publishing. Originally she published a book per month, but as more books poured in, her output increased exponentially, as did the degree of erotica. "We didn't start at the ten level," DeBalko says. "[We] started putting books out and just decided to follow the demand," which meant, in this case, the xrotic novels that were coming in. The company ended up specializing in ménage because that was what was coming over the transom, but also because one "couldn't find ménage anywhere" back then. Ménage was MFM, not FMF, and so it was "a natural progress" to move into m/m fiction. Ménage and male/male have become the specialty, interspersed with a heavy dose of BDSM. DeBalko readily admits that she was at the right time (digital) and in the right place (ménage and m/m). The company puts out a traditional print line of romances for its authors who want to go this route, but it is primarily to placate authors who like to see the hard copy book on their shelf.

Siren's model would be described by mainstream publishers as spaghetti style: throw it all against the wall and see what sticks. It is not a model readily appreciated by mainstream publishers who wring their hands over their limited selection of releases: "I could never figure how the volume business model works," said Stocke at Sourcebook. "You just have to do a lot of books. Less craft, lot of volume." Not that mainstream publishers don't engage in the model. Shawnetelle Madison, an author dropped by Ballantine after two books in her Coveted paranormal romance series (2013), suggests the spaghetti style is fairly common: "They'll toss some books by an author, and if that author sticks, then they'll continue to publish them. If not, they won't."[59] DeBalko would partially agree that the spaghetti metaphor is applicable with Siren. Tried-and-true backlists, which mainstream publishers rely on for steady profits, are of no consequence at xrotic publishers: "The appetite for erotic romance is huge," says DeBalko. "What drives [the market] is new stuff." And so she pretty much publishes whatever comes in. "Yeah, we put them out! Submissions pour in and we're happy to take them." This doesn't mean Siren doesn't do the work. For first-time writers there is "quite a bit" of editorial work to do: first there's content editing portion, line editing, copy editing, and editing aimed at fixing the technical needs side of the work. All the staff is in-house, compared to when the company started and used freelancers. DeBalko argues that they "try to put the quality in by having the editors in-house," while at the same time acknowledging that they are grinding them out. The model works for them.

All major publishers are now doing e-books. Most were slow to get off the mark, though their financial clout is helping them quickly establish a digital presence. It nevertheless remains a fairly small part of a mainstream publisher's means of distribution. It is *the* means for xrotic publishers. Their early digital presence has helped them establish a substantial competitive lead over their larger rivals—one xrotica editor quipped, perhaps a tad hyperbolically but not unrealistically, that management at mainstream houses has told their editors to watch what her house was doing digitally and to mimic her success.

The strong digital presence of xrotic publishers has been helped by the seemingly insatiable demand for erotic content, which they have specialized in from the get-go and which, despite protests to the contrary by management at most mainstream houses, still remains largely untapped by them, at least at the xrotic end of the spectrum. And when mainstream publishers do venture into the xrotica world, it seems they have to explain the "deviancy." The heroine's insatiable sexual appetite in *Dirty* (MIRA) is because of the baggage she carries with her, the result of being repeatedly raped as a teen; in *Laid Bare* (Berkley Heat) the heroine's "kinky" sexual antics is because of "some pretty heavy stuff in her [earlier] life."[60] No "background" psychological explanation is proffered by xrotic writers or publishers for the sexual behavior of their heroines; it's just what some do, and enjoy. The readers clearly enjoy it, and while we might hesitate to pronounce success based on the number of books released—as was done with the short-lived popularity of the bodice-rippers in the late 1970s and the slew of sexually laced contemporary romances that were "all the rage" in the first half of the 1980s—the fact that most xrotic publishers have been in business since around 2005 and are celebrating ten years in the business does hint that readers are enjoying their extreme style of intimacy.

Mainstream publishers are entering the xrotic end of the romance phenomena, but they didn't start until 2005,[61] and did so tentatively. As early as 2010 there was a general feeling by mainstream publishers that the xrotic market was glutted. "There hasn't been a decline [in xrotica]," said Susan Swinwood, who oversees the Carina e-line at Harlequin, "[b]ut there hasn't been a growth spurt" either.[62] She is probably correct insofar as mainstream publishers are concerned. But that's because the *real* market for xrotica is being fulfilled by digital publishers of xrotica, who, if we just use the annual output of three (of the ten) publishers critiqued in this section (Ellora's Cave, Siren, and Samhain), release around 2,000 books per year.[63] To put this into perspective, these *three* xrotic publishers release twice as many books per year than the combined yearly output of Harlequin's entire category lines (12 lines, 768 books).[64] This output remains high even if Siren's prodigious production numbers are held in check—allowing the ten xrotic publishers mentioned at the outset of this section to release an average of eight books per week, which is the industry norm, that amounts to 4,160 novels a year, at least half of which are at the xrotic end of the romance spectrum. Mainstream publishers are simply not players in xrotica, though they may have a presence for those sexual tourists who want to learn more about BDSM love à la the *Fifty Shades* trilogy; but xrotic publishers also

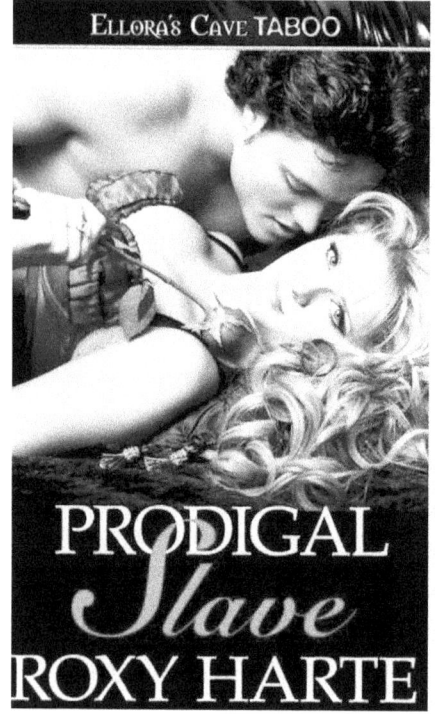 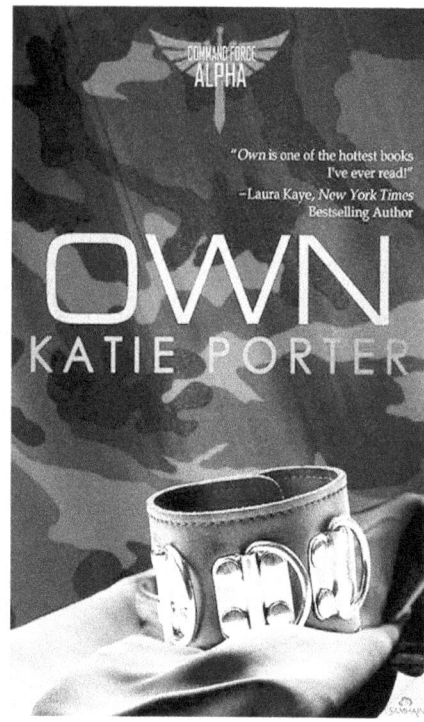

Xrotic covers. From left: *Prodigal Slave* (Ellora's Cave, 2014) and *Own* (Samhain, 2014).

publish novels at the six, seven, and eight level of eroticism. They just have a wealth of books a reader can graduate to when they want to move beyond BDSM-light.

Mainstream publishers might well argue that they are doing some xrotica and not doing more in order to maintain editorial quality. There is some legitimacy in this defense, though all the xrotic publishers are proud of the quality of their novels, even Siren, which boasts that all its editors have bachelor's degrees in English or journalism. Still, cranking out a hundred novels per month (Siren) poses difficulty in maintaining quality control. This is less of an issue with many of the other xrotic publishers, who publish on the average twenty-some books per month with an editorial staff of around five to seven, which is why books by Ellora's Cave and Samhain regularly appear on erotica best-selling charts. It is somewhat ironic that mainstream romance publishers might revert to this charge about "inferior" writing and plotting, considering that it has long been leveled at them by "legitimate" (non-romance) publishers. And when the mainstream houses look at the top-selling erotic romances, they are finding that they are sharing space with the upstart xrotic publishers because the small xrotic books are not just erotic; they are, by and large, well written, well-told romantic stories. Dirty books might sell but quality dirty books sell even better, to paraphrase Adrienne Benedicks, founder of Erotica Readers & Writers Association.[65]

The mainstream houses are still viewing xrotic publishing as a fad—or worse. They are putting some novels out, but most are erotic, not xrotic. The hesitancy of many mainstream publishing houses to tackle this still vibrant field is that they seem to have fallen back into their old "high cultural" malaise. This is perhaps best seen with what happened to Black Lace, which was a series published by Virgin Books. Black Lace novels received little attention in the United States since they were released primarily in the U.K. Founded in 1993, Black Lace was well-known for its cutting-edge line of xrotic novels that explored such themes as BDSM, ménage, and bisexuality. It also produced Idol for gay men and Sapphire for lesbians. In 2007, Random House, through its U.K. division, Ebury, acquired a 90 percent stake in the company. In 2009, Virgin became an independent imprint within Ebury Publishing. Right around this time, Random House announced, to the consternation of many, that they had decided to stop commissioning new titles by Black Lace and its sister imprints.[66] This news, Alison Flood writes in *The Guardian*, "prompted an outpouring of upset online, where it was described as 'a sad day for the world of smut.'"[67]

The key word here is smut. This is a word assiduously avoided by those in xrotic publishing. It does seem to underscore the view of mainstream publishers toward xrotica and is no doubt a reason for Random House abandoning the line in favor of "quality" (romantic) fiction. Random House's decision was also prompted, to be fair, by a downturn in the market for erotica, which was due in part, Flood writes, "because so much material is available for free on the internet, and in part because too many titles had been published." But the real issue, a rival publisher says in *The Guardian* article, is that "the people in the seats of power at Random House don't give a damn about erotica, and the fact it has not been making money [at the moment] is just an excuse to get rid of the lines." One "erotic memoirist" tweeted that it was "terrible news ... erotic fiction—and its writers—will take a hit from this. I do hope something else will arise from the ashes; maybe another publisher will see the niche in the market and set up their own imprint."[68] This person's hopes are being fulfilled by a wide range of xrotic publishers, including Totally Bound in the U.K., which was founded in 2006 and appears to be flourishing since Black Lace had its doors closed.[69]

The major competitors for xrotic publishers are not really the big publishing houses, but self-publishing authors, some of whom are also very savvy in establishing a digital presence and marketing their books. Despite the heavy presence of self-publishers of xrotica, it is a difficult path to plow if only because the more time one spends trying to establish a digital presence, the less time one can devote to writing. This is certainly a strong appeal for self-published authors to gravitate to xrotic publishers, plus the prestige of publishing with an established house. The problem for xrotic publishers is that mainstream houses regularly troll the sales of self-published authors and those at xrotic houses, and when they see an author starting to garner blog attention or sales, they go after them.

Xrotic publishers serve as gatekeeping monitors for the editors at mainstream houses. Agents monitor manuscripts and filter out those that are inappropriate to the house and forward only those would-be authors who have sales potential based on their writing style and theme. Xrotic publishers do more: they edit and market the books, enhancing the potential for the author's success. The mainstream gatekeeper is not just guessing that the manuscript might do well; they actually see how the author is selling so they get to "cherry pick" those whom they are assured are promising when they offer them a contract. And around it goes: just as the xrotic houses entice self-publishers aboard with the promise of better distribution, publicity, and money, mainstream houses are able to entice xrotic authors because they have a more legitimate name, wider distribution beyond the digital world, more promotional clout, and deeper pockets, which means they can provide advances that the digital publishers cannot match. Shoshanna Evers is just one example among many in this regards. Her first BDSM novel, *Punishing the Art Thief*, was published by Ellora's Cave in 2010. It and the subsequent few books she wrote for Ellora's Cave did very well, which is why Simon & Schuster offered her a six-book contract.[70] Her first book, *Enslaved*, was published by Pocket as an e-book in April 2013. To what degree the mainstream publishers "tone down" these xrotic authors is unclear. Entangled, an e-book publisher that is often cited as an xrotic publisher, is more midrange erotica at the five to eight level, which is probably why it was courted by St. Martin's Press. This suggests that mainstream publishers are still not embracing xrotica. A content analysis of those writers who transition from xrotica to the mainstream might prove enlightening.

Xrotic publishers print books, but that is not their preferred format. They do print for those consumers who insist on having a print book or for their authors who like to see the book on their shelf or have something to physically take with them to talks and trade shows. Print on demand (POD), once a dirty word in the industry, has helped digital publishers because they don't have to print and warehouse books that may or may not sell, which the mainstream publishers are still married to. This allows xrotic publishers to easily meet any call for print books. It is very cost-effective. Still, digital sales are why most readers gravitate to xrotic publishers, and more and more people today are adopting digital as a preferred form of reading, on devices such as Kindles, Sony Readers, and Nooks, as well as downloading books to their home computers. The digital book price for mainstream books is about the same as a printed book; for example, the mass-market paperback of Sarah MacLean's *Never Judge a Lady by Her Cover* (Avon, 2014) is priced at $7.99; it is available on Avon's site as an e-book for $6.99, while Amazon has it on Kindle for $6.64.[71] For would-be consumers, xrotic publishers offer a bargain: a e-novel typically costs around $5.99; a novella, $4.45; a quick read, which is gaining favor among digital readers, comes in at around a dollar. The quickies, as they are appropriately referred to by xrotic publishers, are "an easy way for a reader to not only try an author but a genre," said Gorlinsky at Ellora's Cave, where quickies have long been a staple and can be downloaded for as little as $.99, though they typically range between $1.49 to $2.49. "If you don't know whether you'll like futuristic erotic romance," said Gorlinsky, "you can buy a single story [and see if it has appeal]."[72] If a reader is reluctant to spend even this much, most xrotic publishers have free reads across genres available on-line.

Gaining Respect

Recognition by professional associations is a mark of "making it" in any field. The Romance Writers of America (RWA) is *the* gateway for authorial recognition within romance publishing. RWA was founded in 1980 as a nonprofit organization by Vivian Stephens, who was an editor at Dell, and five romance authors who met at a writer's conference at the University of Houston. The idea was to bring romance writers together and provide a network to support career-focused romance writers. Its thirty-seven initial members burgeoned to over 10,000 members by 2014. This membership base gives them considerable clout within the industry. General membership is only open to those who are seriously pursuing a romance writing career; associate membership is open to anyone who supports the organization, but associate members cannot vote or hold office in RWA. One of its stated goals is to lobby for reasonable remuneration for its members and the preservation of authorial and intellectual property rights. They hold an annual conference that promotes networking and seminars for their members. Awards given to members of the industry at the RWA national conference recognize achievement within the romance field and bestow considerable prestige on the recipient. Some 2,000-plus participated in their 34th annual conference, which was held in San Antonio in July 2014.

The RWA has, until recently, resisted the entry of xrotic publishers into their midst.

Susan Edwards at Ellora's Cave as well Christina Brashear at Samhain and Margaret Riley at Changeling, despite their falling-out, share a similar assessment of how their houses have been responded to by RWA, as does Liz Pelletier at Entangled. None were initially recognized as a legitimate publishing house. The resistance appears to be based on their digital format, since most RWA members have historically been print authors. Resistance also appears to be a response to the more explicit xrotic themes, where few RWA members strayed in the early days of xrotica. The digital houses are all publishers of romances, however, and thus meet the general criteria for membership in RWA. But RWA found reasons to hold these publishers at arm's length.

Pelletier says that she was told they were too young of an organization to be invited to participate in the annual conference and those in the field had to be in the business for at least two years. Pelletier rebutted this argument by pointing out that Carina Press was also new and had been invited to participate, though to be fair, Carina was a new imprint of Harlequin, and Harlequin's been around for decades. Then, Pelletier says, they told her she had to prove solvency, which she was able to do because she owned Savvy Authors, which provided workshops to help would-be romance authors. RWA dithered by saying that Savvy Authors was not a publishing firm and that she had no experience in publishing, which was actually true, because Entangled was not launched until 2011. Pelletier did not take this passively. She went to the RWA conference uninvited and told people at the conference that she was holding a seminar for authors at the hotel next door, and over a hundred people showed up. Finally, in 2013, Entangled was invited to attend the RWA conference; she was invited to participate in 2014. Entangled's newly formed alliance with St. Martin's probably helped. Ellora's Cave and Samhain share similar stores about RWA's initial resistance and subsequent attitudinal change. Riley at Changeling is still rankled by her initial treatment at RWA and will have nothing to do with them, not even paying the relatively meager dues, which would be tantamount to supporting them in her eyes.

The other three publishers agree that RWA finally recognized them after RWA realized that digital was not going away and did, begrudgingly, allow xrotic publishers to join; Siren hasn't bothered: "The real benefit [of membership] isn't there [for us] pound for pound." The others acknowledge that they are now embraced by RWA and understand RWA's initial resistance to their firms. Pelletier says that RWA's insistence on having some kind of track record in the field is reasonable since "a lot of e-publishing houses come and go." Brashear elaborates on RWA's initial resistance. "It's difficult to turn away from something and accept something [totally] different. It is hard enough for individuals to do this; it is even harder for organizations. They have to protect the people they were designed to protect." Both digital executives acknowledge that RWA is "becoming more accepting." Edwards sees this acceptance in the recent addition of an erotic chapter within RWA; Brashear even had four of her house's books on the short list for a RITA in 2014, the organization's highest book award; her book didn't win, but that fact that she made the final cut underscores the acceptance of once rogue romance publishers.[73] Xrotic has come a long way, and RWA's recent "accommodation" of those in the industry sends a strong signal that both the genre and format are here to stay.

At a Crossroads

Romance themes are cyclic. The category or subgenre may linger with more or less popularity, but thematic variations within the category come and go. Paranormal romances have been in vogue for a while, but the initial focus on vampires has given way to shape-shifters. If a romance house launched to fulfill consumers' lust for vampires, and vampires gave way to shape-shifters, the house could easily adapt, but if it published exclusively paranormals and the genre itself fell out of favor, the ability to remain financially viable becomes more problematic. This is an issue facing xrotic publishers.

Erotica built slowly between 2000 and 2010. Mainstream publishers did some erotic novels, but they largely left the graphic stuff to xrotic publishers, who flourished by filling the void. As erotica picked up steam after 2010, more mainstream publishers entered the field. This makes it more challenging for xrotic publishers. And if—or perhaps we should say when—the market shifts away from erotica, xrotic publishers may encounter serious problems. Siren and Changeling are probably the most vulnerable in this regard. First, they feel that xrotica is here to stay, and they are probably right, though it remains to be seen whether it will be as strong as it is presently. They also hope that if there is a new wave outside xrotica that "we'll have authors willing and able to write the books," DeBalko at Siren said. Riley feels pretty much the same way and likens Changeling to a sailing ship, in that she "has to catch the wind and see which direction it's pointing." She is not unduly concerned, however, and feels both erotica and the paranormal genre are mainstays in the industry and will endure.

The others seem to intuitively understand they need to diversify their product line. This is done presently by Siren and the others by having a wide variety of subgenres, but the subgenres all pivot on xrotica. It is necessary, then, to move beyond their present xrotic offerings. Most are doing this by filtering more traditional romances onto their lists, but since they are not known for these romances and mainstream competition is fierce, this is somewhat problematic. They are, however, looking at different avenues to expand their business model to go beyond their existing customer base.

Ellora's Cave is approaching this by expanding its xrotic base. Women are the mainstay of romance publishing, even though it is widely acknowledged that some men read romance novels. Men are not the voracious readers women are; they tend to be more visual, which is why "xrotic" Internet sites do so well among men. To reach the male audience, Ellora's Cave has launched EC for Men, with less emphasis on emotional attachment and more on sexual adventure, but this puts it close to what Ellora's Cave already does with its xrotica imprint. More adventurous is its introduction of illustrated manga-type graphic novels. Edwards is proactively going after the male readers who dominate the science fiction field.[74] The company spent five years toying with the idea and talked to "a lot of comic book and manga-type people about producing [this kind of] a book." This was not an easy feat because there's "a lot of technical problems with doing that in e-books format and it is also very expensive. There were a lot of hurdles to cross." The company appears to have overcome them, though, and in mid-2014 launched its illustrated novels. To promote them among potential consumers, the company appeared at the sci-fi trade shows, "where the men are." It is also negotiating with some Japanese publishers to release the illustrated novels in Japan. It remains to be seen how the novels will go over, but the male appetite for these novels in Japan is incredible. It should be pointed out that the romance mangas that Harlequin is releasing in Japan bear little thematic similarity to the male-oriented mangas, which are very chauvinistic, besides being very sexually explicit.[75]

Samhain is still heavily xrotic, but is also venturing further afield. It recently moved into the horror genre. Brashear's interest in this was stimulated by her own addiction to horror novels, but she was prompted to move in this direction after Dorchester, a category publisher that regularly released a series of horror, romance and western novels, folded in 2012. She quickly learned that horror (and sci-fi) enthusiasts don't appreciate digital anywhere to the degree romance readers do, and so moved more into print publishing, at least in this arena. Entangled Publishing is still predominantly an erotic, not an xrotic, digital publisher: most of its books fall on the six to eight on our erotic continuum. They complement St. Martin's predominantly print erotic romance books and have benefitted greatly from association with Macmillan because of Macmillan's international distribution: "We're entering new markets every day around the world." International distribution is often problematic for smaller companies because even in English-speaking countries an alliance has to be formed with a publisher in that country "to gain any traction there." The alliance with

Macmillan means "we don't need to do that anymore." This, in itself, broadens Entangled's customer base.

It is not all about line expansion. It is also about controlling cost. Pelletier has introduced a new model that, for her, controls cost: editors are not paid a salary at Entangled. They earn a royalty on the books that they edit, just like the author. Such an approach not only maintains overhead but provides an incentive for the editors. "If you have a good eye," says Pelletier, "if you're watching the market, if you're anticipating or creating trends, if you're finding fresh voices, and if you're a good solid editor, you can make far more than you could make in New York. Some of our editors make a tremendous amount of money, some make hardly any." The latter stay because of the former. There are about thirty editors at Entangled overseeing eleven imprints. Financial promotion is evenly divided so that all have an equal opportunity of taking off. "It's the American dream," says Pelletier.

Another Kind of Love: GLBT and GLBTQ Romantic Fiction

All the xrotic publishers have a category for gay and lesbian, as do many of the mainstream publishers. Romances by GLBTQ houses are different from those that are here designated GLBT houses: the former is used to designate presses whose books are primarily aimed at others who are gay, lesbian, bisexual or transgendered, while the latter is used to define presses whose audience is largely heterosexual. One thing separating publishers of GLBTQ fiction from straight publishers is the added Q to the acronym GLBT. Queer has long had a pejorative connotation and because of this straight houses seem hesitant to adopt the term. GLBTQ houses in recent years are proud to add the Q. "The community has decided to take [queer] back and claim it for their own," says Sandy Lowe at Bold Strokes Books.[76] She goes on to explain that it is also a more encompassing term: "It is frequently used to encompass the entire [GLBT] community, which is pretty useful. It provides a space for those individuals who do not identify with any of the other terms." This is why I have designated heterosexual xrotic houses as GLBT publishers compared to traditional GLBTQ houses.

Mainstream publishers do most of their GLBT books in e-book format and release a limited number of GLBT books, at least when compared to xrotic publishers of GLBT romances. Bisexual is touched on in most houses. It "used to get bad press," says Aleksandr Voinov, co-founder of Riptide, but he finds they are starting to be treated in "an honest manner,"[77] though outside GLBTQ presses, bisexual typically falls into the ménage category. Transgendered romances are sparse. The xrotic publishers are competing with traditional GLBTQ presses, which heretofore were the primary ones depicting relations among GLBTQ couples that, like their xrotic counterparts, tended to focus on gay and lesbian relationships. The key distinction between GLBTQ traditional novels and GLBT in the xrotic world is that those who are GLBTQ are more likely to look to GLBTQ presses for books on romance entanglements that appeal to them, whereas the primary consumer of xrotic gay (m/m) romances are straight women. At least this is the perception of those who release GLBT and GLBTQ romances.

Traditional GLBTQ publishers would include, among others, Riptide, Bold Strokes, Torquere, Cleis, Dreamspinner, Wilde City, Amber Quill, Less Than Three, and Rocky Ridge. There are certainly GLBTQ writers who write GLBT romances for heterosexual xrotic publishers. Most of the books for straight presses, however, are m/m and ménage (MMF more so than FFM) romances that are written by heterosexual women and generally are penned under a male pseudonym. The male pseudonym is understandable since it a story about two male lovers, which, ostensibly, requires a male to address; this is the same reason males who write traditional heterosexual romances use a female pen name—it is assumed, at least by some editors and readers, that men are not as attuned to the female point of view espoused in the novels.

Those who are GLBTQ are more likely to write for traditional GLBTQ houses where the audience is primarily like-minded GLBTQ readers. The audience for m/m romances by xrotic heterosexual houses is largely female. In a like manner, the editors at most traditional GLBTQ houses indicate that a growing number of their m/m books are similarly read by heterosexual women, though this is not the case with the other pairings. The key difference is that gay men are more likely to drift toward traditional GLBTQ houses since these romances, while obviously dealing with the physical aspects of m/m love, are not just about the physical dimensions of m/m relationships. GLBT xrotica is a strong seller at Ellora's Cave, Samhain, and Changeling; it is the *speciality d'mason* at Siren. It is the *raison d'etre* at ManLoveRomance, which publishes exclusively m/m romances, most of which are written by women for women. Before examining what is being done in GLBTQ publishing, it is first necessary to explain the interest of heterosexual females in m/m bonding.

The heterosexual xrotic m/m romances do not castigate the lovers but, rather, wallow in their romantic tryst. It seems that two is better than one. This has long been the rationale for f/f action enjoyed by heterosexual males. "Why not?" says Constance Penley, who teaches a course in pornography at the University of California (Santa Barbara). "We take it for granted that guys love their girl-on-girl. Why shouldn't women have an appreciation for guy-on-guy?"[78] Linda Williams, who wrote the seminal study on pornography, *Hard Core*, agrees: if the women are heterosexual and they desire men, "then you've doubled the pleasure."[79] It also, Williams argues, solves the problem of who's on top. In this sense, you have the standard alpha male (top) but also the sweet, subservient beta male (bottom). This means the female reader gets to pick which one she identifies with, which allows her in one scene to identify with the "top" and in another with the "bottom." In any event, most in the industry, both traditional publishers of GLBTQ and heterosexual xrotic publishers of GLBT novels, agree that straight books about m/m relationships are about men only superficially.[80] In other words, the books are romance novel because the focus is on finding a soul mate and thus can be enjoyed by heterosexual females even if the plot revolves around two men in love.

GLBTQ publishing houses were founded to provide alternative readings to members of their community. Initially, many GLBTQ books (and related merchandise) were affiliated with small retail outlets that were adjacent to gay/lesbian clubs. The greater acceptance of this lifestyle within the wider society over the last few decades has seen sections in major book retailers devoted to GLBTQ books. The Internet, as it has in many other areas, has vastly expanded the availability of GLTBQ books, since heterosexual readers might hesitate to visit gay/lesbian clubs or venture into "that" section of the bookstore; even for those in the lifestyle, the Internet simply allows greater shopping convenience and options. The greater acceptance of GLBTQ in the wider society, Sandy Lowe feels, has also impacted book publishing. The result is an explosive growth in GLBTQ publishing.

Not surprisingly, personal motivation has sparked the growth of most GLBTQ publishing houses. Those who are GLBTQ wanted to make books depicting GLBTQ relationships available to like-minded others. Cleis Publishing is one of the early GLBTQ presses, which started in 1980; Nalad (1973–2003), which also had its roots during this early period, is now defunct, though its books are still available through Bella Press (1999-present), another GLBTQ house.

The 1970s and 1980s were a time of sexual awakening in the country, and many GLBTQ presses had their origins at this time. Cleis's claim to fame is that it is the only GLBTQ house that is still run by its founders, Felice Newman and Frédérique Delacoste. The founders stated, when asked in 2005 if they were a lesbian press, that they were a queer press, in the same breath acknowledging that their core audience "was and possibly still is lesbians," though a "lot of queer or straight people read us."[81] Cleis's longevity itself ensures a substantive body of gay and lesbian romances among the wide range of fiction and nonfiction it publishes. Many of its gay/lesbian titles are tinted with strong romantic entanglements along traditional erotic lines, such as *Red Velvet* and *Absinthe* (paranormal) and *Carrie's Story* (S/M), along with traditional GLBTQ novels, such as *Active Duty* (gay military erotic romances) and *After Midnight* (true lesbian erotic confessions). Cleis's strong identification as a GLBTQ publisher has helped it establish a strong market presence, but this same identification may hinder its attempt to go beyond its lesbian origins.

Brenda Knight became publisher of Cleis in 2008.[82] When she tried to pitch a gay paranormal or a heterosexual erotic romance, she'd always encounter the question, no matter what the subject matter, "You're still doing lesbian, right?"[83] In order to break out of that pigeonhole, Knight launched a new imprint in September 2014 called Tempted Romances. Its first book, *Cover Him in Darkness*, is a New Adult heterosexual novel with a twenty-three-year-old heroine; those planned over the course of the first year are heterosexual romances, though one three-way has found its way onto the list. Knight is being very careful to ensure quality books to tap into the market for quality romantic fiction, which she herself was raised on. To ensure quality, Tempted is initially limited to one book per month. This is only fifteen percent of the firm's yearly output, so Cleis will remain the main imprint.

There is a paradox here. Knight wants to move beyond the limitations of GLBTQ fiction, which is in line with what many other GLBTQ publishers are doing. Because of Cleis's strong affiliation with GLBTQ books, a new imprint is an understandable way to achieve this goal. At the same time, Knight is relying on Cleis's strong name identification as a producer of quality GLBTQ books to help establish her presence with booksellers. In other words, she wants to break away from the Cleis identification for the new romance line while at the same time building on the Cleis name. This is complicated by her intention, down the road, also to include GLBTQ characters in the new line, which, if done, can only muddy the water and further confuse the issue with consumers and retailers.

Many GLBTQ publishers are of more recent origin and all niche some of their m/m books to attract heterosexual female readers, though their focus remains on books for members of the GLBTQ community: Torquere Press launched in 2003, Bold Strokes Book (BSB) was established in 2004, and Dreamspinner was founded in 2007. Torquere's niche was to focus on GLBTQ e-books; Bold Strokes leans heavily on lesbian fiction, as does Riptide, founded in 2010; Dreamspinner delves exclusively into gay novels. ManLoveRomance Press also focuses exclusively on gay romantic fiction, but it differs from

Dreamspinner because ManLove novels are written by women for consumption by women, while Dreamspinner's novels are niched to gays.

Len Barot is a well-established author of lesbian fiction, so it is not surprising that when she founded BSB, she tended to accentuate fiction in that category: there is the Victory line that accentuates lesbian works, and the Liberty line, which encompasses all the others (GBT). Bold Strokes Books, like most GLBTQ publishers, added a young adult line in 2009, since "YA has infiltrated the mainstream market," and GLBTQ romance subgenres tend to "mimic the mainstream presses."[84]

Sandy Lowe at BSB realizes that there is a large heterosexual female audience for BSB's m/m books, which is why the m/m category has grown in recent years. Ariel Tachna at Dreamspinner says that about sixty percent of those who order m/m books from its website are female, which, because it is a GLBTQ publisher, is slightly lower than the industry average of eighty percent.[85] The lower consumption rate of gay love stories by women at GLBTQ houses seems to be an industry standard, judging from input from GLTBTQ editors; the lower sales are likely owing to the ability of many straight women to find these books at a wide variety of straight xrotic outlets. Sandy Lowe at Bold Strokes Books feels the growth in m/m romances is fostered by the fact that there is no indication of a decrease in the genre's popularity in the foreseeable future. It seems that many GLBTQ publishers are taking advantage of the trend and are now producing more gay romances for a heterosexual audience. This pecuniary motive may seem a bit crass, but these are publishing houses that, while they want to provide books for their primary audience, are businesses that are driven by the profit motive and, just as importantly to many GLBTQ publishers, they are making those outside the community aware of and sensitive to the values of their members. The current vitality of the genre is owing to the fact that the m/m romances, as romances in general, tend to have a very dedicated readership. This is in contradistinction to lesbian fiction, which may have a dedicated following as well but does not have the crossover appeal that gay love does for straight female readers.

Male/male GLBT books are thematically similar to but different from m/m romances released by GLBTQ publishers. This is why Lowe at BSB felt it necessary to differentiate the GLBT books written by straight women for straight women from those written by gay men for a GLBTQ press. The line is called Maverick Books. The BSB website identifies these as books "which feature m/m romance with an emphasis on the developing love relationship." This does not convey authorship or readership. Lowe recognizes, as most GLBT and GLBTQ publishers do, that there is a thematic difference, but there is no way for gays or straight female readers of m/m fiction to distinguish these books at BSB, even though it is a separate line.[86] The rationale for differentiating the books is justifiable, at least for GLBTQ readers: it is widely recognized by GLBTQ publishers that gay men can immediately distinguish a m/m book written by a heterosexual female from one penned by a gay male.[87] For the general heterosexual reader, the thematic distinction probably goes unnoticed. Jessica St. Ama at Torquere feels that authentic m/m novels that truly reflect involvement with the GLBTQ community are based on the author's personal involvement in the lifestyle, which allows the writer "to understand the characters from the [gay] perspective" and therefore tend to "portray [the lifestyle] accurately." The heterosexual m/m publishers "don't do it properly."[88]

There is a valid counterargument, which is articulated nicely by Laura Baumbach, the publisher of ManLoveRomance Press.[89] "You don't have to be a vampire to write a vampire novel. You don't have to be a murderer to write about serial killings. Besides, people who write traditional heterosexual romances write from the male point of view every time they write a book; it's not that big a deal to make it two points of view. If you grow up around men, you know how they react to each other. It's not impossible to write those characters." She does feel that the resistance in the gay community to straight women writing about "the community" is more from older men, primarily those who write gay [non-romance] fiction, who probably shudder at how straights have historically portrayed GLBTQs in print and film. The portrait of GLBTQs is changing, however.

The increased acceptance of same-sex marriages by states is sufficient in itself to underscore the movement for a wider social acceptance of gays and lesbians. This is aptly addressed in Robert Bianco's review of the concluding gay-marriage episode of *Modern Family*. "What's most notable and wonderful," Bianco writes, about *Modern Family*'s spring 2014 special episode "is that it's not trying to be special.... The marriage of two of the show's main male characters is just taken as a given. We've come a long way since the fuss over prime time's first gay wedding, the 1996 *Friends* 'very special episode' marriage of two female secondary characters."[90]

For Baumbach at ManLove, the proof is in the pudding. A number of ManLove's books have been in the finals for best GLBTQ fiction in the Lambda Literary Awards, which recognize published works that celebrate and explore GLBTQ themes. Her own book, *Mexican Heat*, was nominated as a finalist for Best Gay Romance in 2009, and Lynley Wayne's book *Rocky's Road* was nominated in the same category in 2014. Still, Baumbach does agree that there is a different writing style, and some women are able to adopt it in the same manner some men are able to write traditional heterosexual romantic fiction. The operative word is some.

The GLBTQ thematic difference is easier to spot than explain. It is simply that male/male novels tend to have more character development and center more on issues surrounding gay attitudes and values than those depicted in female-written gay romances—the latter can articulate the romance but have little appreciation of the GLBTQ experience. St. Ama articulates the belief held by most GLBTQ publishers: "You're going to find better books by someone who identifies with the GLBTQ alternative lifestyle than [those published] by mainstream publishers, who are just capitalizing on what's in right now." It should also be pointed out that GLBTQ presses tend to produce substantially more GLBT books and market them more widely than straight erotic houses that emphasize xrotica. "Ellora's Cave," says Tachna, "has 238 gay and lesbian books in their Spectrum [gay/lesbian] line; Dreamspinner has 2,800." And because GLBT xrotica is only one aspect of Ellora's larger program, promotion is on their xrotic lines, while GLBTQ publishers focus on their core gay/lesbian clientele. "We've been by [Ellora's Cave's] booth at BEA [Book Expo] for the last four years and have yet to see their gay romances displayed." She is not complaining, just stating a fundamental difference. "We [like most publishers] don't function in our social media and marketing in terms of competing with other publishers. We're all in the same boat…. If Ellora's Cave or one of the others introduces a reader to gay romance, we benefit too."

Most GLBTQ publishers release an array of GLBTQ fiction and nonfiction. Most lean toward fiction. Within the romance category, the novels run the range from none to some sexual activity. They all have an xrotic line where the heat level pushes the limit. None have specific category requirements, though at Bold Strokes they encourage their authors not to "fade to black," because "we believe that in the context of a romance, erotic scenes can enhance character development and reader enjoyment, but every title is unique and some are sweeter than others." *Tigers and Devils* (Dreamspinner, 2012), for example, has only one kiss "on screen," though other novels at Dreamspinner can weigh in at the five, six, or seven level of eroticism. Anything above that at GLBTQ houses is designated for the erotic line, which is akin to our xrotic category.

Many GLBTQ publishers have "spun" some of their romances in recent years to capitalize on the trend in m/m romances among female romance readers. Dreamspinner had little interest in the female market and launched to reach the gay male romance reader. ManLoveRomances was after the heterosexual female reader of m/m romances. In both cases, their secondary market is not insignificant: roughly one-third of Dreamspinner's male/male novels are consumed by straight women, while one-third of ManLoveRomances for women are consumed by gay men. Their romances run the gamut from sweet to sexy, but best-sellers at both houses tend to fall into the xrotic category.

Dreamspinner Press: Male/Male Romances for Gay Men

Elizabeth North started Dreamspinner for two reasons. One was that an author friend had been taken advantage of by a now-defunct unscrupulous publisher. This is not an uncommon complaint in the digital world, but it is not sufficient to be considered motivation to launch a publishing venture. Perhaps a more germane reason for launching the business was that her gay brother-in-law complained of not being able to find gay books with a happy ending: he was getting married at the time and wanted to read books that reflected where he was in his life. This indicated to North that there might be a market for gay romance novels, since the very definition of a romance novel is the requisite happy-ever-after ending, even if that has been somewhat modified today to a happy-at-the-moment ending. North's rationale is similar to Riptide and other GLBTQ publishers. Riptide, for example, was co-founded by Rachael Haimowitz and Alexsandr Voinov. They were less than satisfied with their relationship with other houses and felt there were a lot of other writers in their situation who were looking for "more quality work in the [GLBTQ] genre."[91]

Every publishing house tries to find its special niche. Dreamspinner's is gays, with women m/m devotees a secondary market. It has most of the traditional romance categories, including New Adult, which has long been a mainstay of gay fiction. In fact, GLBTQ publishers had New Adult before New Adult became all the rage (circa 2012) in mainstream fiction. New Adult mainstream novels focus on a young twenty-something-year-old coming to terms with his or her sexual awakening—this may explain the popularity of these novels in YA romantic fiction, since many younger-than-twenty-year-olds have to grapple with this today. Coming of Age stories in gay fiction parallel the New Adult genre, just with a different name. Coming of Age novels in GLBTQ fiction revolve around coming to terms with one's "different" sexuality. But while Coming of Age novels are part of any GLBTQ house's list, Bittersweet Dreams at Dreamspinner is rather unique, especially given the primary reason for starting the press. The name itself suggests that even happy-at-the-moment endings are not a given. Tachna says that's because "not all great love stories have a happy ending, and we got tired of not publishing these books because they weren't traditional romances."

Dreamspinner is similar to but also different from other houses in its international presence. Many publishers, both GLBTQ and even small mainstream ones, as well as many self-published authors, have some international presence today, especially in English-speaking countries. The international presence today has been facilitated by Amazon Europe. But few GLBTQ publishers have the Dreamspinner European presence: its books are translated in-house into French, Spanish, Italian, and German. The reason for such an extraordinary move, Tachna says, is because they saw how well their books were selling in English-speaking markets, such as the U.K. and Australia. By translating the books in-house, they ensure quality control. They also strongly market their translations: "We have a media coordinator in each language who runs our social media accounts and works with reviewers and media outlets in the respective language to publicize the books." Few other publishers outside the mainstream houses take such steps. This may be because the payoff doesn't look that great. Tachna points out the problem with international e-book distribution: "Europe is about five years behind the U.S. in terms of transitioning to digital reading." The rewards can be worth it, though. She notes an interesting European anomaly: "Germany is our most successful market outside the United States, and I believe that's because Germans read. Interesting statistic: more books are published in Germany every year than in the entire English-speaking world."

In a similar vein, Dreamspinner is also seeking to extend its focus to increase readership. This is becoming increasingly common, even if it is still a small part of what GLBTQ houses do. This was seen with the move to snag heterosexual readers of male/male romances. This expansion was also explored with Cleis Press, which is moving into mainstream heterosexual romance publishing to capture a wider slice of the romance pie. Dreamspinner is approaching its brand expansion in a more conventional way by adding subgenres. Dreamspinner will remain a gay publisher of m/m novels but is moving beyond its initial and limited romance focus by launching a line of sci-fi books. Sci-fi books were already part of the offerings at Dreamspinner, but the books were overlooked because of the house's strong romance brand.

DSP Publications was launched in the fall of 2014 to promote and market the non-romance line. The new imprint will have a strong presence at sci-fi and fantasy conferences, which are heavily populated by men, and then will be expanded into the horror genre, an area also well known for its heavy male readership. The books will continue to feature gay characters, but they are now secondary to the primary sci-fi and horror theme. It is felt that the DSP designation, though it obviously stands for Dreamspinner Press, will avoid any off-putting association among potential readers. The DSP designation is meant to appeal to gay men who are not romance readers. Dreamspinner also hopes to tap the heterosexual romance market by relegating gay characters to a less prominent role. "We are attempting," says Tachna, "to make the non-gay market realize our books aren't any different than theirs.... Our goal is to have the idea of 'gay' become a non-issue." This is a lofty goal. It remains to be seen how successful it will be when a heterosexual male is reading one of its sci-fi or horror books and encounters a scene that depicts intimacy between two men.

ManLoveRomance Press: Male/Male Romances for Heterosexual Women

While many GLBTQ publishers are attempting to reach a wider audience by extending their books to tap a heterosexual audience, ManLove is going after those women who read m/m romances. Because it is the only house that specializes in gay novels for female romance readers, it has a greater chance of reaching its intended audience, both in terms of the number of books released yearly and in its focused marketing strategy, which is similar to the strategy used by traditional romance publishers.

Like many publishers, Laura Baumbach started as a writer. She began writing slash fiction[92] in 2010. She took up this "hobby" when she found herself at home taking care of a toddler; she soon gravitated to slash fiction. In slash fiction the characters are same-sex, typically male/male.[93] She focused on this because she saw it as a neglected area, "so I jumped in." Timing was good because soon "slash" (m/m) fiction was gaining ground, if not respectability. Her early works appeared on the GLBT lists of xrotic publishers; she was published by Samhain and Loose Id, among others. She was cheated by one digital publisher who didn't pay her for three books of hers that it published, besides doing "poor quality [work] when they did publish them." The next logical step, taken by many, especially then, before self-publishing gained momentum, was to start her own publishing house: "I felt if they could do it, I can do it, and I can do it better"—the driving reason, it will be recalled, why so many romance authors pick up the pen, or, in this case, start publishing ventures. "So I got together with some best-selling authors within the genre that I was friends with who contributed stories and I opened my first press—there were three of us, now there's 210 of us."

Had she focused on gays and published with a GLBTQ press, she would have experienced little resistance to her m/m romance tales. Baumbach experienced resistance within the industry, however, because she was publishing romances for female romance readers before the subgenre became a staple within the mainstream romance industry. The resistance was similar to that which we saw encountered by xrotic e-book publishers when they first started publishing romances outside the mainstream tradition. *Romantic Times*, a popular fan magazine, refused to review her books, and Romance Writers of America resisted her entry into the organization. Once the subject matter, like xrotica, was seen as a staple within the industry and not just a fad, these organizations have adapted. This is the biggest change she's seen in the male/male fiction industry: acceptance. But that's now because m/m love has become mainstream and every publisher of romances dabbles in the subgenre.

Most mainstreams publishers address m/m romance for women today, though it took them a while to get around to doing it. ManLove, like Ellora's Cave in xrotic publishing, was first out of the chute and established a clear, early identity—*Rolling Stone*, in a feature article, called Baumbach one of the pioneers of the genre. ManLove has a full-time editorial staff of six content editors and publishes between two and three books per week, around 130-plus novels per year. It has, like its xrotic counterparts, started a traditional romance line, but it is mainly to keep its authors happy: "Some of our authors write traditional romance and wanted to stay with me. Probably shouldn't have bothered, but we're family." The m/m books were popular from the get-go, she says, because women "would tell me that they've been reading m/m romances for years," and since they couldn't get m/m romantic fiction, "they were settling for gay fiction." Her success was, in part, timing, but it was also her strong start. She was familiar with m/m xrotic publishing as a writer, so she had some insights as to how things unfolded in the industry and, unlike many, had a strong digital background— her husband is a computer software consultant, so she launched with a high-quality website that pulled people in; she also had strong covers that are a "first attraction" to readers because her good friend

ManLove cover—*Addicted* (MLR Press, 2014).

was a graphic designer and illustrated all of her initial covers. "So," she says, "I had all this talent and zero cost. It helped tremendously."

Love Across the Color Spectrum: African American and Multicultural Romances

It has been a long, somewhat tortuous road for African American romances. Among the first, if not the first, African American romance published by a major house was Elsie Bernice Washington's *Entwined Destinies* in 1980. The book, written under the pseudonym Rosalind Welles, was filtered into the Candlelight Romance line by the new editor at Dell, Vivian Stephens. Stephens was an African American, so no doubt the story resonated with her. They were also about the same age: Stephens was in her forties in 1980; Washington was thirty-eight, so both shared a generational world view. It was the only novel Washington ever published, though she did pen a couple of non-fiction pieces, including *Uncivil War: the Struggle Between Black Men and Women* (Noble Press, 1996). She died at age 66 in 2009.

Entwined Destinies presented a strong black professional heroine (a journalist, like the author) who meets and falls in love with a handsome African American oilman. The book had modest sales, but that had less to do with the merits of the books than with the lackluster performance of the Candlelight line when Stephens came to Dell. The book did open the door for other black authors by challenging the prevalent view by white mainstream publishers that some publishing executives were reputed to have said: "Black women don't read."[94]

Harlequin wooed Stephens away from Dell, and in 1983 she was the launch editor for Harlequin's American Romance line. The fifth book in the series, *A Strong and Tender Thread*, featured African Americans. The author, Jackie Weger, was white. Kathleen Gilles Seidel was one of the launch writers with American Romances and explained what happened.[95] Stephens wanted to publish books by African American authors that featured African American characters but wasn't receiving any submissions, so she asked Weger to make her white characters black. This is insufficient in itself to make the story black: "I can always tell right away when a black woman did not write the book," said Jayha Leigh, co-founder of Beautiful Troubled Publishing, a multicolored romance line that launched in 2010. Stephens no doubt helped "blacken" the book with her strong editorial pen. Not long thereafter, Stephens did receive an African American authored novel by Sandra Kitt, *Adam and Eva*, and published it the following year. There was also a small, short-lived romance series called Heartline Romances that was released circa 1984 by Holloway House (1920–2007), a publisher of traditional African American literature.[96] Holloway is best known for its crime fiction but briefly latched onto the romance craze of the mid-1980s.

One of the historic criticisms of romances by minorities is their whiteness. Until fairly recently, African American women who wanted to read a romance novel had no option but to read about blonde-haired, blue-eyed heroines. The consciousness raising of the 1960s and 1970s, perhaps best encapsulated in James Brown's 1968 funk song, "Say It Loud—I'm Black and I'm Proud," would indicate that blackness among African Americans had moved to the mainstream by the 1980s and blacks embracing "whiteisms" was passé. Indeed, Washington was very outspoken about this, and as senior editor for *Essence*, she lamented the rejection by African Americans of their natural appearance in favor of white European concepts of beauty by even the "just plain folks [who] alter their natural-born God-given dark eyes" by wearing, like Oprah for a short period of time, blue contact lenses.[97]

The blackness of Washington's characters carried over to her first novel and is no doubt one of the reasons Stephens was attracted to it. The subsequent success of Alice Walker's *The Color Purple* (1982 novel, 1985 movie) across the racial divide, as well as Terry McMillan's *Waiting to Exhale* (1992 novel, 1995 film) underscores the diverse audience for African American-themed works. *Waiting to Exhale* (more so than *The Color Purple*) is often mentioned as a catalyst in promoting fiction with African American women. McMillan's subsequent novel, *How Stella Got Her Groove Back* (1996 novel, 1998 movie), which is basically a romance novel about a professional woman who has it all but a man, is more directly related to the surge in romance novels with African American women as the central character. Among the careers that were launched during this period are a number of perennially best-selling African American authors. One is Brenda Jackson, who has published over one hundred novels and novellas since her first novel appeared in 1994 with Kensington Arabesque; in addition to her many other firsts, she was the first African American to publish under the Harlequin/Silhouette Desire line, as well as being the first African American romance author to hit the bestseller lists at both *USA Today* and the *New York Times*. There is also Zane (Kristina Laferne Roberts), whose career was launched with the publication of a collection of erotic romances in 1997 and who continues to specialize in erotica. Her first three self-published titles in 2000 went on to sell more than 250,000 copies and led to an agreement with Atria (Simon & Schuster) in 2001 to launch a series of African American novels under the logo "Zane Presents." There is also Beverly Jenkins, who specializes in African American historical romances and remains with Avon, which launched her first historical romance in 1995. The trail blazed by these and other African American romance authors has helped break the color barrier. In recent years there has been an increased interest in multicultural romances that embrace a wider range of racial and ethnic groups, though African American romances continue to dominate the lists.

The increase of multicultural romance titles should not suggest that romances featuring women of color are in abundance. RWA estimates that approximately eleven percent of African Americans read romance novels, which is in line with the size of the African American population in the United States: thirteen percent in 2014. It can be assumed that the readership for multicultural romances is smaller, despite the size of the minority groups in the United States: minorities compose thirty-six percent of the population.[98] One reason why more minorities don't read romance novels is simply that, while most mainstream publishers of romances filter some multicultural romances into their list, they are not easily identifiable for those seeking to read an African American/multicultural romance. The other reason, just as tellingly, is that there are only a few houses with a dedicated line of romances that feature minorities and the few that do focus primarily on African Americans. Harlequin is one of these. The other is Kensington. There is also Genesis Press, the largest African American-owned-publisher, which produces a line of romances among the books it releases yearly.

The variety of "players" in the African American romance field can be gleaned by reviewing some of the novels on the African American bestseller lists of romance titles. Of the thirty-three top titles listed on Goodreads[99] and the ten on BET's top-ten list, Harlequin dominates with twenty-one, all of which were on Goodreads: Brenda Jackson had ten Harlequin/Silhouette novels listed; most of the others (11) appeared under Harlequin's Kimani imprint. Atria had four, all of which were on BET's list. Kensington followed with three, two of which were released under their African American imprint, Dafina. A few were self-published. Avon had two books, as did NAL, both of which were Terry McMillan's two best-sellers. The rest had only one. Genesis did not make the cut.

Kensington was the first to introduce a dedicated line of African American novels when it launched Arabesque in 1994, which, after a tortured detour by way of BET Books, ended by being the basis for Harlequin's Kimani Press. Kensington, always quick to identify new trends, launched a line of books aimed at this market rather than go with single-title releases, largely because, though Kensington has a single-title program, it tends to specialize in mass-market category novels. The rationale for the sale is in the numbers: the 1994 launch cost is reputed to have been $400,000, and the line was sold to BET in 1998 for a reported $11 million.[100] Stephen Zacharius says the whole thing was serendipitous. They had gone to see Bob Johnson at BET to discuss doing a joint book club with them. Kensington wanted BET to promote it on television and they'd split the revenue. "Bob came back and said, 'Why don't I just buy the imprint from you?' My father [Walter] picked a number out of the air and we had a deal subject to the due diligence, which ended up working out.... It was a chance to sell a line that we started for very little money for a nice profit; so we took the opportunity and the cash to reinvest in the business."[101] Regardless of the sales price, Kensington continued to reap the rewards of the line, which it totally oversaw—from selecting the books to marketing and distributing them, for a separate management fee completely unrelated to the sale price.

A few years after the sale of Arabesque, Kensington introduced (2000) a new line of African American novels dubbed Dafina, which in Swahili means an unexpected gift or treasure. Kensington had a five-year no-compete contract with BET when it sold the Arabesque line. The contract barred them from doing another line of African American romances, but not African American women's fiction, which is how Dafina began: "It was a way to keep our foot in the water," says Zacharius, "without violating the agreement. But when the non-compete [clause] was up, we dived back in. Bigger than ever!" The imprint would subsequently serve as Kensington's African American romance line once the five-year period lapsed, "and now we publish into the African American market in a big way," says Zacharius. Dafina would be followed by K-Dafina in 2006, a YA line of African American romance novels, which would precede Harlequin's Kimani TRU by a good year. Kensington also distributes Urban Books, a growing publishing venture launched in 2001 by African American author Carol Weber that has a strong romance category: "Urban complements our books nicely," says Zacharius.

Other than Harlequin and Kensington, only Genesis Press regularly publishes an African American line of romance novels: Indigo, traditional romance stories featuring African American characters, Indigo Love Spectrum, which capitalizes on the wider move within the industry to introduce cross-cultural relationships, and Indigo Vibe, which takes a close look at life and love among young adults. Genesis appears to have a made a successful transition from print to digital, has a state-of-the-art website, and publishes some sharp, cutting-edge romance novels. Genesis is, nevertheless, simply too small to compete with the two major publishers of African American romance lines and often gets overlooked. The fact that it is one of the few dinosaurs who, on the input side, only take postal manuscript submissions hints that some of its output strategies of disseminating information about its romances may be somewhat dated, which further handicaps its position vis-à-vis the major romance players to make a significant mark in the field. It seldom appears, for example, on Internet searches for African American romance novels.

The advantage of having a dedicated line of African American romances is that African American romance devotees are able to find the books, and there are certainly those African Americans who read only these types of books.[102] It has also helped some small publishing firms that specialize in African American romances to find a niche, and a market, such as Beautiful Trouble Publishing, Sugar and Spice, and Amira. Totally Bound and Changeling can be included on this list because both have a strong multicultural romance presence, even if they don't specialize in African American romances.

The focus on African American characters is constrictive today. The books are more often than not shelved in the African American section in bookstores, segregated from the romance novels, which keeps the general romance reader from reaching for one since, unless they are African American, they are unlikely to gravitate to that section of the bookstore. This is the advantage of mainstream publishers who don't have a category line of African American novels and simply filter an occasional African American author into their generalist romance lists. This increases the chances that a more diverse audience will read the book. This is complicated, however, by the cover illustrations. The cover is likely to feature a picture of an African American if the author is African American, and this can be off-putting to a white reader. "I think," says African American romance novelist Farrah Rochon, "a [white] reader might say [to herself] that this isn't for me if it has a black character on it."[103] Niqui Stanhope's 2014 novel *She's Got to Have It* is a good case in point. Published by St. Martin's, it features a black woman on the cover, and even though the book blurb depicts the typical choice between marrying for love or for money, the picture, which grabs the reader's attention before one reads the blurb, can suggest the book is about the African American experience, even if it is unclear exactly what the African American experience is: "I've been a black woman all my life," quips Farrah Rochon, "and I have no idea what 'the black experience' is."[104] In the end, then, being an African American writer garners sales among African Africans but at the same time prevents them from becoming a success among a wider audience.

In the last few years there has been a move away from the African American focus toward multicultural romances. There are two directions for multicultural romances. One features romantic love among like-cultured individuals—Hispanic-Hispanic, Asian-Asian; the other is to introduce interracial couples, specifically black-white ones. Interracial love has attracted only modest attention.

Romances featuring an Asian heroine-hero are practically nonexistent outside mangas. There is an understandable demographic rationale for this since the Asian population in the United States is just slightly over four percent. In short, the population is relatively small, and this can cause mainstream publishers to hesitate before devoting a dedicated line to Asian romance novels. The only house with a good sprinkling of truly multicultural characters is Totally Bound in the U.K., where Asian and Indian characters are widely represented; Totally Bound even has a (thin) Bollywood romance category, which seems logical since the Indian population in London is fairly substantial.[105] The Hispanic population in the United States, on the other hand, is demographically strong and the absence of romances featuring Latino(a) characters is somewhat surprising: Atria has an Español line of books, but they are mostly nonfiction works with a heavy dose of fiction that is dotted by an occasional English-translated romance. Publishers are well aware of the growing Hispanic population in the United States and have eyed the potentially lucrative Hispanic romance market.

As early as 2000, the Hispanic population in the United States rivaled the African American population at twelve percent. The date is instructive, because seeing the growth in this market, Kensington launched a mass-market line of Hispanic romances in late 1999 called Encanto (Enchantment). It published four books per month in a bilingual edition and one in Spanish. The books were distributed at traditional book retail outlets as well as bodegas. There were a number of unsuccessful attempts to tweak the books. The line was abandoned at the beginning of 2002. It was the in-house opinion at the time that the books were not connecting because Latino(a)s preferred to read bestsellers in Spanish and not necessarily books that they had never heard of before. Harlequin likewise toyed with the idea of introducing a Hispanic line of romances but, perhaps seeing the problems Kensington had, abandoned the idea. Harlequin does publish its Spanish-translated novels for Latin America on its website, Harlequin Deseo (Desire) and Harlequin Bianca, but Kensington's issues would suggest the Latina market in the United States may not be very strong.[106] The market is even more vibrant today: it is just shy of seventeen percent of the population. The size of the population would suggest that romance novels aimed at this group could have strong market potential.

The problem of attracting the Hispanic audience may be that their fondness for romances is already sated with the telenovelas, which literally translated means television romance novels. Telenovelas are basically romantic soap operas and are popular with both Latinas and Latinos. These shows—

with their recurring romantic storyline that typically unfolds over a twelve-week period—are widely available on Spanish-language television.[107] In Asia, market entry was facilitated by Harlequin adapting its romances to the popular manga format. This is more problematic with Hispanics in the United States because they rely more on television for entertainment than books and get their dose of romance from the telenovelas. In order for American publishers to compete in this market, they would have to adapt their romances to a completely different medium, and they have not had huge success at doing this when they have ventured into the Hollywood system.

Despite the lack of Asian and Hispanic characters in romance novels, multicultural romances are interracially growing, which socially "fits" since interracial marriages reached an all-time high of 8.4 percent of all marriages in 2010.[108] A bit of an anomaly, however, is that most of the interracial romantic relationships in the novels are whites with blacks, but black/white interracial marriages are still relatively rare; 13.8 percent of marriages are between white/Hispanic couples, whereas only 2.7 percent are black/white.[109] This may simply be owing to the fact that the overwhelming majority of writers dealing with interracial relationships are mainly African American, with some whites taking up the interracial romance pen. The black/white relationships depicted—and evident from even the most cursory glance at the covers of these novels—are between black heroines and a white heroes.

Belinda Edmondson, writing on the black intra-racial (black-black) romances before the recent surge in interracial romances, recognizes that the "black romances showcase black social mobility—in particular, black *female* [sic] mobility—in a way that white romances do not."[110] She goes on to argue that it is rare for a black heroine to marry down. She marries a black male equal. Edmondson is arguing that this fosters a kind of national identity among African Americans while at the same time allowing the black hero and heroine to see themselves as individuals. This is clearly the case in those romances that depict romantic stories of like-skinned couples that constitute the body of African American romances at the major houses: Kensington's Dafina, Harlequin's Arabesque and Kimani, any number of lines published by Genesis, and Atria's Zane Presents series. Traditional black hero/black heroine romances dot most mainstream publishers' lists and are also strongly represented by self-published African American authors on Amazon and related sites. The Black Nationalism applauded by Edmondson is undercut in the interracial black-white romances, though the other points remain valid: the heroine is a professional woman with a strong sense of identity who marries a socially equal (albeit richer) hero.

The modern interracial black-white romance reflects contemporary social exigencies in two critical ways. First, more African American women obtain a college education than black men: black women in 2010 earned 68 percent of associate's degrees, 66 percent of bachelor's degrees, 71 percent of master's degrees, and 65 percent of all doctorial degrees awarded to black students.[111] Romantically, this means that educated black women are more likely to rub shoulders with professional white males, and this, in itself, increases the potential of their meeting, and marrying, white males. Black females married to a white male also have a statistically greater chance of remaining married than a white female married to a black male: a white wife/black (or Asian) husband marriage shows twice the divorce rate of white wife/white husband couples by the tenth year of marriage, whereas the divorce rate of black wife/white husband marriage was similar to or actually lower than white wife/white husband marriages.[112]

Interracial romances further tend to accentuate the hero's physical features, and since the hero is a white male, this increases the likelihood that white females will also find the novels of some interest. These romances are also more likely to be carried in the regular romance section of a bookstore, and this enhances the potential of reaching a wider, more diverse audience than those romances shelved in the African American section.

Interracial romances are relatively new, and so tend to be resisted by the kingpin African American category romance publishers who release the majority of novels that feature African American characters. The guidelines for these lines are dated and do not recognize the multicultural phenomenon, let alone the interracial one. The online guidelines for Harlequin's Arabesque series at the outset of 2014 specified only African American characters. When this point was addressed with Dianne Moggy, she intimated that the guidelines were incorrect and that Harlequin had filtered a number of multicultural romances into the Kimani line. That may be, but at the end of 2014, the guidelines still say the line features "realistic African American characters," so any would-be author writing for Harlequin is likely to be dissuaded from submitting a multicultural romance since the guidelines specified African American characters. In a similar vein, Kimani Romances specify that the line features African American characters exclusively,[113] effectively shutting out an author who is considering submitting an interracial black/white romance. The mainstream editors at non-category houses appear to operate under the same principle, even if they have no specific guidelines, though black/white interracial romances are beginning to appear more frequently, even if not enough to garner any strong presence on the shelves.[114] This opens the door, as it did with xrotica, to independent houses to fill a gap vacated by mainstream houses, and their success may push more mainstream publishers to filter more interracial romances onto their lists.

There are four small, relatively new e-book publishers that specialize in interracial romances, most of which portray an African American heroine and a white hero: Beautiful Trouble, Sugar and Spice, Changeling, and Amira. Totally Bound, based in the U.K. (Lincoln, England), whose books are starting to gain a foothold in the United States, is also relatively new and should be included in the interracial category because interracial romances are well represented among their wider romance offerings.

Neither Beautiful Trouble nor Sugar and Spice set out to feature interracial love. It is what the co-founders wrote. Jayha Leigh co-owns Beautiful Trouble with Janie Johnson; Kelly Ann Pearson is co-owner of Sugar and Spice with Jordyn Tracey.[115] Leigh and Tracey are both romance authors and initially started self-publishing on the Internet. The response was so good, says Leigh, that they thought about and subsequently started Beautiful Trouble Publishing after cashing in their 401-K. One reason for going this route is because "Amazon takes such a big cut," and to be Amazon-competitive she would have to sell her romances for under a dollar, which means that "after everyone takes their cut, there's nothing left."

Leigh says they really didn't know what direction they would go. They didn't even intend to focus on African American romances, let alone interracial ones, a point also made by Pearson. It happened because that's where their personal interest lay: Leigh, an African American, has a stepmother who is white and has biracial siblings, while co-founder Johnson is also from a multicultural family and is herself of mixed race; Pearson, who hails from the U.K., is black and comes from a biracial family, while her American husband is white. This background made them more attuned to and "appalled" by "the stereotypes in books. If it's a white female with a black male, he must be Mandingo," says Leigh. "So disrespectful!" This dissatisfaction, as has been seen innumerable times, is why many women initially pick up the romance pen, and why some graduate to starting publishing ventures.

Their personal interest led to selecting other authors who wrote similarly: "We have a Canadian author, her heroines are black Jamaicans; we have a Latina author who writes about Hispanic heroines; a Somalian." Pearson mentions having an Asian line at Sugar and Spice and that numerous books they've released feature Native American characters. The personal aspect was also a driving reason for Nina Perez's novel *Sharing Spaces*: "I was in an interracial relationship with my now husband and wanted to write about the complexities of such a relationship, but also the humor and love of one."[116] Perez and Leigh's African American female characters tend to be savvy and educated: "I get a lot of pushback about my black females," says Leigh, remarking on blog reviews by readers of her house's books. "Too smart! College educated! Have a skill set!" Pearson concurs: "Places like Kimani—and it's not just me that says it—want the usual weak woman, strong male.[117] That's not how it works in this day and age…. I'm a strong woman, my husband is a strong man. In small publishing, we get to write the women we want. We don't have subservient women. Our women are on an even keel [with the man]."

"We get criticized all the time when we publish really smart women of color," says Leigh. Her remarks, we'll see in the next section, are echoed by self-published authors; it is one of their reasons for going solo. Leigh remarks on one book in particular that received an unfair amount of criticism because the heroine was mean. The heroine's meanness, it seems, was her self-sufficiency. The hero had enough money and wanted the heroine to quit her job because she was spending too much time at it (and, hence, not with him). She refused because her job meant a lot to her and she didn't appreciate his cavalier attitude toward it. Some readers apparently didn't like it "because it interfered with their fantasy of having the [billionaire] male come save them." This is the kind of heroine that "we can identity with and respect and like [instead of] the porcelain-skinned, flaxen-haired virgins who need saving." Explicit in this statement is not just the strong heroine but the focus on the heroine's white features. The drift to interracial was based on personal factors, but also an analysis of market placement: "We picked genres we like but, more specifically, genres that sell. There was an easier opening into the interracial, multicultural genre because at the time [2010] it did not have enough authors to fill the need," said Leigh.

Sugar and Spice closed in 2015 and Beautiful Trouble Publishing has temporarily (2016) stopped accepting new manuscripts because of overwhelming personal issues, though the co-founders continue to publish their own novels. The interracial niche, even with the addition of Amira and interracial lines at Totally Bound seems underserved when one considers how vibrant the interracial multicultural market is. Of those newlyweds who married a spouse of a different race in 2010, 9 percent of whites married "out," as did 17 percent of blacks, 26 percent of Hispanics and 28 percent of Asians.[118] These numbers would suggest that there is tremendous market potential for interracial marriages beyond the present focus on black heroine/white hero that currently demarks the genre. The high number of Hispanic and Asian intermarriages suggests a means by which romance publishers can incorporate more Asian characters into the romance and a way to tap the growing Hispanic market that they have eyed for so long, but hesitated to substantively develop, for fear of losing white romance readers.

Self-Publishing: Finding One's Own Way

Self-publishing has emerged in the last few years as a legitimate outlet for many writers. Self-publishing was given a big push with *Fifty Shades of Grey*

(2011).[119] The novel was not self-published. E L James's[120] (Erika Mitchell) novel first appeared as (free) fan fiction by The Writer's Coffee Shop in Australia. Fan fiction readers boosted her profile, and soon word of mouth made her a hot topic, eventually landing her a book contract with Vintage Anchor (Random House).

It doesn't matter that the book was not self-published. It matters only that many would-be writers thought of it as a self-published book and witnessed Mitchell's phenomenal success. If nothing else, it helped legitimate publishing outside the mainstream, even if she ended up with a mainstream publisher. Mitchell helped reduce the stigma long associated with self-publishing. "The biggest obstacle I had to overcome," said Donna Fasano in an interview about the four million copies she's sold in her romance self-publishing venture, was "the ingrained idea that becoming an Independent Author, as we tend to call ourselves, meant that I was lowering the bar, that I was moving to the seedy side of town, that I would be looked upon as a hack."[121]

Rejected authors now have an alternative means to publish their novels. Since their manuscripts have been rejected, the general view has been that the novels have little worth; otherwise they would have been published by a mainstream house. This view is increasingly being challenged by those who have self-published successfully, including those who have gone on to success after being dropped for lack of sales by a mainstream publisher or who have walked away from lucrative contracts to self-publish. Brenna Aubry illustrates just one successful self-published author. Aubry turned down a $120,000 contract with one of the Big Five mainstream houses. It should be pointed out that this was an exceptional offer from a mainstream house for a first-time author: the normal advance, Damien Walter points out in *The Guardian*, is $5,000.[122] Even after discounting the agent's fifteen percent, Aubrey had a guarantee of $34,000 per book. She ran the numbers though and felt that self-publishing offered a more lucrative return. One of her main concerns was the reversion clause in her contract that would give the publisher control of her work for up to thirty-five years. Her sales for the first month on Amazon's Kindle netted her $28,000, well above the "less than $500 a year" projection that traditional publishers flag to discourage writers from self-publishing. Success stories like Aubrey's are rampant in the popular press and on blogs; these stories tend to encourage more authors to self-publish, which is why *The Guardian* headline that featured Aubrey's story on Valentine's Day 2014 screamed, "Self-Publishing: Is It Killing the Mainstream?" The answer is no, but it does have the potential to change the rules of the game.

At the moment, self-publishing is relatively small and as of 2012 composed only three percent of all books purchased in the United States, though it did account for eight percent of all e-book purchases.[123] These numbers would increase if we include those independent digital publishers, like The Writer's Workshop, Ellora's Cave, and Beautiful Trouble Publishing, who also promise their authors a hefty slice of the pie, substantially more than that offered by traditional publishers: thirty-five percent of the cover price if the digital book is purchased from the publisher's website, twenty percent if it is purchased from a third-party site, and the more traditional eight percent of the cover price if it is purchased in print format. Self-published authors get to keep substantially more. Amazon, for example, takes thirty percent, and if one discounts another ten percent for cost relating to the production of the book (cover art, editing, and so forth), the self-published author often nets sixty percent of the cover price.

The recommended competitive list price for an e-romance online is between $2.99 and $3.99. Megan Mulry, a self-published romance author, figures that at $3.99 she makes $2.80 (70 percent) per unit, but has to sell 1,000 copies after costs associated with the book are deducted before she starts making a profit.[124] The online competition is getting stiffer today, too, which makes it harder for an unknown author who doesn't have name recognition to generate sales: there were over 391,000 self-published titles in 2012, an increase of 422 percent from 2007,[125] when self-publishing first started to percolate.

Self-publishing success stories are easy to come by but don't necessarily represent the experience of the average self-published author. One recent study attempts to shed light on the self-publishing cottage industry. The study was conducted by Beverly Kendall, who entered the self-publishing world after her second novel did not generate enough sales to warrant Kensington renewing her contract. She is one of the success stories: she published her third book herself and in less than a year had earned over $100,000. She posted a survey online in an attempt to get a reading on what other self-publishing authors were doing. The survey, conducted in 2013, received 822 responses.[126] It cannot be considered a representative sample, and therefore, her results have to be taken with a grain of salt. On the other hand, she received responses from those who self-published across genres, and the results tend to reflect industry standards: sixty-one percent of those responding wrote romances, and of those writing romances, sixteen percent wrote contemporary romances, nine percent wrote paranormals; the other major genres (mystery/thrillers, science fiction, fantasy) and several other romance categories (suspense, erotic, new adult and historical) are pretty evenly split with percentages of six to seven percent. At the lower end, averaging around one percent, were YA, inspirational and "miscellaneous" romances, with a smattering (<1 percent) writing GLBTQ romances.

Self-publishing is not a guaranteed route to riches, but many do very well: 52 percent earned less than $10,000, 15.67 percent earned between $10,000 and $25,000, which Kendall thought was "a significant amount"; the remaining 32 percent earned over $25,000 a year, nearly half of whom (13.5 percent) earned over $100,000. Fifty-three percent of the authors who had one to eleven books out with a traditional publisher earned more by self-publishing. Only when the author had twelve or more books out do the percentages shift and more traditional published authors earn more with their publisher than they did self-publishing. Of those respondents (266) who did not have their books edited by an editor with a publishing background, sales dipped: 59.8 earned less than $10,000 compared to 49.2 percent who used a professional editor. Similar results were found among those who did not use a graphic artist or professional designer for their cover illustration compared to those who did. Of the 88 authors who fell into this category, 39.2 percent earned more than $10,000 when they did not use a professional compared to 52.5 percent who did. These and related findings are reflected among the self-published authors I interviewed for this study, including what we've already seen, the advantage of having a professional editor and graphic artist, plus the importance of coming from a traditional publishing background—Kendall found no advantage "at *all*" [emphasis original] if the author came from a digital-first publishing background. She also found it advantageous for self-published authors to offer books free to hook the reader, and not to get greedy by pricing one's books too steeply.

This study is on the publishing industry and does not typically delve deeply into individual authorial stories. This "rule" is abandoned in this instance because self-publishing is becoming an industry unto itself. Five self-published authors were interviewed. The authors, inclusive of Beverly Kendall, were Courtney Milan (historicals), Melody Anne (contemporary and New Adult), Farrah Rochon (African American/multicultural), and Michelle Monkou (African American/multicultural). Input from these authors is only suggestive of trends in self-publishing. Their input, however, does suggest some issues within self-publishing. It also posits some of the difficulties facing mainstream publishers in the new digital age where authors, for the first time, are not totally dependent on mainstream houses to earn a living.

All five authors are members of RWA, who assisted me in identifying perspective interviewees; four of the five had been published by a mainstream house before going solo. Their experiences reflect those anecdotal tales appended to Kendall's study and those frequently found on blog posts, more so than media stories that tend to suggest that self-publishing is an easy road to fame and fortune. The road to successful self-publishing is hard work, perhaps even harder than in mainstream publishing, though the financial rewards, if these obstacles are overcome, are far greater.

Like xrotic publishers and many of the smaller e-book publishers, such as Beautiful Trouble and Sugar and Spice, there is a digital learning curve. This learning curve is aborted when going with a traditional publisher. The advantage of mainstream houses is that after a writer writes a book, the minutiae of getting it into print and promoting and distributing it are the responsibility of the publisher, and the writer can go about her business, which is writing. One may feel she's an author once she "publishes" online, and maybe that makes her an author, but it doesn't necessarily sell books. Monkou mentions an acquaintance who lauded her recently published (online) novel: "Her measure of success was that she published. It didn't matter if she sold one or a hundred books. For some people, that's all they want: they want to say 'I'm published.' It's like a grain of sand in the desert. You have to do a lot more if you expect people are going to be able to find you." Author and romance e-book publisher Margaret Riley at Changeling Press would agree: "Many [would-be authors] figure that if it's online, it's easy. Throwing it up unedited on Amazon for $.99 isn't the way to do it. You have to have some idea of how you're going to market your book." Few self-publishers out of the gate seem prepared for the effort that is involved after writing a book, which means understanding and utilizing digital space.

All the authors talked to in this study admit to not being very digitally savvy when they started. Only Milan had a computer background—she designed websites in college to help "pay the bills." She was probably more digitally savvy than the average person, but even she acknowledges there was "still a huge learning curve" and that many of the critical skills she needed were learned over time. Most authors, with considerable effort, learned how to utilize digital space. If they were confronted with digital sophistication from the mainstream publishers, they would have a more difficult time establishing an online presence. Their success is the failure of mainstream publishers, who now all have a digital presence, but for most it is rather haphazard. Riley articulates the voice of many small digital publishers and self-published authors: "Most [mainstream publishers] have been dragged kicking and screaming into the digital age, and they're [still] dragging their heels at it. If there's any proof of that, check their prices. They're still trying to price e-books at print prices. The medium isn't the same." Milan rephrases the problem: "The number one thing I had to learn was that you're selling a digital book. This is the first time that the place people buy the books is the place where they read them, and that's something I don't think [mainstream] publishers have completely caught onto yet."

Four of the five authors in this study were published by traditional mainstream publishers, and all feel that generated some name recognition, as did most of the self-published authors who added comments to Kendall's study. Readers have favorite authors, and when that author releases a new book, they are in line to buy it. This is why a series is so important, regardless of the genre. Two of the authors had strong name recognition, and both turned down subsequent contracts to continue the series with their publishers and opted to self-publish the next book in the series. Two of the others had modest series sales, but even that, they felt, helped garner subsequent readers when they went solo. It is generally argued that readers today follow authors, not publishers; indeed, many mainstream covers and spines don't even carry the publisher's name.[127] This, in itself, underscores the authorial name over the houses.' The only real advantage that mainstream houses offer today, many authors argue, including those in Kendall's study, is hard-copy distribution.

Mainstream publishers offer print distribution, which, while it is not likely to go away any time soon, is not what it once was before the new digital age. There are at least two other areas that mainstream publishers tout that don't carry the weight they once did: editing and cover design. Successful self-published authors generally feel that they can do as good a job, if not better, than publishing houses in both of these areas.

The editorial pen, long considered a strong suit of mainstream houses—especially for neophyte writers whose work might be a little choppy—is readily addressed by an author hiring a professional editor. The editor cannot make the story better—that responsibility lies with the author—but she can make sure the story flows. Melody Ann, who has a bachelor's degree in business management, says she is far from stupid, "but you cannot edit your own material." She didn't do this initially and is surprised that her books sold as well as they did, but realizes they could have done a lot better if professionally edited. She is in the process of having her earlier works professionally edited before rereleasing them. She now has a strong editorial team. Melody Ann starts by storyboarding her ideas with her team: "This and this is going to happen but I need some stuff in the middle. What would be a fun thing for them to do?" Then, after her first draft is completed, she has a story editor, who's familiar with the characters in her series, look it over to make sure there is continuity—"she doesn't do grammar, but she makes sure the eyes, and such, are right." Then, the manuscript goes to a line editor "who rips it apart." She revises accordingly and has it looked at one more time before uploading it. It is as polished as any book by a major house. Monkou mentions an acquaintance who is a really good storyteller and has successfully self-published, but is not technically proficient. This problem has been solved for this individual with a lucrative contract from one of the Big Five, whose editorial staff will definitely fix this minor fault, and this, in turn, will strengthen an already good story.

Covers sell books. They are the first thing one sees and can pull the prospective reader in or push them away. The self-published authors whom I spoke with that had dealings with mainstream houses tended to deride the covers put on their novels. At the same time, they acknowledge the right cover is problematic and not an easy task. Covers with African American characters, for example, can push white readers away. Rochon talks about a Christmas anthology published by Dorchester before the house failed. The cover just had a poinsettia on it. "It did better than any of the other books." The same with African American author Brenda Jackson. The first book she had that hit the *New York Times* best-seller list had a cover that depicted a window with curtains waving in the breeze.[128]

It is not just that black characters on the cover can be off-putting to a wider readership. Rochon, who is also African American, says that self-publishing assures her "that I have the best cover I can get. With some [publishers] in New York, you get what you get." Monkou mentions a webinar that showed the same book with the same content but with three different covers, titles, and blurbs. Each successive change prompted greater sales. Monkou doesn't feel the novel will take off just because of the cover, but she is sure it doesn't hurt, which is why she reluctantly shells out even $200 to have a cover designed for her book.[129] Milan is a little blunter, and can afford to be because she, unlike some of the others, has completely severed her relationship with mainstream publishing: "I was *not* going to sign another contract." One of her concerns revolved around the cover:

> MILAN: I think my covers are super different from what they would be traditionally. The difference is this: I have gotten bad covers as a self-published author and my response to bad covers is to create a new one.
> JM: Define bad.
> MILAN: I know it when I see it.
> JM: That's the difference?
> MILAN: Yeah! When publishers make bad covers—they do so many it has to happen—and the author says that it's terrible, they just give it to some lesser author who cannot say no.
> JM: Shouldn't they know about covers? [They've] been making covers for a long time.
> MILAN: Bullshit! Sorry! [They may] have a good idea about some genres; they don't know crap in historicals. [Their] historical covers belong in the 1990s.
> JM: What's changed?
> MILAN: More saturated covers in historical romances; stronger emphasis on the woman. Google the covers [and see].
> JM: Cannot they [the art department under marketing] Google the covers?
> MILAN: I've had this conversation with my [former] editor and she said basically

that all the editors know [the covers don't work] but the art department says that they're right. They're not picky. They don't take criticism well.
JM: Art people!

The criticism toward "the art people" is not confined to them. The biggest issue for many self-published authors is the rigidity of the house. This is especially pronounced at Harlequin with its detailed line constraints, but similar murmurings can be heard from authors at other mainstream houses that don't have dedicated lines but have internal ideas as to what "sells." Far too often authors are simply told when they want to do this or that in their novels that "we just don't do that."[130] Self-published authors, xrotic publishers, and small independent digital presses are all making a mark in areas that nobody "at the top" wanted—male/male fiction and interracial romances being but two excellent examples that have been carved out by small houses at the periphery of the industry and have now, hesitantly, entered the mainstream.

The growth of self-publishing and alternative presses does not spell the end of mainstream publishing, even if the *Huffington Post* received nearly a thousand "likes" for its article proclaiming that self-published authors would capture 50 percent of the e-book market by 2020.[131] The new world may be a hybrid one, where authors publish both in traditional print format and in digital space.

Many self-published authors are finding a middle ground as hybrid publishers. Some of the mainstream publishers are more open to this than others. Melody Ann mentioned a major Big Five house that wanted to digitally publish her books. They'd split the profit fifty-fifty, which at first glance sounds pretty good since the normal authorial print royalty is around eight percent. Melody Anne figured that such an arrangement just didn't make financial sense and that all she would get out of it would be the prestige of the house's name on her books. They'd put the books on Amazon, who'd take their thirty percent, and then they'd split the balance fifty-fifty, which means that instead of getting to keep seventy percent from her Amazon sales, she now would get to keep only thirty-five percent. She also felt that she would actually be selling fewer books with the brand-name publisher because what they do, she explained, is raise the price of the book from $2.99 or $3.99 to $7.99, which is what their mass-market print books sell for, but which few in digital space will pay for a novel. Melody Ann did land with Simon & Schuster Pocket Books, and quite happily: "They just wanted a spin-off from [one of] my series. They weren't saying you have to do this or this or this. They were saying, you know what works, just do what's been making you successful." It's win-win. "My newest e-book has an excerpt from [the print book]" and of course the name recognition from the print book will drive her e-book sales, "and they *want* me to cross-promote."

Farrah Rochon sees the same win-win advantage: "I asked Harlequin if there would be a problem if I did a self-publishing novella that is based on the series I have with them." There wasn't, and one reason is because "when a book at Harlequin comes out, my self-publishing [book] does better; when [I] self-publish, my Harlequin numbers go up. [They're] tied together." Rochon suggests why Harlequin is not bothered by her self-publishing venture. Even though there is story overlap, Harlequin doesn't usually publish the shorter novella format. Monkou also writes novellas, but they are thematically different from those she publishes at Harlequin, which is why Harlequin has no issue with their hybrid relationship. "I didn't have any pushback," from Harlequin, she says, after looking closely at her Harlequin contract and then posting a self-published novella. Her contract with them lays out the general parameters for her books, which is to write a novel in the 60,000-word range that follows a certain [Kimani] format. So she writes interracial novellas. Neither the content nor length of her self-published works conflict with her Harlequin contract.

Hybrid publishing may suggest an emerging industry trend, since romance authors are at the head of the pack in embracing digital, and this has nudged more romance publishers in this direction. There are numerous reasons why hybrid publishers may be the wave of the future. One reason is that it is becoming more difficult for an independent author to establish an online presence. The sheer number of short stories, novellas and novels posted on sites like Amazon makes it difficult for readers to sift through the refuse to find a good self-published romance, though Internet romance reader sites might help some navigate the maze. There is also the prestige of being published by a well-known "legitimate" house that attracts many neophyte authors and draws even already successful self-published romance authors back into the fold, especially if the house is somewhat accommodating by allowing them to pursue their self-publishing ventures. Prestige aside, mainstream publishers still maintain a distribution network that many self-published authors enviously eye—bookstores, to be sure, but also the big-box retailers, who reach a *lot* of people, even if they take only a handful of romances rolling off the presses. And there are simply many authors who are inclined to leave the minutiae of transforming a manuscript into a book to established houses, or who are not disposed to deal with the tedium of establishing an online presence. In short, mainstream publishing is far from its death throes, though publishers are being challenged to adapt to the new digital age and be more accommodating if they want attract new talent and keep their existing, successful authors, a point nicely made by Rochon when discussing the reluctance of some publishers to accommodate digital romance authors: "It is just amazing how much this business has changed in just a few years. Publishers have to work with their authors now [more than they have done] if they want to keep them."[132]

Conclusion

Harlequin's line expansion over the last twenty-odd years only hints at the current complexity of romance publishing detailed in this chapter. The number of publishers, lines, and themes is mind-boggling.

The main rival to Harlequin comes from the Big Eight, who all produce romance novels in some number. The only publisher in this group that releases a multitude of category lines that thematically challenge Harlequin is Kensington, though a number of the Big Eight have a dedicated romance line, like Berkley's Heat and Avon's Red. Most of the other mainstream houses release romances as part of their regular production schedule, though the romance novels, like their other genres, are shelved in the genre-relevant section of the bookstore and are promoted on genre-specific websites and blogs, like allromancebooks.com or smashwords.com/romances.

It is hard to estimate how many romances these houses publish because they are often not delineated by a line, and some houses, like Sourcebooks, may release three or four romances per month as part of their overall fictive titles, while others, like St. Martin's, may release two or three one month and ten to fifteen the next.[133] Whatever the actual yearly numbers may be, they pale in comparison to those released by specialized houses, like the religious publishers, small presses, or legitimate self-published romance novelists.[134] The actual number of releases is not particularly important since any of the mainstream house romance titles are likely to reach a wider audience and garner more sales than the smaller houses.' Mainstream publishers are able to achieve this because they have a better distribution system than most of the small presses and larger advertising budgets to promote their books.

The Young Adult romance market is particularly illustrative in this regard. All the mainstream publishers dabble in YA titles, many of which are generally tinted with romantic elements. These houses regularly release YA novels to critical acclaim and generate significant sales. Scholastic, however, dominates the market, if only because YA is its bread and butter, so it releases substantially more YA novels than their Big Eight counterparts.

The mainstream publishers still hold major sway over the romance field. The books, however, are not distinguished thematically from one another. They are all good, well-written polished stories, and this author may do better than that author on any given month, but the essential romance generally (though not always) unfolds predictably along the lines of any Harlequin. For readers who want something different, they have to go beyond the offerings of mainstream publishers. The consumer is drifting toward the small houses in some number, and this, in itself, suggests the mainstream publishers are thematically lagging.

The mainstream publishers typically ignore the Christian market. Their large, oligopolistic size would suggest they view this as a relatively small market. But it nevertheless generates upwards of $50 million in annual sales, which is not an insignificant sum, even to the Big Boys who are always watching the bottom line. Harlequin is one mainstream publisher that attempts to seriously compete in this market. Harlequin seems to be doing well in it, too, even if the Christian theme of the books is somewhat attenuated, which is why the Christian publishers continue to thrive. HarperCollins is the only secular house whose Christian theme seems attuned to the Christian market, but that's because it bought two established Christian publishers and have not tampered with the novels previously released by Zondervan or Thomas Nelson. The popularity of Christian romance is probably best seen in the phenomenal success of the Amish series, which has become so entrenched and widespread within the Christian market that it is now considered a firmly established subgenre, even if few mainstream houses do more than an occasional Amish romance. One can always be certain that that the Christian storyline will not be strewn with sexual activity, which one is often not sure of among the mainstream releases, where even the "sweet" lines may contain more sexual nuances than any of the Christian romances. The "sweetness" of these novels is a major draw, and with the decreased evangelical slant that previously delineated these novels, they have the potential to reach beyond the Christian market to secular readers who just want a good, sweet, romantic story, which one is not ensured of even getting in a Harlequin Present book anymore.[135]

Those romance readers who enjoy reading about the sexual in more stark terms also have to turn to the smaller houses. Few mainstream publishers venture into the further reaches of what has here been labeled xrotica.[136] Mainstream publishers all have erotic romances, but they tend to pause at the higher level on our ten-point Likert scale. An occasional mainstream novel may step into the xrotic, but an occasional novel here or there gets lost outside the smaller presses that focus on the sexual activities of the heroine. The mainstream publishers still don't seem to appreciate that xrotica is more than a fad. This is clearly seen in the entrenchment of many of the smaller xrotic houses, many of whom are marking their tenth anniversary in 2014–2015. This underscores the stability of xrotica.

The thirst for male/male romances, along with more hardcore BDSM novels that almost mock the sensuality of the *Fifty Shades* books and their mainstream offspring, drives a substantial body of romance titles among xrotic publishers. Gay male/male novels and their LBT siblings are found in some number among GLBTQ publishers. GLBTQ romances don't have to be xrotic, a distinction that is more germane to xrotic male/male romances. GLBTQ presses have long existed to produce novels for other GLBTQs. The difference today is that their books reach a wider audience via the Internet, and this expands their range. This is seen in the number of heterosexual females who gravitate to GLBTQ male/male romances. These books go a long way in presenting the "ordinariness" of homosexuals and can help sensitize heterosexuals to a way of life they are often not otherwise exposed to.

Mainstream publishers don't typically release romantic GLBTQ books, even if they release novels about gay and lesbian relationships. It is almost as if GLBTQ romances are forbidden fruit. This was once the case with African American romances. It wasn't all that long ago that minorities had no option, if they wanted to read a romance, but to read about a white heroine and hero. The thinking among mainstream publishers was that the color really didn't matter to minority readers.[137] And they were right, in the sense that African Americans would read about white romantic relationships, but they only did so because there were no alternatives, which is to say, there were no romances that featured African American couples. Stephens, as editor of Dell Ecstasy and later with Harlequin American Romances, made sure that this changed and filtered a few romances into the respective lines that featured African Americans like herself. Today it is quite common to encounter African American characters in romance novels.

All the mainstream publishers today filter African Americans romance novels onto their lists. The benefit of these mainstream books is that they are placed in the romance section of the bookstore, rather than the African American section, where books from Kensington's and Harlequin's African American lines are more likely to be shelved. The benefit of placing mainstream romances among the other romance novels is that they have the potential to reach a wider (white) audience, though if the covers feature black characters some may be dissuaded from purchasing the book, effectively defeating the purpose of putting the books in the general romance section. The advantage of placing them in the African American section is that African Americans are able to find books that interest them more readily than if the novels are swallowed in the stacks of general romances.

The current vogue of talking about multicultural romances suggests that the modern romance novel goes beyond African American relationships and embraces other minorities. This is taking place but it is infrequent. Most mainstream romances that feature non-white characters are between like-race African American couples. Interracial marriages are sparse outside the smaller houses. Those who have ventured into interracial romance have done so, like almost all the small publishers, because of (1) a feeling of exclusion—they couldn't get their novels published, and (2) they have a personal affinity toward these novels because they are involved in an interracial relationship. Unlike the xrotic publishers, many of these houses are relatively new, so there is no objective yardstick by which to measure their success. Interracial love has extraordinary potential because it allows white readers to identify with the white character but also "speaks" to minority members who can see themselves in the books. Interracial romances with Latina heroines could be a way to break into the demographically strong Hispanic market.

Small romance presses have sprung up in increasing numbers because large capital outlays are not necessary—the cost of printing, warehousing, and distributing the books is overcome in digital space. The digital world has the potential for changing the face of publishing. It has certainly given authors greater control over their works by allowing them an alternative means to publish if (1) their manuscript doesn't make it through the gates, not necessarily because their work is bad, but because mainstream publishers only release a certain limited number of romances per month, (2) the theme doesn't resonate with mainstream houses, or (3) the author is disenchanted with her publisher. Disenchantment with the publisher often occurred because of disaffection with royalty arrangements or, more often than not, because the author feels she was being thematically constrained. The fact that many of these authors have been successful with themes not appreciated by the mainstream houses would indicate that the editorial constraints are misplaced.

Self-publishing has had a stigma, but this is being overcome today in the wake of a wide range of success stories and as more people migrate to, and are comfortable with, digital books. The success stories encourage others to move into self-publishing. There are many, however, who venture here unsuccessfully. It is not just writing a good novel. It is also that the process of getting the novel seen in digital space and getting the novel to the audience (via the bookstore) is one that the publisher has historically fulfilled. Those who realize the work involved beyond just putting their books up on Amazon seem to be doing well. They are not only selling their novels, they are increasingly getting the attention of, and being co-opted by, mainstream publishers.

If one accumulates a certain amount of even modest sales in the digital world, that person is likely going to be approached by an agent or mainstream house, both of whom regularly troll digital in search of potential clients or authors. Many first-time self-published authors are elated with this prospect of being affiliated with an established house, indicating that mainstream publishing is still alive and vibrant. Even those who have left an established house to venture out on their own often return to a mainstream press, but they are, and can be, more demanding in their contract negotiations. Many self-published authors who join the mainstream become hybrid authors: They publish a series for a house but can continue to self-publish shorter forms of the series or a series other than the one stipulated by their contract. Mainstream publishers have been hesitant to move into this area—it's just not what they are used to doing; they are used to controlling the whole process. They are beginning to realize that this hybrid relationship is a win-win situation. The self-published works by an author promote the print series, and the print books refer readers to the author's site, which impact the author's self-published book sales. Hybrid publishing is just one of the adaptive strategies employed by (some) mainstream romance publishers today. These strategies, and the challenges facing publishers today, are addressed more fully in the next chapter, now that there is some understanding as to what is taking place in the romance field at the outset of the new millennium.

CHAPTER 10

Romance Publishing at the Outset of the New Millennium
Market Share, Competition and Content Innovation

The Big Five[1] mainstream publishers control most of the book market and, by default, most of the romance market. The various romance imprints within the Big Five, such as Berkley's Heat and Avon's Red, all have their niches, though most non–Harlequin mass-market romances tend to be released in limited numbers as part of the house's general fiction titles. The novels released by the Big Five, whether category or mainstream romances, are all good, solid, well-written novels that span the subgenre continuum. The vibrancy of their program is underscored by their domination of the RITA Awards.

Most of these books are filtered by editors after the manuscript has been pre-screened by agents since the majority of the large houses do not accept unsolicited manuscripts. The manuscripts the editors receive tend to be those that fit the existing in-house program. The editors do not typically have guidelines but do tend to have an in-house "understanding" of what is working in the market and position their books according to what they have traditionally released and with an eye toward what their major rivals are doing. This holds true even if our definition of the Big Five is extended to include those three major independent houses that round out the Big Eight, though Kensington goes where many of its bigger rivals don't tread, and Scholastic moves a little further than its siblings in the Young Adult market, if only because of the sheer volume of novels that it releases in this market, which itself assures a certain degree of content distinction. Many of the daring departures in romance content come from small, independent, entrepreneurial houses and those authors who move outside the mainstream and self-publish.

The Liability of Newness

Arthur Stinchcombe introduced the now canonical "liability of newness" in his essay "Social Structure and Organizations."[2] Much has been made of this concept since it first appeared in 1965. Most of the works support Stinchcombe's thesis, which is succinctly summarized by Strodomskyte, Dai and Hauge[3]:

> [S]tart-ups suffer from the "liability of newness" and have a greater risk of failure than older organizations, because they depend on the cooperation of strangers, have low levels of legitimacy, and are unable to compete effectively against [large] established firms. In this light, new firms face a variety of barriers they must overcome on their way to success, and these challenges pose serious threats to organizational success for young enterprises.

There were a lot of entrepreneurial failures in digital publishing in the early years, but most of these, anecdotal information would suggest, were shyster start-ups that were simply trying to bilk would-be romance authors. Many of the legitimate houses that were examined in the last chapter remain. One reason is that, as Stinchcombe himself observed, the liability for new firms was particularly germane to new organizations of a new form. One could argue that many of the small digital firms that entered the market were not radically new and built on the basic publishing model and hence were at less risk of failure. It may also be that the liability of newness raised by Stinchcombe is not as relevant today since major funding is not as crucial in launching a new business in the digital age. The relatively reasonable cost of entry was cited as a major reason by the rival upstarts for entering the publishing fray in digital rather than print form, where they knew they could not compete against mainstream publishers. Stinchcombe also argued that new organizations suffer a learning curve because it takes time to build strategic networks. Strodomskyte, et al., and Krackhardt both take issue with this argument and feel this is less an issue in the current environment.[4] Their points are validated in this analysis. The new entrepreneurial digital managers are able to rapidly build strategic resources by tapping a wide range of writers to fill their rosters that "the system" has excluded. They are also able to hire experienced freelance editors, illustrators, and web designers who can ensure that the works produced are competitively positioned.

Stinchcombe's major argument was less in the liability of newness than in appraising how organizations respond to shifting social conditions, something he urged could best be achieved by a historical process like the one utilized in this analysis of romance publishing. The broader social processes shaping organizations received considerable attention when the argument was first formulated, but over the years organizational analyses have shifted to managerial processes within organizations.[5] Lounsbury and Ventresca argue for a return to the original societal dimensions that shape organizations, which they feel is a frequently neglected area in the current research on organizations.[6] There are two primary postulates put forward by Stinchcombe surrounding the intricate relationship between social conditions and organizational. One is that social conditions affect the degree of motivation for starting new organizations; the other is that social conditions affect the likelihood that a new organization will succeed or fail. Both these points are the rationale for starting digital romance enterprises and are a major explanation for their success.

Most entrepreneurial digital firms focus on romances more than any other genre. One reason is that many of the publishers were frustrated authors or romance devotees who couldn't find the novels they wanted among the mainstream offerings. It is also because of the voracious appetite for novels among romance readers, who were among the first to embrace the new format. This ensured a degree of success since there was a large audience there, and this audience was left untapped by mainstream publishers, both in content variations and in digital form. The digital issue will be returned to in the next section, because mainstream publishers are making some effort to establish a digital presence today. They lagged behind the small digital romance presses, however, by at least five years, which gave the entrepreneurial firms time to establish their presence in the marketplace. Entrepreneurial reliance on digital to launch enterprises underscores another Stinchcombe postulate: organizations bear the imprint of their times.[7]

The entrepreneurial publishers also had some experience in publishing.[8] This gave them an intuitive appreciation that there was a vast, underserved market. In most cases, this experience was from a writer's perspective. It was the hesitancy of mainstream publishers to publish their novels that prompted them to start their own house in the belief that if they liked to write these kinds of novels, there must be others out there who would like to read them, a variant of the editor's perspective that if she liked the book, the reader would too.

Mainstream historical publishers in the 1970s were not in sync with changing sexual mores and thus did not meet the needs of those women who wanted a more erotic romance. Changing social mores also dated the generally sweet contemporary romances of the 1970s. The demand for more "sexy" romances would be sated when Avon introduced Woodiwiss in 1972 and when Dell debuted Ecstasy in 1980. In both cases, readers flocked to the books because they couldn't get them anywhere else. The general consensus by mainstream publishers at both periods was that the sweet romances they were publishing were meeting the needs of romance readers since readers were buying the books. But romance readers were buying them because they had no alternative. The romance reader enthusiastically embraced the new erotically charged historical romances when they were offered them, and then the new liberated contemporary romances.

At the outset of the new millennium, mainstream publishers were again not satisfying the needs of the romance reader. This is obvious because when offered an alternative product, the romance reader enthusiastically responded. The key difference between earlier content innovation and that which occurred at the outset of the new millennium is that the internal gatekeeper tradition of sifting manuscripts into the system was voided by the entrepreneurial one.

Religious publishing houses were in a better position than most digital startups, which is why they relied on releasing romances in the tried-and-true print format. They met their constituents' need for clean, more Christian-themed romances. It was getting harder and harder in the secular realm to find these kinds of romances since most mainstream secular publishers had upped the eroticism of their romances. It was left largely to the Christian houses to sate the need for "sweet" contemporary romances. Harlequin is the only major secular publisher that has attempted to tap the Christian market—HarperCollins's Christian books are still promoted via their Christian orientation as Zondervan and Thomas Nelson romances. The Christian message in Harlequin novels, however, is somewhat attenuated, so the smaller Christian publishers still dominate the market for romances with a strong Christian theme, even if this theme is itself toned down from its earlier, evangelical roots.[9]

Many of the mainstream houses believed their romances to be "quite erotic." In a sense, this was true. The eroticism of twenty-first century romances was distinctly more pronounced than those that closed the twentieth century. But they were not erotic enough, or at least not enough for some romance readers. This is the primary reason xrotic publishing was born. Most mainstream publishers have still not ventured into the xrotic realm, which is one reason many of the small houses are still flourishing. Some of the eroticism, especially in male/male romances, spilled over to the GLBTQ presses. The GLBTQ presses didn't hesitate to take advantage of the new heterosexual romance reader of these books, even if they were not their traditional clientele. Others who wrote erotic or male/male novels moved into the new lucrative field of self-publishing their novels.

Multicultural romances are a misnomer since few romances are really multicultural. The buzzword is not as encompassing as it sounds: senior editorial staff at Harlequin, for example, talks about the multicultural dimension of the Kimani and Arabesque books, but the guidelines still stress that the characters be African American. Mainstream publishers release some "multicultural" romances as part of their mainstream titles, but they only pepper the house lists. They seem to feel that Harlequin and Kensington dominate the market since both have a variety of African American lines. Interracial love is another matter and is left primarily to the small houses. Most of these are relatively new, and the liability of newness has taken its toll. Those who have not faired well have suffered from their organizational newness, not the liability of new content, at least judging by those who continue to publish novels with an interracial love story. The survival of the remaining small digital publishers is enhanced, not only because their digital competition is thinner, but because few mainstream publishers are tapping this potentially vibrant market.

Self-publishing is not going to destroy mainstream publishing, but it is changing the rules of the game. In the past, authors had little recourse but to accept whatever conditions the publisher required if they wanted to get their books legitimately published.[10] The stigma of self-publishing has largely disappeared in the wake of the outpouring of success stories by some who have ventured into this field. It is now a viable option for authors to explore, not just the ones who have been rejected by a mainstream house, but by those who are tired of the restrictions imposed by the publisher, or who are dissatisfied with their royalty arrangement. The change is already felt. Hybrid romance authors are becoming increasingly common. It seems that self-published romance authors can have their cake and eat it too. It would not be surprising if authors in other genres started to follow.

Adaptive Strategies within the Mainstream

Bertelsmann is the largest of the Big Eight. It had worldwide gross revenues in 2013 just shy of $22 billion with over $1.164 billion in gross profit.[11] The Penguin Random House group within Bertelsmann was responsible for roughly 10 percent of this worldwide revenue ($2.2 billion), half of which was accounted for by sales in the United States.[12] The loose pocket change ($164 million) at Bertelsmann is likely less than the combined gross sales of all the romance publishers outside the mainstream. Termites, however, can destroy any foundation over time if not treated.

The merits and demerits of large versus small organizations is a complex one. The body of research supporting hierarchal rigidity appears applicable to the Big Five more than the three mainstream independent firms, which also have a hierarchy, but not anywhere near as vast and complex as the Big Five. Increases in organization size tend to slow an organization's response to changes in its environment.[13] This can be compounded when no competitive threat is perceived. This can lead to an "if it ain't broke" mentality, which itself is reinforced by doing the same thing over and over[14] with what appear to be satisfactory (sales) results. Conglomerates, then, tend to embrace change slowly. Even Harlequin, which has released a slew of new lines over the last ten to twenty years, has often made only minor modifications in existing products, leading to a potpourri of lines that are thinly differentiated from one another. The other mainstream publishers also release a substantial body of romance novels that sell well. This is why it seems like there is a lot of new stuff out there, but there really isn't. Content innovation that is markedly different has come from outside the mainstream, and the mainstream publishers, if they notice the small houses, don't appear to take their threat seriously, despite some disgruntlement among romance consumers about the romances offered by the mainstream houses. This could change, however.

The New Digital Age

The one area the mainstream publishers have woken up to is the new digital age, in a somnambulist kind of way. The format has changed, but it has had little effect on content. E-books appear to have simply replaced print sales. Romance publishers are not really building market share, though without making the digital adjustments the publisher would likely lose it. This problem was remarked on by Craig Swinwood at Harlequin, who told *Forbes* reporter Jeremy Greenfield that one of Harlequin's problems, digitally savvy as it was, was that the company didn't replace shrinking paperback sales fast enough.[15]

Mainstream publishers have lagged behind the entrepreneurial romance publisher in this area, so it is not surprising that they are monitoring the activity of the small romance houses. This is most evident in their scanning of self-published authors and those who are making a mark with the smaller digital houses. Many of these authors have been enticed away from their alternative universe by big advances and lucrative contracts.

Digital was embraced by the smaller romance publishers between 2000 and 2005; mainstream houses began to eye digital more critically after 2005 but really didn't start to seriously "get into the game" until 2010.[16] The only Big Eight publisher that placed its digital product alongside the smaller house was Sourcebooks, though its e-books didn't do as well as the smaller houses' for almost a decade. Sourcebooks started looking at digital in the early 2000s, even if few consumers were purchasing in digital. They were set to go in 2010 when digital hit because, Todd Stocke says, "We had the system built. We didn't have to go back and digitalize our backlist, didn't have to figure out what we owned, didn't own, had rights to—we'd done all that work. So we were right there when things struck."[17] It was rather unusual for Sourcebooks to have had the leisure to work in digital when no one else was because the costs didn't appear to warrant the return. Stocke says he was given more latitude because the publisher had a shared computer background and saw the future potential of e-books. It would pay off when "digital struck." The other publishers are starting to catch up because they have a strong financial base to rely on for investment.

Digital sales were modest between 2000 and 2009, which is why one industry analyst who was assessing the industry circa 2003[18] would write that after a careful review of basic consumer data, the "widespread acceptance of electronic books and the widespread distribution of book content via Web-base sites will not occur before 2015 and possibly not before 2020."[19] Albert Greco's assessment seems to have been widely shared by those in the print media, and with good reason. E-book sales represented only about 0.1 percent of books sold by mainstream publishers in 2006, and this rose infinitesimally in 2007 to around 0.5 percent, which was "still an insignificant number."[20] An analysis of the industry by another veteran a few years later shows how quickly the publishing world had changed. "By the autumn of 2009," John Thompson writes, "the decade of confused anticipating [regarding digital] was over: when the change began, it happened more quickly and decisively than most commentators had expected. The sales of e-books had risen sharply.... What had changed? One word: Kindle."[21]

E-book sales would rise exponentially over the next few years with Kindle and similar spin-offs, such as Nook and iPads, and the accessibility of e-books on popular sites such as Amazon and Barnes & Noble. By 2013, e-books accounted for over a quarter (27 percent) of all adult trade sales, even if e-book sales slowed to single-digit growth in 2013.[22] Genre fiction drove the digital revolution since it fit the e-book format perfectly. "These are categories," explained the head of one of the leading executives at a large print corporation, "where people consume a lot of books and they are always waiting for the next one."[23] It is not surprising that when the mainstream publishers seriously started to look at digital, they first moved to where the sales have always been: romance novels.

The benefit of size is economy of scale. Even proponents of small over large concede that this gives large organizations a distinct advantage because they can produce more goods at a lower cost. A small press, for example, may print 1,000 books. The print cost might be $10.00 a book, which means they will have to sell the book for $20.00 to make a profit. A large company can print 5,000 books, but because they are printing more books it actually costs less per unit, say $5.00 per book, which they can sell for $10.00 to make a profit; they could even sell it for $15.00 and undersell the smaller competitor and make a handsome profit.

Small presses are constrained because it takes a lot of money to start a digital press, whereas the amount to start a digital press for a major corporation is a relatively meager amount of their overall budget. Laying out $100,000 is big money to a small start-up entrepreneur. Shelling out a few million to start a new digital imprint is pocket change when Penguin Random House had revenue, just in the United States, of $1.1 billion. This means the millions it spent to start a digital press in the United States, even if it cost $10 million, is one-one-hundredths of one percent. This infinitesimal amount would shrink even more if the new digital imprint went global because international sales for Penguin Random House were twice that of the U.S. market and there would be no start-up costs since the imprint already has an international presence.

Harlequin was one of the first to go digital with women.com in 1999–2000. Like many others at that time, it was prompted to contemplate digital publishing because industry insiders were adamantly prompting it. But soon, John Thompson writes, many in the business started to realize that the levels of uptake in the early 2000s were much lower than were being projected. This was complicated by the dot-com bubble bursting around the same time, and these two reality checks ushered in "a new mood of skepticism … about [the e-book's] capacity to transform traditional business models."[24]

Harlequin was ahead of the pack in going digital. It saw the trend toward digital because the romance reader was the first group to embrace digital. The jump-start association with women.com didn't work, and Harlequin took its losses and moved digital internally. This was largely limited to website design, however. Like many others, it was inflicted with the new mood of uncertainty that continued to surround e-books through at least the first half of the 2000s. It was quicker to get up to speed than many other houses when e-books started to show results in 2010 because it had, like Sourcebooks, at least a rudimentary e-books infrastructure in place. The other houses rushed to enter the market after 2010.

Corporate heads started to encourage e-book developments when the e-book market started to percolate. They do not seem to have directed houses within their sphere to go in this or that direction. There are two reasons many houses moved into e-book romances. First, it is widely recognized within the publishing industry that romance readers are avid readers and it was clear, after even the most cursory review of the romance consumer in 2010, that they had already embraced digital. The implication: the market was there. The second follows from the first: since few other mainstream publishers were doing anything in digital, they looked to those who were successful in the new format. This is why one xrotic romance e-book publisher said she was told by an editor at a mainstream house that the editor was instructed to watch what her house was doing digitally and imitate it. This story gains credence when one recognizes the pressure mainstream publishers were under to get into the e-book game. The logic was inescapable: if these little guys could do it, we, with all our financial clout and publishing acumen, should be able to blow them away. They haven't, though they have made their mark.

There are a number of ways to enter a new market. One approach is to start your own digital press. This is perhaps the most cost-effective way to enter the market over the long term: up-front costs can be amortized over years, so a $5 million outlay, when amortized over five years, is only $1 million per year; if amortized over ten years the start-up cost becomes negligible; if shared with other house presses, the amortization is stretched even further. The house also controls the press, ensuring quality control and product consistency. This was the method chosen by Harlequin, where other lines (more so than non-romance genres) could use the same digital format; it was also the method selected by many others.

Penguin Random House (Bertelsmann) selected this route in North America. Ballantine Bantam Dell (BBD), for example, reintroduced Bantam's Loveswept from the 1980s in digital form. The Loveswept line, defunct since January 1999, still has strong name recognition among romance aficionados. This gave it immediate presence when BBD reintroduced the line in digital form in August 2011; it also relied on the original tagline: "Love stories you'll never forget by authors you'll always remember." It was cost-effective because it mainly re-released old titles, like Iris Johansen's *This Fierce Splendor* (1998, re-released 2011) but gave it a fresh new packaged look. This made it appear new, though the content vocabulary, rooted to the 1990s, would date it.

The marketing rationale camouflaged the driving economic gain to BBD: "Ballantine Bantam Dell has a *treasure trove* of romance *classics*," BBD senior vice present of Digital Content said, "we want to *share* with a new generation of readers [author's italics]."[25] They have interwoven new original titles into the line, which, alongside the old, makes the old look new. The content remains basically the same, despite the disclaimer that "much has changed in the last 20+ years."[26] The change appears to be limited to form over content. The change, says Sue Grimshaw of Romance at Random, is that today "there are no restrictions—shelf space is unlimited in the clouds; there is no upfront cost for online retailers to merchandise their books, so as you can see the environment is perfect for a new digital imprint such as Loveswept."[27] The new novels are the same length as the re-released ones, between 40,000 and 60,000 words. A shorter variant of Loveswept, aptly named Flirt, is also available. Flirt romances run 15,000 to 30,000 words. Loveswept novels cost between $2.99 and $4.99, and at the lower cost are about what a romance reader would pay for one of the original novels at a used bookstore.

Berkley/NAL, also part of the Penguin Random House group, has done pretty much the same thing under the InterMix imprint, launched in January 2012. InterMix has repackaged the cover art for its original Signet Regency romances. It's a new way to get old novels to the public, despite Leslie Gelbman's statement that it is a "way for original voices to reach readers."[28] InterMix ensured a strong launch positioning by publishing eleven Nora Roberts titles that originally had been published by Silhouette. There was nothing new about the Roberts novels except that it would be the first time they were available in e-book format. The price point, however, was not digitally competitive: $6.99. Avon's digital-first Impulse line, created in-house, is much more competitively priced at $1.99.

Another way to "get into the game" is to partner with another firm. Joint overseas ventures, we saw, were a quick way for Harlequin to establish an international presence during its early expansion years. More recently, St. Martin partnered with Entangled. The deal seems more to Entangled's benefit than St. Martin's. Macmillan, which is owned by Holtzbrinck, will distribute all new Entangled English-language e-books (which are considerable) in both domestic and international markets. A new St. Martin's/Entangled imprint will publish a "select number of Entangled digital first titles."[29] It will shore up St. Martin's somewhat anemic digital romance presence.[30]

Another way to enter a new market is to merge with or buy out an existing competitor. Of the two, buyouts tend to be favored.[31] This was the method selected by Kensington, and while it had a line of erotic romances, Aphrodisia, it vastly extended its digital-first erotic romances across subgenres with the purchase in 2014 of e-book publisher Lyrical Press,[32] which had been founded only a few years earlier in 2007. The rationale for the purchase, according to Steven Zacharius, was the synergic fit between "Renee Rocco's cutting-edge expertise in running a small independent press and Kensington's team of talented professionals."[33] This is how big companies think like a small company, which Campbell's president R. Gordon McGovern believes is necessary for large corporations to survive.[34] The recent purchase of Harlequin by Harper-Collins is yet another example of a corporate buyout.

HarperCollins: Buying into the Romance Market BIG Time

Avon is HarperCollins's romance imprint. It releases a respectable number of books each year under Avon Romance, Avon Red, and Avon Impulse, its more recent digital-first line. Avon made its romance "mark" when it discovered Kathleen Woodiwiss in 1972 and introduced romance readers to a radically different type of historical romance novel. It has maintained a solid, respectable but unremarkable program since. With the purchase of Harlequin, HarperCollins became, overnight, the world's leading romance publisher. The deal was announced in May 2014, and it was finalized a scant three months later. HarperCollins's website lost no time in promoting its new acquisition. Two links appeared in August under the romance heading on the HarperCollins's home site: one took the browser to Avon, the other to Harlequin. The only likely change is that the two imprints will be "rebranded" as separate units under the HarperCollins Romance moniker.

Mergers and buyouts are two traditional corporate acquisition strategies that are used to help a company gain better access to markets, products, technology, resources, and management talent. The distinction is a fine one. Mergers are when two companies agree to join each other and become one entity, which was the case in 2013 when Penguin in the U.K. and Random House in the U.S. merged to form one monolithic publishing house. Takeovers, when they are friendly, as they were in the case of HarperCollins's acquisition of Harlequin, occur when one company acquires the other but the purchased company continues to exist as an independent entity. The HarperCollins acquisition of Harlequin is similar to what occurred a few decades ago when Harlequin acquired Silhouette. There were no major changes in Silhouette's organization structure, nor was there any major product tampering by Harlequin with Silhouette's romances. Indeed, many of the Silhouette lines continued to coexist with Harlequin products. Even after the rebranding that took place a few years ago, the original imprint name remained: Silhouette's Desire and Special Editions simply were renamed Harlequin Desire and Special Editions. A similar situation is the likely forecast for Harlequin under HarperCollins.

Harlequin corporate headquarters will remain in Toronto. This assuages any immediate concerns by corporate employees that their jobs may be in danger. There is some concern regarding the location of Harlequin's separate New York offices. This is largely a logistics issue and will have little to do with the content of those novels filtered into the system from New York—economy of scale would suggest that it is simply more economical to have offices at the same location than in separate facilities a few blocks from one another. The only really surprising thing about the sale is that there are so few rumblings about content concerns from romance consumers.[35] This is most likely because the HarperCollins-Harlequin marriage is a good fit.

Acquisitions are sometimes problematic when there is a clash between corporate cultures, which can lead to an "us" versus "them" attitude among staff. The most successful fit is when the companies are in related businesses.[36] The fit between HarperCollins and Harlequin is actually better than the fit between Harlequin and Torstar. Torstar, in fact, had little interest in Harlequin's overseas component except that it added to the bottom line. This is precisely HarperCollins's interest, which further underscores the likelihood that HarperCollins will encourage Harlequin's efforts in this area and not interfere with existing arrangements, since most overseas arrangements are built on Harlequin's English-language product lines. It was, after all, the international arm of Harlequin's product that attracted HarperCollins as a suitor in the first place.[37] HarperCollins's international presence was shallow. Its presence, via Harlequin, is now substantial—it has added 11 countries—and this opens up economy of scale ventures for related HarperCollins products in the international arena. It is now internationally competitive with the other Big Four.

Craig Swinwood took the position of Harlequin's CEO to shepherd the sale of Harlequin to fruition. The only change in his life, now that the sale is completed, is that he will report to Brian Murray at HarperCollins rather than David Holland at Torstar. Swinwood will prove critical in providing stability at Harlequin during the transition process. He will help ensure a state of calm within Harlequin over the next few years. His thirty-some years of experience within Harlequin will also provide a keystone to HarperCollins's understanding of the myriad products Harlequin has to offer and how they reach their market.

This is not to suggest that changes won't take place within Harlequin, instituted by its new owner. Economy of scale itself would suggest some streamlining of duplicate products will take place at some point down the road. This is something that was absent at Torstar. It is a positive "outside" eye that HarperCollins brings to Harlequin.

Torstar was not intimately involved with product at Harlequin, which is why, whenever Harlequin sales dipped, there were rumblings in the industry that Torstar might divest itself of Harlequin.[38] Product placement was not Torstar's area, and it let Harlequin proceed pretty much unhampered. HarperCollins, as a trade, mass-market publisher, will bring more critical product oversight. Many Harlequin lines are thinly differentiated from one another. These lines may look distinct within Harlequin but may not be that distinct, or there may be a way to roll two lines together to save money but also meet consumer needs. More problematic is the continued existence of Avon, whose romance product stands weakly next to Harlequin's lines.[39]

Gatekeeping Monitors

This analysis of the romance industry has pivoted on the decision-making process of gatekeeping editors and in-house managers who are responsible for determining what books to publish and what lines to launch or discontinue. This follows the well-established path of others who have examined those in strategic positions within an industry who decide what products to offer the public and, by default, what and why other products are excluded. The only departure from the tried-and-true evaluation of gatekeepers was to recognize that during turbulent times in the product environment, gatekeepers have to be more active than reactive and temporarily move into gatemaking roles.

Studies of gatekeepers have long acknowledged that there are those whose actions also modify the product, even if they are outside the industry. Since they are not classically gatekeepers, they have escaped substantive critical attention. Naming something (or someone) is the first step in the process of identifying an issue.[40] Lacking an identifier, we will call them gatekeeping monitors. These monitors are critical interrupters at the input and output stages in the publishing industry. Agents are clearly monitors, ones that are becoming more important to the gatekeeping process since mainstream publishers rely on them rather extensively to filter products today. This is the result of mega-building. Corporate consolidation has increased the workload of editors, forcing them to rely, James Thompson writes, "increasingly on agents to provide the initial screening of projects: editors have, in effect," he concludes, "outsourced the initial selection process to agents.... For the most part, it's agents, not editors or publishers, who are expected to discover new talent ... who they think are promising" and to work with them to draft ideas or draft manuscripts into a potentially successful book.[41] The direct (non-agented) means of acquiring new authors at Harlequin may be one of its features most at risk now that it is under the business-driven model fostered by HarperCollins.[42]

Professional organizations are also monitors. We've seen how the Romance Writers of America has acted at a number of critical junctions to hinder the acceptance of books by romance authors who don't fit their established criteria, which until recently meant authors published in print by mainstream romance presses. RWA's role was to protect its members. Its initial resistance is reminiscent of the publishing industry itself in adapting to change. The distinction is that the RWA has now adapted to the new social world and has accepted into the fold those romance authors who approach the romantic story from a "different" perspective, whereas many mainstream houses continue to be resistant to the content advanced by those authors affiliated with the small romance presses and those who self-publish. This parallels changes within the GLBTQ community, which adapted to heterosexual writers addressing gay themes. In 2010, straight romance writers became eligible to compete in the coveted Lambda (GLBTQ) literary awards. It may be a while, one heterosexual author of male/male romances said, before a heterosexual author is going to stand a chance of winning an award in the male-male category, but at least the Lammys are now open and willing to screen manuscripts by those who are not themselves GLBTQ. The acceptance by these gatekeeping monitors goes a long way in legitimating these "upstart" authors. RWA's recognition of digital authors is just one instance of how it helped nudge—or at least reinforced—mainstream houses to move to digital. RWA's effect on the market is best exemplified by its mustered support against a Harlequin project a few years ago.

In November 2009, Harlequin announced that it would team with the self-publishing Penguin Random House subsidiary Author Solutions to form Harlequin Horizon. Horizon was basically a vanity press where authors pay to have their novels printed. By carrying the Harlequin logo, Horizon would give the impression that it was a screened Harlequin book. It was an obvious exploitative attempt to generate an income from would-be romance authors who could tout their "novels" as a Harlequin product. The response by professional organizations, including RWA, but also related writer's groups, such as Mystery Writers of American (MWA) and the Science Fiction & Fantasy Writers of America (SFWA) was swift and negative. They all voiced strong objection to the project. RWA went so far as to strip Harlequin of eligibility for RWA conference resources, which would prohibit Harlequin from entering any award categories for its authors and lines. Such an extreme measure caught then-CEO Donna Hayes by surprise, but she was quick to respond and said Harlequin's name would be removed from the self-publishing venture.[43] Hayes nevertheless felt the reaction was unfair. She wrote,

> It is disappointing that the RWA has not recognized that publishing models have and will continue to change. As a leading publisher of women's fiction in a rapidly changing environment, Harlequin's intention is to provide authors access to all publishing opportunities, traditional or otherwise.

John Scalzi satirically interpreted Hayes's comment, which goes to the heart of what many felt Harlequin was doing.[44]

> It is disappointing that the RWA has not recognized that in a recession, our company's commitment to its bottom line trumps any ethical or moral consideration when it comes to the treatment of writers who haven't figured out that we're

10. Romance Publishing at the Onset of the New Millennium 279

supposed to be paying *them*, not the other way around. Harlequin's intention is to suck money off these rubes in every way possible, so there.

RWA's drastic action kept Harlequin from launching Horizon. It did launch the venture as DellArte Press, but all Harlequin identifiers have been removed from the website. DellArte Press thus lost "one of the key advantages that the venture had in its efforts for convincing aspiring romance writers to subsidize their own publications,"[45] making it, in effect, "just another rookie self-publishing imprint."[46]

The output process also has its monitors. These, too, have fallen largely outside the scope of this analysis, though their role, like the agents, has sometimes been glimpsed in this critique of the romance industry. Reviewers have long been recognized as critical output monitors for their role in making people aware that a new product has been released. Just getting a review is often sufficient to ensure sales because it brings the book to the attention of prospective readers.[47] In the romance field, *Romantic Times* exerts tremendous influence. It is one of the few popular fan-based magazines that has survived from the early 1980s; it is still overseen by its rather colorful founder, Kathryn Faulk. *RT* reviews over 300 romances every month and is peppered with human-interest stories from authors (see RT cover on following page). It has a print and digital subscription base of 50,000 readers. It is very popular with romance aficionados: just shy of 3,000 romance fans attended the 2014 Romantic Times booklovers annual convention in New Orleans; the Saturday Book Fair was attended by 3,700 fans who were there to meet nearly 700 authors.[48] Some of the smaller digital publishers have their own fan conferences; Ellora's Cave, for example, hosts Romanticon in Canton, Ohio, in the fall of each year. Other critical monitors at this output stage would include such sites as Smart Bitches, Trashy Books, All About Romances at likesbooks.com, smashwords.com/romances, and GoodReads, whose romance reader posts have been relied on any number of times in this analysis.

Conclusion

It is always difficult for small, independent entrepreneurs to gain traction against their larger, more established rivals. There has been some suggestion in the literature in recent years that the "liability of newness," which has historically plagued the newcomer, is less pronounced today than when the concept was first formulated a half-century ago. The present analysis of the romance industry would support this assessment. One reason that newness is less of a liability today is that market entry in the digital age does not require the capital expenditures once necessary to launch a new venture. The Internet also vastly accelerates a firm's ability to reach and establish legitimacy with potential consumers.

The ability of small romance firms, such as Siren and Totally Bound Publishing, to establish a market presence was augmented by two related factors. One was that they tapped market niches that were not being addressed by mainstream houses—xrotica and interracial romances, for example—or were not being substantively addressed by the mainstream houses—Christian romances, for instance. The other factor that helped the small houses gain traction over their larger rivals was the slow response by mainstream houses to the new digital format for delivering novels.

There was a five- to ten-year lag before mainstream houses caught on to the digital revolution, by which time the small houses (and self-published authors) had established a market presence. The plodding response to shifting market conditions by conglomerates is related to their size. Large-scale organizations tend to have a very complex bureaucratic structure that hinders their quick response to emerging market trends. This handicap is offset, however, because larger firms have deep pockets and benefit from an economy of scale, which allowed them, once they moved into the digital age, to rapidly establish a presence and compete with the smaller houses. Some have done this internally by establishing digital books; others have purchased existing digital publishers to jumpstart their digital entry.

Mainstream publishers all have a digital presence today, though some are further ahead of the curve than others. Their

Romantic Times October 2014 cover.

entrance into digital space might have seriously challenged the small firms' ability to stay solvent. Curiously, the economy of scale that one would expect to see from the larger houses has not dramatically affected the price of their digital product, so many larger houses are not price-competitive with the smaller ones. This is because they are still locked to the old print model of pricing. It appears that many of the larger firms assumed that all they had to do was "go digital." Their pricing has not dramatically changed, and while it has gone down in recent years, many houses are still not at the price point of many of the smaller digital publishers. The failure of mainstream houses to adjust to the new pricing model is related to their failure to adapt their product line. Few have modified their product to tap the market segments that the smaller presses cater to.

There is considerable attention in the public domain to the challenge facing mainstream publishers today. This is often related to the disappearance of bookstores. But brick and mortar stores are not as necessary in the digital age, and people have moved to alternative means of reading: Kindle, Nook, iPads, and so forth. In short, people are still reading. Publishing will remain vital; it just won't be the same. Mainstream publishers are adapting to the new reading habits. This adaption is largely limited to format, not content. Content is slowly being addressed, however.

Mainstream editors regularly scan the sales of "rising digital stars." Many new authors who have established a digital presence through the Internet or with a small digital press are quick to accept contracts from one of the traditional publishing houses. The prestige of being associated with a mainstream house is still pronounced. The mainstream houses have better digital and print distribution systems than the smaller presses; they also appeal to some self-published authors by taking the drudgery of digital off their shoulders and allowing them to concentrate on their writing. The gatekeeper role of the editor is also made easier since they can see that the author is generating sales and don't have to guess at the sales potential of the manuscript. At the same time, the editorial role is less critical in shaping manuscripts because the author has gained more power. The author can insist that her themes are not to be tampered with; this control was unheard of in the past except for a handful of high-grossing authors. This can pressure the publisher to filter books onto the market that they might otherwise not have accepted. The end result is that new content is slowly making its way into mainstream houses.

It would seem that the forecast of publishing's demise is greatly exaggerated. Mainstream houses may not be doomed, but they do have to change the way they do business, and they are. The major immediate change, embraced to varying degrees across houses, is to allow authors to self-publish while at the same time publishing variations of their work in print and digital within the house. Some firms have been slow to adapt to this unprecedented model. Other houses have embraced the new hybrid style and have learned that it is a win-win situation. Other changes remain to be seen, but mainstream houses are survivors, and they are adapting. Those that don't will go by the wayside. Some of the more astute smaller digital houses might evolve into major publishing firms. After all, Zebra started as a small publisher of historical romance novels in the midst of the bodice-ripper craze of the 1970s and is now Kensington, one of the Big Eight.

Harlequin is likely to persist in the new world order simply because it is so strongly identified by consumers with the romance novel. It has evolved and adapted to market conditions over the years and is likely to continue to do so under HarperCollins. HarperCollins's expertise in the publishing business (versus Torstar's) is likely to press Harlequin to embrace further adaptive strategies. One change that inevitably follows a merger is a tightening of costs, which the new parent often insists on to help defray the expenses of purchasing its rival. This can result in a streamlining of Harlequin's often thinly differentiated lines that may actually strengthen its already strong market position.

This analysis of the industry has primarily looked at key insiders, but some glimpses have been caught of key others in the industry who stand at the input or output gates. These gatekeeping monitors have historically received sparse attention. They are critical in the shaping of the contemporary romance novel, however.

The agent's role today has basically supplanted the decision-making process once the near exclusive domain of editors. This is limited largely to mainstream houses. The agents bear a certain degree of responsibility by filtering out manuscripts that have successfully made their way over the transom at smaller digital houses. At the same time, they often come to the aid of digital writers who are negotiating contracts with mainstream houses. How their intervention affects the content of the subsequent mainstream novel has escaped attention. Their increasingly critical position in the gatekeeping tradition requires greater scrutiny.

The role of other gatekeeping monitors similarly suggests their role is increasingly important. Writer associations have always attempted to intervene with publishers on behalf of their members. The RWA's eventual acceptance of "fringe" romance writers helped nudge mainstream houses to more critically appraise works by these writers. RWA's check-and-balance role was particularly significant in reining in Harlequin when the corporate behemoth decided to move in a direction that might have negatively impacted romance writers. They actually saved Harlequin from itself, since its product would have been diluted if it started to promote vanity "Harlequin authors."

The role of reviewers has always historically garnered a certain amount of critical gatekeeping attention because their assessment of a new book can shape sales. They appear to have gained even more prominence today with Internet access, and readers considering this or that novel are turning more frequently to blog posts to decide whether to purchase this book or that.[49] The role of these bloggers in supplanting traditional critics has escaped scholarly attention.

These areas all suggest that, as this analysis comes to a close, there is still much that needs attention in the ever-evolving, ever-changing romance industry.

Conclusion

Contemporary mass-market publishing emerged in the wake of Pocket Books' successful entry into the market, which was fostered by a lethargic hardback industry that persisted in doing business the way it always had and saw no reason to change with the times. Pocket Books showed there was a demand for more economical books that were distributed to reach an audience beyond bookstores. Most of the paperback houses that started during the 1940s and 1950s are still in existence, though they might have been subsumed by other firms or changed their original thematic focus.

Initially, mass-market publishers simply reprinted a wide array of fiction already on the market in the more costly hardback format. Harlequin in Toronto fit this mode. It was no different from other paperback houses in North America, except that its market was confined primarily to Canada. It was one of the first mass-market houses to move to a specialized product. The slow shift to romance publishing was purely serendipitous. The publisher's wife, who served as editor, liked the "sweet" novels by Mills & Boon. The alignment with Mills & Boon in London was beneficial to both publishers. Mills & Boon had been publishing hardback romance novels for decades, but with the decline in the library market during the 1950s, it was looking for a new outlet for its books. Harlequin, in turn, was assured a steady stream of already proven novels. The arrangement was obviously satisfactory because Mills & Boon romances began to appear ever more frequently on Harlequin's list until 1964 when Mills & Boon romances became Harlequin's primary product. Harlequin sales were solid but not spectacular throughout the remainder of the 1960s. This would change in the 1970s after it hired Lawrence Heisey to run the company. One of the first things done under Heisey was to purchase Mills & Boon in 1971, thereby ensuring that Harlequin would have continued access to the novels published in the U.K.

Heisey was unencumbered with the "high culture" malaise that permeated the book industry during the 1950s and 1960s. He escaped this judgmental standard because he did not have a publishing background. He was, however, conversant with marketing to women in his former position at Proctor and Gamble. This experience translated well to Harlequin's product. One of the first things he recognized was that the books released by Harlequin did not have to be promoted by a single title but could be marketed as an identifiable product—romance novels. This helped identify the line to a wide audience once Heisey achieved distribution in the United States through Pocket Books in 1970. Sales soon soared. The success of Harlequin in penetrating the market in the United States can be ascertained by the relinquishing of domain to Harlequin by other publishers of romances in North America.

Genre fiction has never been held in high regard by those in the industry. Genre fiction started to garner more respect in the 1970s and 1980s, but this regard never spilled over to the romance genre. Publishers in the United States released romances, but this was done to round out the list, and though some authors were well received, most romance novels did not generate significant sales. The condescending attitude toward the genre and the relatively modest sales of romance novels would result in publishers conceding domain to Harlequin, at least in the contemporary romance market. Some houses would still release a few contemporary novels, but as we saw when Vivian Stephens joined Dell Candlelight in 1980, they didn't pay them much attention. Other houses continued to publish some romances, however, though most were historicals. The assumption was that since Harlequin didn't publish historical romances, publishers in the United States could still pick up some romance readers who were not served by Harlequin.

The content of Harlequin's romance also changed under Heisey during the 1970s. This change was atypically initiated by management.

The editors were still operating under the hardcore decency standard imposed by Mary Bonnycastle in the straight-laced 1950s, screening out steamier romances published by Mills & Boon in the U.K. Their assumption appears to have been that since the more staid romances were selling, readers were satisfied with the content and might resist any thematic changes. This is a fairly common practice: producers of consumer products generally assume that customers are satisfied because they are buying the product. It is only after a new product (or thematic variation) is enthusiastically embraced when it is introduced that it becomes obvious the demand for something different was not being sated.

Heisey's decision to overrule his editors was based on the success of the novels in the U.K. Still, Heisey was careful to determine whether his editors were correct or not, so he reverted to another tried-and-true testing pattern that is common in retailing but not common in publishing: blind sampling. The reader response to the test books showed that "it was clear they [the more sensual novels] should be published." Moreover, Heisey said that "some very good books had been held back from the basic series. They should have been published earlier." The new, bolder books intimated that couples in committed relationships had sexual activity before marriage. To make sure the new novels would not be off-putting to dedicated romance readers, the more sensual romances were introduced as a separate line. Presents novels stopped at the bedroom door, however. This was a bold step at Harlequin, but it paled compared to the sensuality of historical romances appearing in the United States during the 1970s.

The new sensual historical themes that dotted publishers' romance lists in the United States in the mid–1970s, christened bodice-rippers in the popular media, were introduced by Avon in 1972. Kathleen Woodiwiss's now classic *The Flame and the Flower* fit the direction Avon was taking: it was looking for and starting to publish original mass-market paperbacks, instead of simply reprinting hardback editions. Woodiwiss's novel slipped through the gates because it did not look (or read) like a traditional slim-tomed category romance. It was a best-seller and soon Avon was publishing other novels in the Woodiwiss style. Because the focus at Avon remained on single-title quality fiction, it never entered the fray that Woodiwiss's novel sparked in other houses in the United States.

A new product that garners consumer attention is often soon imitated by others. In order for this to happen, however, others must be closely monitoring the market, looking for a hot new trend. The delay in responding to the success of the new sensual historical format at Avon further underscores the frivolous attitude toward romances by other houses. Newly formed Zebra Books (1974)[1] strategically positioned its product to take advantage of emerging market trends—Walter Zacharius was surveying the mass-market field more closely than most because he was specifically looking for a competitive niche and recognized the interest surrounding Avon's sensual historical romances. It was a relatively small house, however, and was not looked at by the other houses as a serious player. It would only be after Playboy's successful mid-decade entry that others seemed to wake up. The success of Playboy prompted other publishers to enter the "hot" new market. It was, Mary Ann Stuart at Playboy observed, as if others were saying, "Hey, if Playboy can do it, so can we." It was management that was saying this, not the editors, since there were few editors overseeing romances at the time.

Stuart's desire to publish the more sensual historical novels was based on the classic gatekeeper traditional: she liked Rosemary Rogers's books and wanted to do some herself. Her ten years with Playboy Press carried some weight and helped her position the new line of books at Playboy. Other editors were not as astute. Most were new to publishing and had functioned mainly at the editorial assistant level for a year or two. They were suddenly promoted to editors on the managerial assumption that the only real qualification one needs to be able to evaluate a romance is to be female. It soon became apparent that management was wrong, and most of the lines that appeared in the second half of the 1970s would disappear within a few years. These young editors might have adapted if they had been allowed to settle in and sift romances into the production queue as good manuscripts came across their desk. Management, however, by setting arbitrary production quotas, forced editors to publish more manuscripts than they could find. The result was that the quality of the novels soon deteriorated. It didn't help that many late entries overly accentuated the sexual (versus the sensual) and pushed the rape theme, which, as Judy Sullivan at Walker Books observed, had become more socially problematic by the end of the decade.

The rape theme of the sensual historicals had always been somewhat problematic. Indeed, male managers at houses in the late 1970s were often aghast when they learned that the novels being released by their houses depicted rape. The rape theme in *The Flame and the Flower* was not a central focus of the romance, however. The rape theme was more pronounced in Rosemary Rogers's subsequent Avon books. Nevertheless, the rape theme was set in the distant past and so was not as "threatening" as it might have been in a contemporary novel. Rape also was not a raging social issue at the outset of the 1970s, but it became one by the close of the decade as feminist concerns about the disenfranchised position of women in society gained wider social currency. There were, then, not only too many poorly written and edited books chasing too few readers, but the focal point on which many sensual historical pivoted in the late (versus the early) 1970s just didn't resonate with readers by the close of the decade.

The failure of historical romance lines to capture sales was offset at outset of the 1980s by the market entry of Silhouette, the first major publishing house to directly challenge Harlequin's supremacy in the contemporary romance market. The decision to launch Silhouette was prompted by the termination of Pocket Books' distribution contract with Harlequin and Simon & Schuster's inside knowledge of just how lucrative Harlequin's product was. Simon & Schuster was able to respond so promptly to the termination in 1980 because Harlequin had given forewarning three years earlier that this might happen, so when it did, Silhouette was ready to go. Silhouette had no trouble getting products because Harlequin had for years been turning down would-be romances by budding American authors; the overwhelming majority of its novels were written by women in Great Britain who were filtered into the system by editors in London. The only exception to this "rule" was the introduction of best-selling author Janet Dailey to the Harlequin stable in 1974. This appears to have been done in London as a sop to pressure from management in Toronto to move beyond authors from the U.K. Once Dailey was introduced, no subsequent American romance novelist was published by Harlequin. London had done its duty. The failure of Toronto management to take advantage of Dailey's successful American format and push for more American-themed romances was due to their diverted attention to expanding Harlequin's empire beyond the romance market during the second half of the 1970s. This would later be viewed as a critical mistake and be rectified in the 1980s as Harlequin sold off its ancillary ventures and returned to basics in order to battle it out with Silhouette for market share.

Fred Kerner, Harlequin's editorial director, bridged the gap between gatekeeper and gatemaker in 1980 when he introduced Superromance shortly after the debut of Silhouette. It would be the first new romance product at Harlequin since the introduction of Presents in 1973. Superromance was an attempt to compete with Silhouette by introducing a longer, 100,000-word romance novel. Kerner can be viewed as a gatemaker because he actively developed Superromance; at the same time, Kerner fulfilled the more traditional role of gatekeeper because he simply built on the successful formula already in existence in the shorter Presents line. This suggests the gatekeeper/gatemaker role is not an either/or position inhabited by key decision-makers but exists on a continuum and posits a fruitful area for subsequent research on the decision making process.[2]

The new Superromance line was an initial success, so marketing pushed for more books to be released, despite Kerner's resistance. The quality of the books deteriorated, and sales declined. Marketing, which carried considerable clout at Harlequin, more so than most publishers at the time, felt the problem was not poor writing or editing but that the novels were too long for people to read and therefore unappealing. The decision was to cut the books to 80,000 words. Kerner objected that this would ruin the concept and that the loss of 20,000 words would inhibit character development and sub-plotting. Marketing didn't see how 20,000 words would make any difference in content. The customer did.

The introduction of Superromance was a qualified success. Books were longer but not thematically different from the central theme of Presents. It was the spark, however, that ignited the romance wars. Over the next few years, Silhouette and Harlequin vied with one another by introducing a potpourri of competitive products to stay on top of the market. The romance wars would prove too costly for generalist publisher Simon & Schuster, who acceded dominance back to Harlequin in 1984 by selling Silhouette to Harlequin, shifting attention to some of its other publishing ventures. Harlequin's very existence, however, was at stake; it had to win the romance wars since it had no alternative product to fall back on. The sales price was relatively modest, but Simon & Schuster was satisfied with the arrangements because it regained the lucrative Harlequin distribution contract in North America.

The romance wars of the 1980s were exacerbated by the introduction at Dell of the new liberated, contemporary Ecstasy line of romances. It would be the first thematic content change in the romance format since Avon introduced the so-called bodice-rippers in 1972 and Harlequin introduced Presents in 1973 to indicate that sexual activity occurred outside marriage.

The new theme was discovered in the best gatekeeping tradition by Vivian Stephens at Dell. Stephens had little publishing experience, but unlike some of her younger editorial colleagues in the historical field, she was in her midforties and more worldly wise. She was also under no pressure from management to generate significant sales. Management didn't expect anything from her except to keep releasing a few contemporary romances. Stephens herself did not feel compelled to impress management by trying to do something important. She was quite happy to just do "something I could enjoy without any competition." She did, however, feel that the sweet contemporaries did not accurately depict gender relationships at the outset of the 1980s but was unsure exactly how she could "update" the existing Candlelight line at Dell. The fact that she recognized that the novels didn't quite work for her—the women at Woolworth's that she talked to really didn't tell her much—meant that she would be open to submissions that didn't fit the established Candlelight format, so when she read Joan Hohl's *Morning Rose, Evening Savage*, she thought she found a way to introduce change in the content of the romance novel.

Stephens tentatively published Hohl's novel and was encouraged to do more like it because she received no negative feedback about the sex in it. The next book, Jane Castle's *Gentle Pirate*, surpassed the merely sensual and ultimately liberated the romance novel. This novel, more than its predecessor, captured for Stephens "all the things that are ... right now, the world today." It helped that the book was released under the Ecstasy imprint. This set the book apart from other books in the Candlelight line. The name itself differentiated it from the sweeter contemporary romances then on the market. This time there was little lag by other publishers in imitating the new product.

Three factors had changed between 1972 and 1981 that prompted publishers to more expeditiously spark the so-called romance revolution of the

1980s. First, publishers became aware during the 1970s of just how lucrative the romance market could be. The second feature ties into the first: Harlequin was vulnerable. Silhouette proved this and in the process reinforced the seemingly insatiable consumer habits of the romance reader—management at other houses made this assumption because it saw all the novels that Silhouette and Harlequin had on the market. And third, there were editors in place at the outset of the 1980s who could take advantage of market trends and competitively position products. The problem was that management, by again arbitrarily setting production quotas and requiring editors to move *now*, before they had a chance to survey the market, pushed editors into the uncomfortable role of gatemakers. Gatekeepers filter products into the market; gatemakers make the product before they can assess consumer likes and dislikes.

One of the more astute in-place editors was Carolyn Nichols. Her experience launching Second Chance at Love for Berkley/Jove in June 1981 and then Loveswept two years later at Bantam (May 1983) underscores how rapidly the market was changing. Nichols acted in the new role of gatemaker when she launched Second Chance but was quick to return to the gatekeeper tradition at Loveswept.

Nichols was slightly older than her twenty-something editorial counterparts at many other houses. This gave her some experience in the field that allowed her to immediately recognize the thematic changes introduced at Dell. In fact, she had wanted to do something along these lines a few years earlier (1978), but management at Berkley-Jove was not open to the suggestion, which Nichols didn't push because she seemed unsure herself as to exactly how the romance needed to be "updated." Seeing what Dell did with Ecstasy, she recognized that the new liberated format went beyond the merely sensual, and management, seeing the activity in the marketplace, now wanted to get a line on the market. Nichols homed in on one dimension of the new romance theme: love rediscovered. This was an astute understanding of the new demographics. Divorce had been slowly rising from its all-time low in 1960 to its peak between 1979 and 1981.[3] There was, in short, an upsurge in divorced women (and men) who were not soured on marriage because of their first experience and who still desired to find love "the second time around." Nichols set out to cater to this audience. She knew what she wanted; the problem was that there were few writers conversant with her desired thematic focus or the new sensual liberated format at this early junction. This prompted Nichols to become a gatemaker to "guide" would-be writers on what the new romance novel should entail. These guidelines ran five single-spaced pages and detailed elements of plot, setting, sexuality, and point of view, as well as a detailed composite of characteristics for the new hero and heroine.[4] A year later, when she moved to Bantam and replaced the moribund Circle of Love with Loveswept, she abandoned guidelines and returned to the traditional role of gatekeeper. This was done, she says, because guidelines were no longer necessary since there were now a wealth of romance novels on the market to which would-be writers could turn to assess successful storylines.

Many editors overseeing lines at the outset of the 1980s were not as astute as Nichols and started developing guidelines without a clear understanding of what it was in the Ecstasy novels that worked. They followed Nichols's lead by homing in on one dimension of the romantic theme. Some, like the packagers for Finding Mr. Right, just "miscued" the theme, trying too hard to thematically differentiate their line. Others, like Grunder at Rapture, misread the sensual liberated element and overly accentuated the sexual. These editors seemed to feel that if "x" line had three degrees of sex it in, and "y" line had four degrees of sex in it, then what they needed to do was to notch the sexual up to the fifth degree.

The romance revolution of the 1980s was a short-lived phenomenon. It was dubbed a revolution in the popular presses because of all the romances flooding the market. The books were definitely there during the first half of the 1980s, but the sales weren't. Most secular lines were gone within a few years. The romance market appeared to remain vibrant because Christian publishers entered the fray in the second half of the 1980s to meet their constituents' need for cleaner books. They did not last long either. Lack of sales in a highly competitive market prompted most who moved into romance publishing or increased romance production in the 1980s to either exit the romance field or cut product to a trickle, relinquishing dominance back to Harlequin. Harlequin regained supremacy over the romance market during the 1980s and maintained it without much trouble during the 1990s, even if it did drift away, once again, from its primary product.

Harlequin regained its competitive edge with the purchase of Silhouette in 1984, by which time most secular romance publishers in the United States had already concluded that their lines were not going anywhere. This helped shore up Harlequin's domination of the secular romance market. Harlequin also now owned Silhouette's Inspirational line. It was one of the few lines discontinued by Harlequin after the purchase, presumably because of poor sales. The Christian romance market was just beginning to burgeon, but management at Harlequin felt that it was a rather small niche and it would be more fruitful to focus on its secular romances. Their decision to exit the Christian romance market was no doubt internally viewed as an astute move since many of the Christian lines that appeared in the mid- to late 1980s would, like their secular counterparts, either discontinue or drastically reduce production. By the end of the 1980s, Harlequin was again the dominant romance publisher in North America. Indeed, its foray into the international arena that began in earnest in the late 1970s would make it the dominant romance publisher in the world as early as 1982. This was achieved by allowing editors in the respective countries to exercise their editorial judgment in selecting novels and lines that best suited their countrywomen and seeing that the translations were culturally nuanced.

Harlequin's dominant position in the 1990s is reminiscent of its drift away from romances in the second half of the 1970s, with similar consequences. There were a few successful new lines developed during Brian Hickey's tenure as chief executive officer of Harlequin during the 1990s. One was MIRA; another was Red Dress Ink. Both were overseen by Harlequin's subsequent CEO, Donna Hayes. Steeple Hill, Harlequin's Christian line, was also developed under Hickey. The international expansion continued as new markets in Eastern Europe started to open after the fall of the Berlin Wall in 1989–1990. Hickey was overly optimistic about these ventures, and many of Harlequin's forays into Eastern Europe would not be particularly successful. The real problem for Hickey was moving away from Harlequin's primary product, something Galloway once vowed never to do again. But Galloway, now Torstar's CEO, was busy fighting the newspaper wars in Canada and appears to have given Hickey a free hand, at least until the losses started to mount.

Hickey's decision to enter the children's educational publishing market was based on his personal experiences in failing to find adequate educational materials for his son. His subsequent justification for this "lucrative market" came after the fact: like Stuart at Playboy, Hickey had decided what he wanted to do and then filled in the blanks to justify his decision. It seemed like a sound move, thanks in part to Hickey's overoptimistic sales forecasts, but by the end of the 1990s, the losses were mounting and many of the acquisitions made in the 1990s were sold off at a loss. Complicating Harlequin's market position— which was still sound, largely because no one was attempting to seriously compete with it—was that many key Harlequin executives had been siphoned off from their strategic positions at Harlequin to shore up Children's Supplementary Educational Publishing (CSEP); their absence no doubt contributed to weak sales at Harlequin during the latter 1990s. This would change once Torstar decided to get "out of the money losing business" and return its focus to its primary product. Hayes would take over as CEO. She was, as Galloway said, a "real publisher," mainly because she was the first CEO to come from a publishing, versus a marketing, background. Her publishing credentials were bolstered by her development of MIRA and Red Dress at Harlequin before she was "kicked upstairs" to CSEP.

Hayes's executive role during the outset of the new millennium was instrumental in bringing Harlequin products into the twenty-first century. During her twelve years as Harlequin's CEO (2002–2013), Harlequin developed a potpourri of new, competitive lines; her only major misstep would be toward the end of her tenure, when she introduced the idea for a vanity line of romances, which she promptly withdrew after fierce opposition by Romance Writers of America. She also oversaw a major rebranding, which resulted in the eventual replacement of the separate Silhouette identifier, though she wisely kept many of the successful Silhouette lines: Silhouette Desire, for example, was simply renamed Harlequin Desire.

Hayes departed rather abruptly at the end of 2013. Her departure was preceded by accolades about her accomplishments from senior management at Torstar. These accolades also followed Hickey's departures. This led to some speculation on my part based on an assessment of the industry.

Sales were weak during the latter part of Hayes's tenure, but not enough to warrant nudging her out. My initial personal assessment was that she might be ill.[5] Events that followed her departure have led to a different conclusion.

Swinwood is amply qualified to take the helm at Harlequin after twenty-six years with the company. His mission, however, appears to have been to sell Harlequin. Every time corporate profits were off at Harlequin, the industry buzz was that Torstar was considering selling Harlequin. This time, Torstar followed through with the sale. The influx of capital was clearly desired to bolster Torstar's bottom lines, and the stock rose precipitously immediately after the sale was announced. I suspect that Hayes might not have been totally on board with Torstar's decision to sell Harlequin, and this facilitated her sudden decision to step down. Swinwood's job, then, was to finalize the sale of Harlequin, which had to be in the works at the time of his appointment to CEO, since Harlequin was sold within months of Swinwood's promotion.[6] The transition will likely temporarily stymie any product development. This may be an issue since the industry outside the mainstream is particularly vibrant, and this could keep Harlequin from developing new themes that are competitive with emerging trends. Harlequin under HarperCollins, however, will survive and remain vibrant. It would be fatuous for HarperCollins to seriously tamper with Harlequin's strong market position, though some "belt tightening" will no doubt occur, as it typically does after any costly acquisition.

The real developments in romance publishing at the outset of the twenty-first century have been outside the mainstream. Small publishers are not really challenging the position of mainstream publishers, but they are revitalizing the romance field. It has only been in the last few years that the Big Five have begun to respond to these developments and are making some attempts to reposition their romances to remain competitive. Their strong market position may be why they did not adapt sooner and why their response to "the threat" is still rather anemic.

The 1980s were referred to as a revolution in the romance industry because of the wealth of titles on the market. The real revolution started at the outset of the new millennium and continues to unfold. Indeed, there are more titles and themes on the market than ever today. The small houses are enduring, too; many have been competitively positioned since at least 2005. This is much different from the 1980s, when many lines disappeared within a few years. Most of the developments taking place today are occurring outside the major romance houses.

The New Digital Age

Digital books looked like an emerging new trend in 2000. Then the dot-com bubble burst, and most mainstream houses that had initially flirted with digital moved away from it, or, at least, didn't move dramatically forward. Only Sourcebooks among the Big Eight maintained a digital presence, and this was primarily because the executive editor and the publisher shared a computer background. Sourcebooks still didn't do much digitally because the market was off, but when digital started to percolate around 2010, it was one of the few among the Big Eight to have a digital program in place, and this enabled it to quickly establish a digital presence. Other mainstream publishers followed. They are quickly gaining traction by (1) pumping millions into developing digital internally or (2) acquiring smaller digital publishers. The early aughts, however, were left mainly to small publishers and self-published romance authors to fill the digital void. Ease of entry for them was facilitated by relatively modest start-up expenses. They capitalized on themes that were not embraced by most mainstream houses. Their books were also more reasonably priced in digital formats than what was available at most mass-market print romance publishers. The success of these entrepreneurs suggests the demand was there, just as it was once there when Pocket Books introduced a cheaper product that reached the consumer in a much more convenient manner than traditional bookstores. *Plus ça change, plus c'est la même chose!*

Strong inroads were initially made by those writing erotic novels, which have been dubbed xrotic in this analysis of the industry to separate them out from the degree of sexuality being filtered into mainstream houses. Ellora's Cave, Samhain, and Siren were among those that promptly garnered a digital presence; their romances quickly became known for their heightened eroticism.

Their early presence gave them a competitive edge over mainstream houses that mostly still hesitate to move into the xrotic digital world.[7] Xrotic male/male novels, paranormal ménage (MFM more so than FMF), and BDSM are particularly strong, and though mainstream publishers have ventured into BDSM love in the wake of *Fifty Shades*, their novels, including (and perhaps because of) *Fifty Shades*, don't go as far into this lifestyle as those published by xrotic presses. GLBTQ houses, traditional publishers of m/m novels for gays, are also catering to the interest of heterosexual women in male/male novels. Both xrotic and GLBTQ publishers understand that to stay competitive, they have to go beyond their traditional xrotic titles, which is why Cleis has recently launched a straight line of romance novels and Samhain is venturing into the horror genre left vacant with the exit of Dorchester. In other words, the "marginal"[8] presses are heading into the mainstream. This situation is reminiscent of maverick Kensington (Zebra) when it launched with a series of bodice-rippers in 1974, expanded its line over the years, and today has nudged its way into the Big Eight. Kensington maintains a strong line of romances and is Harlequin's major rival, which is why Harlequin twice attempted to purchase it. The implication is that one or more of the xrotic publishers may maintain their xrotic focus but successfully expand into other genres. It may also suggest that they are ripe to be co-opted by the major houses, much like digital publishers Entangled or Lyrical Press: the former is now part of St. Martin; the latter is now part of Kensington.

Digital publishing has also been embraced by self-published romance authors. Many of these novelists were interested in writing xrotica, but mainstream presses wouldn't publish them. Some went with the small digital publishers; others ventured out on their own into the world of self-publishing. The early years of self-publishing were somewhat problematic, but over the years the doors have opened wider and a host of sites, including the ubiquitous Amazon, now market their works. Self-published authors who are making their presence felt in digital space are now being approached by mainstream houses. Some hesitate, feeling that they can make more of a profit on their own, while others decline and do not want to have thematic restrictions (re)imposed on them. Still others are happy to strike a balance and (re)enter the mainstream. They are likely to do so on their own terms, however. This is atypical in the industry where you either played the game the way the house wrote the rules or you didn't get to play.

Traditionally, only well-established best-selling authors could stand up to their publishers.[9] This is beginning to change, though some houses still resist allowing the authors to "call the shots" or let them continue to self-publish when they are under contract. How far this will go and what impact it will have on the publishing industry are moot points at this early juncture. It does seem to be forcing romance publishers to examine more critically some thematic variations that they might not otherwise have considered publishing. The end result of this, and the self-publishing phenomenon, is to put more romances in the hands of more readers with a wider variety of themes than have traditionally been available from mainstream houses. If, as some have suggested, romance writers and readers were among the first to embrace digital, and romance publishers are now struggling to catch up digitally, the trends that are now emerging in the romance industry are likely to trickle out and affect publishers in other genres.

Mainstream Niches and the Little Guy

Mainstream publishers dominate the Young Adult market. There are two reasons for this. First, most mainstream publishers have a strong YA presence, even if romances are a small part of their overall list. The demand for YA books, and YA romances, appears to be met, though there are a few self-published authors who have made a mark in the field. Exactly how their books differ from those published by mainstream houses has not been addressed and poses a fruitful area for a content appraisal. Xrotic publishers who form the core of the small digital houses have a hands-off approach to YA fiction. They seem to recognize that the material they publish is on the fringe and take great strides to ensure that they do not attract attention for publishing socially inappropriate material. Sexual activity with children under eighteen is verboten, and this means, one publisher emphasized, not someone who is 17.9999 years of age. There are, however, two areas that small presses share with mainstream houses: Christian romances and multicultural romances.

Christian Publishing

To counterbalance the overt sexuality of xrotica and the increasing sexual dimension of the overwhelming majority of mainstream romances today, the Christian market has undergone revitalization. Christian houses are entering the market more cautiously than they did in the 1980s, increasing the number of titles available but not doing so exponentially. Harlequin has made a successful reentry into this niche, but its novels are largely confined to secular big-box retailers frequented by romance aficionados with a Christian orientation. Despite the two years Harlequin spent developing the Love Inspired series, it was not successful in making inroads into Christian outlets, try as it might.

Harlequin has recently made an attempt to nuance its books toward a more traditional Christian market with Heartsong. Harlequin purchased the Heartsong series from Christian publisher Barbour in 2012, but the line is not available at retail outlets and is sent by direct mail, primarily to Barbour customers, without any apparently off-putting secular (Harlequin) identifier.

The Christian market is more successfully developed by Christian publishers who accentuate the Christian element more than Harlequin but don't push it to the degree they did in the 1980s. This makes their novels more attractive to an audience that just wants to read good, clean romance novels. This is why the Amish novels that they produce are so successful: these novels reflect old-world values more than they do a Christian theme, though the Amish lifestyle is, by default, a Christian one. The Internet has helped to expand market entry for Christian-themed romances by Christian publishers because they are not marketed so much as "Christian" romances, but just as good, wholesome romances to an audience that might not frequent Christian bookstores, which, at any rate, are going the way of their secular counterparts.

HarperCollins is a mainstream publisher that is particularly strong in this market, largely because it has purchased traditional Christian publishers and has not tampered with the Christian theme. Harlequin's inspirational romances would be a good fit with HarperCollins Christian. The Harlequin moniker would be kept, much as HarperCollins has done with Zondervan and Thomas Nelson, but editorial and marketing would be coordinated under the Christian umbrella without necessarily trimming existing Harlequin editorial staff. It might also "crank up" the Christian theme that is a bit attenuated in the Love Inspired series at Harlequin, since the editorial staff at HarperCollins is more "attuned" to the Christian market because of their association with traditional Christian publishing such as Zondervan and Thomas Nelson. This could be a serious challenge to the smaller Christian publishers who don't have the financial clout that HarperCollins has.

Multicultural Love

African American romances are extensively developed by mainstream houses. Vivian Stephens filtered a few romances with African American couples into the system at Dell and a few more titles when she became editor at Harlequin American Romance. Kensington, however, is the one that initially developed an African American line of romances in 1994. It sold the Arabesque line to BET books a few years later (1998) because it generated a significant sum when it was needed at Kensington. Kensington stayed in the romance game with women's fiction that featured African American characters, and when its no-compete contract with BET expired, it reentered the African American romance market with Dafina in 2000.

Harlequin was planning to start a line of African American romances and had actually begun acquiring manuscripts in 2005. It was quicker off the mark than the company expected to be because it was able to purchase BET's romance line. Harlequin not only jump-started its foray into African American romance publishing with this purchase, but it was also fortunate to hire most of BET's experienced editorial staff. The strong market presence of Kensington's Dafina series and Harlequin's Kimani line has prevented smaller African American romance publishers like Genesis from garnering much attention. These small traditional African American publishers are also overshadowed by the host of mainstream houses that release romances with African American characters as part of their general romance offerings. Regardless of who publishes these stories, however, they all tend to be intra-racial rather than interracial. Interracial love is left largely to the small digital publishers.

Multicultural romances get a lot of attention today, and most houses release some novels that revolve around romantic relationships between couples of disparate racial backgrounds. Since these novels are filtered onto the list with the other titles, those interested in reading about interracial couples may have difficulty finding these stories. This is less problematic with small digital presses where interracial love is their *raison d'être*. Most of these relationships depict love between a black woman and a man of another race. The hero is often (though not always) Caucasian. This reflects the romantic relationships of many of the women who started the presses and found, like their counterparts in other areas, that the books they liked to read and write were not being released by mainstream houses. Few mainstream publishers have followed the small presses into interracial love, despite lip service that some of their romances involve multicultural couples. A line featuring a Latina heroine and a hero of another race may open the door for romance publishers to break into the fast-growing Hispanic market, but Kensington's earlier failure to make headway with intra-racial (Latino/Latina) romances may discourage other mainstream houses from considering such an interracial venture, leaving the field open to the small digital houses, at least for the time being.

*****

Tracing the history of the romance publishing industry puts into perspective the complexity and vibrancy of the industry. This is sometimes lost sight of when critics focus only on one house, more often than not Harlequin or Mills & Boon, or on a particular line of books, assuming that the line under scrutiny is representative of all romance novels. The focus on Harlequin is understandable, but Harlequin's market position has always taken into account what other (mainstream) publishers in the romance field are doing, or, more specifically, not doing. This is truer today than at any other earlier point in time. Nevertheless, Harlequin does not publish, or publishes infrequently, xrotic romances, m/m romances, or interracial romances. Any critical analysis that loses sight of what others are doing in the romance field is to misread, and misunderstand, the romance market.

Harlequin has kept abreast of market trends in the romance field because romance publishing is its *raison d'être*, even if it, like most mainstream publishers, has not paid much attention to the small digital romance houses. Some in the field have expressed concern over the acquisition of Harlequin by HarperCollins and how this might affect the content of Harlequin's product. Major thematic changes are not likely to occur, at least for the foreseeable future, since a key reason for purchasing Harlequin was to strengthen HarperCollins's foray into the romance field. Indeed, with Avon and HarperCollins Christian, and now Harlequin, HarperCollins is positioned to be the dominant player in the romance industry, with upstart Kensington holding a distant second-place position in the romance market, at least in terms of titles released. Challenges abound, however. It will be interesting to see if some of the smaller houses, now at the periphery of the industry, gain traction and become serious contenders in the years ahead and how their competitive positions, and the realignment of Harlequin within HarperCollins, give rise to developments within mainstream romance publishing.

Key insiders, such as editors, have been studied as gatekeepers before. These pivotal decision makers are typically looked at as *the* ones who decide what products enter the production cycle. This analysis goes a step further and examines the influence of management in shaping the gatekeepers' response to products they examine. It was found that when management presses for more products than the gatekeeper can find in their traditional filtering role, gatekeepers may be forced into the uncomfortable position of gatemaker. In the case of the romance industry, it appears to have been a temporary adaptive strategy employed by editors to address a rapidly changing task environment. The degree to which the gatemaker role is applicable to other industries remains to be seen, and, if it does exist, whether it is always a temporary adaptive measure fostered on them by management. This analysis also recognizes other gatekeepers beyond those inhabiting positions within publishing houses, though it does so only briefly since the focus was on events within the industry. Changes taking place within romance publishing suggest the growing importance of at least three related gatekeepers: (1) the increased prominence of agents as gatekeepers within the mainstream houses today, and how this affects the traditional role of editors in selecting products; (2) the surge in blogs that evaluate novels, once the near-exclusive domain of a handful of literary critics; and (3) the influence of formal organizations, such as Romance Writers of America and *Romantic Times*, in resisting or embracing emerging writers and organizations, such as self-published authors and xrotic publishers, and how this affects or retards the acceptance of these same authors or organizations in the overall market.

It would appear that the story of the romance industry is not completed with this analysis. Indeed, it appears the story is just beginning.

Chapter Notes

Introduction

1. John Tebbel, *A History of Book Publishing in the United States, Vol. 3, The Golden Age Between Two Wars: 1920–1940*. New York: R. R. Bowker, 1978: 59.

2. John Tebbel, *A History of Book Publishing in the United States, Vol. 3*: 59.

3. Leonard Shatzkin, *In Cold Type: Overcoming the Book Crisis*. Boston: Houghton Mifflin, 1982: 194.

4. Kenneth Davis, *Two-Bit Culture: The Paperbacking of America*. Boston: Houghton Mifflin, 1984: 266.

5. Kenneth Davis, *Two-Bit Culture*, 351.

6. John Tebbel, *A History of Book Publishing in the United States, Vol. 3*: 352.

7. John Tebbel, *A History of Book Publishing in the United States, Vol. 3*: 352. See also Walter W. Powell, "From Craft to Corporation: The Impact of Outside Ownership on Book Publishing," in *Individuals in Mass Media Organizations: Creativity and Constraints*, eds. James S. Ettema and C. Charles Whitney. Beverly Hills: Sage, 1983: 33–52.

8. Eighty percent of all mass-market fiction is genre fiction.

9. The serious investigation of popular culture only began to take on the trappings of a distinctly scholarly and concomitantly academic enterprise with the founding of the *Journal of Popular Culture* in the summer of 1967. See Dennis R. Hall, "The Study of Popular Culture: Origin and Developments," *Studies in Popular Culture* 6 (1984): 16–25.

10. This information is compiled by Simba Information, which regularly tracks book industry statistics. "Focus on RWA: 2011 ROMStatReport," November 2012: 8. www.rwa.org/trends. Accessed 7 July 2013.

11. Ron Charles, "Romance Novels Still Fighting for Respect," *The Washington Post*, 4 July 2009, www.voices.washingtonpost.com/sortstack/2009/07/4-roamnce-novels-a-crying-shame. Accessed 25 May 2013.

12. Sara Fitzgerald, "Romance, Writ Large," *The Washington Post*, 30 April 2006, www.washingtonpost.com/article/2006/04/29/AR20060429000280. Accessed 15 June 2013.

13. "Romance Industry Statistics." *Romance Writers of America*, www.rwanational.org/statistics. Accessed 15 June 2013.

14. In 2011, 474 titles by 236 authors under 80 imprints appeared on the consolidated (2007–2011) best-seller rankings (*New York Times*, *USA Today*, and *Publishers Weekly*), with 51 new authors hitting best-seller status in that one year. "Focus on RWA: 2011 RomStatReport," November 2012: 8, www.rwa.org/trends. Accessed 7 July 2013.

15. Lewis Coser, Charles Kadushin and Walter W. Powell, *Books: The Culture and Commerce of Publishing*. New York: Basic Books, 1982: 264–265.

16. Interview with Leonard Shatzkin, author of *In Cold Type*, September 1983.

17. It has been argued that the novel has its roots much earlier than this (see *The Guardian*), though the triumvirate mentioned is still largely viewed as responsible for developing, or at least popularizing, the "modern" novel (see Ian Watt). www.theguardian.com/books/booksblog/2010/jul/23/novel-centuries-older. Accessed 16 October 2014; Ian Watt, *The Rise of the Novel*. London: Chatto and Windus, 1957.

18. Ian Watt, *The Rise of the Novel*.

19. Cited by Ian Watt, *The Rise of the Novel*, 219.

20. Jean Jacques Rousseau, *Emily*. London: J. M. Dent & Sons, 1957: 331.

21. See Bernard I. Murstein, *Love, Sex, and Marriage*. New York: Springer, 1974: 260–261.

22. John Markert, *The Social Impact of Sexual Harassment*. Spokane, WA: Marquette Books, 2010: 26. Myra Marx Ferree and Beth B. Hess, *Controversy and Coalition: The New Feminist*

Movement Across Four Decades of Change, 3rd edition. New York: Rutledge, 2000: 41–42. J. McLaughlin, *Feminist Social and Political Theory*. New York: Palgrave Macmillan, 2003: 9.

23. John Cawelti, *Adventure, Mystery, and Romance*. Chicago: University of Chicago Press, 1976.

24. His chapter on best-selling melodramas touches on the "classic" gothic romance but doesn't address mass-market romance novels, despite the book's title, *Adventure, Mystery, and Romance*.

25. S. Brown, "Consumption Behavior in the Sex and Shopping Novels of Judith Krantz: A Post-Structuralist Perspective," *Advances in Consumer Research* 23 (1996): 43–48.

26. Tania Modleski, *Loving with a Vengeance: Mass-Produced Fantasies for Women*. New York: Methuen, 1982: 83.

27. Janice A. Radway, *Reading the Romance: Women, Patriarchy, and Popular Culture*. Chapel Hill: University of North Carolina Press, 1984: 33. Gothic romances have undergone a recent revival, though they have been updated to incorporate contemporary elements into the traditional storyline.

28. Laura Vivanco has recently addressed these distinctions. Laura Vivanco, *For Love and Money: The Literary Art of the Harlequin and Mills & Boon Romance*. Tirril Hall, Tirril, Penrith, CA: Humanities-Ebooks, 2011. See also Laura Vivanco, "Feminism and Early Twenty-First-Century Harlequin and Mills & Boon Romances," *Journal of Popular Culture*, Vol. 45, no. 5 (2012): 1060–1089.

29. Cited by Christopher Cerf and Victor Navasky in *The Experts Speak*. New York: Pantheon, 1984: 160.

30. Bob Minzesheimer, "Best-Seller List Surprise Destination for 'Orphan Train': Unlikely Tale Punches Author's Ticket to Top," *USA Today*, 17 July 2014: 7B.

31. Walker Percy discusses the manuscript's plight in his forward to the original edition.

32. David Manning White, "The Gatekeeper: A Case Study in the Selection of News," *Journalism Quarterly* 27 (1950): 383–90.

33. Howard Becker, *Art Worlds*. Berkeley: University of California Press, 1982. M. Csikszemtmihalyi, *Creativity: Flow and the Psychology of Discovery and Invention*. New York: HarperCollins, 1996. M. D. Regan, "Physicians as Gatekeepers," *New England Journal of Medicine* (Dec. 1987): 1731–34. M. Rothenberg, "New Information Gatekeepers Arising," *Public Relations Journal* 50 (1994): 22–25.

34. D. Berkowitz, "Refining the Gatekeeping Metaphor for Local News," *Journal of Broadcasting & Electronic Media* 90 (1990): 55–72. Herbert Gans, *Deciding What's News*. New York: Random House, 1980. T. K. Chan and J. W. Lee,

"Factors Affecting Gatekeepers' Selection of Foreign News: A National Survey of Newspaper Editors," *Journalism Quarterly* 69 (1992): 554–62. W. Smith, "Seducing the Gatekeepers: Statistics Canada's Daily and the News Media," *Statistical Journal of the UN Economic Commission for Europe* 13 (1992): 132–62.

35. Lewis Coser, "Publishers as Gatekeepers of Ideas," *The Annals of the American Association of Political and Social Sciences* 421 (1975): 14–22. Lewis Coser, Charles Kadushin and Walter W. Powell, *Books: The Culture and Commerce of Publishing*. R. Simon and J. Fyfe, *Editors as Gatekeepers: Getting Published in the Social Sciences*. Lanham, Maryland: Rowman & Littlefield, 1992. A.S. Berg, *Max Perkins: Editor of Genius*. New York: Washington Square Press, 1978.

36. Herbert Gans, *Deciding What's News*.

37. Harrison C. White, "Where Do Markets Come From?" *American Sociological Review* 48 (1981): 147–60.

38. Harrison C. White, "Where Do Markets Come From?" Paul DiMaggio and Walter W. Powell, "The Iron Cage Revised: Institutional Isomorphism and Collective Rationality in Organizational Fields," *American Sociological Review* 48 (1981): 147–60.

39. Paul DiMaggio and Walter W. Powell, "The Iron Cage Revised."

40. John Ryan and Richard A. Peterson, "The Product Image: The Fate of Creativity in Country Music Song-Writing," in *Individuals in Mass Media Organizations*, edited by J. Eltma and D. Charles Whitney. Beverly Hills: Sage, 1980: 137–162.

41. S. Cohen and J. Young. *Manufacturing of News: Social Problems, Deviance and the Mass Media*. Beverly Hills: Sage, 1981. Howard Becker, *Art Worlds*. Wendy Griswold, "The Writing on the Mud Wall: Nigerian Novels and the Imaginary Village," *American Sociological Review* 57 (1992): 709–24.

42. Joseph Schumpeter, *Capitalism, Socialism and Democracy*, 3rd edition. Cambridge: Harvard University Press, 1950.

Chapter 1

1. Kenneth Davis, *Two-Bit Culture: The Paperbacking of America*. Boston: Houghton Mifflin, 1984: 15–17.

2. Kenneth Davis, *Two-Bit Culture*, 31–44.

3. John Tebbel, *A History of Book Publishing in the United States, Vol. 1: The Creation of an Industry, 1630–1865*. New York: R. R. Bowker, 1972: 203.

4. John Tebbel, *A History of Book Publishing in the United States, Vol. 1*, 207.

5. John Tebbel, *A History of Book Publishing in the United States, Vol. 1*, 207.

6. Richard D. Brown, *Modernization: The Transformation of American Life, 1600–1865.* New York: Hill and Wang, 1976: 103, 137–40.
7. John Tebbel, *A History of Book Publishing in the United States, Vol. 1,* 241.
8. John Tebbel, *A History of Book Publishing in the United States, Vol. 1,* 207. Madeleine B. Stern (ed.), *Publishers for Mass Entertainment in Nineteenth-Century America.* Boston: C. K. Hall, 1980.
9. The term "pirated" is somewhat of a misnomer because it is widely used to describe the unauthorized, but not illegal, reprinting of English novels prior to the International Copyright Act of 1891.
10. John Tebbel, *A History of Book Publishing in the United States, Vol. 1,* 252–54.
11. John Tebbel, *A History of Book Publishing in the United States, Vol. 1,* 242–44. John Tebbel, *The Media in America.* New York: Thomas Y. Crowell, 1974: 11–13. John Dessauer, "Book Publishing: What It Is, What It Does," in *American Mass Media,* eds. Robert Atwan, Barry Orton and William Vesterman. New York: Random House, 1982: 107.
12. John Tebbel, *A History of Book Publishing in the United States, Vol. 2: The Expansion of an Industry, 1865–1919.* New York: R. R. Bowker, 1972: 507.
13. John Tebbel, *A History of Book Publishing in the United States, Vol. 2.* New York: R. R. Bowker, 1972: 245–47. Madeleine Stern (ed.), *Publishers for Mass Entertainment in Nineteenth-Century America,* 229–34.
14. John Tebbel, *A History of Book Publishing in the United States, Vol. 1,* 246.
15. Wendy Griswold, "American Character and the American Novel," *American Journal of Sociology* 86 (1981): 740–65.
16. John Tebbel, *A History of Book Publishing in the United States, Vol. 1,* 246–48; John Tebbel, *The Media in America,* 248–50.
17. John Tebbel, *A History of Book Publishing in the United States, Vol. 1.* New York: R. R. Bowker, 1972: 245–47; Madeleine Stern (ed.), *Publishers for Mass Entertainment in Nineteenth-Century America,* 229–34.
18. John Tebbel, *A History of Book Publishing in the United States, Vol. 2: The Expansion of an Industry, 1865–1919.* New York: R. R. Bowker, 1975: 485–86. Robert Escarpit, *The Book Revolution.* London: George G. Harrap, 1966: 23.
19. John Tebbel, *A History of Book Publishing in the United States, Vol.2:* 486.
20. Wendy Griswold, "American Character and the American Novel."
21. Charles Kindleberger, *Manias, Panics, and Crashes: A History of Financial Crises.* New York: Basic Books, 1978: 133, 153–60, 211–26.
22. Allen Crider, *Mass Market Publishing in America.* Boston: G. K. Hall, 1982: 218. Leonard Shatzkin, *In Cold Type; Overcoming the Book Crisis.* Boston: Houghton Mifflin, 1982. John Tebbel, *The Media in America;* Robert Escarpit, *The Book Revolution;* Kenneth Davis, *Two-Bit Culture.*
23. Robert Escarpit, *The Book Revolution,* 26; Allen Crider, *Mass Market Publishing in America,* 204.
24. John Tebbel, *A History of Book Publishing in the United States, Vol. 3: The Golden Age Between Two Wars, 1920–1940.* New York: R. R. Bowker, 1978: 508.
25. Leonard Shatzkin, *In Cold Type,* 193; John Dessauer, "Book Publishing," 108.
26. Kenneth Davis, *Two-Bit Culture,* 12–29.
27. Leonard Shatkin, *In Cold Type,* 194.
28. John Tebbel, *A History of Book Publishing in the United States, Vol. 4: The Great Change, 1940–1980.* New York: R. R. Bowker, 1981: 376.
29. Allen Crider, *Mass Market Publishing in America,* 223.
30. John Tebbel, *A History of Book Publishing in the United States, Vol. 4,* 32.
31. John Dessauer, "Book Publishing," 108; Allen Crider, *Mass Market Publishing in America,* 222–23.
32. John Tebbel, *A History of Book Publishing in the United States, Vol. 4,* 348.
33. John Dessauer, "Book Publishing," 108; Allen Crider, *Mass Market Publishing in America,* 222–23.
34. Lewis Coser, Charles Kadushin and Walter W. Powell, *Books : The Culture and Commerce of Publishing.* New York: Basic Books, 1982: 97–117.
35. Kenneth Davis, *Two-Bit Culture,* 101–141.
36. Ian Watt, *The Rise of the Novel.* Berkeley: University of California Press, 1967: 171.
37. John Tebbel, *A History of Book Publishing in the United States, Vol. 4:* 695–720; Allen Crider, *Mass Market Publishing in America,* 26.
38. Charles Rembar, *The End of Obscenity.* New York: Random House, 1969.
39. Though we often don't look directly at the reader or writer of romances in this analysis of the industry, one of the recurring complaints of both is their hesitancy—until recently, but still lingering—to indicate that they read or write romance fiction.

Chapter 2

1. Allen Crider, *Mass Market Publishing in America.* Boston: G. K. Hall, 1982: 139. Phyllis Berman, "They Call Us Illegitimate," *Forbes,* 6 March 1978: 37; Rosemary Guiley, *Love Lines: A Romance Reader's Guide to Printed Pleasures.* New York: Facts on File Publications, 1983; *Thirty Years of Harlequin 1949–79.* Toronto: Harlequin Books, 1979.
2. Allen Crider, *Mass Market Publishing in America,* 136.

3. Rosemary Guiley, *Love Lines*, 156; Kenneth Davis, *Two-Bit Culture: The Paperbacking of America*. Boston: Houghton Mifflin, 1984.

4. See Donald Creighton, *Canada's First Century: 1867–1967*. New York: St. Martin's Press, 1970. Ronald Cheffins, *The Constitutional Process in Canada*. Toronto: McGraw-Hill, 1969.

5. These shows, wrote Betty Friedan in 1964, quoting MGM producer Irving Elman, are built around two men: a young bachelor and a middle-aged widower. The bachelors, such as Dr. Kildare and Ben Casey, are available for a fantasy affair with the young housewife [viewers]; the widowers, like Dr. Starke in *The Eleventh Hour*, are available for the older housewives. Betty Friedan, "Television and the Feminine Mystique, Part I," *TV Guide: The First 25 Years*, edited by Jay S. Harris. New York: New American Library, 1980: 93–95. See also Richard Gehman, "Caseyitis," *TV Guide: The First 25 Years*, edited by Jay S. Harris. New York: New American Library, 1980: 63–65.

6. The wholesome depiction of domestic life, with the husband as patriarch solving the children's various dilemmas while the wife serves the family meal in a spic-and-span house, can be found in such long-running popular family situation comedies as *The Donna Reed Show* (1958–1966), *The Adventures of Ozzie and Harriet* (1942–1966), and *Leave It to Beaver* (1957–1963). In Part 2 of her "Television and the Feminine Mystique" for *TV Guide*, Friedan asks producer Norman Felton why the moronic housewife image in these and similar prime-time programs dismisses the twenty-four million women who work outside the home. "He explained: 'If you have a woman lead in a television series, she has to be either married or unmarried. If she's unmarried, what's wrong with her? After all, it's housewives we're appealing to, and marriage is their whole life. If she's married, what's her husband doing in the background? He must not be very effective. He should be making the decisions...For a woman to make decisions, to triumph over anything, would be unpleasant, dominant, masculine. After all, most women are housewives, at home with children; most women are dominated by men, and they would react against woman who succeeded at anything.'" Such an attitude goes a long way to explain the typecasting of unmarried working romance heroines during the period. Betty Friedan, "Television and the Feminine Mystique, Part II: Monsters n the Kitchen," *TV Guide: The First 25 Years*, edited by Jay S. Harris. New York: New American Library, 1980: 95–98.

7. Interview with W. Lawrence Heisey. See also Margaret Ann Jensen, *Love's Sweet Return: The Harlequin Story*. Toronto: The Women's Press, 1984.

8. One of the editors interviewed in the 1980s said she could (almost) always spot a romance written by a man under a female pseudonym, because men always assessed the heroine in overly flattering terms, while women, no matter how attractive, always find some aspect of their physical appearance imperfect.

9. Margaret Ann Jensen, *Love's Sweet Return: The Harlequin Story*. Rosemary Guiley, *Love Lines*. Allen Crider, *Mass Market Publishing in America*.

10. Elaine Showalter (ed.), *The New Feminist Criticism: Essays on Women, Literature, and Theory*. New York: Pantheon Books, 1985: 5.

11. Judith Fetterley, *The Resisting Reader: A Feminist Approach to American Fiction*. Bloomington: Indiana University Press, 1978: 1–11, 72–100.

12. Rosalind Coward, "Are Women's Novels Feminist Novels?" *Feminist Review* 5 (1980): 53–64. See also Elizabeth Abel (ed.), *Writing and Sexual Difference*. Chicago: University of Chicago Press, 1982.

13. Peter Mann, *The Romance Novel: A Survey of Reading Habits*. London: Mills & Boon, 1968.

14. In his two-page introduction to his survey of reading habits, Mann reviews the problems with his sample. He expressly cautions against accepting his findings as representative of all Mills & Boon/Harlequin purchasers. The publishers in the preface, however, indicate an acceptance of Mann's study and view his findings as indicative of Mills & Boon/Harlequin readers.

15. *Women in America: Indicators of Social and Economic Well-Being, March 2011*. U.S. Department of Commerce, Economics and Statistic Administration and Executive Office of the President, Office of Management and Budget. www.whitehouse.gov/administration/eop/cwg/data-on-women. Accessed 30 June 2012.

16. I have chosen to use the term "fifties" romances for these novels produced in the 1960s to avoid confusion. The term "sixties" often connotes changes in attitudes taking place on college campuses during this period; "fifties" more adequately reflects the content of these early, sweet romances.

17. Rosemary Guiley, *Love Lines*, 155; Allen Crider, *Mass Market Publishing in America*, 138.

18. Information in this section is based on interviews with W. Lawrence Heisey unless otherwise specified.

19. John Tebbel, *A History of Book Publishing in the United States, Vol. 4: The Great Change, 1940–1980*. New York: R. R. Bowker, 1981: 35.

20. Joseph McAleer shows that Mills & Boon also capitalized on the branding of its novels as romances, but it would not be until the affiliation with Harlequin that Mills & Boon would begin to promote its books as a line, which is where McAleer's history of Mills & Boon (1908 through 1972) leaves off. See Joseph McAleer,

Passion's Fortune: The Story of Mills & Boon. Oxford: Oxford University Press, 2000.

21. *Statistical Abstract of the United States,* 1980. Washington, DC: U.S. Government Printing Office, 1981.

22. See also Allen Crider, *Mass Market Publishing in America.*

23. Benjamin M. Compaine, *The Book Industry in Transition: An Economic Study of Book Distribution and Marketing.* White Plains, N.Y.: Knowledge Industry Publications, 1978.

24. Interview with Katherine Orr, who at the time (1980s) was director of public relations at Harlequin.

25. A study of audience television viewership in 1977–1978 by Frank and Greenberg indicates that soap opera viewership was extremely high (80 percent) among adult female married homemakers. Ronald E. Frank and Marshall G. Greenberg, *The Public's Use of Television: Who Watches and Why.* Beverly Hills: Sage, 1980: 109–110. See also Thomas Skill and Mary Cassata, "Soap Opera Women: An Audience View," *Life on Daytime Television,* edited by Mary Cassata and Thomas Skill. Norwood, N.J.: Ablex Publishing, 1983: 23–36.

26. Yankelovich, Skelly and White, Inc., *Consumer Research Study on Reading and Book Purchasing.* New York: Book Industry Study Group, 1982.

27. Jay Dixon, *The Romance Fiction of Mills & Boon, 1909–1990s.* London: UCL Press, 1999.

28. Interview with Katherine Orr.

29. Information in this section is based on interviews with Katherine Orr unless otherwise specified. See also *Harlequin Annual Report: Ten Years of Harlequin.* Toronto: Harlequin Enterprises, 1980.

30. Rosemary Guiley, *Love Lines.*

31. Rosemary Guiley, *Love Lines.*

32. Rosemary Guiley in *Love Lines.* Mills & Boon did publish non–British authors, such as New Zealand romance novelist Essie Summers. It had not previously published a romance novelist from the United States, however.

33. Harlequin would introduce an American line, but not until the American theme had met with overwhelming success among romance readers in the 1980s.

34. John Cawelti, *Adventure, Mystery, and Romance.* Chicago: University of Chicago Press, 1976. Gillian Beers, *The Romance.* London: Methuen, 1970. Heather Dubrow, *Genre.* London: Methuen, 1982. Rosemary Guiley, *Love Lines.*

35. Rosemary Guiley, *Love Lines*: 156–57.

36. Interview with David Galloway.

37. Thomas J. Peters and Robert H. Waterman Jr., *In Search of Excellence: Lessons from America's Best-Run Companies.* New York: Harper & Row, 1982: 293–94.

Chapter 3

1. Allen Crider, *Mass Market Publishing in America.* Boston: C. K. Hall, 1982.

2. Allen Crider, *Mass Market Publishing in America.* See also Walter W. Powell, "From Craft to Corporation, The Impact of Outside Ownership on Book Publishing," in *Individuals in Mass Media Organizations: Creativity and Constraints,* edited by James S. Ettema and C. Charles Whitney. Beverly Hills: Sage, 1983.

3. Rosemary Guiley, *Love Lines: A Romance Reader's Guide to Printed Pleasures.* New York: Facts on File Publications, 1983: 84. Elizabeth Mansfield, "Elizabeth Mansfield's Personal Guide to Romantic Fiction," *Romantic Times* 2 (1981): 15.

4. Rosemary Guiley, *Love Lines,* 85.

5. Rosemary Guiley, *Love Lines.* See also Elizabeth Mansfield, "Tell Me a Tale of Love...," *Romantic Times* 10 (1983): 18–19; Katherine Falk and Elena Kolb, "Telling the Romance Styles Apart," *Publishers Weekly,* 13 November 1981: 39.

6. Rosemary Guiley, *Love Lines,* 89; Vivian Jennings, "At Long Last, Love," in *Writing Romantic Fiction: For Love and Money,* edited by Susan Whittlesey Wolf. Cincinnati: Writer's Digest Books, 1983: 2.

7. Judith Murray, "Call of the Cliffhangers," *Romantic Times* 9 (1983): 11, 34. See also Rosemary Guiley, *Love Lines.*

8. Kenneth Davis, *Two-Bit Culture: The Paperbacking of America.* Boston: Houghton Mifflin, 1984: 356–59.

9. Kenneth Davis, *Two-Bit Culture.*

10. Information in this section is based on interviews with Nancy Coffey unless otherwise cited.

11. See also Rosemary Guiley, *Love Lines,* 65.

12. See also Rosemary Guiley, *Love Lines,* 228.

13. See also Rosemary Guiley, *Love Lines,* 65.

14. See also Rosemary Guiley, *Love Lines.* Lila Frelicher, "Millions of Women Avid for Avon's Erotic Historical Romances," *Publishers Weekly,* October 6, 1974: 44.

15. Kenneth Davis, *Two-Bit Culture,* 361.

16. Rosemary Guiley, *Love Lines,* 220–221.

17. Cited by Rosemary Guiley in *Love Lines,* 127.

18. Lila Frelicher, "Millions of Women Avid for Avon's Erotic Historical Romances."

19. Lila Frelicher, "Millions of Women Avid for Avon's Erotic Historical Romances."

20. Zebra (and Pinnacle would be redubbed Kensington when it began to expand beyond the romance field.

21. Information about Zebra is from the founder's son, Stephen Zacharius, who is now the President and Chief Executive Officer of Kensington. Stephen Zacharius says Mr. Stein

was a distributor of Lancer Books; however, an interview with Irwin Stein by John Benson has him as a partner. See John Benson, "Interview with Irwin Stein," *Confessions, Romances, Secrets, & Temptations: Archer St. John and the St. John Romance Comics*. Seattle, WA: Fantagraphics Books, 2007.

22. He was among the first to publish the *Conan the Barbarian* series, long before Arnold Schwarzenegger made the comic book character famous in a movie of the same name in 1982, as well as "marginal" men's magazines, such as *Swank* and *Gallery*.

23. Information in this section is based on interviews with Mary Ann Stuart unless otherwise cited.

24. Stuart specifically mentions the movie *McCabe and Mrs. Miller*, though it was released in 1971 and, despite modest box-office success, never achieved widespread popularity. This movie, like many of Robert Altman's, is biting social commentaries, typically years ahead of the more "popular appeal" movies of the day. See David A. Cook, *A History of Narrative Film*, 3rd edition. New York: W. W. Norton, 1996: 638–41.

25. Interview with Nancy Coffey.

26. Interview with Mary Ann Stuart.

27. Allen Crider, *Mass Market Publishing in America*, 121.

28. Information in this section is based on interviews with Leona Nevler unless otherwise cited.

29. See also Daisy Maryles, "Fawcett Launches Romance Imprint with Brand Marketing Techniques," *Publishers Weekly*, 3 September 1979: 69–70.

30. Information in this section is based on interviews with Judy Sullivan unless otherwise cited.

31. Interview with Kate Duffy.

32. The sexual needs of women were a major tenet of the feminist movement. This idea is incorporated into many of the 1970s sensual historical novels. From this perspective, these romances espoused a strong feminist angle.

33. Carol Thurston, "Popular Historical Romances: Agent for Social Change? An Exploration of Methodologies," *Journal of Popular Culture* 19, no. 1, 1985: 35–50.

34. Daniel Yankelovich, *The New Morality: A Profile of American Youth in the Seventies*. New York: Random House, 1974. Daniel Yankelovich, *New Rules*. New York: Random House, 1981.

35. Joan Mondale, *Women and Social Change in America*. Princeton: Princeton Book, 1978.

36. Joan Mondale, *Women and Social Change in America*. William Chafe, *Women and Equality: Changing Patterns in American Culture*. Oxford: Oxford University Press, 1977: 110.

37. Ben J. Wattenberg, *The Real America*. New York: Doubleday, 1974: 214.

38. John Corry, "A U.S. Sex Revolt, It's Mostly Talk," *Social Profile: USA Today*. New York: Van Nostrand Reinhold, 1970. Robert Bell and Jay Clarke, "Pre-marital Sexual Experience among Coeds, 1958 and 1968," *Journal of Marriage and the Family* 32 (1970): 81–84.

39. P. Sorenson, *Adolescent Sexuality in Contemporary America*. New York: John Wiley, 1973.

40. William Chafe, *Women and Equality*, 122.

41. Daniel Yankelovich, *The New Morality*; William Chafe, *Women and Equality*.

42. Keith Melville, *Marriage and the Family Today*, 2nd edition. New York: Random House, 1980: 82; J. Ross Eshleman and Barbara G. Cashion, *Sociology*. Boston: Little, Brown, 1983: 326.

43. Carol Traynor Williams, *The Dream Beside Me: The Movies and the Children of the Forties*. Rutherford: Fairleigh Dickinson University Press, 1980.

44. Sara McCarthy, "Pornography, Rape, and the Cult of Macho," *The Humanist*, September/October 1980: 11–20.

45. Sex callousness is a term used by Donald Mosher for men who approve of and engage in the use of physical aggression and exploitative tactics, such as falsely professing love or getting their dates drunk, as a means of gaining coitus. Donald Mosher, "Sex Callousness toward Women," *Technical Report of the Commission on Obscenity and Pornography*, Vol. 8. Washington, D.C., 1970: 313–25.

46. See Ann Garry, "Pornography and Respect for Women." In *Pornography and Censorship*, edited by David Copp and Susan Wendell. New York: Prometheus Books, 1983: 61–80. Susan Brownmiller, *Against Our Will: Men, Women and Rape*. New York: Simon & Schuster, 1975.

47. Sara McCarthy, "Pornography, Rape, and the Cult of Macho."

48. Molly Haskel, "The 2,000-Year-Old Misunderstanding—'Rape Fantasy,'" *Ms.*, November 1976: 84–86.

49. Romance author Catherine Coulter, cited in Rosemary Guiley, *Love Lines*, 127.

50. See Sara McCarthy, "Pornography, Rape, and the Cult of Macho."

51. Lenard Shatzkin, *In Cold Type: Overcoming the Book Crisis*. Boston: Houghton Mifflin, 1982.

52. Coser et al. in *Books* cite the 50/50 sex ratio of mass-market publishing during the 1970s. Most of the female editors interviewed do not dispute this sex differential but indicate that it was substantially less during the first half of the decade. Lewis Coser, Charles Kadushin and Walter W. Powell, *Books: The Culture and Commerce of Publishing*. New York: Basic Books, 1982.

53. Lewis Coser Charles Kadushin and Walter W. Powell, *Books*, 148–74.

54. See Harrison C. White, "Where Do Mar-

kets Come From?" *American Journal of Sociology* 87 (1981): 517–47.

55. Lewis Coser Charles Kadushin and Walter W. Powell, *Books*, 97–117, 148–74.

Chapter 4

1. Arthur Bedeian, *Organizations: Theory and Analysis*. Hinsdale, Ill.: Dryden Press, 1980.
2. James Thompson, *Organizations in Action*. New York: McGraw-Hill, 1967: 40–42.
3. Interview with Richard Snyder.
4. Leonard Shatzkin, *In Cold Type: Overcoming the Book Crisis*. Boston: Houghton Mifflin, 1982.
5. This group included Lawrence Heisey, Fred Kerner, Richard Bellringer (operations), and William Wilson (finance).
6. Interview with Fred Kerner.
7. See Terrence E. Deal and Allen A. Kennedy, *Corporate Cultures: The Rites and Rituals of Corporate Life*. Reading, MA: Addison-Wesley, 1982. Stanley M. Davis, *Managing Corporate Culture*. Cambridge, MA: Ballinger, 1984.
8. Information in this section is based on interviews with Richard Snyder unless otherwise cited.
9. Lewis Coser, Charles Kadushin and Walter W. Powell, *Books: The Culture and Commerce of Publishing*. New York: Basic Books, 1982: 97–117.
10. Interview with Richard Snyder. Heisey said much the same thing in a separate interview.
11. Leonard Shatzkin, *In Cold Type*, 138.
12. Wholesaling books to retailers other than the biggest chains was already anachronistic in the 1980s before the decline of the bookstore and the rise of computer e-books in the twenty-first century. A book sales rep would often have to cover 50,000 miles annually and visit 150–250 accounts. In thirty minutes or less—often the maximum time the bookseller allows for the "pitch"—the rep might have to review 50–150 books. N. R. Kleinfield, "On the Road with a Book Salesman," *The New York Times Book Review*, August 24, 1980. See also Leonard Shatzkin, *In Cold Type*; Lewis Coser, Charles Kadushin and Walter W. Powell, *Books*.
13. Interview with Fred Kerner.
14. Daisy Maryles, "S & S to Debut Silhouette with $3-Million TV Ad Campaign," *Publishers Weekly*, 11 May 1980: 51–52.
15. Daisy Maryles, "S & S to Debut Silhouette with $3-Million TV Ad Campaign."
16. Interviews with Richard Snyder, Kate Duffy, and Karen Solem. See also Rosemary Guiley, *Love Lines: A Romance Reader's Guide to Printed Pleasures*. New York: Facts on File Publications, 1983.
17. Arthur Johnson, "Heartbreak at Harlequin: New Entries Distorting Blissful Profit Picture at Romance Fiction Firm." *The Globe and Mail*, 28 October 1983: P.1.
18. A loss leader is when a product (e.g., Janet Dailey) actually loses money because the cost (royalties) outweighs the sales. Loss leaders, however, are widely used because they bring in consumers who might purchase other products. In the case of Dailey, her name would generate interest in the Silhouette line because of her fans, and once familiar with Silhouette, her fans were likely to buy other Silhouette novels.
19. Daisy Maryles, "S & S to Debut Silhouette with $3-Million TV Ad Campaign."
20. Rosemary Guiley, *Love Lines*.
21. Madalynne Reuter, "Judge Rules Silhouette Cover Too Similar to Harlequin's," *Publishers Weekly*, 26 September 1980: 42–43.
22. Lawrence Kilman, "Look-Alike Package Out to Fool Buyer," *Associated Press Wire Service*, July 14, 1987.
23. In many cases, the quality is equal to that of the national brand. The brand-name illusion for many products is sustained by advertisers comparing their products to other brand-name products, not the generics.
24. Interview with Richard Snyder.
25. Michael Schudson, *Advertising, The Uneasy Persuasion: Its Dubious Impact on American Society*. New York: Basic Books, 1984: 58.
26. Michael Schudson, *Advertising, The Uneasy Persuasion*. See also Stephen Fox, *The Mirror Makers: A History of American Advertising and Its Creators*. New York: William Morrow, 1984.
27. Daisy Maryles, "S & S to Debut Silhouette with $3-Million TV Ad Campaign."
28. Daisy Maryles, "S & S to Debut Silhouette with $3-Million TV Ad Campaign."
29. Interview with Karen Solem.
30. Interview with Kate Duffy.
31. Interview with Karen Solem.
32. Information in this section is based on interviews with Fred Kerner unless otherwise cited.
33. The name, though never changed, underwent numerous variations. "We played with the logo quite a bit," says Kerner. "We tried it with two R's going together like the two R's in Rolls Royce. We also tried it by dropping one of the R's and making the other a capital R. For a time the two r's were done in a diphthong style. Eventually it just became one word."
34. Michael Schudson, *Advertising, The Uneasy Persuasion*, 29. See also Stuart Ewen, *Captains of Consciousness: Advertising and the Social Roots of the Consumer Society*. New York: McGraw-Hill, 1976.
35. Michael Schudson, *Advertising, The Uneasy Persuasion*, 21.
36. Michael Schudson, *Advertising, The Uneasy Persuasion*, 19.

37. Howard Aldrich, *Organizations and Environments*. Englewood Cliffs, NJ: Prentice Hall, 1979: 112–115.
38. Michael Hanan and John Freeman, "The Population Ecology of Organizations," *American Journal of Sociology* 82, no. 5 (1977): 929–64.
39. Interview with Richard Snyder.
40. In a separate interview, Heisey confirmed Snyder's recollection of events leading to the meeting and the meeting itself.
41. Interview with David Galloway.

Chapter 5

1. Rosemary Guiley in *Love Lines* cites the sales figures monitored by the romance newsletter *Boy Meets Girl*. These figures appear high since Guiley includes the 11 percent of the market in best-seller sales on the pretext that best-sellers "include many romance titles." Nevertheless, if we use the production estimates for mass-market fiction, we do move toward the 50 percent figure. My production estimates are tabulated in as tabulated in the figure on page 91. Rosemary Guiley, *Love Lines: A Romance Reader's Guide to Printed Pleasures*. New York: Facts on File Publications, 1983: 6.
2. Interviews with Vivian Stephens and Kate Duffy. Interviews conducted separately.
3. Information in this section is based on interviews with Vivian Stephens unless otherwise cited.
4. Time-Life puts out a number of nonfiction series books on a range of subjects from cooking to the Civil War. Stephens was one of a number of individuals who researched background information used in these books. The Time-Life position was her first job in publishing.
5. Harrison White, "Where Do Markets Come From?" *American Journal of Sociology* 87 (1981): 517–47.
6. Walter Powell cites Senator Howard Metzenbaum's charges reported in *Publishers Weekly* (1980) about his concern over the domination of the book industry by a handful of firms: "Eight publishers have over eighty percent of the paperback market and the two largest general interest book clubs have a market share over fifty percent." See Walter Powell, "From Craft to Corporation: The Impact of Outside Ownership on Book Publishing," in *Individuals in Mass Media Organizations: Creativity and Constraint*, edited by James Ettema and D. Charles Whitney. Beverly Hills: Sage, 1982: 36.
7. Coser et al. found that trade publishing is much more likely than other types of publishing to mix business with socializing. This regular socializing of trade editors connects the different units of the industry and provides the opportunity for editors to exchange information on manuscripts. Lewis Coser, Charles Kadushin and Walter W. Powell, *Books: The Culture and Commerce of Publishing*. New York: Basic Books, 1982: 81–86.
8. Lewis Coser, Charles Kadushin and Walter W. Powell, *Books*, 109–111.
9. Paul DiMaggio and Walter Powell, "Institutional Isomorphism," *American Sociological Review* 48 (1983): 147–60.
10. DiMaggio and Powell are citing Armen Alchian's article, "Uncertainty, Evolution and Economic Theory," *Journal of Political Economy* 58 (1950): 311–21.
11. Lewis Coser, Charles Kadushin and Walter W. Powell, *Books*, 108.
12. Interview with Kate Duffy.
13. Interview with Vivian Stephens.
14. Interview with Ellen Edwards.
15. Information in this section is based on interviews with Carolyn Nichols unless otherwise cited.
16. Joann Giusto-Davis, "Jove to Bid for Female Readers with 'Second Chance at Love' Romance Line," *Publishers Weekly*, 16 January 1981: 43–45.
17. Prior to coming to Berkley-Jove, Nichols had worked for some years in television production, where she won an Emmy in news and public affairs. Nichols was one of the "older" women in the romance industry in the early 1980s, "somewhere," she says, "between thirty-five and death."
18. Interview with Ellen Edwards.
19. Joann Giusto-Davis, "Jove to Bid for Female Readers with 'Second Chance at Love' Romance Line."
20. Interview with Ellen Edwards.
21. Catherine Kirkland, *For the Love of It: Women Writers and the Popular Romance*, Ph.D. Dissertation. Philadelphia: University of Pennsylvania, 1984.
22. The more sexually experienced heroines of the 1980s should not be interpreted as the result of promiscuity but, rather, the increased appearance of divorced characters in these novels.
23. Joseph Schumpeter, *Capitalism, Socialism and Democracy*, 3rd edition. New York: Harper and Row, 1950. Joseph Schumpeter, "Economic Theory and Entrepreneurial History," in *Explorations in Enterprise*, edited by H. G. J. Aiken. Cambridge: Harvard University Press, 1965.
24. Rosemary Guiley, *Love Lines*, 177.
25. Information in this section is based on interviews with Carolyn Nichols unless otherwise cited.
26. See also Rosemary Guiley, *Love Lines*, 177.
27. Interview with Carolyn Nichols; see also Rosemary Guiley, *Love Lines*, 177.
28. *Boy Meets Girl*, Vol. 3, No. 33 (1983).
29. Ibid.
30. Other, "older" (thirtyish) women editors

would include Nancy Coffey at Avon, Mary Ann Stuart at Playboy, and Judy Sullivan at Gallen, who would go on to put her stamp on the romance series at St. Martin's, as well as Carolyn Nichols, who was responsible for launching both Second Chance at Love and Loveswept.

31. Lewis Coser, Charles Kadushin and Walter W. Powell, *Books*.

32. Though many of the unsuccessful editors, as we'll see in the next chapter, were young recent college graduates who were promoted from editorial assistants to editors, no correlation is found between previous publishing experience and success with romance lines. Half the older editors, such as Mary Ann Stuart and Nancy Coffey, had been in the publishing business for some years, while the other half, like Vivian Stephens and Carolyn Nichols, were relative newcomers to publishing.

33. Stephens was also instrumental in founding the Romance Writer's Association, and in 2006 she was honored by the RWA by having the Industry Award named after her.

Chapter 6

1. Robert Kearns, "Galloway Rekindles Flame at Harlequin." *Chicago Tribune*, 16 April 1986. www.articles.chicagotribune.com/1986-04-16/business/8601270950/romance-novels. Accessed 2 February 2014.

2. Cited by Margaret Ann Jensen in *Love's Sweet Return: The Harlequin Story*. Toronto: Women's Educational Press, 1984: 57

3. Information in this section is based on interviews with Robin Grunder unless otherwise cited.

4. *Boy Meets Girl* III, No. 19 (1983).

5. *Boy Meets Girl* III, No. 17 (1983); III, no. 44 (1983).

6. Grunder, cited in *Boy Meets Girl* III, no. 44 (1983).

7. Jaffe, cited in *Boy Meets Girl* IV, no. 10 (1984).

8. Interview with Vivian Jennings, publisher of *Boy Meets Girl*. See also *Boy Meets Girl* III, No. 37 (1983).

9. Interview with Ellen Edwards.

10. Ibid.

11. *Boy Meets Girl* III, no. 37 (1983).

12. *Boy Meets Girl* III, no. 37 (1983).

13. Ibid.

14. Edwards, cited in *Boy Meets Girl* IV, no. 39 (1984).

15. James T. Carey, "Changing Courtship Patterns in the Popular Song," in *The Sounds of Social Change*, edited by R. Serge Denisoff and Richard A. Peterson. Chicago: Rand McNally, 1972: 198–212.

16. "Something Old, Something New," reached number 77 on the chart in the summer of 1963. It could be said that Paul and Paula's rapid rise to and fall from rock and roll stardom was already in progress, as each of the four songs appeared lower than its predecessor on the musical charts. However, they did release one other record in the fall of that year, a non-romance ditty entitled, "First Day Back at School," which reached number 60 on the charts, a fair jump above their ill-fated and poorly placed song of marital love. My thanks to Dave Walton at Nashville's WKDF for this information.

17. Information in this section is based on interviews with Pamela Strickler unless otherwise cited.

18. Interview with Joan Schulhaver, director of public relations, Silhouette Books.

19. Information in this section is based on interviews with Denise Marcil unless otherwise cited.

20. Marcil is referring to a theme popular in the gothic romances in the late 1960s/early 1970s. This is not true of contemporary sensual romance publishing in the 1980s, which suggests Marcil was not fully conversant with what was taking place in the romance industry and like so many had jumped into the field to cash in on the romance craze of the period.

21. Information in this section is based on interviews with Page Cuddy unless otherwise cited.

22. *Boy Meets Girl* III, no. 41 (1983).

23. O'Shea, cited in *Boy Meets Girl* III, no. 41 (1983).

24. *Boy Meets Girl* III, no. 36 (1983).

25. *Boy Meets Girl* IV, no. 9 (1984).

26. Reported in *Boy Meets Girl* IV, no. 35 (1984).

27. Anne Severance, "A New Language of Love," *West Coast Review of Books*, 1984.

28. Information in this section is based on interviews with Anne Severance unless otherwise cited.

29. Glenn R. Carroll, "Concentration and Specialization: Dynamics of Niche Width in Populations of Organizations," *American Journal of Sociology* 90, no. 6 (May 1985): 1262–1283. See also Glenn Carroll and Yangchung Paul Huo, "Organizational Task and Institutional Environments in Ecological Perspective: Findings from the Local Newspaper Industry," *American Journal of Sociology* 91, no. 4 (Jan. 1986): 838–73.

30. Walter W. Powell, *Getting Into Print: The Decision-Making Process in Scholarly Publishing*. Chicago: University of Chicago Press, 1985: 18.

31. Walter W. Powell, *Getting Into Print*, 18–19.

32. See *1978 Consumer Research Study on Reading and Book Purchasing*, by Yankelovich, Skelly and White, Inc., prepared for The Book Industry Study Group. GISG Report No. 6 (1978).

33. The line was terminated by Harlequin shortly after the purchase of Silhouette. Karen Solem at Silhouette, however, indicated the line was doing poorly and would likely have been killed in any event. Interview with Karen Solem.
34. Mystery-suspense romances were rooted to the gothic tradition. These novels are distinct from the new romance mystery-suspense, which are contemporary romances overlaid with an element of mystery-suspense.
35. The show's original focus on the heroine was lost in later years as the hero began to take a more active role in the crime-solving. It was not long before the hero became equal to the heroine and then eclipsed her. The romantic tension was likewise lost as heroine and hero grew closer and closer over the years and eventually married. The show was cancelled not long after they tied the knot.
36. Interview with Ellen Edwards.
37. Interview with Pamela Strickler.
38. Cited in *Boy Meets Girl* III, no. 24 (1983).
39. Ibid.
40. Interview with Page Cuddy.
41. Cited in *Boy Meets Girl* V, no. 43 (1985).
42. Ibid.
43. Interview with Vivian Jennings.
44. *Boy Meets Girl* IV, no. 30 (1984).
45. Ibid.
46. *Boy Meets Girl*, V, no. 27 (1985).
47. How Intrigue would be tweaked in the coming decades to remain vibrant will be addressed in Chapter 8.
48. *Boy Meets Girl* IV, no. 30 (1984).

Chapter 7

1. Herbert Gans, *Deciding What's News: A Study of CBS Evening News, NBC Nightly News, Newsweek and Time*. New York: Random House, 1980.
2. Herbert Gans, *Deciding What's News*, 230.
3. Herbert Gans, *Deciding What's News*, 231.
4. Interview with Kate Duffy.
5. The following is the personal observation of this author, who attended the described event. See also Vickie Kilgore East, "Harlequin Fans Praise 'Wholesome' Books." *The Tennessean*, March 11, 1983: 10D.
6. Carol T. Williams, *The Dream Beside Me: The Movies and the Children of the Forties*. Vancouver: Fairleigh Dickinson University Press, 1980.
7. Fred Ferretti, "Romance Authors Have a Queen for 3 Days," *New York Times*, April 22, 1983: 14. Though it is not clear in her comment, we will charitably assume that Cartland is referring to sex in romance novels and not sexual relations between committed unmarried couples.
8. John Markert, "Romancing the Reader," *Romantic Times* 18 (Fall), 1984. The survey was conducted of 500 women who were subscribers to the romance magazine *Romantic Times* in September 1983; forty-two percent responded. See also John Markert, "Challenging the Stereotype: Demographics and Lifestyles of Romance Readers," presented at the Southern Popular Culture Association Conference in Nashville, TN (October 1993).
9. Catherine Kirkland, *For the Love of It: Women Writers and the Popular Romance*. Ph.D. dissertation, University of Pennsylvania, 1984.
10. Lewis Coser, Charles Kadushin, and Walter W. Powell, *Books: The Culture and Commerce of Publishing*. New York: Basic Books, 1982: 233.
11. The year 1979 marks the first year there were more women working full-time than not working (50.8 percent). This has since been increasing at roughly one percent per year. *Statistical Abstracts of the United States*. Washington, D.C.: U.S. Department of Commerce, 2000.
12. John Markert, "Romancing the Reader." See also Catherine Kirkland, *For the Love of It*.
13. Catherine Kirkland, *For the Love of It*, 145.
14. Catherine Kirkland, *For the Love of It*, 134.
15. A. Scott Berg, *Max Perkins: Editor of Genius*. New York: Washington Square Press, 1978: 537.
16. John Markert, "The Language of Love," *Nashville* (February 1984): 26–29.
17. John Markert, "The Language of Love."
18. Catherine Kirkland, *For the Love of It*, 277.
19. Catherine Kirkland, *For the Love of It*, 195, 197.

Chapter 8

1. Jay Dixon, *The Romance Fiction of Mills & Boon, 1909–1990s*. London: UCL Press, 1999: 180.
2. Tony Van Alphen, "Harlequin Head Retiring," *Edmonton Journal*, 19 June 1990: C9. "Lawrence Heisey Retiring as Harlequin Chairman," *Toronto Star*, 18 June 1990: C3.
3. Tony Van Alphen, "Harlequin Head Retiring."
4. Harlequin Annual Report, 2010.
5. This story may be apocryphal—though Alan Boon, according to Jay Dixon, did fancy doing business at the Ritz. Nevertheless, the story underscores the informality of doing business on a handshake that once characterized the "old school" way of doing business. Jay Dixon, *The Romance Fiction of Mills & Boon*, 180.
6. Peter Foster, "No Deal: Torstar's David Galloway Insists They Were Talking Takeover. Sun Media's Paul Godfrey Thought They Were Just Talking. In the End, Quebeco Won the Day, Leaving Godrey Rich and Galloway Bruised," *Toronto Life* 33, no. 3 (March 1999): 49–56.

7. Galloway was well known in the business world for his fair-minded business practices. Ross Oakland, "It's the Balance that Counts: As His Retirement Approaches, Torstar CEO David Galloway is Praised as an Ethical Businessman Who Always Did the Right Thing," *Toronto Star*, 28 April 2002: C.3.

8. Support for the contention that Galloway was destined for "greater things" was offered by David Olive writing in *Canadian Business* as early as 1982, when he speculated that "media analysts" thought that Heisey or Galloway would replace Torstar chairman Beland Honderich when he retired. This is quite a forecast, given the fact that Galloway had only been with Torstar for two years at that point. David Olive, "Lust or Bust: Only Harlequin Can Nurse Torstar Back to Health," *Canadian Business* 55, no. 8 (August 1982): 25–26.

9. Heisey died at seventy-eight in May 2009.

10. Ross Oakland, "It's the Balance that Counts," *Toronto Star*, 28 April 2002: C3.

11. Robert Kearns, "Galloway Rekindles Flame at Harlequin," *Chicago Tribune*, 26 April 1986. www.articles.chicagotribune.com/1986-04-16/business/8601270954/romance-novels. Accessed 16 December 2013.

12. Heisey also had an MBA from Harvard, but it was from another era.

13. Galloway looks back at his accomplishments after being named President of Torstar. "David Galloway Named President of Torstar Corp," *Toronto Star*, 1 September 1988: A4.

14. Galloway is quoted as saying direct sales were the "real [profit] magic" at Harlequin. Robert Kearns, "Galloway Rekindles Flame at Harlequin."

15. Robert Kearns, "Galloway Rekindles Flame at Harlequin."

16. Paul Grescoe, *The Merchants of Venus: Inside Harlequin and the Empire of Romance*. Vancouver: Raincoast Books, 1996: 173–174.

17. "David Galloway Named President of Torstar Corp."

18. American Romance debuted in 1983; Temptation in 1984. Both these lines were strategically positioned to compete with Silhouette lines. Intrigue, Harlequin's one unique line, was already in development when Galloway became CEO. Silhouette's First Love (1981) became Crosswinds (1987). Silhouette's Inspiration line was terminated after the buyout, but it was already on the fast track at Silhouette to be terminated because of lack of sales.

19. Paul Grescoe, *The Merchants of Venus*, p. 178.

20. "Harlequin Readers Hardly Romantic," *Edmonton Journal*, 20 February 1990: C6. See also, "Harlequin: Safe in Print, Wild at Work," *Orlando Sentinel*, 17 April 1990: C6.

21. "Harlequin: Safe in Print, Wild at Work," C6.

22. Hickey announced to the Torstar board as early as 1989 that Harlequin had developed a *proposal* with a potential partner to test-market one of its books in China. Donna Hayes, Hickey's successor, suggested in 2004 that China *might* be a new market for Harlequin sometime in the next two years. In 1998, Galloway announced that there were distribution issues in Russia that he hoped to [finally] address. John Partridge, "Harlequin Eyes China, Torstar Shops in Vain," *The Globe and Mail*, 6 May 1989: B.3. Michelle DaCruz, "Is It Time for Torstar to End Harlequin Fling?" *National Post*, 12 April 2014: FP1. Rob Ferguson, "Torstar to Expand Harlequin Operations in Russia, Says Chairman." *Canadian Press Newswire*, 29 April 1998.

23. "Harlequin Ends Talks on Buying Zebra Books," *Toronto Star*, 3 July 1992: D2.

24. In 1993, Harlequin signed an agreement with Alliance, the Canadian film production and distribution conglomerate, to turn at least four romance novels into television movies. Only CBS appeared interested. Though Harlequin DVD films would subsequently do moderately well under CEO Hayes in the late aughts, the venture under Hickey does not appear to have gone very far. Carol Off, host, "Hot Off the Press," *The National Magazine—CBC Television*. Toronto: Southam, Inc., 8 July 1999. See also Jerry Horton, "Harlequin Alliance: Romance on Screen," *Quill & Quire* 59, no. 6 (June 1993): 9. Christopher Harris, "Harlequin Finds Its Match: Alliance Deal to Put Stream of Passion-Filled Movies on TV, Video," *The Globe and Mail*, 8 April 1993: B.1. Margaret Ann Jensen catalogues the problem with the first movie in 1978. See Margaret Ann Jensen, *Love's Sweet Return: The Harlequin Story*. Toronto: Women's Educational Press, 1984: 48.

25. Harlequin, like many companies, was enticed by the dot-com craze of the late 1990s. The dot-com bubble burst, however, in 2000, not long after Harlequin's embrace of women.com, and over the next twelve months many start-up dot-com organizations that were "all the rage" had disappeared. This may explain why, after a flurry of media coverage between June 1999 and February 2000 announcing Harlequin's partnering with women.com, coverage completely disappeared, as did women.com. See Jack Willoughby, "Burning Up," *Barrons*, 20 March 2000; "Smoldering: Net Companies, Still Burning Cash, Try to Conserve Their Tinder," Barrons, 2 October 2000. See also Eric Janszen commentary on Willoughby's article, "Are 'Net Co's Running Out of Cash?" *Bank Rate.com*, 4 April 2000. www.bankrate.com/brm/news/investing/20000404f.asp. Accessed 24 January 2014.

26. Harlequin purchased Los Angles-based Frank Schaffer Publications for $56 million in

1994. D. A. Galloway, "Torstar Corp. Subsidiary Harlequin Enterprises Ltd. to Purchase Frank Schaffer Publications Inc.," *Business Wire*, April 26, 1994: 1.
27. John Lorinc, "Harlequin Goes to School: With Its Recent Acquisition of Troll, the Romance Giant Aims to Challenge Scholastic at Its Own Game," *Quill & Quire* 63, no. 10 (Oct 1997): 1.
28. John Lorinc, "Harlequin Goes to School...": 1.
29. John Lorinc, "Harlequin Goes to School...": 1.
30. "Learning, and Loving It," *Financial Post*, 15 February 1997: 30–31.
31. John Lorinc, "Romance Language: How Harlequin Became Synonymous with Romance and Then Translated that Success Around the World," *Quill & Quire* 60, no. 5 (May 1994): 13.
32. Ross Oakland, "It's the Balance that Counts."
33. Jim Milliot, "Sales, Earnings Slip at Harlequin; Spinoff Possible?" *Publishers Weekly* 248, no. 33 (August 13, 2001): 156.
34. www.tomsnyder.com. Accessed January 20, 2014
35. "Learning and Loving It," *Financial Post*, 15 February 1997: 30, 31.
36. Nicolas van Rijn, "Happy Ending at Harlequin: Book Publisher Turns Page with First Woman CEO," *Toronto Star*, 20 November 2001: C.3.
37. "Storybook Ending: Harlequin Romance Novels CEO Hickey Takes Early Retirement," *Canadian Press NewsWire*, 19 November 2001. Sales actually rose at Harlequin during the third quarter of 2001, but profits slipped, due in part to issues beyond Hickey's control: higher postage and distribution costs. Still, sales did not significantly increase in the third quarter after falling some 7.1 percent the previous quarter. See Jim Milliot, "Sales, Earnings Inch Ahead at Harlequin," *Publishers Weekly* 248, no. 46, 12 November 2001: 12. Jim Milliot, "Sales, Earnings Slip at Harlequin; Spinoff Possible?" *Publishers Weekly* 248, no. 33, 13 August 2001: 156.
38. "Storybook Ending: Harlequin Romance Novels CEO Hickey Takes Early Retirement," *Canadian Press NewsWire*, 19 Nov. 2001.
39. Elena Cherney, "Harlequin Books Court Young, Single Readers—Canadian Publisher Creates a New Series—Flirting with New Kind of Romance," *Wall Street Journal* [Brussels edition], 6 August 2001: 18. Torstar Corporation, Annual Report 2001, page 2.
40. Richard Blackwell, "How Harlequin Kept the Romance Alive," *The Globe and Mail*, 11 June 2005: B.3.
41. "Harlequin CEO Fell in Love with Books When She was Teen," *Daily Press*, 25 July 2001: 18.
42. "Harlequin CEO Fell in Love with Books."

43. "Harlequin CEO Defends Romance Fiction Saying, 'It Sells,'" *North Bay Nugget*, 28 July 2001: B4.
44. Nicolas van Rijn, "Happy Ending at Harlequin."
45. Richard Blackwell, "How Harlequin Kept the Romance Alive."
46. Nicolas van Rijn, "Happy Ending at Harlequin."
47. Ross Oakland, "It's the Balance that Counts."
48. The category/noncategory distinction was made in Chapter 2 and 3 but bears repeating. Noncategory novels do not have a template; they are released as single titles and promoted by author rather than line. Category fiction has a template. This template may be quite detailed, as it was at many houses in the 1970s, but it does not have to be. Most houses, including Harlequin, have some kind of general writer's guidelines that do little more than delineate the overall theme. Category is here looked at as any line or imprint that has a basic "formula," regardless of whether the formula is spelled out in writer guidelines or is in the mind of the editor, who filters books into the system because they fit her idea of what works within the imprint. In this sense, many mainstream houses also have category romances, though they are not in a numbered series, as Harlequin novels are, and they may or may not have a predetermined number of books they release monthly. Harlequin category novels are also called series because they are consecutively numbered. Since most mainstream publishers of romance lines do not number their books, they are not called series. These books, however, are promoted more by line identification than as single-titled authors—a basic "category" distinction.
49. Richard Blackwell, "How Harlequin Kept the Romance Alive."
50. Jim Milliot, "U.S. Hurts Harlequin, Though Digital Sales Jump 73 Percent," *Publishers Weekly*, 3 November 2010. See also "Sales Down, Earnings Up at Harlequin; Raises E-book Royalty," *Publishers Weekly*, 11 August 2012. "Harlequin Expands Digital First Efforts," *Publishers Weekly*, 14 August 2013.
51. It is curious that *Publishers Lunch: The Publishing Industry's Daily Essential Read*, put this in quotation marks (e.g., "Harlequin CEO and publisher Donna Hayes 'has decided to retire' at the end of the year..."), which suggests that the decision was rather sudden and hints that there may be more to her retirement than meets the eye. www.publishersmarketplace.com/3013/12/people-172. Accessed 10 January 2014.
52. "Swinwood to Succeed Hayes at Harlequin," *Publishers Weekly*, 4 December 2013. See also Leslie Scrivener, "Harlequin CEO Donna Hayes Retires, Craig Swinwood Takes Over,"

Toronto Star, 4 December 2013. www.thestar.com/business/2013/12/04/harlequin_ceo donna_hayes_reties. Accessed 25 January 2014. "Torstar Announces Craig Swinwood to Succeed Donna Hayes as publisher and CEO of Harlequin," *Marketwired*, 4 December 2013. www.finance.yahoo.com/news/torstar-announces-craig-swinwood-succeed-. Accessed 25 January 2014.

53. I am indebted to Laura Vivanco for bringing this to my attention. Personal correspondence.

54. Laura Vivanco addresses the thematic difference in greater detail in her assessment of the romance novel. See Laura Vivanco, *For Love and Money: The Literary Art of the Harlequin Mills & Boon Romance*. Tirril-Hall, Tirril, Penrith, CA: Humanities-Ebooks, 2011.

55. Margaret Ann Jensen, *Love's Sweet Return*, 80–93, 134–39.

56. Information in this section is based on interviews with Dianne Moggy unless otherwise cited. Ms. Moggy has spent thirty years with Harlequin and has been the vice president over all the series lines at Harlequin since 2011. Before that, she was vice president of overseas editorial strategic development.

57. *Romance Writers of America's 2005 Market Research Study on Romance Readers*. www.rwanational.org/eweb/doc/05MarketResearch. Accessed 3 February 2014.

58. *Romance Writers of America's 2005 Market Research Study on Romance Readers*.

59. I am using the midpoint (1995) to calculate when the Millennials transition to their twenties with 2015 my baseline. See John Markert, "Demographics of Age: Generational and Cohort Confusion," *Journal of Current Issues and Research in Advertising* XXVI, no. 2 (Fall 2004): 11–26.

60. This is mentioned in the online guidelines to the line, suggesting to the would-be author that this theme has a certain amount of favor with readers.

61. The Historical line may be similarly erotic, but the Historicals were not released in the United States at this time.

62. Margaret Ann Jensen, *Love's Sweet Return*, 62–64.

63. Jay Dixon, *The Romance Fiction of Mills & Boon*.

64. Established lines may already have incorporated some of these changes into their novels, but the success of a new line that pivots on the new dimension causes established lines to lift their already existing focus and dwell on it to a greater degree. Harlequin Presents is an excellent example of this tendency.

65. Quoted and refuted in Maryanne Fisher and Anthony Cox, "Man Change Thyself: Hero versus Heroine Development in Harlequin Romance Novels," *Journal of Social, Evolutionary, and Cultural Psychology* 4, no. 4 (2010): 305–316.

66. Nora Krug, "Nora Roberts's Three Decades of Writing Have Led to 200 Books," *The Washington Post*, 16 April 2012. www.washingtonpost.com/lifestyle/style/nora-roberts-three-decades…. Accessed 3 January 2014. See also Lev Grossman and Andrea Sachs-Seattle, "Rewriting the Romance," *Time Magazine*, 3 February 2003. www.time.com/time/printout/0,8816,1004160, 00. Accessed 20 December 2013.

67. This does not mean the heroines aren't described in any physical detail. The reader can visualize the heroine's looks: the color of her hair and her eyes, for example. It is just that the hero is described in much more detail than the heroine. See A. Dana Ménard and Christine Cabrera, "'Whatever the Approach, Tab B Still Fits Into Slot A': Twenty Years of Sex Scripts in Romance Novels," *Sexuality & Culture*, 15 (2011): 240–255. Laura Vivanco, *For Love and Money*.

68. Carol Thurston, *The Romance Revolution: Erotic Novels for Women and the Search for a New Sexual Identity*. Urbana: University of Illinois Press, 1987: 56.

69. Pamela Regis, *A Natural History of the Romance Novel*. Philadelphia: University of Pennsylvania Press, 2003: 112.

70. Maryanne Fisher and Anthony Cox, "Man Change Thyself," 305. It should be mentioned that the evolutionary explanation is rejected by some.

71. Heather Schell, "The Love Life of a Fact," in *The Dissemination of Reliable Knowledge*, edited by Peter Howlett and Mary S. Morgan. Cambridge: Cambridge University Press, 2010. Laura Vivance, "The Evolution of the Alpha Male," *Teach Me Tonight: Musings on Romance Fiction from an Academic Perspective*. www.teachemetonight.blogspot.com/2010/07/evolution-of-alpha-male. Accessed 20 October 2014.

72. Personal correspondence with Laura Vivanco. See also Kathleen Gilles Seidel, "Judge Me by the Joy I Bring," 159–179 in *Dangerous Men and Adventurous Women: Romance Writers on the Appeal of the Romance*, edited by Jayne Ann Krentz. Philadelphia: University of Pennsylvania, 1992.

73. Pamela Regis, *A Natural History of the Romance Novel*, 113.

74. Maryanne Fisher and Anthony Cox, "Man Change Thyself." A. Dana Ménard and Christine Cabrera, "'Whatever the Approach, Tab B Still Fits Into Slot A.'"

75. Lawrence B. Finer, "Trends in Premarital Sex in the United States, 1954–2003," *Public Health Reports*, Vol. 122 (January–February) 2007: 73–78. See also Rebecca Wind, "Premarital Sex is Nearly Universal among Americans, and Has Been for Decades," *Guttmacher Institute: Media Center*, 19 December 2006. www.guttmacher.org/media/nr/2006/12/19/index. Accessed 6 March 2014.

76. Justin R. Garcia, Chris Reiber and Ann Merriwether, "Sexual Hook-Up Culture," *American Psychological Association* 44, no. 2, February 2013: 60. www.apa.org/monitor/2013/02/ce-corner. Accessed 6 March 2014.

77. The parental attitude toward their school-aged children's sexual behavior is aptly caught in the title of Dave Barry's 2013 book, *You Can Date Boys When You're Forty: Dave Barry on Parenting and Other Topics He Knows Very Little About.*

78. *Romance Writers of America's 2005 Market Research Study on Romance Reader.*

79. See John Markert, *Post–9/11 Cinema: Through a Lens Darkly.* Lanham, MD: Scarecrow Press, 2011.

80. A few days after Osama bin Laden was killed, Annys Shin with *The Washington Post* wrote, "Publishers are already bracing for a flurry of Navy SEAL-themed pitches and manuscripts in the coming weeks" but went on to acknowledge that this was a widespread phenomena not limited to romance publishing. Annys Shin, "SEALS Go from Superhero to Sex Symbol," *Washington Post*, May 6, 2011. www.articles.washingtonpost.com/2011-05-06/local/35232588_1_navy-seal-navy-udt-seal-musemm-seal-teamsix. Accessed 15 March 2014.

81. Paul Grescoe, *The Merchants of Venus*, 137–144; see also Gold Eagle Books, www.readgoldeagle.blogspot.com. Accessed 10 February 2014.

82. Paul Gresco quotes Harlequin's Dick Bellringer and Fred Kerner on their mistake in overpaying Pendleton. Paul Gresco, *The Merchants of Venus*, 139.

83. See also "Pinnacle Books, Inc., Plaintiff, v. Harlequin Enterprises Limited, Defendant," U.S. District Court, S. D. New York, No. 81, Civ. 0641, May 13, 1981. Trans-Lex.org: Law Research. www.translex.uni-koeln.de/output.ph/?docid+309400. Accessed 13 March 2014.

84. Plot summary on Wikipedia. www.wikipedia.org/wiki/Rogue_Angel. Accessed 3 August 2013.

85. The early history of Kimani is based on an interview with Glenda Howard, who is Harlequin's senior executive editor in New York and came to Harlequin from BET when BET was sold.

86. Richard Blackwell, "How Harlequin Kept the Romance Alive."

87. Ridley, "An Open Letter to Harlequin," *Love in the Margins*, 5 September 2013. www.loveinthemargins.com/2013/09/05/an-open-letter-to-harlequin. Accessed 15 February 2014.

88. "Harlequin's First YA Line," *Publishers Weekly* 253, no. 41 (16 October 2006): 19.

89. Joe Woodard, "God Starts Cleaning Up the Pulp-Romance: Harlequin Brings Out an 'Inspiration' Series to Feed a Growing Hunger for Religion," *Alberta Report*, 25, no. 4: (12 January 1998): 36.

90. Joe Woodard, "God Starts Cleaning Up the Pulp-Romance."

91. Karen Hold, "Harlequin Launching Inspirational Line," *Publishers Weekly* 250, no. 41 (13 October 2003): 8.

92. Quoted by Lisa Peryman, "Harlequin Launches New Spiritual Imprint," *Quill & Quire*, Vol. 63, No. 12 (December 1997): 17.

93. Karen Hold, "Harlequin Launching Inspirational Line," 8.

94. Laura Clawson, "Cowboys and Schoolteachers: Gender in Romance Novels, Secular and Christian," *Sociological Perspectives* 48. no. 4 (Winter 2005): 461–479.

95. Laura Clawson, "Cowboys and Schoolteachers," 476.

96. Jim Millot, "Harlequin Pushes to Boost Single-Title Sales," *Publishers Weekly* 249, No. 5 (4 February 2002): 16.

97. Like most mainstream lines at Harlequin, Teen only accepts agented manuscripts.

98. This year, 1998, is the U.S. release date. The books actually appeared in print in the U.K. a year earlier.

99. Even Kensington, which tends to "push the [content] envelope" (see Chapter 9), balks at going beyond an 8 level in print. Interview with Stephen Zacharius.

100. Author Maureen Lee, an Australian grandmother aged 57, is discussing her explicit sex scenes in Blaze's *A Man For the Night*. Quoted by Geraldine Bedell, "Mills & Boom Boom," *The Guardian*, 14 December 2002. www.guardian.co.uk/books/2002/dec/15/fiction.features1. Accessed 17 December 2013.

101. Meghan Daum, "The Recession Heats Up Romance Novels," *Los Angeles Times*, 4 April 2009. www.articles.latimes.com/print/2009/apr/04/opinion/oe-daum4. Accessed 21 February 2013. Andrea Sachs, "The Global Boom in Bodice-Rippers," *Time*, 21 September 2009. www.time.com/time/printout/0,8816,1921627,00. Accessed 25 February 2013.

102. The "dated" rape theme is another reason the bodice-rippers have passed into oblivion. Nevertheless, the description of sexuality that we saw in the excerpt from *Sweet Savage Love* in Chapter 3 pales in its depiction of the sexual act when compared to many romance novels of today (2014).

103. Personal conversations with some in the BDSM lifestyle about the *Fifty Shades* books.

104. In "Old Dogs," (2005) Doc Martin is concerned about an accident-prone fisherman in the village whom he is regularly treating for various bruises and contusions. In the end, the fisherman's lifestyle is revealed as the reason for his multiple injuries. It is a lifestyle that he and his wife "discovered" they rather enjoyed after the children grew up and moved away—she is the dominatrix; he is "the slave" who is frequently beaten.

105. Elena Cherney, "Harlequin Books Court Young, Single Readers—Canadian Publisher Creates a New Series—Flirting with New Kind of Romance," *The Wall Street Journal, Europe.* 6 August 2001: 18.
106. Elena Cherney, "Harlequin Books Court Young, Single Readers."
107. Quote by Elena Cherney, "Harlequin Books Court Young, Single Readers."
108. Quoted by Andrea Zoe Aster, "How Harlequin Woos Women," *Marketing Magazine* 108, no. 12 (31 March 2003). See also Megan Turner, "Harlequin Gets Hip: Pulp-Fantasy Publisher Woos Young City Women with New Line of Books," *New York Post* (26 November 2001): D.1. www.nypost.com/2001/11/26/harlequin-gets-hip.... Accessed 2 April 2014.
109. Carol Memmott, "NASCAR, Harlequin Gear Up for Love Stories," *USA Today*, 30 January 2006. www.usatoday30.usatoday.com/sports/motor/nascar/2006-01-30-harlequin. Accessed 20 March 2014. Charles McGrath, "In Harlequin-Nascar Romance, Hearts Race," *New York Times*, 19 February 2007. www.nytimes.com/2007/02/19/books/19nasc. Accessed 19 March 2014.
110. Carol Memmott, "NASCAR, Harlequin Gear Up for Love Stories."
111. Alison Flood, "Mills & Boon Whisper Sweet Nothings in Cauliflower Ears," *The Guardian*, 5 January 2009. www.guardian.co.uk/books/2009/jan/06/mills-boon-rugby. Accessed 20 March 2014.
112. Alison Flood, "Mills & Boon Whisper Sweet Nothings in Cauliflower Ears."
113. It debuted in the U.K. a few months earlier in 2010.
114. See also, Allison Flood, "Mills & Boon Goes Behind National Trust's Bedroom Doors for Racy Novels," *The Guardian* 2 May 2010. www.guardian.co.ukbooks/2010/may03/mills-boon-national-trust-novels. Accessed 20 March 2014.
115. It may well be, Laura Vivanco points out, that it was more of a public relations exercise than a revenue-raising one, perhaps with the idea that the association with the National Trust would make Mills & Boon books seem more respectable. Personal correspondence.
116. Kelli Korducki, "For Love and Money: Harlequin and the Mainstreaming of Erotic Fiction," *Quill & Quire*, 9 May 2013. www.quillandquire.com/blog/index.php/industry-news/for-love-and-money-harlequin. Accessed 21 March 2014.
117. Focusing too much on casual sex dulls the central premise of the romance, which is to focus on a romantic relationship with a hero that has a happy ending.
118. Tom Peck and Sophie Mills, "Sex Sells: Mills & Boon Marks Centenary with Move to Hardcore Erotica," *The Independent*, 8 March 2014. www.independent.co.uk/arts-entertainment/books/news/sex-0sells-mills-boon.... Accessed 8 March 2014.
119. The pornographic would have its own Likert scale. At the 10 romantic level discussed here, the books step over into a Level 1 in the pornographic realm and the scale graduates upward from there, depending on the the "crudity" of sexual activity depicted.
120. Victoria Dahl, "10 Dirty Romance Novels," *Publishers Weekly*, 7 February 2014. www.publishersweekly.com/paper-copy/by-topic/industry-news/tip-sheet/article/6095. Accessed 8 April 2014.
121. Tom Peck and Sophie Mills, "Sex Sells."
122. Richard Blackwell, "How Harlequin Kept the Romance Alive."
123. Garry Chick, Careen Yarnal and Andrew Purrington, "Play and Mate Preference: Testing the Signal Theory of Adult Playfulness," *American Journal of Play*, Vol. 4, No. 4 (spring 2012): 407–441; Willow Lawson, "Humor's Sexual Side," *Psychology Today* 38, no. 5 (September/October 2005): 17–18. Elizabeth McGee and Mark Shevlin, "Effect of Humor on Interpersonal Attraction and Mate Selection," *The Journal of Psychology* 143, no. 1 (January 2009): 67–77.
124. Paul Grescoe, *The Merchants of Venus*, 80.
125. Torstar Annual Report, 2001, 2010.
126. Paul Grescoe, *The Merchants of Venus*, 80.
127. "Global Publishing Leaders 2013: Harlequin," *Publishers Weekly*, 19 July 2013. www.publishersweekly.com/paper-copy/by-topic/industry-news/financial-reporting.... Accessed 14 February 2014.
128. Jim Millot, "Harlequin Pushes to Boost Single-Title Sales."
129. "Global Publishing Leaders 2012: Harlequin," *Publishers Weekly*, 25 June 2012. www.publishersweekly.com/paper-copy/by-topic/industry-news/financial-reporting/.... Accessed 11 February 2014.
130. "Global Publishing Leaders 2013: Harlequin," *Publishers Weekly*, 19 July 2013.
131. Paul Grescoe, *The Merchants of Venus*, 80.
132. Paul Grescoe, *The Merchants of Venus*, 106.
133. See Abbass F. Alkhafaji, *Restructuring American Corporations: Causes, Effects, and Implications*. New York: Quorum Books, 1990. Robert Hayes, Gary Pisano, David Upton, and Steven Wheelwright. *Operations, Strategy and Technology: Pursuing the Competitive Edge*. Hoboken, NJ: Wiley, 2005. Bennett Harrison, *Lean and Mean: The Changing Landscape of Corporate Power in the Age of Flexibility*. New York: Basic Books, 1994.

134. "Harlequin Enterprise Pty Ltd: Publishing of Romance Books." www.australianexporters.net/companyID3131. Accessed 23 February 2014.
135. Glen Thomas, "Romance: The Perfect Creative Industry? A Case Study of Harlequin-Mills & Boon Australia," in *Empowerment versus Oppression: Twenty-First-Century Views of Popular Romance Novels*, edited by Sally Goade. Newcastle: Cambridge Scholars Publishing, 2007: 20–29. See also Fay Weldon, "I Still Hide the Cover When I Read a Mills & Boon," www.telegraph.co.uk/comment/3553925/I-still-hide-the-cover.... Accessed 2 April 2014.
136. Interview with Diane Moggy.
137. The rugged Australian rancher travels just as well the other way, as evident in *Crocodile Dundee* (1986), *Crocodile Dundee II* (1988), and *Crocodile Dundee in Los Angeles* (2001).
138. *Hard Jacka* would be offered as a case study by Harlequin Enterprises Australia before the Australian Productivity Commission to argue against restrictions to a proposal to surrender territorial copyright. www.pc.gov/au/data/assets/pdf_file/0008/85814/sub239. Accessed 3 February 2014. See also www.hardjacka.com/reviews. Accessed 23 February 2014.
139. Margaret Ann Jensen, *Love's Sweet Return*, 33.
140. Paul Grescoe, *The Merchants of Venus*, 108–109.
141. Gresco quotes Horst Bausch, a former foreign editor with *Der Spiegel*, who was then acquiring novels for Springer: "The top editorial echelons in Springer were really quite snobbish. They simply didn't like the romance genre." Paul Grescoe, *The Merchants of Venus*, 108.
142. Grescoe is quoting Ralf Kläsener, then divisional editor at Springer. Paul Grescoe, *The Merchants of Venus*, 108.
143. "Global Publishing Leaders 2013: Harlequin."
144. "Harlequin Expands Business in Germany," *Book Business* 2013. www.bookbusinessmag.com/article/harlequin-expands-business-germany. Accessed 14 February 2014.
145. "Romance Inc.: Why the Love Industry Flourishes," *The Independent*, 23 September 2008. www.indpendent.co.uk/life-style/love-sex/clture-of-llove/romance-inc-why.... Accessed 3 February 2014.
146. Paul Grescoe, *The Merchants of Venus*, 110.
147. Paul Grescoe, *The Merchants of Venus*, 110–111.
148. Paul Grescoe, *The Merchants of Venus*, 112–113.
149. Paul Grescoe, *The Merchants of Venus*, 113.
150. Beverly Slopen, "Harlequin Girdles the Globe with Women's Romance," *Toronto Star*, 25 June 1989: C7.
151. Paul Grescoe, *The Merchants of Venus*, 111–113.
152. Eva Hemmungs Wirtén, *Global Infatuation: Explorations in Transnational Publishing and Texts, The Case of Harlequin Enterprises and Sweden*. Dissertation for the Degree of Doctor of Philosophy in Literature, Uppsala University, 1998. See also Eva Hemmungs Wirtén, "'They Seek It Here, They Seek It There, They Seek It Everywhere': Looking for the 'Global' Book," *Canadian Journal of Communication* 23, no. 2 (1998). www.cjc-online.ca/index.php/journal/article/view/1034/940. Accessed 5 January 2014.
153. Margaret Ann Jensen, *Love's Sweet Return*.
154. Margaret Ann Jensen, *Love's Sweet Return*, 119.
155. Writes one reviewer of the novel on Goodreads: "This was a train wreck.... The Hero is a brute. A tyrant who manhandles the heroine at the drop of his hat." The same today can be said of Emile Bronte's novel; one reviewer of *Wuthering Heights* comments, "I often wonder how Heathcliff, whose acts are often mean-spirited bullying, is often seen as a Byronic hero...?" A study of sexual violence in romance novels has not, to my knowledge, been undertaken, but would be instructive. Modern sensibilities to violence in romantic relationships would suggest that it is rarer in contemporary romances, but it would be interesting to track this change, if, indeed, it has changed in the Alpha hero. www.goodreads.com/book/show/7889086-the-devils-mistress; www.goodreads.com/topic/show/1019195-i-often-wonder-how-heathcliff. Accessed 21 February 2014.
156. Eva Hemmungs Wirtén, *Global Infatuation*, 150.
157. Eva Hemmungs Wirtén, *Global Infatuation*, 148.
158. The wall was technically breached on 9 November 1989 when East Germans were allowed the freedom to travel; the wall was not destroyed until 1990, paving the way for German reunification in October 1990.
159. "Harlequin: Safe in Print, Wild at Work," *Orlando Sentinel*, 17 April 1990: C6. This may be journalistic hyperbolic rounding; Paul Grescoe reports the number actually distributed was 720,000 books, a still not insignificant number. Paul Grescoe, *The Merchants of Venus*, 249.
160. "Harlequin: Safe in Print, Wild at Work."
161. Tony Van Alphen, "New Plant Vital, Torstar Says," *Toronto Star*, 9 May 192: D3.
162. Ton Van Alphen, "New Plant Vital, Torstar Says." "Harlequin Makes Love in the East," *The Globe and Mail*, 4 May 1991: B6. Paul Grescoe, *The Merchants of Venus*, 249–51.
163. Beth Hale, "Mills & Boon to Publish Novels in Polish to Cash in on Eastern European

Immigration," *MailOnline* (28 January 2008). www.dailymail.co.uk/news/article-510755/Mills-Boon-publish-novels-Polish-cash... Accessed 20 January 2014.

164. John Lorinc, "Romance Language..."

165. Paul Grescoe, *The Merchants of Venus*, 250.

166. The first recession hit in March 2001 and lasted eight months; the second struck when the stock market declined by 54 percent and ran from December 2007 through June 2009, though the stock market would not fully recover for a few more years and some areas are arguably still struggling economically as late as 2014.

167. John Lorinc, "Romance Language..." Rob Ferguson, "Torstar to Expand Harlequin Operations in Russia, Says Chairman," *Canadian Press NewsWire*, 29 April 1998.

168. Rob Ferguson, "Harlequin Eyes China, Torstar Shops in Vain."

169. "Publishing—Books; Harlequin Announces New Licensee in Russia," *Leisure & Travel Business* (4 July 2010): 62.

170. John Partridge, "Harlequin Eyes China, Torstar Shops in Vain," *The Globe and Mail*, 6 May 1989: B.3; Rob Ferguson, "Torstar to Expand Harlequin Operations in Russia, Says Chairman," *The Canadian Press NewsWire*, 29 April 1998.

171. Donna Hayes in 2005 reiterated the interest in China that was announced by Brian Hickey a decade earlier. See Richard Blackwell, "How Harlequin Kept the Romance Alive."

172. Interview with Diane Moggy.

173. The Japanese manga romances are translated into simplified Chinese characters and made available for mobile digital distribution by Celsy, one of the largest mobile portals and E-channel providers in China."Harlequin Comics Go Mobile in China," *Downthetubes.net: Mobile and Digital Comics News Blog* (23 May 2009). See also "Harlequin Harem Romance Novels: To Be or Not to Be," *China.org.cn* (27 January 2014). www.china.org.cn/english/Books&Magazines/22147. Accessed 25 February 2014.

174. Paul Grescoe, *The Merchants of Venus*, 115–117.

175. K. A. Adams and L. Hill, "Protest and Rebellion: Fantasy Themes in Japanese Comics," *Journal of Popular Culture* 25, no. 1 (Summer 1991): 99–128.

176. "Harlequin Romance, Manga-Style," *MediaBistro: The Pulse of the Media*, 9 January 2006. www.mediabistro.com/galleycat/harlequin-romance-manga-style. Accessed 20 February 2014. See also Charles Bodsworth, "How Mills & Boon Turned to Manga Comics," *BBC News*, 12 April 2004. www.news.bbc.co.uk/2/hi/uk_news/magazine/3614229. Accessed 20 February 2014.

177. The titles and release years are found at baka-updates manga harlequin, www.mangaupdates.com/publishers.html?id=362. Accessed 20 February 2014.

178. "Harlequin to Launch New Romance manga Mag in Japan," *AnimeNewsNetwork*, 19 January 2009. www.animenewsnetwork.com/news/2009-01-19/harlequin-to-launch.... Accessed 20 February 2014.

179. Deb Auki,"Harlequin Romance Comics Debut on eManga.com," *About.com Manga*, 14 December 2009. www.manga.about.com/b/2009/12/14/8-harlequin-romance-comics-debut-on-emanga. Accessed 20 February 2014.

180. A selection of Harlequin manga romance covers can be examined on Goodreads. www.goodreads.com/list/show/40290.Harlequin_Manga. Accessed 18 February 2014.

181. Diana Palmer is best known for her romantic westerns. It should not be surprising that the cowboy travels well; he is akin to the samurai tradition in Japan. The transmigration of the cowboy-samurai may best be exemplified in the East-to-West transformation of the *Seven Samurai* (1954) into *The Magnificent Seven* (1960).

182. Jayashree Kamble, "Female Enfranchisement and the Popular Romance: Employing an Indian Perspective," in *Empowerment versus Oppression: Twenty-First-Century Views of Popular Romance Novels*, edited by Sally Goade. Newcastle: Cambridge Scholars Publishing, 2007: 148–191.

183. The author gave the title of the book and the publisher. The fact that they were "sweets," including those from Avon that were examined, escaped the author's attention.

184. John Markert, "The Globalization of Sexual Harassment," in *Advances in Gender Research, Volume 9—Gender Realities: Local and Global*, edited by M. T. Segal and V. Demos. Amsterdam: Elsevier: 133–160.

185. John Markert, *The Social Impact of Sexual Harassment*. Spokane: Marquette Books, 2010: 23–33. See also L. S. Chancer, *Reconcilable Differences: Confronting Beauty, Pornography, and the Future of Feminism*. Berkeley: University of California Press, 1998. N. F. Cott, editor, *History of Women in the United States: Feminist Struggles for Sex Equality*. Munich: K. G. Saur.

186. Some of the novels available on hqindia.com are more current, but it is unclear how well these novels are selling or who is purchasing these more erotic novels.

Chapter 9

1. Line sales figures are proprietary information. It can reasonably be deduced, however, that the line is financially successful if it endures, just as it can be surmised that many lines in the 1980s did not generate significant sales because they were eliminated in relatively short order.

2. John B. Thompson, *Merchants of Culture*. New York: Plum (Penguin USA), 2012. The book was originally published by Polity Press in London, 2010.

3. The entrepreneurial phase actually began in the 1920s, but the mass-market paperback phase would not begin until the 1940s, so I am using the later date.

4. John B. Thompson, *Merchants of Culture*, Appendix I. The other media groups discussed in this section are itemized by Thompson in the appendix with more recent acquisitions noted by me.

5. "Letter from the President" in the "About Us" section from Kensington's website. www.kensingtonbooks.com/page.aspx/about. Accessed 12 July 2014.

6. Senior management at all these publishing firms indicate that they regularly fend off offers from the Big Five.

7. Cited by Albert N. Greco, *Book Publishing Industry*, 2nd edition. Mahwah, NJ: Lawrence Erlbaum Associates, 2005: 64. See Ben H. Bagdikian, *The Media Monopoly*, 6th edition. Boston: Beacon Press, 2000.

8. The recent case (July 2013) involving the "price fixing" of e-books that transpired between Penguin, Hachette, HarperCollins, Simon & Schuster, and Apple underscores the interdependence of the Big Five. Judge Cotes ruled, "The plaintiffs have shown that the publisher defendants conspired with each other to eliminate retail price competition in order to raise e-book prices, and that Apple played a central role in facilitating and executing that conspiracy." www.bbc.co.uk/news/business-23259935. I am indebted to Laura Vivanco for bringing this case to my attention.

9. Albert N. Greco, *The Book Publishing Industry*, 65.

10. Diane Patrick, "The State of African-American Publishing," *Publishers Weekly*, 10 December 2012. www.publishersweekly.com/...-publishing-african-american-interest-books-2012-13. Accessed 14 July 2014.

11. Diane Patrick, "The State of African-American Publishing."

12. Harrison White, "Where Do Markets Come From?" *American Journal of Sociology* 87 (1981): 517–547. See also Paul DiMaggio and Walter Powell, "Institutional Isomorphism," *American Sociological Review* 48 (1983): 147–160.

13. Robert Hayes, Gary Pisano, David Upton, and Steven Wheelwright, *Operations, Strategy, and Technology: Pursuing the Competitive Edge*. Hoboken, NJ: Wiley, 2005: 287.

14. Mentioned by Latoya Smith at Grand Central in an interview with Diane Patrick, "The State of African-American Publishing." It is worth noting that while Smith specifically said this, most of those interviewed in this article and mainstream editors interviewed in the course of this study acknowledge that a primary source of finding new authors is to search online sites.

15. Tami M. Bereska, "Adolescent Sexuality and the Changing Romance Novel Market," *The Canadian Journal of Human Sexuality* 3, no. 1 (Spring 1994): 35–44.

16. Tami M. Bereska, "Adolescent Sexuality and the Changing Romance Novel Market."

17. L. K. Christian-Smith, *Becoming a Woman Through Romance*. New York: Rutledge, Chapman, and Hall, 1990.

18. The three Scholastic lines could still be found in the book club but were no longer available in retail outlets. They would finally be terminated. K. Christian-Smith, *Becoming a Woman Through Romance*. Interview with Aimee Friedman, executive editor at Scholastic.

19. Naomi R. Johnson summarizes the prevailing literature of the period in "Consuming Desires: Consumption, Romance, and Sexuality in Best-Selling Teen Romance Novels," *Women's Studies in Communication* 33, No. 1 (2010): 54–73.

20. Tami M. Bereska, "Adolescent Sexuality and the Changing Romance Novel Market."

21. Julie Naughton, "YA Romance Makes the Honor Roll: Focus on Romance 2012," *Publishers Weekly* 259, no. 23 (1 June 2012): 21.

22. References to Scholastic in this section are based on interviews with executive editor Aimee Friedman, unless otherwise cited

23. Interview with Todd Stocke, editorial director at Sourcebooks. References to Sorucebooks in this section are based on interviews with Todd Stocke unless otherwise cited.

24. John Markert, "Demographics of Age: Generational and Cohort Confusion," *Journal of Current Issues and Research in Advertising* XXVI, no. 2 (Fall 2004): 11–26.

25. Kate Pavao, "Out of the Closet: Now More than Ever, Gay and Lesbian Characters are Prominently Featured in YA Fiction," *Publishers Weekly*, 1 December 2014.

26. "Letters to the Editor," *The Tennessean*, 7 May 2014: A10.

27. Julie Naughton, "YA Romance Makes the Honor Roll."

28. Naomi R. Johnson, "Consuming Desires: Consumption, Romance, and Sexuality in Best-Selling Teen Romance Novels," 58.

29. Ibid., 58.

30. This assessment is based on comments by readers remembering books in the series that appear in reviews on Goodreads.

31. Bob Minzesheimer, "Teen Novels Tear Up USA TODAY Best-Seller List," *USA Today*, 8 July 2014: 7B.

32. Interview with David Long, senior acquisitions editor of fiction at Bethany House. Ref-

erences to Bethany House in this section are based on interviews with David Long unless otherwise cited.

33. Interview with David Long at Bethany.
34. *Fleming H. Revell Company: The First 125 Years, 1870–1995.* Grand Rapids, MI: 1995.
35. Interview with David Long at Bethany.
36. Thomas Nelson has never been as overtly evangelical as Zondervan.
37. Interview with Ramona Richards, senior acquisition editor with Abingdon Press, United Methodist Publishing. References to Abingdon Press in this section are based on interviews with Ramona Richards unless otherwise cited. www.religionfacts.com/christianity/denominations/amish. Accessed 12 May 2014.
38. Peter Darbyshire, "The Politics of Love: Harlequin Romances and the Christian Right," *Journal of Popular Culture*, 35, no. 4, 2002: 75–87.
39. Rebecca Kaye Barrett, "Higher Love: What Women Gain from Christian Romance Novels," *Journal of Religion and Popular Culture*, 4 (Summer) 2003: 1–11.
40. Clawson analyzed the content of Barbour's Heartsong line and Harlequin's Love Inspired line and contrasted them to Harlequin's Romance, American Romance, and Desire lines.
41. Laura Clawson, "Cowboys and Schoolteachers: Gender in Romance Novels, Secular and Christian," *Sociological Perspectives* 48, no. 4, 2006: 461–479.
42. Rebecca Barrett-Fox, "Hope, Faith and Toughness: An Analysis of the Christian Hero," in *Empowerment versus Oppression: Twenty-First-Century Views of the Popular Romance Novel*, edited by Sally Goade. Cambridge: Cambridge Scholars Publishing, 2007: 93–102.
43. See also Lynn S. Neal, *Romancing God: Evangelical Women and Inspirational Fiction.* Chapel Hill: University of North Carolina Press, 2006.
44. The Golden Medallion was the initial name of the award for best romance before it was renamed RITA.
45. *Religion Facts: The Amish.* www.religionfacts.com/christianity/denominations/amish, Accessed 12 May 2014. These facts are augmented by my personal knowledge of the Amish, having grown up in the heart of Amish country (Lancaster, PA).
46. Interview with David Long.
47. Interview with Ramona Richards.
48. Prairie romances (sometimes referred to as Americana) are set in the 1800s. They are still popular; they have just been shoved to the side by the sheer volume of Amish romances. Interview with David Long.
49. See Valerie Weaver-Zercher, "Why Amish Romance Novels Are Hot," *The Wall Street Journal*, 6 June 2013. www.online.wsj/articles/SB 10001424127887324063304578525410241734 112#. Accessed 14 May 2014. Weaver-Zercher has also penned a book on the Amish romance novel, *Thrill of the Chase: The Allure of Amish Romance Novels.* Baltimore: Johns Hopkins University Press, 2013.
50. One little-known aspect of Amish life that was mentioned as a potential theme by Ramona Richards was the Pinecraft beach resort in southern Florida, where the Amish and Mennonites go to vacation (the season runs December through April). The resort is on the outskirts of Sarasota and has been refereed to as an Amish Las Vegas. See also Miki Meed, "Where Amish Snowbirds Find a Nest," *New York Times*, 13 April 2012. www.nytimes.com/2012/04/15/travel/pinecraft-fla-where-amish-snowbirds-find-a-nest. Accessed 15 May 2014. Luren Selsky, "'Amish Las Vegas': What Happens in Pinecraft Stays in Pinecraft," *NBC News*, 28 April 2013. www.today.com/amish-las-vegas-what-happens-in-Pinecraft-stays-in-Pinecraft. Accessed 15 May 2014.
51. Victoria Dahl, "10 Dirty Romance Novels," *Publishers Weekly*, 7 February 2014. www.publishersweekly.com/…tip-sheet/article 60950–10-best-dirty-novels. Accessed 10 May 2014. Jennifer Porter, "10 Erotic Romance Novels You Should Read (An Opinionated Opinion)," *Heroes and Hearbreakers.com*, 5 November 2013. www.heroesandheartbreakers.com/blogs/2013/11/10-erotic-romance-novels-you-should-read…. Accessed 7 February 2014.
52. These are among the mainstream publishers who have any presence on iBookstore's Top 50 Erotic Romance Ebooks, May 2014. www.popvortex.com/books/charts/erotic-romance-ebooks. Accessed 20 June 2014.
53. These names appeared with some frequency on iBookstore's Top 50 list of erotic books.
54. "The Quick and Dirty History of Erotic Romance," *The Adventures of … Super Librarian.* www.wendythesuperlibrarian.blogspot.com/…the-quick-and-dirty-history… Accessed September 5, 2014.i
55. As of May 2014.
56. Interview with Christina (Cris) Brashear, publisher at Samhain. References to Samhain in this section are based on interviews with Brashear unless otherwise specified.
57. Interview with Margaret Riley, co-founder and publisher with Changeling Press. References to Changeling Press are based on interviews with Riley unless otherwise specified.
58. Interview with David DeBalko, CEO of Siren. References to Siren in this section are based on interviews with DeBalko unless otherwise specified.
59. Trisha Telep, "Second Life in Self-Publishing: For Romance Writers, Getting

Dropped Midseries Is No Longer the End of the World," *Publishers Weekly*, 18 April 2014. www.publishersweek.com/author/pw-select/article/61925-series-interrupted. Accessed 5 June 2014.

60. Both analyses are based on reviewer comments about the books on Goodreads.

61. Sara Robbins, "Erotica—Fanning the Flames," *Publishers Weekly* Vol. 257, No. 30 (August 2, 2010). www.publishersweekly.com/.../article/44013-erotica-fanning-the-flames. Accessed 13 May 2014.

62. Quoted by Sara Robbins in "Erotica—Fanning the Flames."

63. Even if we discount the excessive number of books released monthly by Siren (100) and base our calculations on the other nine xrotic publishers, who publish on the average 10 books a week, we're still talking a phenomenal number of xrotic romances: nine publishers releasing an average of ten books a month results in a yearly output of some 4,680 books, which is double the total number of romances published by all the mainstream houses, including Harlequin.

64. Output was calculated based on the number of novels released in each of the following Harlequin category romances: American Romances, Blaze, Desire, Historical, Intrigues, Medical, Presents, Romance, Romantic Suspense, Special Editions, Superromance and Nocturne.

65. Her actual quote is "the hands-down most important component of successful erotica is quality." Sara Robbins, "Erotica—Fanning the Flames."

66. Benedicte Page, "Erotica on hold for Black Lace and Nexus at Virgin," *The Bookseller*, 6 July 2009. www.thebookseller.com/news/erotica-hold-black-lace-and-nexus-virgin. Accessed 1 July 2014.

67. Alison Flood, "Uproar as Erotica Publisher Black Lace Withdraws from Market," *The Guardian*, 7 July 2009. www.theguardian.com/books/2009/jul/07/erotica-publisher-black-lace. Accessed 1 July 2014.

68. Alison Flood, "Uproar as Erotica Publisher Black Lace Withdraws from Market."

69. Claire Siemaszkiewicz, "Yes, Yes, Yesssss...! Erotic Romance Sales Still Sizzle," *Publishing Perspective*, 7 January 2014. www.publishingperspectives.com/.../01/yes-yes-yesssss-erotic-romance-sales-still-sizzle. Accessed 1 July 2014.

70. Julie Naughton, "Anything Goes: Focus on Romance, Fall 2012," *Publishers Weekly* 259, no. 46 (12 November 2012. www.publishersweekly.com/.../54762-anything-goes-focus-on-romance-fall-2012. Accessed 17 August 2014.

71. These are the pre-launch prices quoted in late October for the November 2014 release of the book.

72. Quoted by Sarah Robbins in "Erotica—Fanning the Flames."

73. One book was in the erotic category. The other categories Entangled was represented in include Best First Book, Best Historical, and Best Short Contemporary.

74. Riley at Changeling is a dedicated science fiction reader and feels that the genre greatly neglects women readers, which may be why her sci-fi paranormal erotic romances are doing so well at Changeling. Nevertheless, it is still viewed by most in the industry as predominantly a male-oriented genre.

75. A content analysis of manga was undertaken by the Tokyo Metropolitan Government. It found that 50 percent portrayed sexual acts; 96 percent of the females in the colored pictures were between 13 and 32, with one-third barebreasted and nearly one-fifth fully naked. V. Fic, "Sexual Harassment Still a Fixture in the Japanese Office," *Tokyo Business*, December 1994: 24–26. See also K. Adams and L. Hill, "Protest and Rebellion: Fantasy Themes in Japanese Comics," *Journal of Popular Culture* 25 (1991): 99–128. John Markert, *The Social Impact of Sexual Harassment*. Spokane, Wash.: Marquette Books, 2010: 159.

76. Interview with Sandy Lowe, senior editor, Bold Strokes Books. Information relating to BSB in this section is based on comments by Lowe unless otherwise specified.

77. Julie Naughton, "Anything Goes."

78. Quoted by Gendy Alimurung, "Man on Man: The New Gay Romance...Written By and For Straight Women," *L.A. Weekly*, 17 December 2009. www.laweekly.com/printVersion/799568." Accessed 5 May 2014.

79. Quoted by Gendy Alimurung, "Man on Man: The New Gay Romance." Williams wrote the definitive work on contemporary pornography, *Hard Core: Power, Pleasure, and the "Frenzy of the Visible."* Berkeley: University of California Press, 1989.

80. Gendy Alimurung goes so far as to say that the m/m characters are actually women: "They may look like boys, and make love with male bodies, but they think and act and love like girls." Gendy Alimurung, "Man on Man: The New Gay Romance."

81. Interview with the authors, published on Cleis's home site. www.cleispress.com. Accessed 7 June 2014.

82. Knight was hired to oversee the day-to-day running of the press.

83. Interview with Brenda Knight, publisher, Cleis Press. Information relating to Cleis in this section is based on comments by Knight unless otherwise specified.

84. Interview with Sandy Lowe.

85. Interview with Ariel Tachna at Dreamspinner Press. Information relating to Dreamspinner in this section is based on comments by Tachna unless otherwise cited.

86. Books are divided into lesbian, GBT, and YA on the website. Under GBT there is no way to single out books by heterosexual women, nor were results found when entering the search for "Maverick Books" on the website.

87. Heterosexual women readers of m/m romances often say that they could tell when an author was a man even if he used a female pen name. They may not have been able to do with this 100 percent accuracy, but more often then not they could.

88. Interview with Jessica St. Ama, editor, Torquere Books. Information relating to Torquere in this section is based on comments by St. Ama unless otherwise cited.

89. Interview with Laura Baumbach, founder and publisher of ManLoveRomance Publishing. Information relating to ManLove in this section is based on comments by Baumbach unless otherwise cited.

90. Robert Bianco, "'Modern Family' Wedding Special Because It's Not," *USA Today*, 20 May 2014: 8B.

91. Information on Riptide is from the "about us" section on their website. www.riptidepublishing/faq. Accessed 20 May 2014.

92. Flash fiction is a short-short story that typically runs 100 to 1,000 words.

93. Many fans consider female slash (f/f) a separate genre.

94. "Nordette Adams, First Black Romance Novelist, Elsie B. Washington, Dies at 66," *The Examiner*, 2 June 2009. www.examiner.com/article/first-black-romance-author-novelist-elsie-b-washington-dies-at-66. Accessed 10 August 2013. See also "How Black Romance—Novels, That Is—Came to Be," *The Free Library* 1 January 2002. www.thefreelibrary.com/How+black+romance-novels,+that+is-came+to+be. Accessed 10 August 2013.

95. Rachel Potter, "Kathleen Gilles Seidel: Thoughtful Writer, Buried Treasure," *All About Romance: The Back Fence For Lovers of Romance Novels*, 17 June 2003. www.likebooks.com/seidel. Accessed 2 June 2014.

96. Kensington acquired Holloway House's backlist in 2008 to complement its African American imprints: Dafina, Urban Soul, and Vibe Street Lit. Calvin Reid, "Kensington Acquires Holloway House Backlist," *Publishers Weekly*, 20 February 2008. www.publishersweekly.com/pw/by-topic/industry-news/book-deals/article/831-kensington-acquires-holloway-house-backlist. Accessed 1 June 2014.

97. "How Black Romance—Novels, That Is—Came to Be."

98. The African American population composes just under 14 percent of the population, Asian slightly over 4 percent, Hispanics around 17 percent, and Native Americans, including Pacific Islanders, 1 percent.

99. There were thirty-three books listed on the home page for African American romance novels on Goodreads: four were new releases, sixteen (after discounting the one repetitive novel from new releases) were listed as "most read," and twelve were listed as "perennially popular."

100. Gwendolyn E. Osborne, "The Color of Love: Harlequin Courts African American Women with Its Own New Lines and Elopes with BET/Arabesque Imprint," *The Free Library*. www.thefreelibrary.com/...quin+courts+African+American+women+with.... Accessed 5 February 2014. The information is based on Osborne's article "Women Who Look Like Me: Cultural Identity and Reader Responses to African-American Romance Novels," in *Race/Gender/Media: Considering Diversity Across Audience, Content, and Producers*, edited by Rebecca Ann Lind, Longman Press, 2003.

101. Interview with Stephen Zacharius, president of Kensington Publishing. Information related to Kensington in this section is based on interviews with Zacharius unless otherwise specified.

102. Interview with Michelle Monkou.

103. Interview with Farrah Rochon.

104. Interview with Farrah Rochon.

105. The Indian population is the largest non-white ethnic minority in the city and composes 6.4 percent of London's population.

106. Further hindering U.S. sales among Latinas is that the English-language novels are translated in Spain for the Latin American market and do not "adapt" the Spanish to that which is spoken in Latin America.

107. John Markert, "Superstitious Peasants: Religious Images on Spanish-Language Television in the United States," *Sociological Imagination* 43, no. 2 (2007): 21–35. John Markert, "Divergent Gender-Role Messages on Spanish-Language Television in the Untied States: Cracks in the Edifice, Unlatching the Window of Change," *Sociological Imagination* 45, no. 1 (2009): 41–61.

108. Sharon Jayson, "U.S. Rate of Interracial Marriage Hits Record High," *USA Today*, 16 February 2012. www.usatoday.com/30.usatoday.com/health/wellness/marriagehistory2012-02-16/US-rate-of-interracial-marriage-hits-record-high/53109980/1. Accessed 6 June 2014.

109. Calculation based on Pew Research report that breaks down racial marriages on a state-by-state base. Sharon Jayson, "U.S. Rate of Interracial Marriage Hits Record High."

110. Belinda Edmondson, "The Black Romance," *Women's Study Quarterly* 35 (Spring 2007: 191–211).

111. "Fast Facts: Degrees Conferred by Sex and Race," *Institute of Education Sciences, National Center for Educator Statistics*. www.nces.ed.gov/fastfacts/display/asp?id+72. Accessed 10 June 2014.

112. Jenifer L. Bratter and Rosalind B. King,

"'But Will It Last?': Marital Instability Among Interracial and Same-Race Couples," *Family Relations*, 57 (April 2008), 160–171.

113. Harlequin's Arabesque line no longer emphasizes the exclusivity of the character's race but does say that it focuses on African American relationships, leaving the door somewhat ajar for the potential of filtering black-white interracial romances into the series.

114. Maisy Yates published *The Highest Price to Pay* with Mills & Boon in 2011. The cover featured a black man and a white woman. The Australian version muted the hero's skin tone on the cover. I could not find a North American cover on the Harlequin home site. There are certainly other interracial romances by mainstream publishers, but they are few and far between.

115. Interview with Jayha Leigh, co-founder of Beautiful Trouble Publishing, and Kelly Ann Pearson, co-founder of Sugar and Spice. Information in this section is from Leigh and Pearson unless otherwise cited.

116. Jackie C. Horne, "Color-Aware Interracial Romance: Nina Perez's *Sharing Space*," *Romance Novels for Feminists: For Readers Who Like a Little Equality with Their Love*, 1 April 2014. www.romancenovelsforfeminists.blogspot.com/color-aware-interracial-romance-nina. Accessed 1 June 2014.

117. Pearson acknowledges that the heroines at Kimani are strong characters; it's just that "ours are stronger."

118. Wendy Wang, "The Rise of Intermarriage: Rates, Characteristics Vary by Race and Gender," *Pew Research: Social and Demographic Trends*, 16 February 2012. www.pewsocialtrends.org/2012/02/16/the-rise-of-intermarriage. Accessed 21 June 2012.

119. Chris Berube, "How 'Fifty Shades of Grey' Is Shaking Up the Business of the Romance Genre," *The Daily Beast*, 6 June 2012. www.thedailybeast.com/articles/2012/06/06/how-fifty-shades-of-grey-is-shaking…. Accessed 5 July 2014.

120. She does not use a period after her initials, though the *New York Times* "corrects" this oversight and typically puts a period after E. L.

121. Valeria Peterson, "From Traditional Publisher to Indie Author," *About.com Book Publishing* (n/d). www.publishing.about.com/od/SelfPublishingAndVanityPresses/a/From-Tradtioanl-Pbulisher-To Indie-Author. Accessed 12 July 2014.

122. Damien Walter, "Self-Publishing: Is It Killing the Mainstream?" *The Guardian*, 14 February 2014. www.theguardian.com/…/2014/feb/14/self-publishing-mainstream-genre-fiction. Accessed 16 May 2014.

123. The numbers are generated from Nelson data. See Erin Burnett, "Romance Writer Megan Mulry Takes a Risk on Self-Publishing," *Out-Front*, CNN.com Blogs. 27 November 2013. www.outfront.blogs.cnn.com/2013/11/27/romance-writer-megan-mulry-takes-a-risk-on-self-publihsing. Accessed 16 June 2014.

124. Erin Burnett, "Romance Writer Megan Mulry…"

125. The numbers are generated from Bowker, which tracks industry trends. See Erin Burnett, "Romance Writer Megan Mulry…"

126. I am indebted to Beverly Kendall for allowing me to discuss, often verbatim, her findings. The interested reader can access the complete study, "The Self-Publishing Survey Results—It's a Brave New Word," at www.theseasonforromance.com/wordpress/2014/01/the-self-publishing-survey-results-its-a-brave-new-world.

127. Many times in the course of this study when I needed to identify who published a specific book, I had to search for the copyright page to identify the house.

128. Interview with Farrah Rochon.

129. Monkou was concerned about the high cost ($200) for a cover and has now found someone to do a professional job for a lot less: $45 a cover.

130. Interview with Courtney Milan.

131. Mark Coker, "10 Reasons Self-Published Authors Will Capture 50 Percent of the Ebook Market by 2020," *Huffington Post*, 7 March 2014. www.huffingtonpost.com/mark-coker/10-reasons-self-publsihed_b_491594. Accessed 28 August 2014.

132. In October 2014, as this analysis was coming to a close, Barbara Freethy, a successful self-published author, has pioneered another first in the industry, not just within romance publishing. Her e-book will be printed and distributed to retails outlets via Ingram Publishing Services, a subsidiary of Ingram Content Group, which provides books to booksellers, librarians, educators, and specialty retailers across the United States. Kristin Ramsdell considers this the "missing link for many indie authors," who now have the ability to have their print titles distributed though a major vendor. See www.publishersweekly.com/pw/by-topic/industry-news/publisher-news/article/64405-kdp-star-freethy-launches-print-imprint. Accessed 3 November 2014. Personal correspondence with Kristin Ramsdell.

133. Even for those houses that have a dedicated line of romances, there is often no monthly number of books they are committed to like Harlequin.

134. I am using the term "legitimate" here to distinguish the serious self-published romance authors from those who just throw up one book, one time, on Amazon.

135. Harlequin's Heartwarming, launched in 2011, is the one secular line that is specifically positioned to develop the sweet themes; its tagline reads: "Heartwarming celebrates whole-

some, heartfelt relationships imbued with the traditional values so important to you: home, family, community and love."

136. Kensington does xrotica but only in e-books. In fact, its purchase of e-book publisher Lyrical Press was to expedite its entry into xrotica. Interview with Stephen Zacharius.

137. This was a self-justification for not releasing romances featuring minorities; it mattered to whites, who, the editors felt, wouldn't want to read about minorities. So color did matter.

Chapter 10

1. This would normally be extended to six in order to include Harlequin, but since Harlequin has now been bought and subsumed by HarperCollins, it remains the Big Five.

2. Arthur Stinchcombe, "Social Structure and Organizations," in *Handbook of Organizations*, edited by James G. March. Chicago: Rand McNally, 1965: 142–193.

3. Ieva Strodomskyte, Xin Dai and Stian Hauge, "'All You Need is Trust'—To Overcome the Liability of Newness by Forming Alliances," master's thesis in Innovation and Entrepreneurship, Centre for Entrepreneurship: University of Oslo (December 2012). www.duo.uio.no/handle/10852/12893. Accessed 4 August 2014.

4. Ibid. David Krackhardt, "Social Networks and the Liability of Newness for Managers," *Trends in Organizational Behavior* 3 (1996): 159–173.

5. Charles Perrow. *Complex Organizations: A Critical Essay*, 3rd edition. New York: Random House, 1986.

6. Michael Lounsbury and Marc J. Ventresca. *Social Structure and Organizations Revised: Research in the Sociology of Organizations* 19. Oxford: JAI Press, 2002.

7. Arthur Stinchcombe, "Social Structure and Organizations." See also Elisabeth S. Clemens, "Invention, Innovation, Proliferation: Explaining Organizational Genesis and Change," in *Social Structure and Organizations Revisited*, 397–441.

8. In most cases, this experience was from a writer's perspective. It was the hesitancy of mainstream publishers to publish their novels that prompted them to start their own house in the belief that if they liked to write these kinds of novels, there must be others out there who would like to read them, a variant of the editors' perspective that if they liked the book, the reader would too.

9. Harlequin's Heartwarming does provide "wholesome reads," but it is shorn of the Christian message. www.romanceuniveristy.org/2013/10/11/fifty-shades-of-sweet-with-heartwarming-editor-victoria-curan. Accessed 5 October 2015.

10. Vanity presses have been the traditional recourse for "failed" authors before the digital age, but these presses seldom had a pronounced impact on the sale of the books. Typically, the author pays a set fee for a certain number of books to be printed and is then given the responsibility of promoting and distributing their print work.

11. I am translating euros into dollars. The currency conversion rate used was 1.338 euros to the dollar. The figures are based on their annual report for 2013. See investor relations at www.bertelsmann.com. Accessed 12 August 2014.

12. The Random House group's sales are base on 2007 sales figures. John B. Thompson in *Merchants of Culture*, 2nd edition. New York: Plume, 2012: 113.

13. Robert Hayes, Gary Pisano, David Upton, and Steven Wheelwright, *Operations, Strategy and Technology: Pursuing the Competitive Edge*. Hoboken, NJ: Wiley, 2005: 287.

14. Robert Hayes et al., *Operations, Strategy and Technology*, 317–321.

15. Jeremy Greenfield, "Ebook Growth Slows to Single Digit in U.S. in 2013," *Digital Book World*, 1 April 2014. www.digitalbookworld.com/…/ebook-growth-slows-to-single-digits-in-u-s-in-2013. Accessed 12 August 201.

16. David Stocke at Sourcebooks confirms my assessment: "In 2010, suddenly people wanted digital and wanted them in large quantities." Interview with David Stocke, Editorial Director, Sourcebooks.

17. Interview with Todd Stocke.

18. Greco's book was published in 2005, so, given the publishing lag, he would likely be relying on data from 2003. Albert N. Greco, *The Book Publishing Industry*, 2nd edition. Mahwah, N.J.: Lawrence Erlaum, 2005.

19. Ibid., 289.

20. John B. Thompson, *Merchants of Culture*, 2nd edition, 315.

21. Ibid., 318.

22. Jeremy Greenfield, "Ebook Growth Slows to Single Digit in U.S. in 2013."

23. John B. Thompson. *Merchants of Culture*, 2nd edition, 322.

24. Ibid., 314.

25. "Random House Revives Loveswept as E-only Imprint," *Publishers Weekly*, 22 June 2011. www.publishersweekly.com/…07-random-house- Accessed 13 August 2012revives-loveswept-as-e-only. Accessed 13 August 2014. See also, "Random House Revives Romance Imprint as Digital Exclusive," *The Bookseller*, 23 June 2011. www.thebookseller.com/…/random-house-revives-romance. Accessed 11 August 2014.

26. Joyce Lamb, "Interview: Sue Grimshaw, Loveswept Editor at Large," *USA Today*, 12 November 2011. www.books/usatoday.com/happyeverafter/post/2011–11-12/interview-loveswept-editor-at-large-sue grimshaw/5644455/1. Accessed 11 August 2014.

27. Ibid.

28. "Berkley/NAL to Launch E-book Imprint,

InterMix," *Publishers Weekly*, 19 October 2011. www.publishersweekly.com/...49162-berkley-nal-to-launch-e-book-imprint-intermix. Accessed 12 August 2014.

29. "Macmillan and Entangled Sign Distribution Partnership," *Publishers Weekly*, 8 January 2013. www.publishersweekly.com/macmillan-and-entangled-sign-distribution-partnership. Accessed 10 August 2014.

30. In late 2014, St. Martin's website shows only nine novels under the digital romance category; none bear the new imprint name.

31. Abbass F. Alkhafaji. *Restructuring American Corporations: Causes, Effects, and Implications*. New York: Quorum Books, 1990.

32. Interview with Stephen Zacharius.

33. Dianna Dilworth, "Kensington Publishing has Acquired eBook Publisher Lyrical Press." *Galleycat*, 3 January 2014. www.mediabistro.com/galleycat/kensington-publishing-has-acquired... Accessed 4 December 2013. See also "Kensington Buys Digital Pub, Lyrical Press," *Publishers Weekly*, 3 January 2014. www.publishersweekly.com/kensington-buys-digital-pub.... Accessed 3 January 2014.

34. Abbass F. Alkhafaji, *Restructuring American Corporations*, 11.

35. Jane Little at Dear Author expresses "dismay" over the sale, but this had less to do with concerns about content than her feeling that Harlequin has very author- and reader-friendly policies and HC not so much. www.dearauthor.com/.../essays/harpercollins-acquistion-harlequin-means-to-readers. Accessed 10 September 2014.

36. Ibid., 23–29, 51–55.

37. Jeremy Greenfield, "Three Reasons News Corp Bought Harlequin, World's Biggest Romance Book Publisher," *Forbes*, 2 May 2014. www.forbes.com/sites/jeremygreenfield/2014/05/02/news-corp-buys-harlquin... Accessed 7 June 2014.

38. Torstar needed the cash to shore up its newspaper syndicate, whose print sales have been plummeting in the digital age. The sale of Harlequin will help Torstar management address the $158.5 million they have in debt and provide some needed cash resources for them to move forward.

39. Avon romances are marked by their quality. Many of Avon's contemporary romances could be incorporated into Harlequin's existing MIRA or HQN lines; other Avon romances might fit into some of Harlequin's category lines. Avon's historical novels are particularly well received, and rolling them into Harlequin's Historicals would shore up this Harlequin line, which, though they have done well in the U.K., has not been a strong performer in North America. See my concluding remarks regarding mergers and acquisition, 492.

40. Julia Wood, "Saying It Makes It So: The Discursive Construction of Sexual Harassment," in *Conceptualizing Sexual Harassment as Discursive Discourse*, edited by S. G. Bingham, 17–32. Westport, CT: Praeger.

41. John B. Thompson, *Merchants of Culture*, 2nd edition, 75.

42. See endnote 35.

43. Lynn Andriani, "Harlequin Horizons Now DellArte Press," *Publishers Weekly*, 25 November 2009. www.publishersweekly.com//.../27076-harlequin-horizons-now-dellarte-press. Accessed 10 August 2014.

44. John Scalzi, "Writer's Organizations to Harlequin: If You're Not Going to Act Like a Real Publisher, We're Not Going to Treat You like One," www.whatever.scalzi.com/2009/11/20/writers-organizations-to-harlequin... Accessed 11 August 2014.

45. Lynn Andriani, "Harlequin Horizons Now DellArte Press."

46. Ron Hogan, "Harlequin's Lost Horizons: Self-Publishing Imprint Renamed," *GalleyCat*, 25 November 2009. www.mediabistro.com/galleycat/harelquins-lost-horizons-self-publishing-imprint-renamed. Accessed 10 August 2014.

47. Albert N. Greco. *The Book Publishing Industry*, 197.

48. E-mail communication with Carol Stacy, Publisher, *Romantic Times*.

49. Discussion with various sources in the field suggests that there are a lot of shenanigans in blog reviews. These machinations deserve serious scholarly attention since they can have a tremendous impact on sales. See www.theguardian.com/books/2012/sep/04/sock-puppertry-pubish-be-damned. Accessed 12 October 2014.

Chapter 11

1. When Zebra started to develop lines outside the historical romance genre, it was rechristened Kensington.

2. Many scholars have indicated that key personnel often do more than simply filter products onto the market and that they sometimes tweak the product based on their assessment of market conditions (see Introduction, page 9). The idea of gatekeepers existing on a continuum, from very loose filtering to actually making the product, has not been raised.

3. *Statistical Abstract of the United States, 2011*. Washington, D.C.: U.S. Census Bureau, 2012: Table 78 (Divorce Trends, 1960–2007).

4. Second Chance at Love's guidelines were among the most detailed of any house during the 1980s.

5. This would have been sidestepped in this analysis of the industry, since there was no foundation for this assessment, had events not taken an immediately different course under Swinwood.

6. Senior management at Torstar, HarperCollins, and Harlequin were all contacted (mul-

tiple times) but would not consent to an interview relating to the sale.

7. Kensington is the exception and has a strong xrotic digital presence.

8. I am using the term "marginal" simply to suggest that these houses cater to an audience beyond those typically addressed by mainstream publishers.

9. Even perennial best-selling novelist Stephen King was stymied by his publisher Doubleday, which would not publish *The Stand* until he cut it by 400 pages from the original 1,153 pages. Gilbert Cruise, "Stephen King on His 10 Longest Novels," *Time*, 6 Nov. 2009. www.entertainment.time.com/2009/11/09/stephen-king-on-his-10-longest-novels.

Bibliography

Abel, Elizabeth, ed. *Writing and Sexual Difference*. Chicago: University of Chicago Press, 1982.
Alchian, Armen. "Uncertainty, Evolution and Economic Theory," *Journal of Political Economy* 58 (1950): 311–21.
Aldrich, Howard. *Organizations and Environments*. Englewood Cliffs, N.J.: Prentice Hall, 1979.
Balle, Helen T. "Blood Ties: The Vampire Lover in the Popular Romance," *The Journal of American Culture* 34 (2), 2011: 141–148.
Barber, John. "Harlequin's Manly Masterpieces," *The Globe and Mail*, 29 May 2009.
_____. "Romancing the Tablet: How Harlequin is Revolutionizing the E-book Market," *The Globe and Mail*, 24 Aug. 2012.
Barrett, Rebeca Kaye. "Higher Love: What Women Gain from Christian Romance Novels," *Journal of Religion and Popular Culture* 4 (Summer), 2003. www.utpjournals.metapress.com/index/484H263478158331.
Bedeian, Arthur. *Organizations: Theory and Analysis*. Hinsdale, Ill.: Dryden Press, 1980.
Berg, A Scott. *Max Perkins: Editor of Genius*. New York: Washington Square Press, 1978.
Berman, Phyllis. "They Call Us Illegitimate," *Forbes*, 6 March 1978.
Bosman, Julie. "Lusty Tales and Hot Sales: Romance E-Books Thrive," *New York Times*, 8 Dec. 2010.
Brownmiller, Susan. *Against Our Will: Men, Women and Rape*. New York: Simon & Schuster, 1975.
Carroll, Glenn R. "Concentration and Specialization: Dynamics of Niche Width in Populations of Organizations," *American Journal of Sociology*, 90 (6), 1985: 1262–1283.
_____. "The Specialist Strategy," *California Management Review* 26 (Spring) 1984: 131–32.
Cawelti, John. *Adventure, Mystery, and Romance*. Chicago: University of Chicago Press, 1976.
Chafe, William. *Women and Equality: Changing Patterns in American Culture*. Oxford: Oxford University Press, 1977.
Charles, Ron. "Romance Novels Still Fighting for Respect," *The Washington Post*, 22 July 2009.
Clawson, Laura. "Cowboys and Schoolteachers: Gender in Romance Novels, Secular and Christian," *Sociological Perspectives*, 48 (4), 2006: 461–479.
Compaine, Benjamin M. *The Book Industry in Transition: An Economic Study of Book Distribution and Marketing*. White Plains, NY: Knowledge Industry Publications, 1978.
Coser, Lewis, Charles Kadushin and Walter W. Powell. *Books: The Culture and Commerce of Publishing*. New York: Basic Books, 1982.
Coward, Rosaland. "Are Women's Novels Feminist Novels?" *Feminist Review* 5, 1980.
Crider, Allen. *Mass Market Publishing in America*. Boston: G. K. Hall, 1982.
Danford, Natalie, et al. "Toujours l'Amour: Publishers are Seeking to Increase Readership by Diversifying Subgenres and Adding New Category Niches," *Publishers Weekly*, 1 Dec. 2003.
Daum, Meghan. "The Recession Heats up Romance Novels," *Los Angeles Times*, 4 April 2009.
Davis, Kenneth. *Two-Bit Culture: The Paperbacking of America*. Boston: Houghton Mifflin, 1984.

Bibliography

Deal, Terrence E., and Allen A. Kennedy. *Corporate Cultures: The Rites and Rituals of Corporate Life*. Reading, MA: Addison-Wesley, 1982.
Dessauer, John. "Book Publishing: What It Is, What It Does," in *American Mass Media*, edited by Robert Atwan, Barry Orton and William Vesterman. New York: Random House, 1982: 119–137.
DiMaggio, Paul, and Walter Powell. "Institutional Isomorphism," *American Sociological Review* 48 (1983): 147–160.
Dixon, Jay. *The Romance Fiction of Mills & Boon, 1909–1990s*. London: UCL Press, 1999.
Edmondson, Belinda. "The Black Romance," *Women's Studies Quarterly* 35 (1/2), 2007: 91–111.
Falk, Katherine, and Elene Kolb. "Telling the Romance Styles Apart," *Publishers Weekly*, November 13, 1981: 39.
Fetterley, Judith. *The Resisting Reader: A Feminist Approach to American Fiction*. Bloomington: Indiana University Press, 1978.
Fisher, M., and A. Cox. "Man Change Thyself: Hero Versus Heroine Development in Harlequin Romance Novels," *The Journal of Social, Evolutionary, and Cultural Psychology* 4 (4), 2010: 305–316.
Flood, Alison. "Mills & Boon Goes Behind National Trust's Bedroom Doors for Racy Novels," *The Guardian*, 2 May 2010.
Foster, Guy Mark. "How Dare a Black Woman Make Love to a White Man! Black Women Romance Novelists and the Taboo of Interracial Desire," in *Empowerment Versus Oppression: Twenty-First-Century View of Popular Romance Novels*, edited by Sally Goode. Newcastle: Cambridge Scholars Publishing, 2007: 103–128.
Frantz, Sarah S. G., and Selinger, Eric Murphy, eds. *New Approaches to Popular Romance Fiction: Critical Essays*. Jefferson, NC: McFarland, 2012.
Frelicher, Lila. "Millions of Women Avid for Avon's Erotic Historical Romances," *Publishers Weekly*, 6 October 1974: 44.
Gans, Herbert. *Deciding What's News: A Study of CBS Evening News, NBC Nightly News, Newsweek and Time*. New York: Random House, 1980.
Garry, Ann. "Pornography and Respect for Women," in *Pornography and Censorship*, edited by David Copp and Susan Wendell. New York: Prometheus Books, 1983: 61–80.
Gignac, Tamara. "Romancing the Net," *E Business Journal* 1 (10) 1993: 13.
Giusto-Davis, Joann. "Jove to Bid for Female Readers with 'Second Chance at Love' Romance Line," *Publishers Weekly*, 16 January 1981: 43–45.
Glenn, Carroll, and Paul Huo Yangchung. "Organizational Task and Institutional Environments in Ecological Perspective: Findings from the Local Newspaper Industry," *American Journal of Sociology* 91 (4), 1986: 838–73.
Greco, Albert N. *The Book Publishing Industry*, 2nd edition. Mahwah, N.J.: Lawrence Erlbaum, 2005.
Grescoe, Paul. *The Merchants of Venus: Inside Harlequin and the Empire of Romance*. Vancouver: Raincoast Books, 1996.
Griswold, Wendy. "American Character and the American Novel," *American Journal of Sociology* 86 (1981): 740–765.
Guiley, Rosemary. *Love Lines: A Romance Readers Guide to Printed Pleasures*. New York: Facts on File Publications, 1983.
Hanan, Michael, and John Freeman. "The Population Ecology of Organizations," *American Journal of Sociology* 82 (5), 1977: 929–64.
Haskel, Molly. "The 2,000-Year-Old Misunderstanding—'Rape Fantasy,'" *Ms.*, November 1976: 84–86.
Holt, Karen. "Harlequin Launching Inspirational Line," *Publishers Weekly* 250 (41), 2003: 8.
Jennings, Vivian. "At Long Last, Love," in *Writing Romantic Fiction: For Love and Money*, edited by Susan Whittlesey Wolf. Cincinnati: Writer's Digest Books, 1983: 2.
Jensen, Margaret Ann. *Love's Sweet Return: The Harlequin Story*. Toronto: The Women's Press, 1984.
Johnson, Naomi. "Consuming Desires: Consumption, Romance, and Sexuality in Best-Selling Teen Romance Novels," *Women's Studies in Communication* 33 (1), 2010: 54–73.

Kirkland, Catherine. *For the Love of It: Women Writers and the Popular Romance*. Ph.D. dissertation, Philadelphia: University of Pennsylvania, 1984.

Mann, Peter. *The Romance Novel: A Survey of Reading Habits*. London: Mills & Boon, 1968.

Mansfield, Elizabeth. "Tell Me a Tale of Love...," *Romantic Times* 10 (1983): 18–19.

Markert, John. "Challenging the Stereotype: Demographics and Lifestyles of Romance Readers," Presented at the Southern Popular Culture Association Conference in Nashville, TN, October 1993.

_____. "The Language of Love," *Nashville* (February 1984): 26–29.

_____. "The Publishing Decision: Managerial Policy and Its Effect on Editorial Decision-Making," *Book Research Quarterly* 3 (Summer), 1987: 33–59.

_____. "Romancing the Reader," *Romantic Times* 18 (Fall), 1984.

_____. "Romance Publishing and the Production of Culture," *Poetics: International Review for the Theory of Literature*, Special Edition on Empirical Sociology of Cultural Productions, Vol. 14 (April 1985): 69–94.

_____. "Unsated Demand: An Explanation for the Growth in Romance Publishing," presented at the Modern Language Association Conference in Washington, D.C., December 1985.

Maryles, Daisy. "Fawcett Launches Romance Imprint with Brand Marketing Techniques," *Publishers Weekly*, 3 September 1979: 69–70.

_____. "S & S to Debut Silhouette with $3-Million TV Ad Campaign," *Publishers Weekly*, 11 May 1980: 51–52.

McAleer, Joseph. *Passion's Fortune: The Story of Mills & Boon*. Oxford: Oxford University Press, 2000.

McCarthy, Sara. "Pornography, Rape, and the Cult of Macho," *The Humanist*, September/October 1980: 11–20.

McCaukey, Mary. "McDaniel College Offers New Minor in Genre Fiction," *The Baltimore Sun*, 22 March 2012.

McMahon, Jim. "Harlequin Takes a Novel Approach," *In-Plant Graphics* 62 (3), 2012: 34–35.

Memmott, Carol. "Romance Novels for Women Get Frankly Sexual," *USA Today*, 20 Feb. 2006.

Menard, A. Dana, and Christine Cabrera. "'Whatever the Approach, Tab B Still Fits Slot A': Twenty Years of Sex Scripts in Romance Novels," *Sexuality & Culture* 15, 2001: 240–255.

Modleski, Tania. *Loving with a Vengeance: Mass Produced Fantasies for Women*. North Haven, CT: Achon, 1982.

Mondale, Joan. *Women and Social Change in America*. Princeton: Princeton Book, 1978.

Morgan, P. "'Like Bush Fire in My Arms': Interrogating the World of Caribbean Romance," *Journal of Popular Culture* 36 (4), 2003: 804–827.

Mosher, Donald. "Sex Callousness Toward Women," *Technical Report of the Commission on Obscenity and Pornography*, Vol. 8. Washington, D.C., 1970: 313–25.

Neal, Lynn S. *Romancing God: Evangelical Women and Inspirational Fiction*. Chapel Hill: University of North Carolina Press, 2006.

Nehring, Cristina. *A Vindication of Love: Reclaiming Romance for the Twenty-first Century*. New York: HarperCollins, 2009.

Pavao, Kate. "Out of the Closet: Now More than Ever, Gay and Lesbian Characters are Prominently Featured in YA Fiction," *Publishers Weekly*, 1 Dec. 2003.

Peryman, Lisa. "Harlequin Launches New Spiritual Imprint," *Quill & Quire* 63 (12), 1997: 17.

Peters, Thomas J. and Robert H. Waterman Jr. *In Search of Excellence: Lessons from America's Best-Run Companies*. New York: Harper & Row, 1982: 293–94.

Powell, Walter P. "From Craft to Corporation: The Impact of Outside Ownership on Book Publishing," in *Individuals in Mass Media Organizations: Creativity and Constraints*, eds. James S. Ettema and C. Charles Whitney. Beverly Hills: Sage, 1983: 33–52.

Powell, Walter W. *Getting Into Print: The Decision-Making Process in Scholarly Publishing*. Chicago: University of Chicago Press, 1985.

Radway, Janice. *Reading the Romance: Women, Patriarch and Popular Literature*. Chapel Hill: University of North Carolina Press, 1984.

Regis, Pamela. *A Natural History of the Romance Novel.* Philadelphia: University Pennsylvania Press, 2003.
Reuter, Madalynne. "Judge Rules Silhouette Cover Too Similar to Harlequin's," *Publishers Weekly,* 26 September 1980: 42–43.
Schumpeter, Joseph. *Capitalism, Socialism and Democracy,* 3rd edition. New York: Harper & Row, 1950.
———. "Economic Theory and Entrepreneurial History," in *Explorations in Enterprise,* edited by H. G. J. Aiken. Cambridge: Harvard University Press, 1965: 45–64.
Severance, Anne. "A New Language of Love," *West Coast Review of Books,* 1984.
Shatzkin, Leonard. *In Cold Type: Overcoming the Book Crisis.* Boston: Houghton Mifflin, 1982.
Shodzinski, Noelle. "Publishing Innovator of the Year: Harlequin," *Book Business* 12 (3): 22–24.
Showalter, Elaine, ed. *The New Feminist Criticism: Essays on Women, Literature, and Theory.* New York: Pantheon Books, 1985.
Tebbel, John. *A History of Book Publishing in the United States, Vol. 1: The Creation of an Industry, 1630–1865.* New York: R. R. Bowker, 1972.
———. *A History of Book Publishing in the United States, Vol. 2: The Expansion of an Industry, 1865–1919.* New York: R. R. Bowker, 1972.
———. *A History of Book Publishing in the United States, Vol. 3: The Golden Age Between Two Wars: 1920–1940.* New York: R. R. Bowker, 1978.
———. *A History of Book Publishing in the United States, Vol. 4: The Great Change, 1940–1980.* New York: R. R. Bowker, 1981.
———. *The Media in America.* New York: Thomas Y. Crowell, 1974.
Thompson, James. *Organizations in Action.* New York: McGraw-Hill, 1967
Thompson, John. *Merchants of Culture: The Publishing Business in the Twenty-First Century.* New York: Plume, 2012.
Thurston, Carol. "Popular Historical Romances: Agent for Social Change? An Exploration of Methodologies," *Journal of Popular Culture,* Vol. 19 (2), 1985: 35–49.
———. *The Romance Revolution: Erotic Novels for Women and the Quest for a New Sexual Identity.* Urbana: University of Illinois Press, 1987.
Vivanco, Laura. "Feminism and the Early Twenty-First-Century Harlequin Mills & Boon Romance," *Journal of Popular Culture* 45 (5), 2012: 1060–1089.
———. *For Love and Money: The Literary Art of the Harlequin Mills & Boon Romance.* Tirril Hall, Tirril, Penright CA: Humanities-Ebooks, 2011.
Watt, Ian. *The Rise of the Novel.* Berkeley: University of California Press, 1967.
White, Harrison C. "Where Do Markets Come From?" *American Journal of Sociology* 87 (1981): 517–47.
Wirten, Eva Hemmungs. *Global Infatuation: Explorations in Transnational Publishing and Texts: The Case of Harlequin Enterprises in Sweden.* Ph.D. dissertation, Department of Literature, Uppsala University. Uppsala, Sweden, 1998.
Yankelovich, Skelly, and White, Inc. *Consumer Research Study on Reading and Book Purchasing.* New York: Book Industry Study Group, 1982.

Index

African American romances 131, 152, 165–167, 195, 197, 201–203, 242–250, 254, 257, 262–263, 269, 297–298, 322*ch*10*n*137; *see also* multicultural romances; self-publishing
alpha male hero *see* hero/heroine characteristics
Asian-themed romances 190–191, 246–251; *see also* manga romances
audience demographics 31, 129–131, 154, 157, 173, 179, 190–191, 204, 207, 206 230–233, 235, 240, 243, 249, 263, 290
author income 131, 252–254
Avon 11, 24–25, 44–51, 53–55, 57–58; Finding Mr. Right 98, 113–115, 122, 291; Impulse 274–275; Red 275; Velvet Glove 80, 122–123; *see also* bodice-rippers; Coffey, Nancy

BDSM *see* Fifty Shades of Grey; xrotic romances
BET romances *see* African American romances
bodice-rippers 4, 7, 11, 47–53, 58–64, 90, 98, 103, 108, 114, 125, 131, 155–156, 175–177, 223, 275, 282, 286–287, 295
Bonnycastle, Mary 27, 41, 285
Bonnycastle, Richard Gardyn 26–28
Boon, Alan 145–146, 310*ch*8*n*5; *see also* Mills & Boon
Boy Meets Girl newsletter 151, 176, 307*ch*5*n*1
Bridget Jones's Diary 151, 176; *see also* chick-lit

Candlelight romances *see* Dell; *see also* Stephens, Vivian
chick-lit 151, 168–169, 176–178, 182, 195, 204, 208
Christian romances: publishers 80, 106, 116–119, 125, 138–139, 166, 168–171, 198–199, 201–202, 207–212, 261, 268, 291–292, 296–297, 318*ch*9*n*36, 323*ch*10*n*9, 319*ch*9*n*48, 319*ch*9*n*49; themes 166–167, 212–216, 261, 268, 323*ch*10*n*9; *see also* distributing the romance novel, Christian retailers
Circle of Love 11, 98–100, 109, 291
Coffey, Nancy 7, 47–48, 50–51, 55, 57, 103, 111, 125, 127–128, 308*ch*5*n*30 32; *see also* Avon

competitive market threat *see* market niche
Cosmo Red Hot reads 179, 196
cover art 16, 20, **23**–24, 36–**37**, 51, 53–**54**, 57, 70–73, 76, 111–113, 158, **160**, 177, 187, 190–192, **216**, 220, **224**, 241–242, 246, 248, 254, 256–258, 262, 274, 321*ch*9*n*114

Dailey, Janet 10–11, 36–39, 42–43, 70, 74, 83, 157, 288, 307*ch*4*n*18
Dell Candlelight romances 14, 86–89, 103, 127, 137, 242, 285, 289; *see also* Stephens, Vivian
Dell Ecstasy romances 7, 9–11, 14, 62, 79–80, 83–86, 88–90, 91–95, 97–100, 102–106, 116, 124, 126–127, 136–138, 158, 162, 177, 194, 262, 268, 289–291; *see also* Stephens, Vivian
digital publishing *see* e-books
distributing the romance novel: Amazon 175, 191, 221, 227, 238, 248, 250, 253, 258–259, 263; big box retailers 166, 175, 208, 212, 259; Christian retailers 118–119, 169, 208, 211–212, 297; traditional bookstores 155, 157, 173, 181, 187, 189, 233, 246, 249, 262, 281, 294, 307*ch*5*n*12; *see also* e-books
Duffy, Kate 14, 59, 75, 89, 93, 129

e-books 12, 138–139, 146, 152–153, 155, 170–175, 190, 196, 200–202, 207, 211, 214, 219, 250, 253, 255, 258, 263, 266–275, 278–282, 294–296, 298–299, 324*ch*11*n*7; *see also* self-publishing; xrotic romances
economy of scale of large houses over small 271–272, 275–276, 280–281
Ecstasy romances *see* Dell Ecstasy
editors: the editorial pen 135, 242, 256; establishing submission guidelines 39–40, 53, 89–90, 95–98, 101, 103–104, 107, 111, 115, 117, 123, 134, 136–138, 158, 166–167, 170, 188, 210, 218, 249, 265, 269, 290–291, 312*ch*8*n*48, 313*ch*8*n*6; as gatekeepers 98; as gatemakers 9, 98, 290; personal taste in selection process 8–9, 27, 95, 102, 145, 149, 210, 250–251, 263, 292, secretaries as 64, 93–94; selecting manuscripts *see* gatekeepers; gatemakers; sifting

331

332 Index

reader input 52, 87–88, 100, 126–131, 137, 289; in stable environments 8, 98; transediting 188–189; in turbulent environments 8–9, 97, 194, 277, 299; *see also* Coffey, Nancy; GLBTQ romances; product monitoring; Stephens, Vivian; xrotic romances
Edwards, Ellen 94–95, 109–110, 228–230
erotic Likert scale 154, 156–159, 175, 180, 261
erotic romances 154, 156–158, *160*, 162–163, 168, 175–181, 193, 196, 201, 205, 208, 213, 234, 237, 243, 267, 268, 274; *see also* erotic Likert scale; xrotic romances
evangelical romances *see* Christian romances

Fawcett romances 22, 44, 55, 75; *see also* Nevler, Leona
feminist criticism of romances 4, 30, 42, 59–61, 193, 306*ch*4*n*29
Fifty Shades of Grey 176, 223, 251–252, 262, 295

Galloway, David 40, 70, 82, 106, 144–148, 150–152, 189, 194, 292, 310*ch*8*n*7, 310*ch*8*n*8
gatekeepers 6, 8–9, 277, 290, 299; *see also* editors, as gatekeepers; literary agents; Romance Writers of America; *Romantic Times*
gatemakers *see* editors, as gatemakers
GLBTQ romances 202, 205, 231–242, 253, 262, 268, 278, 295, 310*ch*9*n*80
gothic romances 4, 45–46, 52, 55–56, 96, 108, 120, 302*ch*1*n*33

Harlequin, 1949–1979: advertising 31–34, 41–42, 56, 70, 83, 305*ch*2*n*25; audience targeting 30–34; blind sampling 35–36, 285–286; break with Pocket Books 66–69; expansion beyond romances 40, fiction in good taste 16, 27, 29, 34; Mills and Boon, initial relationship 26–28, 31–32, 25, 38, 41–42, 144–146, 184–186; romance identity established 7, 10–11, 26, 63, 66, 147, 285; sex in novel, introduction of 31, 35–37, 42, 73
Harlequin, 1980–2015: Children's Supplementary Education Publishing (CSEP) 149–150, 292; digital market entry and developments 152–153, 155, 174–175, 196, 202 (*see also* e-books); fan parties 129, 131; Harlequin/Silhouette lawsuit 70–73; HarperCollins, purchase of 10, 12, 153, 184, 194, 198–199, 275–277, 286, 293, 297, 299, 324*ch*10*n*39; Mills & Boon relationship 144–146, 148, 195; rebranding 152, 157–158, 195, 275, 293
Harlequin, international expansion 40, 184–193, 197, 274, 276, 292, 311*ch*8*n*22
Harlequin lines/subsidiaries: American Romance 14, 80, 156–158, 183, 194–195, 262, 297; Arabesque *see* African American romances; Blaze 154, 158–160, 162–163, 175, 185, 196; Bombshell 179, 196; Cosmo Red Hots 179, 197; Crosswinds 173; Deseo/Bianco 247; Desire 154, 158, 243, 275 (*see also* Silhouette, launch lines); Duets/Flipside 151, 182–183; First Love 80–81, 173, 182, 202–203; Ginger Blossom 191; Gold Eagle Books 163–165, 183–184; Heartsong 170, 197, 322*ch*9*n*135; Heartwarming 322*ch*9*n*134, 323*ch*10*n*9; Inspirational 291; Intimate Moments 80, 98, 157, 195 (*see also* Romance Suspense); Intrigues 80, 123, 157–158, 174, 195; Kimani *see* African American romances; KISS 174; Love & Laughter 151, 182; Love Inspired 80–81, 173, 182, 202–203; Masquerade 155–156; Medical Romance 15, 157–158, 185, 194; MIRA 150–152, 171–172, 176, 178, 185–186, 195, 219, 223; Mystique 163–164; NASCAR 178, 195; NEXT 152, 181; Nocturne 174, 179, 196; Presents 4, 10, 28, 31, 35–40, 42–43, 73–74, 76, 88–89, 94, 97, 116, 129, 152–154, 156, 158, *160*, 180–181, 188, 193–195, 261, 286, 288–289; Red Dress Ink 150–152, 176–178, 182–183, 195; Rogue Angel 163, 165, 179, 196; Romance 28–30, 34–37, 39–42, 74, 153–154, 158, 188, 194–195; Romance Suspense 121, 157–158; Shadows 151, 179, 196; Special Edition 158–159, 275 (*see also* Silhouette, launch lines); Spice 159, 179–181, 196; Steeple Hill Books 151, 168–169, 292; Superromance 75–80, 83, 103, 111–112, 129, 158, 188, 194–195, 288, 307*ch*4*n*33; Teen 173, 203; Temptation 79–80, 116, 159, 162, 194, 196; Worldwide Library 163–164, 171; Yours Truly 151, 182
Hayes, Donna 145, 150–153, 177, 194–195, 278, 292–293, 311*ch*8*n*22, 311*ch*8*n*24, 312*ch*8*n*51
Heisey, W. Lawrence 145–148, 172, 184, 189, 194, 284–286, 311*ch*8*n*9, 311*ch*8*n*37
hero/heroine characteristics 29–30, 60, 73–74, 91, 95–96, 119–120, 161, 214, 290, 313*ch*8*n*67, 316*ch*8*n*155
Hickey, Brian 145, 148–152, 189, 194–195, 292–293, 311*ch*8*n*22, 311*ch*8*n*24, 312*ch*8*n*37
Hispanic romances: lines 246–247, 298; market for 247–248, 251, 263; *see also* multicultural romances
Howard, Glenda 14, 165–166
humor in romances 88, 101–102, 116, 121, 135, 151, 182–183, 196, 250
hybrid publishing 258–259, 264, 269, 282

inspirational romances *see* Christian romances
interracial romances *see* multicultural romances
intra-racial romances *see* African American romances

Jackson, Brenda *see* African American romances

Kensington Publishing 13–14, 51, 149, 165, 167, 200, 202–203, 243–245, 247–248, 253, 260, 262, 265, 269, 274, 282, 295, 297, 312*ch*9*n*136, 314*ch*8*n*99, 322*ch*9*n*136, 324*ch*11*n*1; *see also* African American romances; multicultural romances
Krentz, Judith 161

Index

Latino-themed romances *see* multicultural romances
liability of newness 266–269, 279
literary agents, as gatekeepers 77, 107, 171, 207, 210, 226, 263–265, 277, 279, 282, 299–300
Love and Life 105–106, 110–114, 125
Loveswept 11, 59, 98–102, 119, 136–138, 273–274, 290–291, 308*ch*5*n*30

male/male romances *see* GLBTQ publishers
manga romances 191–**192**, 197, 230, 247–248, 317*ch*8*n*173, 320*ch*9*n*75
market control, monopolies and oligopolies 99, 187, 200–201, 261
market niche 8, 10, 12, 63, 80–81, 100–101, 106, 113, 118–119, 125, 127, 138–140, 158, 163, 168–169, 176, 179, 201, 203, 225, 234–235, 236, 246, 251, 265, 280, 186, 191, 296
medical romances 154–155, 157–158, 185, 194; *see also* nurse novels
military in romances 163, 234, 313*ch*8*n*80
Mills & Boon 27–28, 35, 37–38, 41, 67, 75–77, 82, 144–146, 148, 153, 195–196, 284–285; historical romances 155–156, 159; medical romances 154; rugby novels 178; *see also* Boon, Alan; Harlequin, international expansion
multicultural romances 201–202, 246–251, 258, 263, 269, 298–299, 321*ch*9*n*106, 321*ch*9*n*113
mystery-suspense romances 2, 24, 39, 45–46, 55–56, 80, 119–124, 174, 183, 204, 253, 309*ch*6*n*34

Nevler, Leona 56–57, 64, 127
New American Library *see* Rapture romances
Nichols, Carolyn *see* Circle of Love; Loveswept; Second Chance at Love
nurse novels **28**–29, 86, 154

packagers of romances lines 55, 57–59, 113, 122–123, 309*ch*6*n*20
paperback book revolution: first 16–17; second 17–19; *see also* Pocket Books, introduction of mass market paperbacks
paranormal romances 112, 174–175, 179, 196, 204, 218, 221–222, 229, 234, 253, 295, 320*ch*9*n*74
Playboy Press romances 45, 51–55, 57–58, 89, 98, 105, 164, 286–287, 292
Pocket Books 1, 7, 10–11, 14–16, 53, 58–59, 129, 210, 258; Harlequin distribution arrangement with 26, 32, 41, 66–69, 82–83, 147; introduction of mass market paperbacks 19–25, 284–287
product homogeneity 8, 92
product monitoring 7–8, 12, 64–65, 92, 94, 103, 105, 127, 140, 201, 226, 270, 277–279, 282, 286

Rapture romances 106–108, 124
readers to writers *see* writers as readers

Regency romances 45–46, 55–57, 87, 127, 208, 274
RITA award(s) *see* Romance Writers of America
Roberts, Nora 56–57, 64, 127
Rogers, Rosemary *see* bodice-rippers
romance novel: condescending attitude toward 2–5, 25, 60, 65, 93–94, 97, 186–187, 285, 303*ch*2*n*39 (*see also* editors, secretaries as; feminist criticism of romances); percent of market 1, 26, 63, 66, 69, 85, 148, 150–152, 171, 178, 184, 186, 189, 195, 198, 203–204, 220, 235, 244, 247, 252–253, 258, 269, 271–272, 307*ch*5*n*1
romance revolution of 1980s 6, 8, 43, 65, 134, 137–138, 198, 208, 289, 291, 294
Romance Writers of America (RWA) 214, 227–229, 244, 254, 277–279, 282, 309*ch*5*n*33
Romantic Times magazine 211, 240–241, 279–**280**, 300, 310*ch*7*n*8

science-fiction romances *see* paranormal romances
Second Chance at Love 11, 94–96, 98–99, 103, 105–106, 108–109, 111, 115, 124–125, 127, 136–138, 181, 196, 290
self-publishing 176, 200, 202, 217, 238, 240, 243–244, 251–260, 263–266, 268–269, 278–281, 294–296, 300, 322*ch*10*n*132; *see also* hybrid publishing; xrotic romances
sensual historical romances *see* Avon; bodice-rippers
Silhouette Books: cover infringement 70–73; formation 7, 11, 66, 70; launch lines 37, 73–75, 79–80, 83, 106, 128, 158, 162, 194, 293; purchase by Harlequin 10–11, 79–82
Solem, Karen 74–75, 127, 137; *see also* Silhouette Books, formation
Stevens, Vivian 227, 242–243, 262, 308*ch*5*n*32, 308*ch*5*n*33; *see also* Dell Candlelight; Dell Ecstasy
Stuart, Mary Ann *see* Playboy Press
Sullivan, Judy 59, 62, 287; *see also* packagers of romance lines
Swinwood, Craig 145, 152–153, 194, 223, 270, 276, 293

task environment and effect on product *see* editors, in stable environments; editors, in turbulent environments; gatekeepers; gatemakers
television/film tie-ins 28, 120–121, 165, 154–155, 173–174, 178–179, 183, 203–204, 208, 247–248, 304*ch*2*n*5, 304*ch*2*n*6, 315*ch*8*n*137
To Have and to Hold 106, 108–110
Torstar 12, 144–150, 152–153, 184, 194, 276, 282, 292–293
transediting *see* editors, transediting
transmigration transformation 185, 188

virginal heroines *see* heroes/heroines characteristics

western romances 157, 183, 185, 189, 317ch8n181
Woodiwiss, Kathleen *see* Avon; bodice-rippers
writers as readers 38, 75, 97, 117, 13–14, 216, 218–219, 221, 248, 304*ch*2*n*8, 320*ch*9*n*37; *see also* African American romances; multicultural romances; xrotic romances

xrotic romances 217–231, 232, 235, 237, 240–241, 246, 249, 255, 258, 261–263, 268, 273, 294–296, 299–300, 317*ch*9*n*63, 320*ch*9*n*74, 322*ch*9*n*136, 324*ch*11*n*7; *see also* e-books; self-publishing

young adult romances 167, 173, 201–207, 235, 245, 260, 265, 296

Zane *see* African American romances
Zebra Books *see* Kensington

www.ingramcontent.com/pod-product-compliance
Ingram Content Group UK Ltd.
Pitfield, Milton Keynes, MK11 3LW, UK
UKHW041922140426
5217IPUK00014B/280